Bloom's Classic Critical Views

GEOFFREY CHAUCER

Bloom's Classic Critical Views

Jane Austen

Geoffrey Chaucer

Charles Dickens

Ralph Waldo Emerson

Nathaniel Hawthorne

Herman Melville

Edgar Allan Poe

Walt Whitman

Bloom's Classic Critical Views

GEOFFREY CHAUCER

Edited and with an introduction by
Harold Bloom
Sterling Professor of the Humanities
Yale University

BLOOM'S
LITERARY CRITICISM
An imprint of Infobase Publishing

Bloom's Classic Critical Views: Geoffrey Chaucer Geo

Bloom's Literary Criticism
An imprint of Infobase Publishing
132 West 31st Street
New York NY 10001

Library of Congress Cataloging-in-Publication Data
Geoffrey Chaucer / Harold Bloom, editor.
    p. cm. — (Bloom's classic critical views)
  Includes bibliographical references and index.
  ISBN-13: 978-0-7910-9562-1 (hardcover)
  ISBN-10: 0-7910-9562-2 (hardcover)
  1. Chaucer, Geoffrey, d. 1400—Criticism and interpretation—History. I. Bloom, Harold.
II. Title: Bloom's classic critical views : Geoffrey Chaucer.
  PR1924.G355 2007
  821'.1—dc22
                                    2007012599

Series design by Erika K. Arroyo
Cover design by Takeshi Takahashi

Printed in the United States of America

Bang EJB 10 9 8 7 6 5 4 3 2 1
Chelsea   4/17/08   40.50
This book is printed on acid-free paper.

Contents

Series Introduction

Bloom's Classic Critical Views is a new series presenting a selection of the most important older literary criticism on the greatest authors commonly read in high school and college classes today. Unlike the Bloom's Modern Critical Views series, which for more than twenty years has provided the best contemporary criticism on great authors, Bloom's Classic Critical Views attempts to present the authors in the context of their time and to provide criticism that has proved over the years to be the most valuable to readers and writers. Selections range from contemporary reviews in popular magazines, which demonstrate how a work was received in its own era, to profound essays by some of the strongest critics in the British and American tradition, including Henry James, G.K. Chesterton, Matthew Arnold, and many more.

Some of the critical essays and extracts presented here have appeared previously in other titles edited by Harold Bloom, such as the New Moulton's Library of Literary Criticism. Other selections appear here for the first time in any book by this publisher. All were selected under Harold Bloom's guidance.

In addition, each volume in this series contains a series of essays by a contemporary expert, who comments on the most important critical selections, putting them in context and suggesting how they might be used by a student writer to influence his or her own writing. This series is intended above all for students, to help them think more deeply and write more powerfully about great writers and their works.

Introduction by Harold Bloom

When I muse about the poetry and life of Geoffrey Chaucer, who died in 1400 at about the age of sixty, even I find it odd that I brood first on Immanuel Kant's Third Critique, the *Critique of Judgment* (1790). Chaucer and Kant, even had they a common vernacular, would not have had much to say to each other. Still, Kant inaugurates aesthetics in his Third Critique and Chaucer matters overwhelmingly because he is the only writer in English who approaches Shakespeare in aesthetic eminence.

Shakespeare actually owed more to Chaucer than to any other precursor, including Ovid, Christopher Marlowe, and William Tyndale, the principal translator of the English Bible's Geneva Version. Yet Shakespeare never mentions Chaucer, perhaps for the same reason Chaucer never refers to Boccaccio, his authentic forerunner. Greatest of magpies, Shakespeare cheerfully stole with both hands, Chaucer did also. The strongest authors are the most agonistic, and repress any figures who might induce anxieties of influence. Kant teaches that the Sublime depends upon a negation that is subjective and individual, private rather than social. I am happy to agree, and suspect that pragmatically both Chaucer and Shakespeare might have concurred also.

This anthology of classic critical views of Chaucer includes the major poets, except for Shakespeare, most indebted to "the father of English poetry": Henryson, Dunbar, Skelton, Spenser, Blake, Byron, and William Morris. Major critics here comprise Sidney, Addison, Dryden, Dr. Johnson, Hazlitt, Emerson, Ruskin, Arnold, and Churton Collins (a greatly undervalued exegete).

A crucial legacy of Chaucer's for Shakespeare was an extraordinary fusion of disinterestedness, secularization, and an enormous irony. The Chaucerian-Shakespearean irony pervades the Wife of Bath and her son (as it were), Sir

John Falstaff. That mode of irony is erotic, humane, vitalistic, and sublimely witty. Another strain of irony, darker and less conforting, is transmitted by the Pardoner to Iago, the truly Satanic undoer of Othello.

What precisely did Shakespeare learn from Chaucer? Partly it was an ethos, exemplified by Chaucer's Knight and by several Shakespearean protagonists: we must bear ourselves like the time, because always we will be keeping appointments that we never made. More central even than this ethos is what I have learned to call Chaucer's and Shakespeare's "invention of the human." Dr. Samuel Johnson remarked that the essence of poetry was invention, by which the supreme critic meant the uncovering of realities always present but noticed by us only after reading Chaucer and Shakespeare.

No dramatists or novelists in English have peopled a cosmos for us, except for Chaucer and Shakespeare. And yet this is not a heterocosm, in the visionary mode of Blake, Shelley, and Yeats. Dickens's marvelous caricatures are in the supra-cartoon world of Marlowe, Ben Jonson, and Tobias Smollett. Shakespeare-haunted, Dickens performed public readings of his fictions that mesmerized huge audiences, but the parts he acted out—Fagin, Pickwick, Pip, Lady Dedlock and their cohorts—could not change by the antithetical will or daimon *overhearing* itself and being startled into another nature. A dramatic poet like the Browning of *Men and Women* was far closer to the representation of Chaucerian-Shakespearean personalities than Dickens or George Eliot could be.

It will not do though to judge Chaucer as only a proto-Shakespeare. Chaucer the Pilgrim, a parody of Dante the Pilgrim, plays his own role in the Tales of Canterbury, slyly dramatizing his subtle "gullibility." Enthusiastically innocent, Chaucer allows himself to be charmed by all his companions. In Shakespeare, Chaucer would be bully Bottom or even Feste, entertaining enchantments and practical jokes as though they were one. The uncanny Shakespearean singularity is not quite for the court sophisticate Chaucer, who manifests instead an individuality that finally is a touch cold both towards himself and others. Shakespeare fights perpetual lawsuits, to recover money he had loaned out at Shylock-like rates. Chaucer, a contemporary of Falstaff, is dragged off to court by the lady he has abducted for amorous dalliance, and is fined heavily for his flamboyant lusts.

So far as we can know, nothing external ever happened to the greatest of all dramatists, whereas Chaucer was nimble enough to serve both Richard II and Henry IV, who had usurped Richard and then murdered him. Chaucer's fabled disinterestedness is more defensive than Shakespeare's, perhaps because Chaucer had little choice. A commoner, his livelihood depended upon royal patronage and the largesse of great nobles. Shakespeare, even commoner, cultivated royals and nobles when he had to, but was saved by the huge audiences at the Globe, where as an investor he shared handsomely in the proceeds. Shakespeare's public made him independently wealthy, while Chaucer went on reading out loud in palaces and manor houses.

It remains a miracle that Chaucer's character and personality flowered in a society still caught up in feudalism. Chaucer's world was ending, and he knew it. Whether Shakespeare anticipated the era of Milton and Cromwell we never can know. Whether he cared at all about either literary or political-religious developments after his own career ended, I more than doubt. He lived in the present moment, and seems pragmatically to have been free of both past nostalgia and futurity's doubt.

Chaucer was much given to covert translation, which is something different from Shakespearean appropriation. The subtlest recent critical study I have read on Chaucer is R. Allen Shoaf's *Chaucer's Body* (2001), where Shoaf modulates my now antique notion of "the anxiety of influence" into an "anxiety of circulation" or of contamination.

Shoaf relates this to Chaucer's envy of his never-mentioned precursor Boccaccio, and I have cited earlier Shakespeare's failure ever to refer to Chaucer, in total contrast to Edmund Spenser's description of their joint forerunner as "the well of English undefiled." As a translator Chaucer is unsurpassed, and it is belated for us to call this plagiarism, an idea not extant in the ages before copyright. I conclude here by surmising that Chaucer demonstrates the translation of words and ideas, but not personalities. Chaucer's people were his own creation and thus set a model for Shakespeare's even more astonishing reinvention of the human.

BIOGRAPHY

GEOFFREY CHAUCER
(1340–1400)

Geoffrey Chaucer was born around 1340, the son of a prosperous vintner, probably in London. He received a good education, apparently attending the Almonry
Cathedral School. In the early 1360s he studied law, perhaps at Oxford University.

From 1357 to 1359, he served as a yeoman in the court of Elizabeth, countess of
Ulster, continuing his studies when not occupied with his duties, and writing songs.
In 1359 he traveled to France, the first of many journeys to continental Europe in the
service of the king and various noblemen.

By the mid-1360s, Chaucer had come to the attention of John of Gaunt. It is
probably due to Gaunt's intercession that Chaucer was placed in the king's service
around 1366. Gaunt was not only fond of Chaucer, but of Chaucer's wife as well.
Between 1369 and 1372, Philippa Chaucer bore a child whose father, the evidence
suggests, was John of Gaunt. Some scholars and critics have suggested that
Chaucer's sympathetic portrayal of wayward women in his poetry stems from his
seeming awareness and tolerance of his wife's affair with his best friend. Another
reason for the magnanimity evident in his depiction of characters such as the Wife
of Bath, Alisoun in the Miller's Tale, and "faithless Cressid" may be that Alice Perrers,
King Edward's promiscuous mistress, was Chaucer's patron.

In 1372 Chaucer went to Italy on his first major diplomatic mission. This journey
was a turning point in his career, boosting his favor with the king and providing a
new impetus for his poetry. It was shortly after this trip that Chaucer began writing
short tales similar to those of Petrarch and Boccaccio. The themes and techniques of
his poetry also began to exhibit the influence of Dante. By the mid-1370s, his work
was receiving wide attention: in 1374 he read his poetry at court, at the festival of the
Order of the Garter.

Throughout the 1370s, Chaucer served in a variety of governmental posts,
notably as controller of customs from 1374 to 1386. The years of the Peasants' Revolt
(1377–82) were dangerous for any government official, and the constant travel

throughout England and to continental Europe that his position required made Chaucer's life difficult.

Although he had weathered the revolt and a term in Parliament in 1386 as the member representing Kent, the latter part of the 1380s proved to be no less trying for Chaucer. Philippa Chaucer died in 1387, and Chaucer mourned her deeply. At the height of the duke of Gloucester's power, Chaucer's royalist sympathies caused him to fall into disfavor. In 1388 financial difficulties forced him to sell one of his annuities.

By 1391, however, Chaucer had been given a more leisurely position than clerk of the king's works, an arduous post that he had held beginning in 1389. From 1391 to 1397 he was able to concentrate on his poetry for the first time in his life. It was evidently during these years that he revised and expanded *The Canterbury Tales*. He died in London in 1400.

The establishment of a firm Chaucerian canon is comparatively recent. Works such as the *Flower and the Leaf, Chaucer's Dream,* and the *Court of Love,* once thought to be Chaucer's creations, are now no longer accepted as his. Scholars are still uncertain about the specific dates he produced much of his work. His first completed work, the *Book of the Duchess,* was written between 1369 and 1373. During the 1370s and 1380s, he composed the *House of Fame,* the *Legend of Good Women,* and *Troilus and Criseyde.* The work for which he is best known, *The Canterbury Tales,* represents the labor of a lifetime.

THE FOURTEENTH CENTURY

THOMAS USK (1387)

Thomas Usk (13??–1388) was a medieval writer and direct contemporary of Chaucer's. In the *Testament of Love*, Usk, writing in the persona of Love, notes that Chaucer is a "trewe seruaunt" ("true servant") to Love and that the poet's *Troilus and Criseyde* contains some of the most "noble sayenges" ("noble sayings") about Love. Usk concludes by noting that Chaucer "passeth al other makers" ("passes all other poets"), a statement from Chaucer's own lifetime that indicates the poet's significance.

⎯⎯ ⎯⎯ ⎯⎯

(Quod Loue) I shal tel the
this lesson to lerne myne owne trewe seruaunt
the noble philosophical poete
in Englissh
whiche euermore hym besyeth and trauayleth right sore
my name to encrease
wherefore al that wyllen me good
owe to do him worshyp & reuerence bothe
trewly his better ne his pere in schole of my rules coude I neuer
fynde: he (quod she) in a treatise that he made of my seruant Troylus
hath this mater touched
and at the ful this questyon assoyled. Certaynly his noble sayenges
can I not amende: In goodnes of gentyl manlyche speche
without any maner of nycite of starieres ymagynacion in wytte and
in good reason of sentence he passeth al other makers. In the boke of
Troylus
the answere to thy questyon mayste thou lerne.

—Thomas Usk, Testament of Love, c. 1387, Works,
1532, ed. Thynne, Fol. 359b

JOHN GOWER (1390)

A great friend to Chaucer, John Gower (c. 1330–1408) was a prominent fourteenth-century poet and author who is now best known for his frame poem *Confessio Amantis*. Here, in an excerpt from the end of the work, the character of Venus labels Chaucer "mi disciple and mi poete" ("my disciple and my poet") and instructs Amans, to whom she is speaking, to tell Chaucer to "sette an ende of alle his werk" ("to set an end to all his work"), an

exhortation that critics believe is Gower's way of telling Chaucer to finish his
Legend of Good Women, a frame poem in a similar vein to the *Confessio*.

And gret wel Chaucer whan 3e mete,
As mi disciple and mi poete:
ffor in þe floures of his 3ouþe
In sondri wise, as he wel couþe,
Of Ditees and of songes glade,
The whiche he for mi sake made,
The lond fulfild is oueral:
Wherof to him in special
Aboue alle oþre I am most holde.
fforfþi now in hise daies olde
Thou schalt him telle þis message,
That he vpon is latere age,
To sette an ende of alle his werk,
As he which is myn owne clerk,
Do make his testament of loue,
As þou hast do þi schrifte aboue,
So þat mi Court it mai recorde.

—John Gower, *Confessio Amantis*, c. 1390,
Works, 1901, ed. Macaulay, p. 466

THE FIFTEENTH CENTURY

JOHN LYDGATE (1400)

John Lydgate (circa 1370–1450), a prolific medieval poet known for his magnum opus *Fall of Princes*, was the first and most important of the post-Chaucerian imitators, a group of English and Scottish writers who were highly influenced by Chaucer's stylistics, genres, and themes. A contemporary of Chaucer's for roughly thirty years, Lydgate himself referred to the great poet as his "maister" ("master").

In *The Flower of Courtesy*, Lydgate laments Chaucer's recent passing; he bemoans that "[t]he welle is drie, with the lycoure swete / Bothe of Clye and of Caliope," ("the well is dry with the liquor that is sweet / to both Clio and Calliope," a reference to two Greek Muses.) Lydgate also demonstrates Chaucer's enormous influence over the poets of his generation when he comments that "[w]e may assay forto counterfete / His gay style but it wyl not be" ("we may attempt to counterfeit his gay style but it will not be"), Lydgate's assertion that he and his fellow writers may attempt to mimic Chaucer's style and brilliance, but will come up short in their efforts.

In *The Life of Our Lady*, Lydgate speaks again of Chaucer's great influence on English poetry, noting expressively that Chaucer was the first "to distille and rayne / The golde dewe dropes of speche and eloquence / Into our tunge" ("to distill and rain / The gold dewdrops of speech and eloquence / Into our tongue"). Here, Lydgate is the first to suggest what many others will more directly state, that Chaucer was the father of English poetry. Students writing about Chaucer, especially in an essay that considers the man's significance and influence on later authors, may find it useful to cite that Chaucer's most noteworthy immediate successor understood his great impact as a writer.

Euer as I can supprise in myn herte
Alway with feare betwyxt drede and shame
Leste oute of lose, any worde asterte
In this metre, to make it seme lame,
Chaucer is deed that had suche a name
Of fayre makyng that (was) without wene
Fayrest in our tonge, as the Laurer grene.
We may assay forto countrefete
His gay style but it wyl not be;
The welle is drie, with the lycoure swete
Bothe of Clye and of Caliope.

—John Lydgate, *The Flower of Courtesy*,
c. 1400, ed. Thynne, Fol. 284b

John Lydgate (1410)

And eke my maister Chauser is ygrave
The noble Rethor, poete of Brytayne
That worthy was the laurer to haue
Of poetrye, and the palme atteyne
That made firste, to distille and rayne
The golde dewe dropes of speche and eloquence
Into our tunge, thurgh his excellence
And fonde the floures, firste of Retoryke
Our Rude speche, only to enlumyne
That in our tunge, was neuere noon hym like
For as the sonne, dothe in hevyn shyne
In mydday spere, dovne to vs by lyne
In whose presence, no ster may a pere
Right so his dytes withoutyn eny pere
Euery makyng withe his light disteyne
In sothefastnesse, who so takethe hede
Wherefore no wondre, thof my hert pleyne
Vpon his dethe, and for sorowe blede
For want of hym, nowe in my grete nede
That shulde alas, conveye and directe
And with his supporte, amende eke and corecte
The wronge traces, of my rude penne
There as I erre, and goo not lyne Right
But for that he, ne may not me kenne
I can no more, but with all my myght
With all myne hert, and myne Inwarde sight
Pray for hym, that liethe nowe in his cheste
To god above, to yeve his saule goode reste

—John Lydgate, *The Life of Our Lady*, c. 1410

John Walton "Translator's Preface" (1410)

John Walton was a medieval author who penned a prominent verse translation of Boethius's *De Consolatione Philosophiae*. In his preface to the translation, Walton writes that Chaucer was the "floure of rethoryk / In englisshe tong" ("flower of rhetoric / In the English tongue"). This statement demonstrates that, like Lydgate, the author understood Chaucer's immediate impact and importance as a writer in English.

To chaucer þat is floure of rethoryk
In englisshe tong & excellent poete
This wot I wel no þing may I do lyk
þogh so þat I of makynge entyrmete
And gower þat so craftily doþ trete
As in his book of moralite
þogh I to þeym in makyng am vnmete
3it most I schewe it forth þat is in me.
Noght lyketh me to labour ne to muse
Vppon þese olde poysees derk
ffor crystes feith suche þing schuld refuse,
Witnes vppon Ierom þe holy clerk,
Hit schold not ben a cristenmannes werk
Tho fals goddes names to renewe
ffor he þat haþ reseyued cristes merk
If he do so to crist he is vntrewe.
Of þo þar crist in heuene blis schall,
Suche manere werkes schold ben set on side,
ffor certaynly it nedeþ noght at all
To [whette] now þe dartes of cupide
Ne for to bidde þat Venus be oure gide
So þat we may oure foule lustes wynne,
On aunter lest þe same on vs betide
As dede þe same venus for hyre synne.
And certayn I haue tasted wonder lyte
As of þe welles of calliope
No wonder þough I sympilly endite
Yet will I not vnto tessiphone
Ne to allecto ne to megare
Besechin after craft of eloquence
But pray þat god of his benignyte
My spirit enspire wiþ his influence.

—John Walton, "Translator's Preface" to
De Consolatione Philosophiae, 1410

THOMAS HOCCLEVE (1412)

Thomas Hoccleve (c. 1368–c. 1437) was a Chaucerian imitator and poet known for his works "The Letter of Cupid" and *The Regiment of Princes*. Like many other post-Chaucerian medieval writers, Hoccleve—or Occleve, as his name is sometimes spelled—identified Chaucer as his master and describes Chaucer's "flour of eloquence," echoing Walton's earlier statements about Chaucer's flower of rhetoric. In *The Regiment of Princes*, Hoccleve writes a moving tribute to Chaucer that demonstrates once again how significant his work was to the writers who directly succeeded him.

—∿— —∿— —∿—

What schal I calle the What is thi name?
hoccleue fadir myn men clepen me. . . .
thou were aqueynted with Caucher pardee
God haue his soule best of any Wyght. . . .
O maister deere / and fadir reuerent
Mi maister Chaucer flour of eloquence
Mirour of fructuous entendement
O vniuersal fadir in science
Alias that thou thyn excellent prudence
In thi bed mortel mightist naght by qwethe
What eiled deth / alias Whi wolde he sle the
O deth thou didest naght harme singuleer
In slaghtere of him / but al this land it smertith
But nathelees / yit hast thou no power
His name sle / his hy vertu astertith
Vnslayn fro the / Which ay vs lyfly hertyth
With bookes of his ornat endytyng
That is to al this land enlumynyng
Hast thou nat eeke my maister Gower slayn. . . .
Mi dere maistir / god his soule quyte
And fadir Chaucer fayn Wolde han me taght
But I was dul, and lerned life or naght
Alias my worthi maister honorable
This landes verray tresor and richesse
Deth by thi deth / hath harme irreparable
Vnto vs doon / hir vengeable duresse
Despoiled hath this land of the swetnesse
Of rethorik for vnto Tullius
Was neuer man so lyk amonges vs
Also who was hier in philosophic
To Aristotle / in our tonge but thow
The steppes of virgile in poesie
Thow filwedist eeke men wot wel ynow. . . .
The firste fynders of oure faire langage

Hath seyde in caas semblable & othir mo
So hyly wel that it is my dotage
For to expresse or touche any of thoo
Alasse my fadir fro the worlde is goo
My worthi maister Chaucer hym I mene
Be thou aduoket for hym heuenes quene
As thou wel knowest o blissid virgyne
With louyng hert and hye deuocioun
In thyne honour he wroot ful manye a lyne
O now thine helpe & thi promocioun
To god thi sone make a mocioun
How he thi seruaunt was mayden marie
And lat his loue floure and fructifie
Al thogh his lyfe be queynt the resemblaunce
Of him hath in me so fressh lyflynesse
That to putte othir men in remembraunce
Of his persone I haue heere his lyknesse
Do make to this ende in sothfastnesse
That thei that haue of him lest thought & mynde
By this peynture may ageyn him fynde

—Thomas Hoccleve, *The Regiment of Princes,* 1412

JOHN SHIRLEY "INTRODUCTION" (1450)

John Shirley (1366?–1456) was Chaucer's first known editor. His work with Chaucer helped to preserve the poet's words for future generations. Here, in an introduction to *The Knight's Tale*, Shirley calls Chaucer the "moste famous poete . . . of oure rude moders englisshe tonge" ("the most famous poet . . . of our rude mother tongue, English,") a phrase that identifies not only Chaucer's importance but also the significance of his working in English, a language that had been somewhat neglected by previous medieval authors in England, in favor of Latin and French.

Take þe heed sirs I prey yowe of þis compleynt of *Anelyda* Qweene of Cartage Roote of trouthe and stedfastnesse þat pytously compleyneþe Upon þe varyance of daun *Arcyte* lord borne of þe blood Royal of Thebes, englisshed by Geffrey Chaucier In the best wyse and moost Rethoricyous þe mooste vnkou eþ metre, coloures and Rymes þ' euer was sayde. tofore þis day—redeþe and preveþe þe sooþe. . . .

Loo yee louers gladeþe and comforteþe you of þallyaunce etrayted bytwene þe hardy and furyous Mars þe god of armes and Venus þe double goddesse of loue made by O yee so noble and worthi pryncis and princesse, oþer estatis or degrees, what-euer yee beo, þat haue disposicione or plesaunce to rede or here þe stories of old tymis passed, to kepe yow frame ydelnesse and slowthe, in escheuing oþer folies þat might be cause of more harome filowyng, vowcheth sauf, I beseche yowe to fynde yowe occupacioun in þe reding here of þe tales of Caunterburye wiche beon compilid in þis boke Glowing First foundid, ymagenid and made boþe for disporte and leornyng of all þoo that beon gentile of birthe or of condicions by þe laureal and moste famous poete þat euer was to-fore him as in þemvelisshing of oure rude moders englisshe tonge, clepid Chaucyer a Gaufrede of whos soule god for his mercy have pitee of his grace. Amen.

—John Shirley, "Introduction" to *The Knight's Tale*, c. 1450

ROBERT HENRYSON (1475)

A major Scottish writer of the late fifteenth century, Robert Henryson (1420s–1505) wrote several important works, including *The Testament of Cresseid*, a sequel to Chaucer's own *Troilus and Criseyde*. In this selection from *Cresseid*, Henryson describes his debt to Chaucer's version, calling it "glorious" and detailing why he decided to pen a continuation to Chaucer's work. Any student writing about Chaucer's significance to early English or Scottish writing would do well to quote the words of Henryson or any of the numerous authors cited above, fellow poets who all recognized Chaucer as the foremost writer of his time.

———

I made the fyre and beaked me about
Than toke A drinke my spirites to conforte
And armed me wel fro the colde therout
To cutte the wynter nyght and make it shorte
I toke a queare / and left al other sporte
Written by worthy Chaucer glorious
Of fayre Creseyde / and lusty Troylus
And there I founde. . . .
(Diomede's seduction of Criseyde)
Of his distresse me nedeth nat reherse
For worthy Chaucer in that same boke
In goodly termes / and in ioly verse

Compyled hath his cares who wyl loke
To breke my slepe another queare I toke
In whiche I founde the fatal desteny
Of fayre Creseyde / whiche ended wretchedly
Who wot if al that Chaucer wrate was trewe
Nor I wotte nat if this narration
Be authorysed / or forged of the newe
Of some poete by his inuention
Made to reporte the lamentation
And woful ende of this lusty Creseyde
And what distresse she was in or she deyde

—Robert Henryson, *Testament of Cresseid*, c. 1475

WILLIAM CAXTON "EPILOGUE" (1478)

William Caxton (about 1422–91?) is largely known today as the first English printer, though he was also a minor translator and writer. Caxton most likely printed the first book in the English language in 1474 in Bruges, Belgium, and set up the first printing press in England in Westminster in 1477. Caxton's press was of enormous significance to the literary world in England, as it allowed books to be produced more quickly and more cheaply than previously before, making them more readily available to a growing number of people.

Among his many projects, Caxton printed a slew of Chaucer's works, including *The Parliament of Fowls* (1477), *Troilus and Criseyde* (1483), *The House of Fame* (1483), and *The Canterbury Tales* (1477, second edition 1484–85), which became some of his best-selling texts. For each of these editions, Caxton wrote an introduction or an epilogue to the manuscript, and the three excerpts below are from these introductions. In the first, from an edition of Chaucer's translation of Boethius from 1478, Caxton calls Chaucer the "first foundeur & enbelissher of ornate eloquence in our englissh" ("first founder and embellisher of ornate eloquence in English"), a statement that reflects the opinions of Shirley, Walton, and numerous other medieval critics and writers. In the second excerpt, from *The Book of Fame*, Caxton again praises Chaucer, concluding that he "excellyth in myn oppynyon alle other writers in our Englyssh" ("excels in my opinion all other writers in our English"), a judgment that was shared by many English critics until the latter half of the English Renaissance.

In the third excerpt, from Caxton's second edition of *The Canterbury Tales*, the printer addresses some of the problems inherent to his business.

He notes that the handwritten copies of Chaucer's texts Caxton had to work with were often severely abridged or contain embellishments that were added decades after Chaucer's death. The printer explains that the reason he is producing a second edition of *The Canterbury Tales* is that a man informed Caxton that his family possessed an earlier, more complete, and more accurate edition of it, and that the man would provide Caxton with a copy if he would consent to print a second edition. Caxton readily agreed to this and, a wise businessman, he added twenty-four illustrations to the text, making it even more popular than the first. Caxton's excerpts here provide students with an apt illustration of some of the difficulties of printing works that were copied by hand, and also demonstrate why and how those works were changed over time.

Thus endeth this boke whiche is named the boke of Consolacion of philosophie whiche that Boecius made for his comforte and consolacion he beyng in exile for the comyne and publick wele hauyng grete heuynes & thoughtes and in maner of despayr / Rehercing in the sayde boke howe Philosophie appiered to him shewyng the mutabilite of this transitorie lyfe / and also enformyng howe fortune and happe shold bee vnderstonden / with the predestynacion and prescience of God as moche as maye and ys possible to bee knowen naturelly / as a fore ys sayd in this sayd boke / Whiche Boecius was an excellente auctour of dyuerce bookes craftely and curiously maad in prose and metre / And also had translated dyuerce bookes oute of Greke into latyne / and had ben senatour of that noble & famous cite Rome. And also his two sones Senatours for their prudence & wisedom. And for as moche as he withstode to his power the tyrannye of theodorik thenne Emperour / & wold haue defended the sayde cite & Senate from his wicked hondes / wherupon he was conuict & putte in prison / in whiche prisone he made this forsaide boke of consolacion for his singular comfort, and for as moche as the stile of it / is harde & difficile to be vnderstonde of simple persones. Therfor the worshipful fader & first foundeur & enbelissher of ornate eloquence in our englissh. I mene / Maister Geffrey Chaucer hath translated this sayd werke oute of latyn in to oure vsual and moder tonge. Folowyng the latyn as neygh as is possible to be vnderstande wherin in myne oppynyon he hath deservid a perpetuell lawde and thanke of al this noble Royame of Englond / And in especiall of them that shall rede and vnderstande it. Fqrjn the sayd boke they may see what this transitorie & mutable worlde is And wherto euery mann liuyng in hit / ought to entende. Thenne for as moche as this sayd boke so translated is rare & not spred ne knowen as it is digne and worthy. For the erudicion and lernyng of suche as ben Ignoraunt & not knowyng of it / Atte requeste of a singuler frende and gossib of myne. I william Caxton haue done my debuoir & payne tenprynte it in fourme as is here afore made / In hopyng that it shal prouffite moche peple to the wele & helth of their soules / & for to lerne to haue and kepe the better pacience in aduersitees / And furthermore I desire & require you that of your charite ye wold praye for the soule of the sayd worshipful mann Geffrey Chaucer / first translatour of this sayde boke into englissh & enbelissher in making the sayd langage ornate & fayr whiche shal endure perpetuelly and therfore he ought eternelly to be remembrid. of whom the body and corps lieth buried in thabbay of Westmestre beside london to fore the chapele of seynte benet by whos sepulture is wreton on a table hongyng on a pylere his Epitaphye maad by a poete laureat.

—William Caxton, "Epilogue" to *Chaucer's Boethius,* 1478

WILLIAM CAXTON "EPILOGUE" (1483)

I fynde nomore of this werke to fore sayd / For as fer as I can vnderstonde / This noble man Gefferey Chaucer fynysshyd at the sayd conclusion of the metyng of lesyng and sothsawe / where as yet they ben chekked and maye not departe / whyche werke as me semeth is craftyly made / and dygne to be wreton and knowen / For he towchyth in it ryght grete wysedom & subtyll vnderstondyng / And so in alle hys werkys he excellyth in myn oppynyon alle other wryters in our Englyssh / For he wrytteth no voyde wordes / but alle hys mater is ful of hye and quycke sentence / to whom ought to be gyuen laude and preysyng for hys noble makyng and wrytyng / For of hym alle other haue borowed syth and taken / in alle theyr wel sayeng and wrytyng / And I numbly beseche & praye yow / emonge your prayers to remembre hys soule / on whyche and on alle crysten soulis I beseche almyghty god to haue mercy Amen

—William Caxton, "Epilogue" to *The House of Fame,* 1483

WILLIAM CAXTON "PROHEMYE" (1484)

Grete thankes lawde and honour / ought to be gyuen vnto the clerkes / poetes / and historiographs that haue wreton many noble bokes of wysedom of the lyues / passions / & myracles of holy sayntes of hystoryes / of noble and famous Actes / and faittes / And of the cronycles sith the begynnyng of the creacion of the world / vnto thys present tyme / by whyche we ben dayly enformed / and have knowleche of many thynges / of whom we shold not haue knowen / yf they had not left to vs theyr monumentis wreton / Emong

whom and inespecial to fore alle other we ought to gyue a synguler laude vnto
that noble & grete philosopher Gefferey chaucer the whiche for his ornate
wrytyng in our tongue may wel haue the name of a laureate poete / For to fore
that he by hys labour enbelysshyd / ornated / and made faire our englisshe /
in thys Royame was had rude speche & Incongrue / as yet it appiereth by olde
bookes / whyche at thys day ought not to haue place ne be compared emong
ne to hys beauteuous volumes / and aournate writynges / of whom he made
many bokes and treatyces of many a noble historye as wel in metre as in ryme
and prose / and them so craftyly made / that he comprehended hys maters in
short / quyck and hys sentences / eschewyng prolyxyte / castyng away the chaf
of superfluyte / and shewyng the pyked grayn of sentence / vtteryd by crafty
and sugred eloquence / of whom emonge all other of hys bokes / I purpose
temprynte by the grace of god the book of the tales of cauntyrburye / in whiche
I fynde many a noble hystorye / of euery astate and degre / Fyrst rehercyng
the condicions / and tharraye of eche of them as properly as possyble is to be
sayd / And after theyr tales whyche ben of noblesse / wysedom / gentylesse /
Myrthe / and also of veray holynesse and vertue / wherin he fynysshyth thys
sayd booke / whyche book I haue dylygently ouersen and duly examyned to
thende that it be made acordyng vnto his owen makyng / For I fynde many of
the sayd bookes / whyche wryters haue abrydgyd it and many thynges left out
/ And in somme place haue sette certayn versys / that he neuer made ne sette
in hys booke / of whyche bookes so incorrecte was one brought to me vj yere
passyd / whyche I supposed had ben veray true & correcte / And accordyng
to the same I dyde do enprynte a certayn nombre of them / whyche anon
were sold to many and dyuerse gentyl men / of whome one gentylman cam
to me / and said that this book was not accordyng in many places vnto the
book that Gefferey chaucer had made / To whom I answerd that I had made
it accordyng to my copye / and by me was nothyng added ne mynusshyd /
Thenne he sayd he knewe a book whyche hys fader had and moche louyd /
that was very trewe / and accordyng vnto hys owen first book by hym made
/ and sayd more yf I wold enprynte it agayn he wold gete me the same book
for a copye / how be it he wyst wel / that hys fader wold not gladly departe
fro it / To whom I said / in caas that he coude gete me suche a book trewe
and correcte / yet I wold ones endeuoyre me to enprynte it agayn / for to
satysfye thauctour / where as to fore by ygnouraunce I erryd in hurtyng and
dyffamyng his book in dyuerce places in settyng in somme thynges that he
neuer sayd ne made / and leuyng out many thynges that he made whyche ben
requysite to be sette in it / And thus we fyll at accord / And he ful gentylly
gate of hys fader the said book / and delyuerd it to me / by whiche I haue
corrected my book / as here after alle alonge by thayde of almyghty god shal

folowe / whom I humbly beseche to gyue me grace and ayde to achyeue / and accomplysshe / to hys lawde honour and glorye / and that alle ye that shal in thys book rede or heere / wyll of your charyte emong your dedes of mercy / remembre the sowle of the sayd Gefferey chaucer first auctour / and maker of thys book / And also that alle we that shal see and rede therin / may so take and vnderstonde the good and vertuous tales / that it may so prouffyte / vnto the helthe of our sowles / that after thys short and transitorye lyf we may come to euerlastyng lyf in heuen / Amen

—William Caxton, "Prohemye" to
The Canterbury Tales, 2nd ed., 1484

THE SIXTEENTH CENTURY

WILLIAM DUNBAR (1503)

Along with Henryson, William Dunbar (c. 1460–c. 1522) was the most significant Scottish poet of his day. Another poet who was widely influenced by Chaucer, Dunbar writes in *The Golden Targe* of the important authors who have preceded him, and includes Chaucer as the foremost of these individuals.

O reverend Chaucere, rose of rethoris all,
As in oure tong ane flour imperiall
That raise in Britane ewir, quho redis rycht,
Thou beris of makaris the tryumph riall;
Thy fresch anamalit termes celicall
This mater coud illumynit haue full brycht:
Was thou noucht of oure Inglisch all the lycht,
Surmounting ewiry tong terrestriall
Alls fer as Mayes morow dois mydnycht?
O morall Gower, and Ludgate laureate,
Your sugurit lippis and tongis aureate,
Bene to oure eris cause of grete delyte;
Your angel mouthis most mellifluate
Our rude langage has clere illumynate,
And faire our-gilt oure speche, that imperfyte
Stude, on your goldyn pennis schupe to wryte;
This He before was bare, and desolate
Off rethorike, or lusty fresch endyte.

—William Dunbar, *The Golden Targe*, c. 1503,
Poems, 1893, Vol. 2, ed. Small, p. 10

JOHN SKELTON "PHILLIP SPARROWE" (1508)

A poet of the Tudor courts, John Skelton (1463–1529) is best remembered today for his works *The Tunning of Elinor Rumming* and *Phillip Sparrowe*, the latter, excerpted here, written to mark the death of a pet bird that belonged to a young woman named Jane Scrope. In an epitaph that Skelton purports to be writing for the bird's grave, he refers to Chaucer and several of his works, providing interesting early commentary on several key Chaucerian texts.

After quickly referencing both "The Knight's Tale" and "The Nun's Priest's Tale," Skelton pauses to reflect a moment on the popular "Wife of Bath's Prologue and Tale": "And of the Wyfe of Bath, / That worketh moch scath / Whan her tale is tolde / Amonge huswyues bolde, / How she controlled / Her husbandes as she wolde, / And them to despise / In the homylyest wyse, / Brynge other wyues in thought / Their husbandes to set at nought" ("And of the Wife of Bath / Who worked much trouble / When her tale is told / Among housewives bold / [About] How she controlled / Her husbands as she willed / And them to despise / In the homeliest wise / Bring other wives in agreement / Their husbands to set at naught" [not think of]). This is perhaps one of the earliest texts to provide this type of critical commentary on the Wife of Bath and her tale, and students focusing on that particular text might examine how this criticism has been echoed and repudiated over the centuries.

After also writing at some length about Chaucer's *Troilus and Criseyde*, Skelton returns to the man himself, and writes, "His mater is delectable, / Solacious, and commendable" ("His matter is delectable, / Pleasant and commendable"). Skelton laments that his contemporaries feel that the language of Chaucer and his fellow medieval writers Gower and Lydgate is too crude, old fashioned, and impenetrable, and that many feel their language needs updating in order for their works to be useful and appreciated. Skelton agrees that English is, by its very nature, "rude," and not as pleasant sounding as French or Italian; nonetheless, Skelton finds much to admire in Chaucer and the other major writers of his time. Skelton is perhaps the first critic to note what many Chaucerian critics have subsequently commented on: the debate over the Middle English Chaucer used and whether excellent poetry can truly be written in such a tongue. Many students today declare Chaucer to be incomprehensible to them. Skelton, however, argues in favor of Chaucer, ultimately concluding that, "There is no Englysh voyd, / At those dayes moch commended" ("There is no loss of English / [That] in those days many had noted").

An epytaphe I wold haue
For Phyllyppes graue:
But for I am a mayde,
Tymerous, halfe afrayde,
That neuer yet asayde
Of Elyconys well,
Where the Muses dwell;
Though I can rede and spell,
Recounte, reporte, and tell

Of the Tales of Caunterbury,
Some sad storyes, some mery;
As Palamon and Arcet,
Duke Theseus, and Partelet;
And of the Wyfe of Bath,
That worketh moch scath
Whan her tale is tolde
Amonge huswyues bolde,
How she controlde
Her husbandes as she wolde,
And them to despyse
In the homylyest wyse,
Brynge other wyues in thought
Their husbandes to set at nought:
And though that rede haue I
Of Gawen and syr Guy.
And though I can expounde
Of Hector of Troye,
That was all theyr ioye,
Whom Achylles slew,
Wherfore all Troy dyd rew;
And of the loue so hote
That made Troylus to dote
Vpon fayre Cressyde,
And what they wrote and sayd,
And of theyr wanton wylles
Pandaer bare the bylles
From one to the other;
His maisters loue to further,
Somtyme a presyous thyng,
An ouche, or els a ryng;
From her to hym agayn
Somtyme a prety chayn,
Or a bracelet of her here,
Prayd Troylus for to were
That token for her sake;
How hartely he dyd it take,
And moche therof dyd make;
And all that was in vayne,
For she dyd but fayne;

The story telleth playne,
He coulde not optayne,
Though his father were a kyng,
Yet there was a thyng
That made the male to wryng;
She made hym to syng
The song of louers lay;
Musyng nyght and day,
Mournyng all alone,
Comfort had he none,
For she was quyte gone;
Thus in conclusyon,
She brought him in abusyon;
In ernest and in game
She was moch to blame;
Disparaged is her fame,
And blemysshed is her name,
In maner half with shame;
Troylus also hath lost
On her moch loue and cost,
And now must kys the post;
Pandara, that went betwene,
Hath won nothing, I wene,
But lyght for somer grene;
Yet for a speciall laud
He is named Troylus baud,
Of that name he is sure
Whyles the world shall dure.
I am but a yong mayd,
And cannot in effect
My style as yet direct
With Englysh wordes elect:
Our naturall tong is rude,
And hard to be enneude
With pullysshed termes lusty;
Our language is so rusty,
So cankered, and so full
Of frowardes, and so dull,
That if I wolde apply

To wryte ornatly,
I wot not where to fynd
Termes to serue my mynde.
Gowers Englysh is olde,
And of no value told;
His mater is worth gold,
And worthy to be enrold.
In Chauser I am sped,
His tales I haue red:
His mater is delectable,
Solacious, and commendable;
His Englysh well alowed,
So as it is enprowed,
For as it is enployd,
There is no Englysh voyd,
At those dayes moch commended,
And now men wold haue amended
His Englysh, whereat they barke,
And mar all they warke:
Chaucer, that famus clerke,
His termes were not darke,
But plesaunt, easy, and playne;
No worde he wrote in vayne.
Also Johnn Lydgate
Wryteth after an hyer rate;
It is dyffuse to fynde
The sentence of his mynde,
Yet wryteth he in his kynd,
No man that can amend
Those maters that he hath pende;
Yet some men fynde a faute,
And say he wryteth to haute.

—John Skelton, "Phillip Sparrowe" (c. 1508), *Poetical Works
of John Skelton*, 1843, ed. Dyce, pp. 69–75, v. 605–812

GAVIN DOUGLAS "TRANSLATOR'S PROLOGUE" (1513)

A significant poet of the court of Scottish king James IV, Gavin Douglas
(1476–1522) was the author of *The Palice of Honour* and translator of several

important works. Here, in a translation of the *Aeneid*, Douglas praises
Chaucer but notes he "standis beneth Virgill in gre" ("stands beneath Virgil
in greatness"). Douglas takes issue with a story from Virgil that Chaucer
relates in his *Legend of Good Women*, but eventually excuses Chaucer for
his shortcoming in this instance, declaring that Chaucer "was evir . . . all
womanis frend" ("was ever . . . all women's friend"). Douglas is perhaps
the first significant writer to criticize Chaucer, though his criticisms are
pointed, and he widely praises Chaucer as well.

Thoght venerabill Chauser, principal poet but peir,
Hevynly trumpat, orlege and reguler,
In eloquens balmy, cundyt and dyall,
Mylky fontane, cleirstrand and royss ryall,
Of fresch endyte, throu Albion iland braid,
In hys legend of notabill ladeis said
That he couth follow word by word Virgil,
Wisar than I may faill in lakar stile.
I say nocht this of Chauser for offens,
Bot till excuss my lewyt insufficiens,
For as he standis beneth Virgill in gre,
Vndir hym alsfer I grant my self to be.
And netheless into sum place, quha kend it,
My mastir Chauser gretly Virgill offendit.
All thoch I be tobald hym to repreif,
He was fer baldar, certis, by hys leif,
Sayand he followit Virgillis lantern toforn,
Quhou Eneas to Dydo was forsworn.
Was he forsworn? Than Eneas was fals-
That he admittis and callys hym traytour als.
Thus wenyng allane Ene to haue reprevit,
He hass gretly the prynce of poetis grevit.
Bot sikkyrly of resson me behufis
Excuss Chauser fra all maner repruffis
In lovyng of thir ladeis lylly quhite
He set on Virgill and Eneas this wyte,
For he was evir (God wait) all womanis frend.

—Gavin Douglas, "Translator's Prologue" to
Aenead: Eneados, Book I, 1513

Sir Thomas Wyatt (1540)

An author in the court of English king Henry VIII, Sir Thomas Wyatt (c. 1503–42) penned *The Court of Venus* and numerous shorter works. The politics and machinations of court life greatly impacted Wyatt's work, but critics have often noted Chaucer's influence on his writing. Here, in *How to Use the Court*, Wyatt uses Chaucer's character of Pandarus, from *Troilus and Criseyde*, as a simile for how one could use attractive female relations to advance one's cause at court.

In this also se thou be not idle:
Thy nece, thy cosyn, thy sister, or thy daughter,
If she bee faire: if handsome be her middle:
If thy better hath her loue besought her:
Auaunce his cause, and he shall helpe thy nede,
It is but loue, turne it to a laughter.
But ware I say, so gold thee helpe and spede:
That in this case thou be not so vnwise,
As Pandar was in such a like dede.
For he the fole of conscience was so nice:
That he no gaine would haue for all his payne.

—Sir Thomas Wyatt, *How to Use the Court*, c. 1540

Henry VIII (1542–43)

Henry Tudor (1491–1547), more commonly known as Henry VIII, king of England (reigned 1509–47), is perhaps most famous for his many wives, though he was also a formidable politician and, like many monarchs of his day, an occasional author. In the following statute, Henry is something of a critic, excepting Chaucer's works, and *The Canterbury Tales* specifically, from an act of censure, an exception that clearly denotes the continuing popularity and importance of Chaucer's writings, even in the highest of circles.

Provided allso that all bokes in Englishe printed before the yere of our Lorde a thousande fyve hundred and fourtie intytled the Kings Hieghnes proclamacions iniunctions, translacions of the Pater noster, the Aue Maria and the Crede, the psalters prymers prayer statutes and lawes of the Realme,

Cronycles Canterburye tales, Chaucers bokes Gowers bokes and stories of mennes lieues, shall not be comprehended in the prohibicion of this acte.

> —Henry VIII, "An Act for Thaduancement of
> True Religion and for Thabbolisshment of the Contrarie,"
> *Statute 34 and 35 Henry VIII,* 1542–43, Ch. 1, Sec. 5

ROGER ASCHAM (1545)

Roger Ascham (1515/16–1568) was an important educator and writer in sixteenth-century England, a popular rhetorician whose most enduring work is *The Scholemaster.* Ascham refers to Chaucer in each of the three following excerpts. In the first, he makes a reference to Chaucer's Parson while decrying gambling. In the second, Ascham notes Chaucer's praiseworthy ability to create and describe unique characters. In the third, Ascham connotes Chaucer to Petrarch and notes that some individuals make the two poets "their Gods in verses." All three of Ashcam's references note Chaucer's enduring fame and popular reputation during the early years of the English Renaissance.

The Nource of dise and cardes, is werisom Ydlenesse, enemy of vertue, ye drowner of youthe, that tarieth in it, and as Chauser doth saye verie well in the Parsons tale, the greene path waye to hel, hauinge this thing appropriat vnto it, that where as other vices haue some cloke of honestie, onely ydlenes can neyther do wel, nor yet thinke wel.

Whose horriblenes (Gaming) is so large, that it passed the eloquence of our *Englishe Homer,* to compasse it: yet because I euer thought hys sayinges to haue as muche authoritie, as eyther *Sophocles* or *Euripides* in Greke, therefore gladly do I remember these verses of hys. (Not from Thynne's text, 1532)

> Hasardry is Very mother of lesinges
> And of deceyte and cursed sweringes
> Blasphemie of Chist, manslaughter, and waste also,
> Of catel of tyme, of other thynges mo.

Cursed sweryng, blasphemie of Christe, These halfe verses Chaucer in an other place, more at large doth well set out, and verye liuely expresse, sayinge.

> Ey by goddes precious hert and his nayles
> And by the blood of Christe, that is in Hales.

> —Roger Ascham, *Toxophilus,* 1545

Roger Ascham (1552)

Diligence also must be vsed [by an Historian] in kepyng truly the order of tyme: and describyng lyuely, both the site of places and nature of persons not onely for the outward shape of the body: but also for the inward disposition of the mynde, as *Thucidides* doth in many places very trimly, and *Homer* euery-where, and that alwayes most excellently, which obseruation is chiefly to be marked in hym. And our *Chaucer* doth the same, very praise worthely: marke hym well and conferre hym with any other that writeth of in our tyme in their proudest toung, whosoeuer lyst.

—Roger Ascham, A *Report . . . of the Affaires and
State of Germany*, 1552

Roger Ascham (1570)

Some that make *Chaucer* in Englishe and *Petrarch* in *Italian*, their Gods in verses, and yet be not able to make true difference, what is a fault, and what is a just prayse, in those two worthie wittes, will moch mislike this my writyng. But such men be euen like followers *of Chaucer* and *Petrarke* as one here in England did folow *Syr Tho. More:* who, being most vnlike vnto him, in wit and learning, neuertheles in wearing his gowne awrye vpon the one shoulder, as *Syr Tho. More* was wont to doe, would needes be counted like vnto hym.

—Roger Ascham, *The Scholemaster,* 1570

John Foxe "A Protestation to the Whole Church of England" (1570)

John Foxe (1517–87) was a prominent Protestant author and critic during the Elizabethan era who is most renowned for compiling the *Acts and Monuments of These Latter and Perilous Times.* This book contains accounts of the martyrdom of Christians whom Foxe believed kept faith with the "true" Protestant Church and rebuked what Foxe considered the "false" Church under the leadership of the Pope in Rome. It should hardly be surprising, then, that Foxe's perspective on Chaucer is widely colored by his religious beliefs, and any students writing on the topic of Chaucer and religion will find a meaty discussion excerpted here.

Foxe begins by referring to a "certayne other auncient treatise compiled by Geoffray Chawcer by the way of a Dialogue or questions moued in the person of a certaine uplandish and simple ploughman of the countrey." The particular text Foxe is referring to was actually not written by Chaucer, though in Foxe's day many believed it was. The text supported the teachings of John Wycliffe (c. 1320–1384), an English theologian and church reformer and a direct contemporary of Chaucer's. Wycliffe's work was considered a precursor to the Protestant Reformation, and thus it can easily be understood why Foxe was eager to connect the great medieval writer Chaucer to Wycliffe. This connection has been explored by numerous other critics as well, including Frederick Denison Maurice and H. Simon in works excerpted in this volume. Contemporary scholars generally believe that Chaucer was not a follower of Wycliffe's, though there is no indication that Chaucer was wholly unsympathetic to the man's ideas.

Foxe refers to Chaucer's penchant for criticizing the clergy and church of his day, something Chaucer does much of in *The Canterbury Tales*. Foxe labels Chaucer a definitive Wycliffite and even concludes that some medieval individuals, "by readyng of Chausers workes . . . were brought to the true knowledge of Religion." Though Foxe's views on Chaucer and religion are generally considered extreme today, they are provocative, and provide contemporary readers a glimpse of how Chaucer's works were used during the great cultural and social struggles that occurred in England in the centuries after his death.

To discend now somewhat lower in drawing out the descent of the Church. What a multitude here commeth of faithful witnesses in the time of *Ioh. Wickleffe*, as *Ocliffe, Wickleffe*. an. 1376. W. *Thorpe, White, Puruey, Patshall, Payne, Gower, Chauser, Gascoyne, William Swynderby, Walter Brute, Roger Dexter, William Sautry* about the year 1400. *Iohn Badley*, an. 1410. *Nicholas Tayler, Rich. Wagstaffe, Mich. Scriuener, W. Smith, Iohn Henry, W. Parchmenar, Roger Goldsmith*, with an Ancresse called *Mathilde* in the Citie of Leicester, Lord *Cobham*, Syr *Roger Acton* Knight, *Iohn Beuerlay* preacher, *Iohn Hus, Hierome of Prage* Scholemaster, with a number of faithfull Bohemians and Thaborites not to be told with whom I might also adioyne *Laurentius Valla*, and *Joannes Picus* the learned Earle of Mirandula. But what do I stand upon recitall of names, which almost are infinite.

For so much as mention is here made of these superstitious sects of Fryers, and such other beggerly religions, it shall not seme much impartient, being moued by the occasion hereof . . . to annexe . . . a certayne other auncient treatise compiled by Geoffray Chawcer by the way of a Dialogue or questions moued in the person of a certaine uplandish and simple ploughman of the countrey. Which treatise for the same, yᵉ autor intituled Jack vp land. . . .

Moreouer to these two (Linacre and Pace), I thought it not out of season to couple also some mention of Geffray Chaucer, and Iohn Gower:

Whiche although beyng much discrepant from these in course of yeares, yet may seme not vnworthy to bee matched with these forenamed persons in commendation of their studie and learnyng.

Likewise, as touchyng the tyme of Chaucer, by hys owne workes in the end of his first booke of Troylus and Creseide it is manifest, that he and Gower were both of one tyme, althoughe it seemeth that Gower was a great deale his auncient: both notably learned, as the barbarous rudenes of that tyme did geue: both great frendes together, and both in like kind of studie together occupied, so endeuoryng themselues, and employing their tyme, that they excelling many other in study and exercise of good letters, did passe forth their lyues here right worshipfully & godly, to the worthy fame and commendation of their name. Chaucers woorkes bee all printed in one volume, and therfor knowen to all men. This I meruell, to see the idle life of ye priestes and clergy men of that tyme, seyng these lay persons shewed themselues in these kynde of liberal studies so industrious & fruitfully occupied: but muche more I meruell to consider this, how that the Bishoppes condemnyng and abolishyng al maner of Englishe bookes and treatises, which might bryng the people to any light of knowledge, did yet authorise the woorkes of Chaucer to remayne still & to be occupied: Who (no doubt) saw in Religion as much almost, as euen we do now, and vttereth in hys workes no lesse, and semeth to bee a right Wicleuian, or els was neuer any, and that all his workes almost, if they be throughly aduised, will testifie (albeit it bee done in myrth, & couertly) & especially the latter ende of his third booke of the Testament of loue: for there purely he toucheth the highest matter, that is the Communion. Wherin, excepte a man be altogether blynde, he may espye him at the full. Althoughe in the same booke (as in all other he vseth to do) vnder shadowes couertly, as vnder a visoure, he suborneth truth, in such sorte, as both priuely she may profite the godly minded, and yet not be espyed of the craftye aduersarie: And therefore the Byshops, belike, takyng hys workes but for iestes and toyes, in condemnyng other bookes, yet permitted his bookes to be read. So it pleased God to blinde then the eyes of them, for the more commoditie of his people, to the entent that through the readyng of his treatises, some fruite might redounde therof to his Churche, as no doubt, it did to many: As also I am partlye informed of certeine, whiche knewe the parties, which to them reported, that by readyng of Chausers workes, they were brought to the true knowledge of Religion. And not vnlike to be true. For to omitte other partes of his volume, whereof some are more fabulous then other, what tale can bee more playnely tolde, then the talke of the ploughman? or what finger can pointe out more directly the Pope with his Prelates to be Antichrist, then doth the poore Pellycan reasonyng agaynst the gredy Griffon? Under whiche *Hypotyposis* or Poesie, who is so blind that seeth not by the Pellicane, the doctrine of Christ, and of the Lollardes to bee defended agaynst the Churche of Rome? Or who is so impudent that can denye that to be true, which the Pellicane there affirmeth in describyng the presumptuous pride of that pre-tensed Church? Agayne what egge can be more lyke, or figge vnto an other, then yᵉ words, properties, and conditions of that rauenyng Griphe resembleth the true Image, that is, the nature & qualities of that which we call the Churche of Rome, in euery point and degre? and therfore no great maruell, if that narration was exempted out of the copies of Chaucers workes: whiche notwithstandyng now is restored agayne, and is extant, for euery man to read that is disposed.

This Geffray Chauser being borne (as is thought) in Oxfordshire, & dwellyng in Wodstocke, lyeth buried in the Churche of the minster of S. Peter at Westminster, in an He on the South side of the sayd Churche, not far from the doore leading to the cloyster, and vpon his graue stone first were written these ii old verses

> Galfridus Chauser vates et fama poesis
> Maternae, hac sacra sum tumulatus humo.

> —John Foxe, "A Protestation to the Whole Church of
> England," *Ecclesiasticall history contayning the Actes and
> Monumentes of thyngs passed in euery Kinges tyme
> in this Realme* 1570, 2nd enlarged ed., pp. 341, 965–66

George Gascoigne "Certain Notes of Instruction" (1575)

The first and most necessarie poynt that euer I founde meete to be considered in making of a delectable poeme is this, to grounde it upon some fine invention. For it is not inough to roll in pleasant woordes nor yet to thunder in *Rym, Ram, Ruff,* by letter (quoth my master *Chaucer)* nor yet to abound in apt vocables, or epythetes. . . . Also our father *Chaucer* hath vsed the same libertie in feete and measures that the Latinists do vse: and who so euer do peruse and well consider his workes, he shall finde that although his lines are not alwayes of one selfe same number of Syllables, yet beyng redde by one that hath vnderstanding, the longest verse and that which hath most Syllables in it, will fall (to the eare) correspondent vnto that whiche hath fewest syllables in it: and like wise that whiche hath in it fewest syllables, shalbe founde yet to consist of woordes that haue suche naturall sounde, as may seeme equall in length to a verse which hath many moe sillables of lighter accentes. . . .

I had forgotten a notable kinde of ryme, called ryding rime, and that is suche as our Mayster and Father *Chaucer* vsed in his Canterburie tales, and in diuers other delectable and light enterprises.

—George Gascoigne, "Certayne Notes of Instruction,"
The Posies of George Gascoigne, Esquire, 1575

EDMUND SPENSER (1579)

One of England's most revered authors, Edmund Spenser (1552–99) wrote such classics as *The Shepheardes Calendar* and *The Faerie Queene.* Because they are both epic poets and because Spenser himself acknowledged the impact Chaucer had on his own work, the two writers are often compared, and any student discussing the two poets and their major works would do well to begin by uncovering what Spenser himself wrote about Chaucer.

In this excerpt, from *The Shepheardes Calendar* (1579), Spenser, in the guise of the rustic figure Colin Clote, refers to Chaucer as "The God of shepheards *Tityrus.*" Here, Spenser equates Chaucer to the revered Roman poet Virgil, suggesting that Chaucer is as important to English poetry as Virgil is to Latin poetry. Spenser adds that Chaucer "taught me . . . to make," by which he means write; this is the first, but not the last, time that Spenser credited the influence Chaucer had on his own writing.

The God of shepheards *Tityrus* is dead,
Who taught me homely, as I can, to make.
He, whilst he lived, was the soueraigne head
Of shepheards all, that bene with loue ytake:
Well couth he wayle his Woes, and lightly slake
The flames, which loue within his heart had bredd,
And tell vs mery tales, to keep vs wake,
The while our sheepe about vs safely fedde.

Nowe dead he is, and lyeth wrapt in lead,
(O why should death on hym such outrage showe?)
And all hys passing skil with him is fledde,
The fame whereof doth dayly greater growe.
But if on me some little drops would flowe
Of that the spring was in his learned hedde,

I soone would learne these woods, to wayle my woe,
And teache the trees, their trickling teares to shedde.

—Edmund Spenser, *The Shepheardes Calendar*, 1579, Fol. 24

Sir Philip Sidney (1581)

(Poets came before philosophers and historians.) So among the Romans were Liuius, Andronicus, and Ennius. So in the Italian language, the first that made it aspire to be a Treasure-house of Science, were the Poets *Dante, Boccace,* and *Petrarch.* So in our English were *Gower* and *Chaucer.*

After whom, encouraged and delighted with theyr excellent fore-going, others haue followed, to beautifie our mother tongue, as wel in the same kinde as in other Arts. . . .

See whether wisdome and temperance in *Vlisses and Diomedes,* valure in *Achilles,* friendship in *Nisus,* and *Eurialus,* euen to an ignoraunt man, carry not an apparent shyning: and contrarily, the remorse of conscience in *Oedipus,* the soone repenting pride in *Agamemnon,* the selfe-deuouring crueltie in his Father *Atreus,* the violence of ambition in the two *Theban* brothers, the sowre-sweetnes of reuenge in *Medaea,* and to fall lower, the *Terentian Gnato,* and our *Chaucer's* Pandar, so exprest, that we nowe vse their names to signifie their trades. . . .

Thirdly, that it (Poetry) is the Nurse of abuse, infecting vs with many pestilent desires: with a Syrens sweetnes, drawing the mind to the Serpents tayle of sinfull fancy. And heerein especially, Comedies giue the largest field to erre, as *Chaucer* sayth: howe both in other nations and in ours, before Poets did soften vs, we were full of courage, giuen to martiall exercises; the pillers of manlyke liberty and not lulled a sleepe in shady idlenes with Poets pastimes. . . .

Chaucer, vndoubtedly did excellently in hys *Troylus* and *Cresseid;* of whom, truly I know not, whether to meruaile more, either that he in that mistie time, could see so clearely, or that wee in this cleare age, walke so stumblingly after him. Yet had he great wants, fitte to be forgiuen, in so reuerent antiquity.

—Sir Philip Sidney, An *Apologie for Poetrie,* 1581

William Webbe "A Discourse of English Poetrie" (1586)

William Webbe (1550–91?) was an English critic and translator who wrote "A Discourse of English Poetrie." In this work, Webbe speaks of Chaucer as "the God of English Poets," but also notes that many individuals in Webbe's own time consider Chaucer "blunte and course" ("blunt and coarse.") This is one of the first references to Chaucer as a potentially vulgar poet (for another, see Daniel Defoe's entry), but Webbe defends Chaucer. While noting that Chaucer is a product of his time Webbe heaps praise on the man and ultimately concludes that Chaucer wrote of such vices to detract people from indulging in them, not to encourage them.

The first of our English Poets that I haue heard of was Iohn *Gower* . . . his freend *Chawcer* who speaketh of him oftentimes in diuers places of hys workes. *Chawcer,* who for that excellent fame which hee obtayned in his Poetry, was alwayes accounted the God of English Poets (such a tytle for honours sake hath been giuen him), was next after if not equall in time to Gower and hath left many workes, both for delight and profitable knowledge farre exceeding any other that as yet euer since hys time directed theyr studies that way. Though the manner of hys stile may seeme blunte and course to many fine English eares at these dayes, yet in trueth, if it be equally pondered, and with good iudgment aduised, and confirmed with the time wherein he wrote, a man shall perceiue thereby euen a true picture or perfect shape of a right Poet. He by his delightsome vayne so gulled the eares of men with his deuises, that, although corruption bare such sway in most matters, that learning and truth might skant bee admitted to shewe it selfe, yet without controllment myght hee gyrde at the vices and abuses of all states, and gawle with very sharpe and eger inuentions, which he did so learnedly and pleasantly that none therefore would call him into question. For such was his bolde spyrit, that what enormities he saw in any he would not spare to pay them home, eyther in playne words, or els in some pretty and pleasant couert, that the simplest might espy him. Neere in time vnto him was *Lydgate,* a Poet surely for good proportion of his verse and meetely currant style, as the time affoorded, comparable with *Chawcer,* yet more occupied in supersticious and odde matters then was requesite in so good a wytte. . . .

Let thinges that are faigned for pleasures sake haue a neer resemblance of the truth. This precept may you perceiue to bee most duelie obserued of *Chawcer.* for who could with more delight prescribe such wholsome counsaile and sage aduise, where he seemeth onelie to respect the profitte of his lessons and instructions? or who coulde with greater wisedome, or more pithie skill, vnfold such pleasant and delightsome matters of mirth, as though they respected nothing but the telling of a merry tale? so that this is the very grounde of right poetrie, to give profitable counsaile, yet so as it must be mingled with delight. . . .

For surelie I am of this opinion that the wantonest Poets of all, in their most laciuious workes wherein they busied themselues, sought rather by that meanes to withdraw mens mindes (especiallie the best natures) from such foule vices then to allure them to imbrace such beastly follies as they detected.

—William Webbe, "A Discourse of English Poetrie," 1586,
Elizabethan Critical Essays, 1904, Vol. 1, ed. Smith, pp. 241–63

THOMAS NASHE (1589)

Thomas Nashe (1567–1601?), best known as a prose writer during the Elizabethan era, commented often on the literary works and standards of England. In the excerpt below, Nashe responds to a common continental European argument that the Italian authors of the Middle Ages were the finest; Nashe declares he would place Chaucer, Lydgate, and Gower against the finest writers of the Middle Ages from any country.

———— ———— ————

Tut saies our English Italians, the finest witts our Climate sends foorth, are but drie braind doltes, in comparison of other countries: whome if you interrupt with *redde rationem,* they will tell you of *Petrache, Tasso, Celiano,* with an infinite number of others; to whome if I should oppose *Chaucer, Lidgate, Gower,* with such like, that liued vnder the tirranie of ignorance, I do think their best louers, would bee much discontented, with the collation of contraries, if I should write ouer al their heads, Haile fellow well met. One thing 1 am sure of, that each of these three, haue vaunted their meeters, with as much admiration in English, as euer the proudest *Ariosto* did his verse in Italian.

—Thomas Nashe, *To the Gentlemen Students
of both Universities,* 1589

RICHARD PUTTENHAM (1589)

Richard Puttenham (c. 1520–1601) is the author of the influential *The Art of English Poesie,* though his brother George is also sometimes credited as the author of the work. In *Poesie,* Puttenham christens Chaucer "the most renowmed" of all medieval poets, and even places him above those poets who have recently distinguished themselves during "her Maiestis" Queen Elizabeth I's reign. Students can thus see how Chaucer was viewed by critics of the Elizabethan Renaissance shortly before its great writers, including William Shakespeare, rose to prominence.

———— ———— ————

And in her Maiesties time that now is are sprang vp an other crew of Courtly makers, Noble men and Gentlemen of her Maiesties owne seruauntes, who haue written excellently well.... But of them all particularly this is myne opinion, that *Chaucer,* with *Gower, Lidgat* and *Harding* for their antiquitie ought to haue the first place, and *Chaucer* as the most renowmed of them all, for the much learning appeareth to be in him aboue any of the rest. And though many of his bookes be but bare translations out of the Latin and French, yet are they wel handled, as his bookes of *Troilus* and *Cresseid,* and the *Romant of the Rose,* whereof he translated but one halfe, the deuice was *Iohn de Mehunes,* a French Poet, the Canterbury Tales were *Chaucers* owne inuention as I suppose, and where he sheweth more the naturall of his pleasant wit, then in any other of his workes, his similitudes comparisons, and all other descriptions are such as can not be amended. His meetre Hero- icall of *Troilus* and *Cresseid* is very graue and stately, keeping the staffe of seuen, and the verse often, his other verses of the Canterbury tales be but riding ryme, neuerthelesse very well becomming the matter of that pleasaunt pilgrimage in which euery mans part is played with much decency. . . .

But our auncient rymers, as *Chaucer, Lydgate,* and others, vsed these *Cesures* either very seldome, or not at all, or else very licentiously, and many times made their meetres (they called them riding ryme) of such vnshapely wordes as would allow no conuenient *Cesure,* and therefore did let their rymes runne out at length, and neuer stayd till they came to the end.

—Richard Puttenham, *The Art of English Poesie,*
1589, pp. 49–50

ROBERT GREENE (1592)

A Renaissance playwright and author known as much for his riotous living as for his published works, Robert Greene (1558–92) was a colorful and controversial figure and one of England's first professional writers. *Greene's Vision,* which was purportedly written on the author's deathbed, consists of a dream vision in which Greene encounters the spirits of both Chaucer and Gower, who each relate a story that illustrates the dangers of jealousy. Chaucer tells a fabliau, a short often comic or cynical verse tale, a genre he uses in *The Canterbury Tales* in "The Miller's Tale" and "The Reeve's Tale." Gower's contribution is an exemplary tale, a more solemn story designed to demonstrate a good example.

Greene juxtaposes these two tales. Chaucer's work is light and pleasant, whereas Gower's work is serious and erudite. At the end of the two tales, Gower asks Chaucer, "how like you this tale, is it not more full of

humanity, then your vain and scurrulous inuention?" Chaucer responds,
"but these are not plesant, they breed no delight, youth wil not like of
such a long circumstance." Critics have considered Chaucer's frivolous
response reflective of much of the work of Greene himself, an approach
that Greene, in his vision, abandons in favor of the more sober style and
thematics of Gower, promising to focus his own writing on more serious
matters in the future. *Greene's Vision* is not hesitant in launching several
critical jabs at Chaucer. Greene represents Chaucer as foolish and his
work as lighthearted and ultimately unsatisfying. Students may find it
instructive to compare Greene's characterization of Chaucer's work to
that of other writers and critics of his day, to determine whether Greene's
opinion was a popular and commonly held one or not.

I considered, that wee were borne to profit our countrie, not onely to
pleasure our selues: then the discommodities that grew from my vaine
pamphlets, began to muster in my sight: then I cald to minde, how many
idle fancies I had made to passe the Presse, how I had pestred Gentlemens
eyes and mindes, with the infection of many fond passions, rather infecting
them with the allurements of some inchanted Aconiton', then tempered
their thought with any honest Antidote, which consideration entered thus
farre into my conscience. . . .

Being in this deepe meditation, lying contemplating vpon my bed, I
fell a sleepe, where I had not lyne long in a slumber, but that me thought
I was in a faire medowe, sitting vnder an Oake, viewing the beautie of the
sunne which then shewed himselfe in his pride: as thus I sat gasing on
so gorgeous an obiect, I spied comming downe the Meade, two ancient
men, aged, for their foreheads were the Calenders of their yeares, and the
whitenesse of their haires bewrayed the number of their dayes, their pace
was answerable to their age, and *In diebus Mis,* hung vpon their garments:
their visages were wrinckled, but well featured, and their countenance
conteyned much grauitie. . . .

Thou has heere two, whome experience hath taught many medicines for
yong mens maladies, I am sir *Geffrey Chaucer,* this *Iohn Gower,* what we can
in counsaile, shall be thy comfort, and for secrecie we are no blabs. Heering sir
Geffrey Chaucer thus familiar, I tooke heart at grasse to my selfe, and thought
nowe I might haue my doubt well debated, betweene two such excellent schollers:
wherevpon putting of my hat with great reuerence, I made this replie.

Graue Lawreats, the tipes of Englands excellence for Poetry, and the worlds
wonders for your wits, all haile, and happily welcome, for your presence is a
salue for my passions, and the inward greefes that you perceiue by my outward

lookes, are alreadie halfe eased by your comfortable promise: I cannot denie but my thoughts are discontent, and my sences in a great maze, which I haue damd vp a long while, as thinking best to smoother sorrow with silence, but now I will set fire on the straw, and lay open my secrets to your selues, that your sweet counsailes may ease my discontent. So it is, that by profession I am a scholler, and in wil do affect that which I could neuer effect in action, for faine would I haue some taste in the liberall sciences, but *hlon licet cuibis adire Corinthum*, and therefore I content my selfe with a superficiall insight, and only satisfie my desire with the name of a Scholler, yet as blinde Baiard wil iumpe soonest into the mire, so haue I ventured afore many my betters, to put my selfe into the presse, and haue set foorth sundrie bookes in print of loue & such amourous fancies which some haue fauoured, as other haue misliked. But now of late there came foorth a booke called the Cobler of Canterburie, a merry worke, and made by some madde fellow, conteining plesant tales, a little tainted with scurilitie, such reuerend *Chawcer* as your selfe set foorth in your iourney to *Canterbury*. At this booke, the grauer and greater sorte repine, as thinking it not so pleasant to some, as preiudiciall to many, crossing it with such bitter inuectiues, that they condemne the Author almost for an Atheist. Now learned Lawreat, heere lyes the touch of my passions: they father the booke vppon me, whereas it is *Incerti authoris*, and suspitiouslye slaunder me with many harde reproches, for penning that which neuer came within the compasse of my Quill. . . . This father *Chawcer* hath made me enter into consideration of all my former follies, and to thinke how wantonly I haue spent my youth, in penning such fond pamphlets, that I am driuen into a dumpe whether they shall redound to my insuing credit, or my future infamie, or whether I haue doone well or ill, in setting foorth such amourous trifles, heerein resolue me, and my discontent is doone.

At this long period of mine, *Chawcer* sat downe & laught, and then rising vp and leaning his back against a Tree, he made this merry aunswer. Why *Greene* quoth he, knowest thou not, that the waters that flow from *Pernassus* Founte, are not tyed to any particular operation? that there are nine Muses, amongst whom as there is a *Clio* to write graue matters, so there is a *Thalis* to endite pleasant conceits, and that *Apollo* hath Baies for them both, aswell to crowne the one for hir wanton amours, as to honour the other for her worthy labours: the braine hath many strings, and the wit many stretches, some tragical to write, like *Euripedes*: some comicall to pen, like *Terence*: some deepely conceited to set out matters of great import: others sharpe witted to discouer pleasant fantasies: what if *Cato* set foorth seueare censures, and *Quid* amorous Axiomes, were they not both counted for their faculties excellent? yes, and *Ouid* was commended for his *Salem ingenii*, when the other was counted to haue a dull wit, & a slow memory: if learning were knit in one string, and could expresse himself but in one vaine, then should want of variety, bring all into an imperfect Chaos. But sundry men, sundry conceits, & wits are to be praised not for the grauity of the matter, but for the ripenes of the inuention: so that *Martiall*, *Horace* or any other, deserue to bee famoused for their Odes and Elegies, as wel as *Hesiode*, *Hortensius*, or any other for their deeper precepts of doctrines. Feare not then what those Morosie wil murmure, whose dead cinders brook no glowing sparkes nor care not for the opinion of such as hold none but Philosophic for a Subiect: I tell thee learning will haue his due, and let a vipers wit reach his hand to *Apollo*, and hee shall sooner haue a branch to eternize his fame, than the sowrest Satyricall Authour in the worlde. Wee haue heard of thy worke to be amorous, sententious, and well written. If thou doubtest blame for thy wantonnes, let my selfe suffice for an instaunce, whose Canterburie tales are broad enough before, and written homely and pleasantly: yet who hath bin more canonised for his workes, than Sir *Geffrey Chawcer*. What *Green?* Poets wits are free, and their words ought to be without checke: so it was in my time, and therfore resolue thy selfe, thou hast doone Scholler-like, in setting foorth thy pamphlets, and shalt haue perpetual fame which is learnings due for thy endeuour. This saying of *Chawcer* cheered mee vntill olde *Iohn Gower* rising vp with a sowre countenance began thus.

Iohn Gower to the Authour.

Well hath *Chawcer* said, that the braine hath sundrie strings, and the wit diuerse stretches: some bent to pen graue Poems, other to endite wanton fancies, both honoured and praised for the height of their capacitie: yet as the Diamond is more estimated in the Lapidaries shop than the Topace, and the Rose more valued in the Garden than Gillyflowers: So men that write of Morall precepts, or Philosophical! Aphorismes are more highly esteemed, than such as write Poems of loue, and conceits of fancie. . . .

Thou hast applied thy wits ill, & hast sowed chaffe & shalt reape no haruest. But my maister *Chaucer* brings in his workes for an instance, that as his, so thine shalbe famoused: no, it is not a promise to conclude vpon: for men honor his more for the antiquity of the verse, the english & prose, than for any deepe loue to the matter: for proofe marke how they weare out of vse. Therfore let me tel thee, thy books are baits that allure youth, Syrens that sing sweetly, and yet destroy with their notes, faire flowers without smel and good phrases without any profite.

Without any profite (quoth *Chawcer*) and with that hee start vp with a frown: no *Gower*, I tell thee, his labours, as they be amorous, so they be sententious: and serue as well to suppresse vanity, as they seem to import

wantonnes. Is there no meanes to cure sores, but with Corasiues? no helpe
for vlcers, but sharpe implasters? no salue against vice, but sowr satyres? Yes,
a pleasant vaine, quips as nie the quicke as a grauer inuectiue, and vnder a
merry fable can *Esope* as wel tant folly, as *Hesiode* correct manners in his
Heroicks. I tell thee this man hath ioyned pleasure with profite, & though his
Bee hath a sting, yet she makes sweet honny. Hath he not discouered in his
workes the follies of loue, the sleights of fancy, and lightnesse of youth, to be
induced to such vanities? and what more profit can there be to his countrey
than manifest such open mischiefes, as grew from the conceit of beauty &
deceit of women: and all this hath he painted down in his pamphlets. I grant
(quoth *Gower*) the meaning is good, but the method is bad: for by aming at
an inconuenience, he bringeth in a mischiefe: in seeking to suppresse fond
loue, the sweetnes of his discourse allures youth to loue, like such as taking
drink to cool their thirst, feele the tast so pleasant, that they drinke while
they surfeit. *Ouid* drewe not so many with his remedie of Loue from loue,
as his *Ars Amandi* bred amorous schollers, nor hath *Greenes* Bookes weaned
so many from vanity, as they haue wedded from wantonnesse. That is the
reason (quoth *Chawcer*) that youth is more prone vnto euil than to good,
and with the Serpent, sucke honny from the sweetest sirops, and haue not
Poets shadowed waightie precepts in slender Poems and in pleasant fancies
vsed deepe perswations? who bitte the Curtizans of his time and the follies of
youth more than *Horace,* and yet his Odes were wanton. Who more inuaied
against the manners of men than *Martiall,* and yet his verse was lasciuious?
And had hee not better (quoth *Cower*) haue discouered his principles in
some graue sort as *Hesiode* did or *Pindaris,* than in such amorous & wanton
manner: the light-nesse of the conceit cracks halfe the credite, and the vanitie
of the pen breeds the lesse beleefe. After *Ouid* had written his Art of Loue,
and set the youth on fire to imbrace fancy, he could not reclaime them with

Otia si tollas periere cupidinis arcus.

The thoughts of young men are like Bauins, which once set on fire, will
not out till they be ashes, and therefore doe I infer, that such Pamphlets
doe rather preiudice than profite. Tush (quoth *Chawcer*) all this is but
a peremptorie selfe conceit in thine owne humour: for I will shew thee
for instance, such sentences as may like the grauest, please the wisest,
and instruct the youngest and wantonnest, and they be these: first, of the
disposition of women. . . .

Now Sir *Geffrey Chawcer* (quoth *Gower*) how like you this tale, is it
not more full of humanity, then your vain and scurrulous inuention? and
yet affecteth as muche in the mind of the hearers? are not graue sentences

as forcible, as wanton principles? tush (quoth *Chawcer)* but these are not plesant, they breed no delight, youth wil not like of such a long circumstance. Our English Gentlemen are of the mind of the Athenians, that will sooner bee perswaded by a fable, than an Oration: and induced with a merrie tale, when they will not be brought to any compasse with serious circumstances. The more pittie (quoth *Gower)* that they should bee so fond, as to be subiect to the delight of every leud fancy, when the true badge of a Gentleman, is learning ioyned with vallour and vertue, and therefore ought they to read of Martiall Discipline, not of the slight of *Venus:* and to talke of hard labours, not to chat of foolish and effeminate amoures.

—Robert Greene, *Greene's Vision,* 1592

THOMAS NASHE (1592)

Nashe's *Strange Newes of the Intercepting certaine Letters*, which this excerpt is taken from, was a savage and bitter satire of Renaissance author Gabriel Harvey's work *Four Letters* (1592). In it, Nashe reserves higher praise for Chaucer and Edmund Spenser, calling them the "Homer and Virgil of England." Nashe's lament that Chaucer did not write all of his verse in hexameter is likely a sarcastic response to something in Harvey's work.

─────

Proceede to cherish thy surpassing carminicall arte of memorie with full cuppes (as thou dost) let Chaucer *bee new scourd against the day ofbattaile, and* Terence *come but in nowe and then with the snuffe of a sentence, and* Dictum puta, *Weele strike it as dead as a doore naile. . . .*

The Hexamiter verse I graunt to be a Gentleman of an auncient house (so is many an english begger), yet this Clyme of ours hee cannot thriue in; our speech is too craggy for him to set his plough in, hee goes twitching and hopping in our language like a man running vpon quagmiers, vp the hill in one Syllable and down the dale in another, retaining no part of that stately smooth gate, which he vaunts himselfe with amongst the Greeks and Latins.

Homer and Virgil, two valorous Authors, yet were they neuer knighted; they wrote in Hexameter verses: *Ergo, Chaucer,* and *Spencer* the *Homer* and *Virgil* of England, were farre ouerseene that they wrote not all their Poems in Hexamiter verses also.

In many Countries veluet and Satten is a commoner weare than cloth amongst vs, *Ergo,* wee must leaue wearing of cloth, and goe euerie one in veluet and satten, because other Countries vse so.

The Text will not beare it, good *Gilgilis Hobberdehoy.*

Our english tongue is nothing too good, but too bad to *imitate the Greeke and Latine.* . . . In a verse, when a worde of three sillables cannot thrust in but sidelings, to ioynt him euen, we are oftentimes faine to borrowe some lesser quarry of elocution from the Latine, alwaies retaining this for a principle, that a leake of indesinence as a leake in a shippe, must needly bee stopt, with what matter soeuer.

Chaucers authoritie, I am certaine shalbe alleadgd against mee for a many of these balductums. Had *Chaucer* liu'd to this age, I am verily perswaded hee would haue discarded the tone halfe of the harsher sort of them.

They were the Oouse which ouerflowing barbarisme, withdrawne to her Scottish Northren chanell, had left behind her. Art, like yong grasse in the spring of *Chaucers* florishing, was glad to peepe vp through any slime of corruption, to be beholding to she car'd not whome for apparaile, trauailing in those colde countries. There is no reason that shee a banisht Queene into this barraine soile, hauing monarchizd it so long amongst the Greeks and Romanes, should (although warres furie had humbled her to some extremitie) still be constrained when she hath recouerd her state, to weare the robes of aduersitie, iet it in her old rags, when she is wedded to new prosperitie.

Vtere moribus praeteritis, saith *Caius Caesar in Aulus Gellius, loquere verbis praesentibus.*

Thou art mine enemie, *Gabriell,* and that which is more, a contemptible vnder-foote enemie, or else I would teach thy olde *Trewantship* the true vse of words, as also how more inclinable verse is than prose to dance after the horrizonant pipe of inueterate antiquitie.

It is no matter, since thou hast brought godly instruction out of loue with thee, vse thy own destruction, raigne sole Emperour of inkehornisme, I wish vnto thee all superabundant increase of the singular gifts of absurditie, and vaineglory.

—Thomas Nashe, *Strange Newes of the Intercepting certaine Letters,* 1592

EDMUND SPENSER (1590–96)

This excerpt, from Spenser's *The Faerie Queene,* and the excerpt dated 1599, from a later edition of the work, underscore Spenser's respect for Chaucer. By saluting Chaucer, Spenser refutes a common refrain in his day that Chaucer's work was dated, old fashioned, or, at best, a product of a bygone era and thus irrelevant to contemporary authors. William Webbe refers to this same argument in his own defense of Chaucer in "A Discourse of English Poetrie." Spenser resolutely disagrees that Chaucer has become irrelevant in his era. Indeed, by consistently noting his own debt to Chaucer and connecting his own work to the medieval author's, Spenser makes the case that Chaucer is still a distinctly relevant poet, and that his work, far from being dated, is timeless, and that Chaucer had done more to shape and influence the literature of England to that point than any other writer.

Whylome as antique stories tellen vs,
   Those two (Cambell and Triamond) were foes the
   fellonest on ground,
   And battell made the draddest daungerous, That euer shrilling trumpet
      did resound; Though now their acts be no where to be found, As
      that renowmed Poet them compiled, With warlike numbers and
      Heroick sound, Dan Chaucer, well of English vndefiled,
On Fames eternall beadroll worthie to be filed.
But wicked *Time* that all good thoughts doth waste,
   And workes of noblest wits to nought out-weare, That famous
      moniment hath quite defac't, And robd the world of threasure
      endlesse deare, The which mote haue enriched all vs heare.
   O cursed Eld! the canker-worme of writs,
      How may these rimes (so rude as doth appeare)
      Hope to endure, sith workes of heauenly wits
Are quite deuour'd, and brought to nought by little bits?
Then pardon, O most sacred happy spirit,
   That I thy labours lost may thus reviue,
   And steale from thee the meed of thy due merit,
   That none durst euer whil'st thou wast aliue,
   And beeing dead in vaine yet many striue:
   Ne dare I like, but through infusion sweet
   Of thine owne spirit (which doth in me surviue)
   I follow heere the footing of thy feet
That with thy meaning so I may the rather meete.

—Edmund Spenser, *The Faerie Queene* 1590–96,
Book 4, Canto 2, Stanza 9

Thomas Speght (1598)

Thomas Speght was a schoolmaster and an editor of Chaucer, whose initial edition of the writer's works in 1598 was the first to include such features as a glossary of Chaucer's more outdated words, new texts by the author that had not been previously published, and the first biographical information on the author printed in English. The following excerpt is from the biography and includes information on the poet, his education, and his patrons ("Friends").

———⚬⚬⚬——— ———⚬⚬⚬——— ———⚬⚬⚬———

To the Readers

Some few yeers past, I was requested by certaine Gentlemen my neere friends, who loued *Chaucer,* as he well deserueth; to take a little pains in reuiuing the memorie of so rare a man, as also in doing some reparations on his works, which they iudged to be much decaied by iniurie of time, ignorance of writers, and negligence of Printers. For whose sakes thus much was then by me vndertaken, although neuer as yet fully finished. . . . As that little which then was done, was done for those priuat friends, so was it neuer my mind that it should be published. But so it fell out of late, that *Chaucers* Works being in the Presse, and three parts thereof alreadie printed, not only these friends did by their Letters sollicit me, but certaine also of the best in the Companie of Stationers hearing of these Collections, came vnto me, and for better or worse would haue something done in this Impression. Whose importunitie hath caused me to commit three faults: first in publishing that which was neuer purposed nor perfected for open view: then, in putting diuerse things in the end of the booke, which els taken in time might haue bene bestowed in more fit place: lastly, in failing in some of those eight points, which might more fully haue bene performed, if warning and conuenient leisure had bene giuen. But seeing it is as it is, I earnestly entreat all friendly Readers, that if they find anie thing amisse they would lend me their skilfull helpe against some other time, & I wil thankefully receiue their labors, assuring them that if God permit, I wil accomplish whatsoeuer may be thought vnperfect. And if herein I be preuented, those honest and learned Gentlemen that first set me on worke, haue promised to succeed mee in these my purposes. But howsoeuer it happen either in mine or their determination, I earnestly entreat al to accept these my endeuours in best part, as wel in regard of mine owne well meaning, as for the desert of our English Poet himselfe: who in most vnlearned times and greatest ignorance, being much esteemed, cannot in these our daies, wherein Learning and riper judgement so much flourisheth, but be had in great reuerence, vnlesse it bee of such as for want of wit and learning, were neuer yet able to iudge what wit or Learning meaneth. And so making no doubt of the friendly acceptance of such as haue taken pains in writing themselves, and hoping wel also of all others, that meane to employ any labour in reading, I commit our Poet to your fauourable affection, and yourselues to the protection of the Almightie.

The Life of Geffrey Chaucer

This famous and learned Poet Geffrey Chaucer Esquire, was supposed by Leland to haue beene an Oxfordshire or Barkeshireman borne. . . . But as it is euident by his owne wordes in the Testament of Loue, hee was borne in the Citie of London. . . .

The parents of Geffrey Chaucer were meere English, and he himselfe an Englishman borne. For els how could he haue come to that perfection in our language, as to be called, The first illuminer of the English tongue, had not both he, and his parents before him, been born & bred among vs. But what their names were or what issue they had, otherwise then by coniecture before giuen, wee can not declare.

Now whether they were Merchants, (for that in places where they haue dwelled, the Armes of the Merchants of the Staple haue been seene in the glasse windowes) or whether they were of other calling, it is not much necessary to search: but wealthy no doubt they were, and of good account in the common wealth, who brought vp their Sonne in such sort, that both he was thought fitte for the Court at home, and to be imployed for matters of state in forraine countreyes.

His Education

His bringing vp, as *Leland* saieth, was in the Vniuersitie of Oxford, as also of Cambridge, as appeareth by his owne wordes in his booke entituled 'The Court of Loue'.

It seemeth that both these learned men (Chaucer and Gower) were of the inner Temple: for not many yeeres since, Master *Buckley* did see a Record in the same house, where *Geoffrey Chaucer* was fined two shillings for beating a Franciscane fryer in Fleetstreete.

Thus spending much time in the Vniuersities, Fraunce, Flaunders, and Innes of Court, he prooued a singular man in all kind of knowledge.

His Friends

Friends he had in the Court of the best sort: for besides that he alwaies held in with the Princes, in whose daies he liued, hee had of the best of the Nobility both lords and ladies, which fauoured him greatly. But chiefly Iohn of Gaunt Duke of Lancaster, at whose commandement he made the Treatise 'of the alliance betwixt Mars and Venus': and also the booke of the Duchesse. Likewise the lady Isabel daughter to King Edward the third, and wife to Ingeram De Guynes, Lord De Coucy: also the lady Margaret daughter to the same King, maried to Iohn Hastings Earle of Penbrooke, did greatly loue and fauour Geffrey Chaucer, and hee againe did as much honour them, but specially the Lady Margaret, as it may appeare in diuers Treatises by him written. Others there were of great account, wherof some for some causes tooke liking of him, and other for his rare giftes and learning did admire him. And thus hee liued in honour many yeares both at home and abroad.

Yet it seemeth that he was in some trouble in the daies of King Richard the second, as it may appeare in the Testament of Loue: where hee doth greatly complaine of his owne rashnesse in following the multitude, and of their hatred against him for bewraying their purpose. And in that complaint which he maketh to his empty purse, I do find a written copy, which I had of Iohn Stow (whose library hath helped many writers) wherein ten times more is adioined, then is in print. Where he maketh great lamentation for his wrongfull imprisonment, wishing death to end his daies: which in my judgement doth greatly accord with that in the Testament of Loue.

His Bookes

Chaucer had alwaies an earnest desire to enrich & beautifie our English tongue, which in those daies was verie rude and barren: and this he did following the example of *Dantes* and *Petrarch,* who had done the same for the Italian tongue; *Alarns* for the French; and *Iohannes Mena* for the Spanish: neither was Chaucer inferior to any of them in the performance hereof: And England in this respect is much beholden to him, as *Leland* well noteth.

—Thomas Speght, *Scholarly Edition of Chaucer,*
1598, 2nd ed., 1602

EDMUND SPENSER
"THE MUTABILITIE CANTOS" (1599)

So heard it is for any liuing wight,
 All her (Dame Nature's) array and vestiments to tell
 That old *Dan Geffrey* (in whose gentle spright
 The pure well head of Poesie did dwell)
 In his *Foules parley* durst not with it mel,
 But it transferd to *Alane,* who he thought
 Had in his *Plaint of kindes* describ'd it well:
 Which who will read set forth so as it ought,
Go seek he out that *Alane* where he may be sought.

—Edmund Spenser, "The Mutabilitie Cantos,"
The Faerie Queene, 1599

THE SEVENTEENTH CENTURY

Edward Foulis "Prefatory Verse" (1635)

True Poet! Who could words endue
With life, that makes the fiction true.
  All passages are seene as cleare
As if not pend, but acted here:
Each thing so well demonstrated,
It comes to passe, when 'tis but read.
  Here is no fault, but ours: through vs
True Poetry growes barbarous:
While aged Language must be thought
(Because 'twas good long since) now naught.
Thus time can silence *Chaucers* tongue
But not his witte, which now among
The Latines hath a lowder sound;
And what we lost, the World hath found.
  Thus the Translation will become
Th' Originall, while that growes dumbe:
And this will crowne these labours:
None Sees *Chaucer* but in *Kinaston.*

—Edward Foulis, "Prefatory Verse" to *The Loves of Troilus and
Creseide,* tr. into Latin by Sir Francis Kynaston, 1635

Samuel Pepys (1663–64)

14 June 1663 . . . So to Sir W. Penn to visit him; and finding him alone, sent for my wife, who is in her riding-suit, to see him; which she hath not done these many months I think. By and by in comes Sir J. Mennes and Sir W. Batten, and so we sat talking; among other things, Sir J. Mennes brought many fine expressions of Chaucer, which he dotes on mightily, and without doubt is a very fine poet. . . .

8 July 1664 . . . So to Pauls churchyard about my books—and to the binders and directed the doing of my Chaucer, though they were not full neat enough for me, but pretty well it is—and thence to the clasp-makers to have it clasped and bossed. . . .

10 August 1664 . . . Up; and being ready, abroad to do several small businesses; among others, to find out one to engrave my tables upon my new sliding-Rule with silver plates, it being so small that Browne that made it cannot get one to do it. So I found out Cocker, the famous writing-

master, and got him to do it; and I sat an hour by him to see him design it all, and strange it is to see him with his natural eyes to cut so small at his first designing it, and read it all over without any missing, when for my life I could not with my best skill read one word or letter of it—but it is use; but he says that the best light, for his life, to do a very small thing by (contrary to Chaucer's words to the sun: that he should lend his light to them that small seals grave), it should be by an artificiall light of a candle, set to advantage as he could do it.

—Samuel Pepys, *Diary*, 1663–64, pp. 184–237

Sir John Denham (1668)

Old *Chaucer*, like the morning Star,
To us discovers day from far,
His light those Mists and Clouds dissolv'd,
Which our dark Nation long involv'd;
But he descending to the shades,
Darkness again the Age invades.
Next (like *Aurora*) *Spencer* rose,
Whose purple blush the day foreshows.

—Sir John Denham, "On Mr. Abraham Cowlcy,
His Death and Burial amongst the Ancient Poets,"
Poems and Translations, 1668, p. 89

Joseph Addison (1694)

Since, dearest Harry, you will needs request
A short Account of all the Muse possest;
That, down from Chaucer's *days to* Dryden's *Times*
Have spent their noble Rage in British *Rhimes;*
Without more Preface, wrote in formal length,
To speak the Vndertaker's want of Strength
I'll try to make their sev'ral Beauties known,
And show their Verses worth, tho not my own.
  Long had our dull Fore-Fathers slept Supine
Nor felt the Raptures of the tuneful Nine;
'Till *Chaucer* first, a merry *Bard*, arose;
And many a Story told in Rhime and Prose.

But Age has rusted what the Poet writ,
Worn out his Language, and obscur'd his wit:
In vain he Jests in his unpolish'd Strain,
And tries to make his Readers laugh in vain.

—Joseph Addison, "To Mr. H. S(acheverell),
April 3, 1694," 1694, *Miscellany Poems*, 1719,
Vol. 4, ed. Dryden, p. 288

THE EIGHTEENTH CENTURY

JOHN DRYDEN "PREFACE" (1700)

The dominant literary figure of the Restoration era in England, John Dryden (1631–1700) was a renowned poet, playwright, and critic who became the master writer of his generation. One of Dryden's many works was *Fables Ancient and Modern* (1700), a series of works translated from Ovid, Homer, and Boccaccio, as well as "modern" translations of several of Chaucer's texts and original pieces by Dryden himself. For the next century, Dryden's versions of "The Wife of Bath's Tale" (not the prologue, however,) *The Cock and the Fox* (based on "The Nun's Priest's Tale"), *Palamon and Arcite* (based on "The Knight's Tale"), *The Character of a Good Parson* (adapted from Chaucer's description of the Parson in the General Prologue to *The Canterbury Tales*), and *The Flower and the Leaf*, a poem no longer ascribed to Chaucer, were considered by many superior even to Chaucer's own, and thus his comments on Chaucer in the preface to the *Fables* proved highly influential as well.

Dryden begins his preface by comparing Chaucer to Ovid, "with no disadvantage on the Side of the Modern Author." An ardent admirer of Chaucer's, Dryden, like many others before him, considered Chaucer the father of English poetry and one of the key originators of English language and literature, noting that, "From *Chaucer* the Purity of the *English* Tongue began." Dryden also notes Chaucer's affinity for nature in his works, and remarking on Chaucer's Middle English, which he calls "old" English, Dryden writes, "There is the rude Sweetness of a *Scotch* Tune in it, which is natural and pleasing, though not perfect." Dryden's criticisms of Chaucer's meter stem from Dryden's own ignorance of Middle English; his lack of comprehension about how the work was to be pronounced lead him to believe it contained numerous uneven lines.

Speaking of his own translations of Chaucer's work, Dryden writes that not everyone was pleased by his intention to update the work of the medieval author. Abraham Cowley (1618–67), the metaphysical poet, believed that Chaucer's works were "not worth receiving," that Chaucer was a "dry, old-fashion'd Wit," and therefore unworthy of Dryden's attention. Others, Dryden contended, supposed "a certain Veneration due to [Chaucer's] old Language; and that it is little less than Profanation and Sacrilege to alter it." Dryden insists that he venerates Chaucer more than any other, but also notes, "*Chaucer*, I confess, is a rough Diamond, and must first be polish'd, e'er he shines." Dryden's versions of several of Chaucer's key works ultimately helped spark a renewed critical interest in the medieval author's works; students may find it valuable to use Dryden's preface as a springboard to explore his versions of Chaucer's tales and compare them to the originals, and also to note what changes

Dryden deemed were necessary to update and modify Chaucer for a
Restoration era audience.

———◈——— ———◈——— ———◈———

Spencer and *Fairfax* both flourish'd in the Reign of Queen *Elizabeth:* Great
Masters in our Language. . . . *Milton* was the Poetical Son of *Spencer,* and
Mr. *Waller* of *Fairfax;* for we have our Lineal Descents and Clans, as well as
other Families: Spencer more than once insinuates, that the Soul of *Chaucer*
was transfus'd into his Body; and that he was begotten by him Two Hundred
years after his Decease. *Milton* has acknowledg'd to me that *Spencer* was his
Original; . . .

But to return: Having done with *Ovid* for this time, it came into my mind,
that our old *English* poet, *Chaucer,* in many Things resembled him, and that
with no disadvantage on the Side of the Modern Author, as I shall endeavour
to prove when I compare them: And as I am, and always have been studious
to promote the Honour of my Native Country, so I soon resolv'd to put
their Merits to the Trial, by turning some of the *Canterbury* Tales into our
Language, as it is now refin'd: For by this Means, both the Poets being set in
the same Light, and dress'd in the same *English* habit, Story to be compar'd
with Story, a certain Judgment may be made betwixt them, by the Reader,
without obtruding my Opinion on him: Or if I seem partial to my Countryman, and Predecessor in the Laurel, the Friends of Antiquity are not few:
And, besides many of the Learn'd, *Ovid* has almost all the *Beaux,* and the
whole Fair Sex his declar'd Patrons. Perhaps I have assum'd somewhat more
to my self than they allow me; because I have adventur'd to sum up the
Evidence; but the Readers are the Jury; and their Privilege remains entire to
decide according to the Merits of the Cause: Or, if they please, to bring it to
another Hearing, before some other Court. In the mean time, to follow the
Thrid of my Discourse (as Thoughts, according to Mr. *Hobbs,* have always
some Connexion) so from *Chaucer* I was led to think on *Boccace,* who was
not only his Contemporary, but also pursu'd the same Studies; wrote Novels
in Prose, and many Works in Verse; particularly is said to have invented
the Octave Rhyme, or *Stanza* of Eight Lines, which ever since has been
maintain'd by the Practice of all *Italian* Writers, who are, or at least assume
the title of *Heroick Poets:* He and *Chaucer,* among other Things, had this in
common, that they refin'd their Mother-Tongues; but with this difference,
that Dante had begun to file their Language, at least in Verse, before the time
of *Boccace,* who likewise receiv'd no little Help from his Master *Petrarch:* But
the Reformation of their Prose was wholly owing to *Boccace* himself; who is
yet the Standard of Purity in the *Italian* Tongue; though many of his Phrases

are become obsolete, as in process of Time it must needs happen. *Chaucer* (as you have formerly been told by our learn'd Mr. *Rhymer*) first adorn'd and amplified our barren Tongue from the *Provencall,* which was then the most polish'd of all the Modern Languages: But this Subject has been copiously treated by that great Critick, who deserves no little Commendation from us his Countrymen. For these Reasons of Time, and Resemblance of Genius, in *Chaucer* and *Boccace,* I resolv'd to join them in my present Work; to which I have added some Original Papers of my own; which whether they are equal or inferiour to my other Poems, an Author is the most improper Judge; and therefore I leave them wholly to the Mercy of the Reader: I will hope the best, that they will not be condemn'd; but if they should, I have the Excuse of an old Gentleman, who, mounting on Horseback before some Ladies, when I was present, got up somewhat heavily, but desir'd of the Fair Spectators, that they would count Fourscore and eight before they judg'd him. . . .

I proceed to Ovid, and *Chaucer;* considering the former only in relation to the latter. With *Ovid* ended the Golden Age of the *Roman* Tongue: From *Chaucer* the Purity of the *English* Tongue began. The Manners of the Poets were not unlike: Both of them were well-bred, well-natur'd, amorous, and Libertine, at least in their Writings, it may be also in their Lives. Their Studies were the same, Philosophy, and Philology. Both of them were knowing in Astronomy; of which *Ovid's* Books of the Roman Feasts, and *Chaucer's* Treatise of the *Astrolabe,* are sufficient Witnesses. But *Chaucer* was likewise an Astrologer, as were *Virgil, Horace, Persius,* and *Manilius.* Both writ with wonderful Facility and Clearness; neither were great Inventors: For *Ovid* only copied the *Grecian* Fables; and most of *Chaucer's* Stories were taken from his *Italian* Contemporaries, or their Predecessors: *Boccace* his *Decameron* was first publish'd; and from thence our *Englishman* has borrow'd many of his *Canterbury* Tales: Yet that of *Palamon* and *Arcite* was written in all probability by some *Italian* Wit, in a former Age; as I shall prove hereafter: The tale of *Grizild* was the Invention of *Petrarch;* by him sent to *Boccace;* from whom it came to *Chaucer: Troilus* and *Cressida* was also written by a *Lombard* Author; but much amplified by our *English* Translatour, as well as beautified; the Genius of our Countrymen, in general, being rather to improve an Invention than to invent themselves; as is evident not only in our Poetry, but in many of our Manufactures. I find I have anticipated already, and taken up from *Boccace* before I come to him: But there is so much less behind; and I am of the Temper of most Kings, *who love to be in Debt,* are all for present Money, no matter how they pay it afterwards: Besides, the Nature of a Preface is rambling; never wholly out of the Way, nor in it. This I have learn'd from the Practice of honest *Montaign,* and return at my pleasure to

Ovid and *Chaucer*, of whom I have little more to say. Both of them built on the Inventions of other Men; yet since *Chaucer* had something of his own, as *The Wife of Baths Tale, The Cock and the Fox*, which I have translated, and some others, I may justly give our Countryman the Precedence in that Part; since I can remember nothing of *Ovid* which was wholly his. Both of them understood the Manners; under which Name I comprehend the Passions, and, in a larger Sense, the Descriptions of Persons, and their very Habits: For an Example, I see Baucis and *Philemon* as perfectly before me, as if some ancient Painter had drawn them; and all the Pilgrims in the *Canterbury* Tales, their Humours, their Features, and the very Dress, as distinctly as if I had supp'd with them at the *Tabard* in *Southward*. Yet even there, too, the Figures of *Chaucer* are much more lively, and set in a better Light: Which though I have not time to prove; yet I appeal to the Reader, and am sure he will clear me from Partiality. The Thoughts and Words remain to be consider'd, in the Comparison of the two Poets; and I have sav'd my self one half of that Labour, by owning that *Ovid* liv'd when the Roman Tongue was in its Meridian; *Chaucer*, in the Dawning of our Language: Therefore that Part of the Comparison stands not on an equal Foot, any more than the Diction of *Ennius* and *Ovid*; or of *Chaucer* and our present *English*. The Words are given up as a Post not to be defended in our Poet, because he wanted the Modern Art of Fortifying. The Thoughts remain to be consider'd: And they are to be measur'd only by their Propriety; that is, as they flow more or less naturally from the Persons describ'd, on such and such Occasions. The Vulgar Judges, which are Nine Parts in Ten of all Nations, who call Conceits and Jingles Wit, who see *Ovid* full of them, and *Chaucer* altogether without them, will think me little less than mad for preferring the *Englishman* to the *Roman*: Yet, with their leave, I must presume to say, that the Things they admire are only glittering Trifles, and so far from being Witty, that in a serious Poem they are nauseous, because they are unnatural. Wou'd any Man, who is ready to die for Love, describe his Passion like *Narcissus?* Wou'd he think of *inopem me copia fecit,* and a Dozen more of such Expressions, pour'd on the Neck of one another, and signifying all the same Thing? If this were Wit, was this a Time to be witty, when the poor Wretch, was in the Agony of Death? This is just *John Littlewit,* in *Bartholomew Fair,* who had a Conceit (as he tells you) left him in his Misery; a miserable Conceit. On these Occasions the Poet shou'd endeavour to raise Pity: But, instead of this, *Ovid* is tickling you to laugh. *Virgil* never made use of such Machines when he was moving you to commiserate the Death of *Dido:* He would not destroy what he was building. *Chaucer* makes Arcite violent in his Love, and unjust in the Pursuit of it: Yet, when he came to die, he made him think more reasonably: He repents not of his Love, for that had alter'd his Character; but acknowledges the Injustice of his Proceedings, and resigns *Emilia* to *Palamon*. What would *Ovid* have done on this Occasion? He would certainly have made *Arcite* witty on his Deathbed. He had complain'd he was further off from Possession, by being so near, and a thousand such Boyisms, which Chaucer rejected as below the Dignity of the Subject. They who think otherwise, would by the same Reason, prefer *Lucan* and *Ovid* to *Homer* and *Virgil,* and *Martial* to all Four of them. As for the Turn of Words, in which *Ovid* particularly excels all Poets; they are sometimes a Fault, and sometimes a Beauty, as they are us'd properly or improperly; but in strong Passions always to be shunn'd, because Passions are serious, and will admit no Playing. The *French* have a high Value for them; and I confess, they are often what they call Delicate, when they are introduc'd with Judgment; but *Chaucer* writ with more Simplicity, and follow'd Nature more closely, than to use them. I have thus far, to the best of my Knowledge, been an upright Judge betwixt the Parties in Competition, not medling with the Design nor the Disposition of it; because the Design was not their own; and in the disposing of it they were equal. It remains that I say somewhat of *Chaucer* in particular.

In the first place, as he is the Father of *English* Poetry, so I hold him in the same Degree of Veneration as the *Grecians* held *Homer,* or the *Romans Virgil:* He is a perpetual Fountain of good Sense; learn'd in all Sciences; and, therefore speaks properly on all Subjects: As he knew what to say, so he knows also when to leave off; a Continence which is practis'd by few Writers, and scarcely by any of the Ancients, excepting *Virgil* and *Horace.* One of our late great Poets is sunk in his Reputation, because he cou'd never forgive any Conceit which came in his way; but swept like a Drag-net, great and small. There was plenty enough, but the Dishes were ill sorted; whole Pyramids of Sweet-meats for Boys and Women; but little of solid Meat for Men: All this proceeded not from any want of Knowledge, but of Judgment; neither did he want that in discerning the Beauties and Faults of other Poets; but only indulg'd himself in the Luxury of Writing; and perhaps knew it was a Fault, but hoped the Reader would not find it. For this Reason, though he must always be thought a great Poet, he is no longer esteemed a good Writer: And for Ten Impressions, which his Works have had in so many successive Years, yet at present a hundred Books are scarcely purchased once a Twelvemonth: For, as my last Lord *Rochester* said, though somewhat profanely, *Not being of God, he could not stand.*

Chaucer follow'd Nature every where, but was never so bold to go beyond her: And there is a great Difference of being *Poeta* and *nimis Poeta*, if we may believe *Catullus,* as much as betwixt a modest Behaviour and Affectation. The

Verse of *Chaucer,* I confess, is not Harmonious to us; but 'tis like the Eloquence
of one whom *Tacitus* commends, it was *auribus istius temporis accommodata:*
They who liv'd with him, and some time after him, thought it Musical; and it
continues so even in our Judgment, if compar'd with the Numbers of *Lidgate*
and *Gower,* his Contemporaries: There is the rude Sweetness of a *Scotch* Tune
in it, which is natural and pleasing, though not perfect. 'Tis true, I cannot
go so far as he who publish'd the last Edition of him; for he would make us
believe the Fault is in our Ears, and that there were really Ten Syllables in
a Verse where we find but Nine: But this Opinion is not worth confuting;
'tis so gross and obvious an Errour, that common Sense (which is a Rule in
everything but Matters of Faith and Revelation) must convince the Reader,
that Equality of Numbers, in every Verse which we call *Heroick,* was either
not known, or not always practis'd, in *Chaucer's* Age. It were an easie Matter
to produce some thousands of his Verses, which are lame for want of half a
Foot, and sometimes a whole one, and which no Pronunciation can make
otherwise. We can only say, that he liv'd in the Infancy of our Poetry, and
that nothing is brought to Perfection at the first. We must be Children before
we grow Men. There was an *Ennius,* and in process of Time a *Lucilius,* and a
Lucretius, before *Virgil* and *Horace;* even after *Chaucer* there was a *Spencer,*
a *Harrington,* a *Fairfax,* before *Waller* and *Denham* were in being: And our
Numbers were in their Nonage till these last appear'd. I need say little of his
Parentage, Life, and Fortunes: They are to be found at large in all the Editions
of his Works. He was employ'd abroad, and favour'd by *Edward* the Third,
Richard the Second, and *Henry* the Fourth, and was Poet, as I suppose, to all
Three of them. In *Richard's* Time, I doubt, he was a little dipt in the Rebellion
of the Commons; and being Brother-in-Law to *John of Ghant,* it was no
wonder if he follow'd the Fortunes of that Family; and was well with *Henry*
the Fourth when he depos'd his Predecessor. Neither is it to be admir'd, that
Henry, who was a wise as well as a valiant Prince, who claim'd by Succession,
and was sensible that his Title was not sound, but was rightfully in *Mortimer,*
who had married the Heir of *York;* it was not to be admir'd, I say, if that great
Politician should be pleas'd to have the greatest Wit of those Times in his
Interests, and to be the Trumpet of his Praises. *Augustus* had given him the
Example, by the Advice of *Mecaenas,* who recommended *Virgil* and *Horace*
to him; whose Praises helped to make him Popular while he was alive, and
after his Death have made him Precious to Posterity. As for the Religion of
our Poet, he seems to have some little Byas towards the Opinions of *Wickliff,*
after *John of Ghant* his Patron; somewhat of which appears in the Tale of
Piers Plowman: Yet I cannot blame him for inveighing so sharply against the
Vices of the Clergy in his Age: Their Pride, their Ambition, their Pomp, their

Avarice, their Worldly Interest, deserv'd the Lashes which he gave them, both in that, and in most of his *Canterbury Tales:* Neither has his Contemporary *Boccace,* spar'd them. Yet both those Poets liv'd in much esteem, with good and holy Men in Orders: For the Scandal which is given by particular Priests reflects not on the Sacred Function. *Chaucer's Monk,* his *Chanon,* and his *Fryar,* took not from the Character of his *Good Parson.* A Satyrical Poet is the Check of the Laymen on bad Priests. . . .

I have followed *Chaucer,* in his Character of a Holy Man, and have enlarg'd on that Subject with some Pleasure, reserving to myself the Right, if I shall think fit hereafter, to describe another sort of Priests, such as are more easily to be found than the Good Parson; such as have given the last Blow to Christianity in this Age, by a Practice so contrary to their Doctrine. But this will keep cold till another time. In the mean while, I take up *Chaucer* where I left him. He must have been a Man of a most wonderful comprehensive Nature, because, as it has been truly observ'd of him, he has taken into the Compass of his *Canterbury Tales* the various Manners and Humours (as we now call them) of the whole *English* Nation, in his Age. Not a single Character has escap'd him. All his Pilgrims are severally distinguish'd from each other; and not only in their Inclinations, but in their very Phisiognomies and Persons. *Baptista Porta* could not have describ'd their Natures better, than by the Marks which the Poet gives them. The Matter and Manner of their Tales, and of their Telling, are so suited to their different Educations, Humours, and Callings, that each of them would be improper in any other Mouth. Even the grave and serious Characters are distinguish'd by their several sorts of Gravity: Their Discourses are such as belong to their Age, their Calling, and their Breeding; such as are becoming of them, and of them only. Some of his Persons are Vicious, and some Vertuous; some are unlearn'd, or (as *Chaucer* calls them) Lewd, and some are Learn'd. Even the Ribaldry of the Low Characters is different: the *Reeve,* the *Miller,* and the *Cook,* are several Men, and are distinguish'd from each other, as much as the mincing Lady-Prioress, and the broad-speaking, gap-tooth'd Wife of *Bathe.* But enough of this: There is such a Variety of Game springing up before me, that I am distracted in my Choice, and know not which to follow. 'Tis sufficient to say according to the Proverb, that here is God's Plenty. We have our Fore-fathers and Great Grand-dames all before us, as they were in *Chaucer's* Days; their general Characters are still remaining in Mankind, and even in *England,* though they are call'd by other Names than those of *Moncks,* and *Fryars,* and *Chanons,* and *Lady Abbesses,* and Nuns: For Mankind is ever the same, and nothing lost out of Nature, though every thing is alter'd. May I have leave to do myself the Justice, (since my Enemies will do me none, and are so far from granting me to be a good Poet, that they will not allow me so much as to be a Christian, or a Moral Man), may I have leave, I say, to inform my Reader, that I have confin'd my Choice to such Tales of *Chaucer* as savour nothing of Immodesty. If I had desir'd more to please than to instruct, the *Reve,* the *Miller,* the *Shipman,* the *Merchant,* the *Sumner,* and above all, the *Wife of Bathe,* in the Prologue to her Tale, would have procur'd me as many Friends and Readers, as there are *Beaux* and Ladies of Pleasure in the Town. But I will no more offend against Good Manners: I am sensible as I ought to be of the Scandal I have given by my loose Writings; and make what Reparation I am able, by this Public Acknowledgment. If anything of this Nature, or of Profaneness, be crept into these Poems, I am so far from defending it, that I disown it. *Totum hoc indictum volo. Chaucer* makes another manner of Apologie for his broad-speaking, and *Boccace* makes the like; but I will follow neither of them. Our Country-man, in the end of his Characters, before the *Canterbury Tales,* thus excuses the Ribaldry, which is very gross in many of his Novels.

> But first I praye you of youre curteisye
> That ye n'arette it nought my vilainye
> Though that I plainly speke in this matere
> To telle you hir wordes and hir cheere,
> Ne though I speke hir wordes proprely;
> For this ye knowen also wel as I:
> Who so shal telle a tale after a man
> He moot reherce, as neigh as evere he can,
> Everich a word, if it be in his charge;
> Al speke he nevere so rudeliche and large,
> Or elles he moot telle his tale untrewe,
> Or feine thing, or finde wordes newe;
> He may nought spare although he were his brother:
> He moot as wel saye oo word as another.
> Crist spak himself ful brode in Holy Writ,
> And wel ye woot no vilainye is it;
> Eek Plato saith, who so can him rede,
> The wordes mote be cosin to the deede.

Yet if a Man should have enquir'd of *Boccace* or of *Chaucer,* what need they had of introducing such Characters, where obscene Words were proper in their Mouths, but very undecent to he heard; I know not what Answer they could have made: For that Reason, such Tales shall be left untold by me. You have here a *Specimen* of *Chaucer's* Language, which is so obsolete, that his Sense is scarce to be understood; and you have likewise more than one

Example of his unequal Numbers, which were mention'd before. Yet many of his Verses consist of Ten Syllables, and the Words not much behind our present *English:* as for Example, these two Lines, in the Description of the Carpenter's Young Wife:

> Wincing she was, as is a jolly Colt,
> Long as a Mast, and upright as a Bolt.

I have almost done with *Chaucer,* when I have answer'd some Objections relating to my present Work. I find some People are offended that I have turn'd these Tales into modern *English;* because they think them unworthy of my Pains, and look on *Chaucer* as a dry, old-fashion'd Wit, not worth receiving. I have often heard the late Earl of *Leicester* say, that Mr. *Cowley* himself was of that opinion; who, having read him over at my Lord's Request, declared he had no Taste of him. I dare not advance my Opinion against the Judgment of so great an Author: But I think it fair, however, to leave the Decision to the Publick: Mr. *Cowley,* was too modest to set up for a Dictatour; and, being shock'd perhaps with his old Style, never examin'd into the depth of his good Sense. *Chaucer,* I confess, is a rough Diamond, and must first be polish'd, e'er he shines. I deny not likewise, that, living in our early Days of Poetry, he writes not always of a piece; but sometimes mingles trivial Things with those of greater Moment. Sometimes also, though not often, he runs riot, like *Ovid,* and knows not when he has said enough. But there are more great Wits beside *Chaucer,* whose Fault is their Excess of Conceits, and those ill sorted. An Author is not to write all he can, but only all he ought. Having observ'd this Redundancy in *Chaucer,* (as it is an easie Matter for a Man of ordinary Parts to find a Fault in one of greater,) I have not ty'd my self to a Literal Translation; but have often omitted what I judg'd unnecessary, or not of Dignity enough to appear in the Company of better Thoughts. I have presum'd farther in some Places, and added somewhat of my own where I thought my Author was deficient, and had not given his Thoughts their true Lustre, for want of Words in the Beginning of our Language. And to this I was the more embolden'd, because, (if I may be permitted to say it of my self) I found I had a Soul congenial to his, and that I had been conversant in the same Studies. Another Poet, in another Age, may take the same Liberty with my Writings; if at least they live long enough to deserve Correction. It was also necessary sometimes to restore the Sense of *Chaucer,* which was lost or mangled in the Errors of the Press: Let this Example suffice at present in the Story of *Palamon* and *Arcite,* where the temple of *Diana* is describ'd, you find these Verses in all the Editions of our Author:

> There saw I *Dane* turned unto a Tree,
> I mean not the goddess *Diane,*
> But *Venus* Daughter, which that hight *Dane.*

Which, after a little Consideration, I knew was to be reform'd into this Sense, that *Daphne,* the daughter of *Peneus,* was turn'd into a Tree. I durst not make thus bold with *Ovid,* lest some future *Milbourn* should arise, and say, I varied from my Author, because I understood him not.

But there are other Judges, who think I ought not to have translated *Chaucer* into *English,* out of a quite contrary Notion: They suppose there is a certain Veneration due to his old Language; and that it is little less than Profanation and Sacrilege to alter it. They are farther of opinion, that somewhat of his good Sense will suffer in this Transfusion, and much of the Beauty of his Thoughts will infallibly be lost, which appear with more Grace in their old Habit. Of this Opinion was that excellent Person, whom I mention'd, the late Earl of *Leicester,* who valued *Chaucer* as much as Mr. *Cowley* despis'd him. My Lord dissuaded me from this Attempt, (for I was thinking of it some Years before his Death,) and his Authority prevail'd so far with me, as to defer my Undertaking while he liv'd, in deference to him: Yet my Reason was not convinc'd with what he urg'd against it. If the first End of a Writer be to be understood, then, as his Language grows obsolete, his Thoughts must grow obscure, *multa renascuntur, quae nunc cecidere; cadentque quae nunc sunt in honore vocabula, si volet usus, quern penes arbitrium est et jus el norma loquendi.* When an ancient Word for its Sound and Significance deserves to be reviv'd, I have that reasonable Veneration for Antiquity, to restore it. All beyond this is Superstition. Words are not like Land-marks, so sacred as never to be remov'd: Customs are chang'd, and even Statutes are silently repeal'd, when the Reason ceases for which they were enacted. As for the other Part of the Argument, that his Thoughts will lose of their original Beauty by the innovation of Words; in the first place, not only their Beauty, but their Being is lost, when they are no longer understood, which is the present Case. I grant, that something must be lost in all Transfusion, that is, in all Translations; but the Sense will remain, which would otherwise be lost, or at least be maim'd, when it is scarce intelligible; and that but to a few. How few are there who can read *Chaucer,* so as to understand him perfectly? And if imperfectly, then with less Profit, and no Pleasure. 'Tis not for the Use of some old *Saxon* Friends, that I have taken these Pains with him: Let them neglect my Version, because they have no need of it. I made it for their sakes who understand Sense and Poetry, as well as they; when that Poetry and Sense is put into Words which they understand. I will go farther, and dare to add, that what Beauties I lose in some Places, I give to others which had them not originally: But in this I may be partial to my self; let the Reader judge, and I submit to his Decision. Yet I think I have just Occasion to complain of them, who because they understand *Chaucer*, would deprive the greater part of their Countrymen of the same Advantage, and hoord him up, as Misers do their Grandam Gold, only to look on it themselves, and hinder others from making use of it. In sum, I seriously protest, that no Man ever had, or can have, a greater Veneration for *Chaucer* than my self. I have translated some part of his Works, only that I might perpetuate his Memory, or at least refresh it, amongst my Countrymen. If I have alter'd him any where for the better, I must at the same time acknowledge, that I could have done nothing without him: *Facile est inventis addere,* is no great Commendation; but I am not so vain to think I have deserv'd a greater. I will conclude what I have to say of him singly, with this one Remark: A Lady of my Acquaintance, who keeps a kind of Correspondence with some Authors of the Fair Sex in *France,* has been inform'd by them, that *Mademoiselle de Scudery,* who is as old as *Sibyl,* and inspir'd like her by the same God of Poetry, is at this time translating *Chaucer* into modern *French.* From which I gather, that he has been formerly translated into the old *Provencall;* (for, how she should come to understand Old *English,* I know not). But the Matter of Fact being true, it makes me think, that there is something in it like Fatality; that after certain Periods of Time, the Fame and Memory of Great Wits should be renew'd, as *Chaucer* is both in *France* and *England.* If this be wholly Chance, 'tis extraordinary; and I dare not call it more, for fear of being tax'd with Superstition.

Boccace comes last to be consider'd, who, living in the same Age with *Chaucer,* had the same Genius, and followed the same Studies: Both writ Novels, and each of them cultivated his Mother-Tongue: But the greatest Resemblance of our two Modern Authors being in their familiar Style, and pleasing way of relating Comical Adventures, I may pass it over, because I have translated nothing from *Boccace* of that Nature. In the serious part of Poetry, the Advantage is wholly on *Chaucer's* Side; for though the *Englishman* has borrow'd many Tales from the *Italian,* yet it appears, that those of *Boccace* were not generally of his own making, but taken from Authors of former ages, and by him only modell'd: So that what there was of Invention, in either of them, may be judg'd equal. But *Chaucer* has refin'd on *Boccace,* and has mended the Stories which he has borrow'd, in his way of telling; though Prose allows more Liberty of Thought, and the Expression is more easie, when unconfin'd by Numbers. Our Countryman carries Weight, and yet wins the Race at disadvantage. I desire not the Reader should take my Word; and, therefore, I will set two of their Discourses on the same Subject, in the same Light, for every Man to judge betwixt them. I translated *Chaucer* first, and amongst the rest, pitch'd on The Wife of *Bath's* Tale; not daring, as I have said, to adventure on her Prologue, because 'tis too licentious: There *Chaucer* introduces an old Woman of mean Parentage, whom a youthful Knight of Noble Blood, was forc'd to marry, and consequently loath'd her: The Crone being in bed with him on the wedding Night, and finding his Aversion, endeavours to win his Affection by Reason, and speaks a good Word for herself, (as who could blame her?) in hope to mollifie the sullen Bridegroom. She takes her Topiques from the Benefits of Poverty, the Advantages of old Age and Ugliness, the Vanity of Youth, and the silly Pride of Ancestry and Titles, without inherent Vertue, which is the true Nobility. When I had clos'd *Chaucer,* I return'd to *Ovid,* and translated some more of his Fables; and, by this time, had so far forgotten The Wife of *Bath's* Tale, that when I took up *Boccace,* unawares I fell on the same Argument of preferring Virtue to Nobility of Blood, and Titles, in the Story of *Sigismonda;* which I had certainly avoided for the Resemblance of the two Discourses, if my Memory had not fail'd me. Let the Reader weigh both; and if he thinks me partial to *Chaucer,* 'tis in him to right *Boccace.* I prefer in our Countryman, far above all his other Stories, the Noble Poem of *Palamon* and *Arcite,* which is of the *Epique* kind, and perhaps not much inferiour to the *Ilias* or the *Aeneis:* the Story is more pleasing than either of them, the Manners as perfect, the Diction as poetical, the Learning as deep and various; and the Disposition full as artful: only it includes a greater length of time; as taking up seven years at least; but *Aristotle* has left undecided the Duration of the Action; which yet is easily reduc'd into the Compass of a year, by a Narration of what preceded the Return of *Palamon* to *Athens.* I had thought for the Honour of our Nation, and more particularly for his, whose Laurel, tho' unworthy, I have worn after him, that this Story was of *English* Growth, and *Chaucer's* own: But I was undeceiv'd by *Boccace;* for casually looking on the End of his seventh *Giornata,* I found *Dioneo,* (under which name he shadows himself,) and *Fiametta,* (who represents his Mistress, the natural Daughter of *Robert,* King of *Naples)* of whom these Words are spoken. *Dioneo e Fiametta gran pezza cantarono insieme d'Arcita, e di Palemone:* by which it appears, that this Story was written before the time of *Boccace;* but the Name of its Author being wholly lost, *Chaucer* is now become an Original; and I question not but the Poem has receiv'd many Beauties, by passing through his Noble Hands. Besides this Tale, there is another of his own Invention, after the manner of the *Provencalls,* call'd *The Flower and the Leaf;* with which I was so particularly pleas'd, both for the Invention and the Moral; that I cannot hinder myself from recommending it to the Reader.

—John Dryden, "Preface" to *The Fables,* 1700

ALEXANDER POPE (1711)

Short is the Date, alas, of *Modem Rhymes;*
And 'tis but just to let 'em live *betimes.*
No longer now that Golden Age appears,
When Patriarch-Wits surviv'd a *thousand* Years.
Now Length of Fame (our *second* Life) is lost,
And bare Threescore is all ev'n That can boast:
Our Sons their Father's *failing Language* see,
And such as *Chaucer* is, shall *Dryden* be.

—Alexander Pope, *An Essay on Criticism,* 1711

JOHN HUGHES (1715)

A prolific but minor playwright and author who rose to prominence in the latter quarter of the seventeenth century, John Hughes (1677–1720) was also known for translating Molière and editing Shakespeare and Spenser, among others. In his *Essay on Allegorical Poetry*, Hughes, like Ashcam before him, praises Chaucer for his ability to create extraordinary characters, and also labels him a satirist and humorist, "a lively but rough Painter of the Manners of that rude Age in which he liv'd."

———

Notwithstanding the Disadvantage he has mention'd, we have two Antient *English* Poets, *Chaucer* and *Spenser,* who may perhaps be reckon'd as Exceptions to this Remark. These seem to have taken deep Root, like old *British* Oaks, and to flourish in defiance of all the Injuries of Time and Weather. The former is indeed much more obsolete in his Stile than the latter; but it is owing to an extraordinary native Strength in both, that they have been able thus far to survive amidst the Changes of our Tongue, and seem rather likely, among the Curious at least, to preserve the Knowledg of our Antient Language, than to be in danger of being destroy'd with it, and bury'd under its Ruins.

Tho Spenser's Affection to his Master *Chaucer* led him in many things to copy after him, yet those who have read both will easily observe that these two Genius's were of a very different kind. *Chaucer* excell'd in his Characters; *Spenser* in his Descriptions. The first study'd Humour, was an excellent Satirist, and a lively but rough Painter of the Manners of that rude Age in which he liv'd.

—John Hughes, *Essay on Allegorical Poetry*, 1715,
pp. xxvi–xxvii

Daniel Defoe (1718)

Best known for the novel *Robinson Crusoe*, Daniel Defoe (1659/1661?–1731) was a prominent English author and journalist. In this excerpt from a letter Defoe wrote, the author states that Chaucer's work has been neglected because it is considered vulgar by the cultural standards of the day. Defoe also compares the supposed lewdness of Chaucer's work to that of John Wilmot, earl of Rochester, a Restoration playwright; this comparison may be of interest to students, since most contemporary readers would agree that Wilmot's work far exceeds Chaucer's in its vulgarity.

The inimitable brightness of (Rochester's) Wit has not been able to preserve (his poems) from being thought worthy, by wise Men, to be lost, rather than remember'd; being blacken'd and eclips'd by the Lewdness of their Stile, so as not to be made fit for Modesty to read or hear. Jeffrey Chaucer is forgotten upon the same Account; and tho' that Author is excused, by the unpoliteness of the Age he lived in, yet his Works are diligently buried, by most Readers, on that very Principle, that they are not fit for modest Persons to read.

—Daniel Defoe, Letter to *Mist's Weekly Journal*, 1718,
Daniel Defoe: His Life and Recently Discovered Writings,
1869, Vol. 2, ed. Lee, p. 31

Elizabeth Cooper (1737)

The Morning-Star of the *English* Poetry! was, by his own Record, in the *Testament of Love*, born in *London;* in the Reign of *Edward* the Third. His Family is suppos'd to come in with *William* the *Norman,* and, some day, his Father was a Merchant. He had his Education partly at *Oxford,* partly at *Cambridge,* and, by Circumstance, we find he was enter'd a Student of the *Inner-Temple.* He travelled in his Youth, thro' *France* and *Flanders;* and, in the Reign *of Richard* the Second, was famous for his Learning. After this he marry'd the Daughter of a Knight of *Hainault,* by which Alliance he is said to become Brother-in-Law to *John* of *Gaunt* Duke of *Lancaster:* He had several Children, a large, and ample Revenue, resided chiefly at *Woodstock,* was employ'd on several Embassies, received many great Rewards from the Crown, and was in high Esteem with the most Noble and Excellent Persons of his Time.—In the latter Part of his Life, he met with many Troubles, of which he complains, very pathetically, in some of his Pieces; yet liv'd to the Age of Seventy Two Years, and was bury'd at *Westminster*.

All agree he was the first Master of his Art among us, and that the Language, in general, is much oblig'd to him for Copiousness, Strength, and Ornament. It would be endless, almost, to enumerate the Compliments that have been paid to his Merit, by the Gratitude of those Writers, who have enrich'd themselves so much by his inestimable Legacies.—But his own Works, are his best Monument. In those appear a real Genius, as capable of inventing, as improving; equally suited to the Gay, and the Sublime; soaring in high Life, and pleasant in low: Tho' I don't find the least Authority in History to prove it. Ever both entertaining, and instructive! All which is so well known, 'tis, in a Manner, needless to repeat: But the Nature of this Work requires it, and I should not be excus'd for saying less, or omitting a Quotation; tho it is not a little difficult to chuse one that will do him Justice: Most of his principal Tales have been already exhausted by the Moderns, and, consequently, neither of them would appear to Advantage in their antiquated, original Dress; tho' the same in Complexion and Harmony of Parts.

—Elizabeth Cooper, *The Muses' Library*, 1737

GEORGE OGLE "LETTERS TO A FRIEND" (1739)

George Ogle (1704–46) was the editor of a popular collection of Chaucer's work and a prominent translator of "The Clerk's Tale." In his work on "The Clerk's Tale," Ogle, like Hughes and Ascham, praises Chaucer's characterizations, labeling him among "the best Drawers of Characters." Ogle, who was also a prominent translator of Horace and other classical authors, favorably compares Chaucer to numerous earlier writers, including Horace, Juvenal, Aristophanes, and Terence.

All these, I say, are the Strokes of no common Genius, but of a Man perfectly conversant in the Turns and Foibles of human Nature. Observe but his Manner of Throwing Them in, and You will not think I exaggerate, if I say, these Turns of Satire, are not unworthy of PERSIUS, JUVENAL or HORACE himself. Before I cool upon this Subject, I shall venture (as far as the Ludicrous may hold Comparison with the Serious) to rank our CHAUCER with whatever We have of greatest Perfection in this Character of Painting; I shall venture to rank

Him (making this Allowance) either with SALUST or CLARENDON; Who in History are allowed to have been the greatest Masters of the Picturesque; I mean the best Drawers of Characters. Even here some Criticks will not allow that the Persons, so described, are always consistent with themselves, at least that their Actions are always conformable to the Characters given of Them by their Historians; they will never be able to lay that Charge to CHAUCER. A Fault, however, more applicable to CLARENDON than to SALUST.

For it was not to the Distinguishing of Character from Character, that the Excellence of CHAUCER was confin'd; He was equally Master of Introducing them properly on the Stage; and after having introduced them, of Supporting them agreeably to the Part They were formed to personate. In This, He claims equal Honour with the best Comedians; there is no Admirer of PLAUTUS, TERENCE, or ARISTOPHANES, that will pretend to say, CHAUCER has not equally, thro' his *Canterbury Tales,* supported his Characters. And All must allow, that the Plan, by which He connects and unites his Tales, one with another, is well designed, and well executed. You will not think it Loss of Time, if I enter into it, so far as may be requisite to our present Subject.

The Scheme of the *Canterbury Tales* is this. CHAUCER pretends, that intending to pay his Devotions to the Shrine of THOMAS A BECKET, He set up his Horse at the *Tabbard Inn* in *Southwark.*

—George Ogle "Letters to a Friend," *Gaultheris and Griselda: or the Clerk of Oxford's Tale; from Boccace, Petrarch and Chaucer,* 1739, pp. vii–viii

SAMUEL JOHNSON (1755)

Remembered today for his *Dictionary of the English Language,* Samuel Johnson (1709–84) was an important English novelist, poet, biographer, scholar, and author. In his *Dictionary,* Johnson labels John Gower, and not Chaucer, the "father of our poetry," a description that seems at odds with what Lydgate, Caxton, Dunbar, Webbe and others previously denoted. Johnson suggests this because Gower, as Johnson believes, labels Chaucer "his disciple"; however, the line Johnson is referring to in the *Confessio Amantis* is not Gower speaking, but Venus (for more, see the introduction to the John Gower extract, 1390).

This misreading still colors Johnson's reception of Chaucer, whose reputation, Johnson seems to believe, has been overstated: "He does not however appear to have deserved all the praise which he has received." Johnson writes that John Dryden and others have given Chaucer credit for innovations and techniques he did not bring to poetry or the English language. Conversely, Johnson also suggests that Chaucer does not deserve "all the censure that he has suffered" from critics as well. Ultimately, Johnson ascribes to Gower many of the innovations and techniques that are generally credited to Chaucer. Students looking for works prior to the twentieth century that are critical of Chaucer may find Johnson useful, and may wish to further explore Johnson's claims about Gower as well.

The first of our authours, who can be properly said to have written *English,* was Sir *John Gower,* who in his *Confession of a Lover,* calls *Chaucer* his disciple, and may therefore be considered as the father of our poetry. . . .

The history of our language is now brought to the point at which the history of our poetry is generally supposed to commence, the time of the illustrious *Geoffry Chaucer,* who may perhaps, with great justice, be stiled the first of our versifiers who wrote poetically. He does not however appear to have deserved all the praise which he has received, or all the censure that he has suffered. Dryden, who mistaking genius for learning, and in confidence of his abilities, ventured to write of what he had not examined, ascribes to *Chaucer* the first refinement of our numbers, the first production of easy and natural rhymes, and the improvement of our language, by words borrowed from the more polished languages of the Continent. *Skinner* contrarily blames him in harsh terms for having vitiated his native speech by *whole cartloads of foreign words.* But he that reads the works of *Gower* will find smooth numbers and easy rhymes, of which *Chaucer* is supposed to have been the inventor, and the *French* words, whether good or bad, of which *Chaucer* is charged as the importer. Some innovations he might probably make, like others, in the infancy of our poetry, which the paucity of books does (not) allow us to discover with particular exactness; but the works of *Gower* and *Lydgate* sufficiently evince that his diction was in general like that of his contemporaries: and some improvements he undoubtedly made by the various dispositions of his rhymes; and by the mixture of different numbers, in which he seems to have been happy and judicious. I have selected several specimens both of his prose and verse; and among them, part of his translation of *Boetius.* . . . It would be improper to quote very sparingly an author of so much reputation, or to make very large extracts from a book so generally known.

—Samuel Johnson, *Dictionary of the English Language,* 1755

THOMAS GRAY (1760)

Thomas Gray (1716–71) was one of England's most important eighteenth-century poets. In the first selection from his *Commonplace Book*, Gray evaluates the work of the medieval poet John Lydgate, noting that, "I do not pretend to set him on a level with his master Chaucer" and considering Lydgate to be bleaker in his writing than Chaucer. In the second selection from the same work, Gray comments on textual inconsistencies in Chaucer's writing.

―◊◊◊―   ―◊◊◊―   ―◊◊◊―

However little (Lydgate) might be *acquainted* with Homer & Virgil, it is certain he was very much so with Chaucer's compositions, whom he calls his master, & who (I imagine) was so in a literal sense: certain 'tis Lydgate was full 30 years when Chaucer died, but whatever his skill were in either of the learned languages, it is sure he has not taken his 'Fall of Princes' from the original Latin prose of Boccace, but from a French Translation of it by one *Laurence,* as he tells us himself in the beginning of his work; it was indeed rather a Paraphrase than a translation, for he took the liberty of making several additions, & of reciting more at large many histories, that Boccace had slightly passed over.

> And *he* saieth eke, that his entencion   Laurence
> Is to amende, correcten & declare.
> Not to condemne of no presumpcion,
> But to support plainly & to spare
> Thing touched shortly of the storie bare
> Under a stile brief and compendious,
> Them to prolonge when they be vertuous:
>   For a storie which is not plainly tolde,
> But constrained under wordes few,
> For lack of truth wher they ben new or old
> Men by reporte cannot the matter shewe:
> These okes great be not downe yhewe
> First at a stroke, but by long process,
> Ner long stories a word may not expresse.

These *Long processes* indeed suited wonderfully with the attention & simple curiosity of the age, in which Lydgate lived, many a *stroke* have he & the best of his Contemporaries spent upon a sturdy old story, till they had blunted their own edge, & that of their readers, at least a modern reader will find it so; but it is a folly to judge of the understanding & of the patience of those times by our own. they loved, I will not say Tediousness, but length & a train of circumstances in a narration, the Vulgar do so still; it gives an air of reality to facts, it fixes the attention, raises and keeps in suspense their expectation, & supplies the defects of their little & lifeless imagination; it keeps pace with the slow motion of their own thoughts, tell them a story as you would tell it a Man of wit, it will appear to them as an object seen in the night by a flash of lightening; but when you have placed it in various lights & various positions, they will come at last to see & feel it, as well as others, but we need not confine ourselves to the Vulgar & to understandings beneath our own. Circumstance was ever & ever will be the Life & essence both of Oratory & Poetry, it has in some sort the same effect upon every mind, that it has on that of the populace; & I fear, the quickness & delicate impatience of these polish'd times we live in, are but forerunners of the decline of all those beautiful arts that depend upon the imagination, whether these apprehensions are well or ill grounded, it is sufficient for me, that Homer, the Father of Circumstance, has occasion for the same apology I am making for Lydgate & his Predecessors, not that I pretend to make any more comparison between his beauties & theirs, than I do between the different languages they wrote in: ours was indeed barbarous enough at that time, the Orthography unsettled, the Syntax very deficient & confused, the Metre & Number of syllables left to the ear alone, and yet with all its rudeness our Tongue had then aquired an Energy & a Plenty by the adoption of a variety of words borrow'd from the French, the Provengal, and the Italian about the middle of the 14th century, that at this day our best Writers seem to miss & to regret, for many of them have gradually drop'd into disuse, & are only now to be found in the remotest Counties of England. Another thing, which perhaps contributed something to the making our ancient Poets so voluminous, was the great facility of rhiming, which is now grown so difficult, words of two & three syllables being then newly taken from foreign languages did still retain their original accent, & that (as they were mostly derived from the French) fell according to the Genius of that tongue upon the Last Syllable, which, if it still had continued among us, had been a great advantage to our Poetry, among the Scotch this still continues in many words, for they say, Envy, Practise, Pensive, Positive, &c: but we in process of time, have accustom'd ourselves to throw back all our accents upon the Antepenultima, in words of three or more syllables, and of our Dissyllables comparatively but a few are left, as Disdain, Despair, Repent, Pretend, &c: where the stress is not laid upon the Penultima; By this means we are almost reduced to find our Rhimes among the Monosyllables, in which our tongue too much abounds, a defect that will forever hinder it from adapting itself well to Musick, & must be no small impediment consequently to the sweetness & harmony of Versification. . . .

To return to Lydgate, I do not pretend to set him on a level with his master Chaucer, but he certainly comes the nearest to him of any contemporary writer that I am aquainted with, his choice of expression, & the smoothness of his verse far surpass both Gower & Occleve. he wanted not art in raising the more tender emotions of mind, of which I might give several examples, the first is of that sympathy which we feel for humble piety & contrition. . . .

It is observable, that in images of horrour & a certain terrible Greatness, our author comes far behind Chaucer, whether they were not suited to the Genius or the temper of Lydgate I do not determine; but it is sure that, tho' they seem'd naturally to present themselves, he has almost in general chose to avoid them, yet is there frequently a stiller kind of majesty both in his thought & expression, which makes one of his principal beauties. . . .

Lydgate seems to have been by nature of a more serious & melancholick turn of mind than Chaucer: yet one here & there meets with a stroke of Satyr and Irony that does not want humour, & it usually falls (as was the custom of those times) either upon the Women or on the Clergy, as the Religious were the principal Scholars of these ages, they probably gave the tone in writing & in wit to the rest of the nation, the celibacy imposed on them by the Church had sower'd their temper, and naturally disposed them (as it is observed of Old-Bachelors in our days) to make the Weaknesses of the other Sex their theme; & tho' every one had a profound respect for his own particular order, yet the feuds and bickerings between one Order & another were perpetual & irreconcileable: these possibly were the causes that directed the Satyr of our old Writers principally to those two objects. . . .

This kind of satyr I know, will appear to modern Men of Taste a little stale & unfashionable: but our reflections should go deeper, & lead us to consider the fading & transitory nature of Wit in general. I have attempted to shew above the source from whence the two prevailing subjects of our Ancestor's Severity were derived: let us observe their different success & duration from those times to our own. . . .

Metrum

Though I would not with Mr. Urry, the last Editor of Chaucer, insert words & syllables, unauthorized by the oldest Manuscripts, to help out what seems lame and defective in the measure of our ancient writers; yet as I see those MSS, and the first printed Editions, so extremely inconstant in their manner of spelling one & the same word, as to vary continually, often in the compass of two Lines, & seem to have no fix'd Orthography at all, I can not help thinking it probable, that many great inequalities in the metre are owing to the neglect of Transcribers, or that the manner of reading made up for the defects that appear in the writing, thus the y which we often see prefix'd to Participles passive, as *ycleped, yhewe,* &c: is not a mere arbitrary insertion to fill up the verse, but the old Anglo-Saxon augment, always prefix'd formerly to such Participles, as gelufod (loved) from *Lufian* (to love), geraed, from *raedan* (to read), &c. . . . This syllable, tho' (I suppose) then out of use in common speech, our Poets inserted, where it suited them, in verse, the same did they by the final syllable of verbs, as *bren-nin, correctin, dronkin* . . . this termination begun to be omitted, after the Danes were settled among us . . . the transition is very apparent from thence to the English, we now speak, as then our writers inserted these initial and final syllables, or omitted them; & where we see them written, we do not doubt, that they were meant to fill up the measure, it follows that these Poets had an ear not insensible to defects in metre; & where the verse seems to halt, it very probably is occasion'd by the Transcriber's neglect who seeing a word differently spelt from the manner then customary, changed or omitted a few letters without reflecting on the injury done to the measure, the case is the same with the genitive case singular, & nominative plural of many nouns, which by the Saxon inflexion had an additional syllable, as *word,* a word, *wordes,* of a word: *smith,* a Smith, *smithes,* of a smith; *smithas,* Smiths, which (as Hickes observes) is the origin of the formation of those cases in our present tongue; but we now have reduced them by our pronunciation to an equal number of syllables with their Nominatives-singular, this was commonly done (I imagine) too in Chaucer & Lydgate's time; but in verse they took the Liberty either to follow the old language in pronouncing the final syllable; or to sink the vowel, and abridge it, as was usual; according to the necessity of their versification, for example, they would read either vlolettes with four syllables, or violets with three; *bankis,* or banks, *triumphys,* or triumphs, indifferently. I have already mention'd the *e* mute & their use of it in words derived from the French and imagine, that they did the same in many of true English Origin, which the Danes had before rob'd of their final consonant, writing *bute,* for the Saxon *butan* (without) . . . here we may easily conceive, that tho' the n was taken away, yet the *e* continued to be pronounced faintly, and tho' in time it was quite drop'd in conversation, yet, when the Poet thought fit to make a syllable of it, it no more offended their ears, than it now does those of a Frenchman to hear it so pronounced, in verse. . . .

These reflections may serve to shew us, that Puttenham, tho' he lived within about 150 years of Chaucer's time, must be mistaken with regard to what the old Writers call'd their *riding* ryme, for the Canterbury Tales, which he gives as an example of it, are as exact in their measure & their pause as the Troilus and Creseide where he says *the meetre is very grave and stately*; and this not only in the Knight's Tale, but in the comic introduction and characters. . . .

I conclude, he was misled by the change words had undergone in their accents since the days of Chaucer, & by the seeming defects of measure that frequently occur in the printed copies.

—Thomas Gray, *Commonplace Book*, c. 1760, Volume 2, pp. 743–57

Thomas Warton (1778–81)

Thomas Warton (1728–90) was an English literary historian and scholar, as well as the poet laureate of England from 1785–90. Writing of Chaucer in *The History of English Poetry*, Warton declares, "Chaucer manifestly first taught his countrymen to write English; and formed a style by naturalising words from the Provencial, at that time the most polished dialect of any in Europe, and the best adapted to the purposes of poetical expression." Warton demonstrates the validity of this statement by comparing Chaucer and Boccaccio, with an emphasis on the latter's *Teseide* and the former's "The Knight's Tale"; similar work will be done by Ker, Brink, and Borghesi, and students are encouraged to examine their excerpts and compare what these four critics each say on the matter.

After a brief discussion of *Troilus and Criseyde*, Warton launches into a longer discussion of the general construct of *The Canterbury Tales* and many of the specific pilgrims on the trip. This is the part of the excerpt students will likely find the most useful. Warton's work with "The Miller's Tale," a tale thought too vulgar to be taken seriously by many in Warton's day, should prove of enormous benefit, as many contemporary readers find the crude humor of the text particularly endearing. Warton's work on Chaucer's humor in the *Tales* is also particularly informative in regard to "The Tale of Sir Thopas," the first tale Chaucer himself tells on the pilgrimage. Warton and his brother, Joseph Warton, were the first to declare that "Thopas" is actually a parody: "Chaucer, at a period which almost realized the manners of romantic chivalry, discerned the leading absurdities of the old romances: and in this poem, which may be justly called a prelude to *Don Quixote*, has burlesqued them with exquisite ridicule." Most contemporary critics now agree with Warton, that this tale was meant to mock the genre and style of medieval romances.

Warton's observations on humor in *The Canterbury Tales* lead him into brief but interesting discussions of many of the pilgrims, including the Prioress, the Wife of Bath, the Summoner, the Monk, and the Franklin. Warton ends this essay with an examination of a text known as the *Marchaunt's Second Tale*, or the *History of Beryn*. It is one of several medieval texts that appeared after Chaucer's death, often ascribed to the poet himself, which purported to have originated in *The Canterbury Tales*. Students examining this text or others like it will find Warton's perspective here of interest. Warton ends his essay by greatly praising Chaucer, noting that "his genius was universal." Warton's essay, with its emphasis on humor, satire, and genre, demonstrates not only an intriguing shift in how *The Canterbury Tales* was starting to be perceived but also a growing understanding of Chaucer's accomplishment in this single text alone.

The revival of learning in most countries appears to have first owed its rise to translation. At rude periods the modes of original thinking are unknown, and the arts of original composition have not yet been studied. The writers therefore of such periods are chiefly and very usefully employed in importing the ideas of other languages into their own. They do not venture to think for themselves, nor aim at the merit of inventors, but they are laying the foundations of literature; and while they are naturalising the knowledge of more learned ages and countries by translation, they are imperceptibly improving the national language. This has been remarkably the case, not only in England, but in France and Italy. In the year 1387, John Trevisa, canon of Westbury in Gloucestershire, and a great traveller, not only finished a translation of the Old and New Testaments, at the command of his munificent patron Thomas lord Berkley, but also translated Higden's *Polychronicon,* and other Latin pieces. But these translations would have been alone insufficient to have produced or sustained any considerable revolution in our language: the great work was reserved for Gower and Chaucer. Wickliffe had also translated the Bible: and in other respects his attempts to bring about a reformation in religion at this time proved beneficial to English literature. The orthodox divines of this period generally wrote in Latin: but Wickliffe, that his arguments might be familiarised to common readers and the bulk of the people, was obliged to compose in English his numerous theological treatises against the papal corruptions. Edward the Third, while he perhaps intended only to banish a badge of conquest, greatly contributed to establish the national dialect, by abolishing the use of the Norman tongue in the public acts and judicial proceedings, as we have before observed, and by substituting the natural language of the country. But Chaucer manifestly first taught his countrymen to write English; and formed a style by naturalising words from the Provencial, at that time the most polished dialect of any in Europe, and the best adapted to the purposes of poetical expression.

It is certain that Chaucer abounds in classical allusions: but his poetry is not formed on the antient models. He appears to have been an universal reader, and his learning is sometimes mistaken for genius: but his chief sources were the French and Italian poets. From these originals two of his capital poems, the *Knight's Tale,* and the *Romaunt of the Rose,* are imitations or translations. The first of these is taken from Boccacio. . . .

In passing through Chaucer's hands, this poem has received many new beauties. Not only those capital fictions and descriptions, the temples of Mars, Venus, and Diana, with their allegorical paintings, and the figures of Lycurgus and Emetrius with their retinue, and so much heightened by the bold and spirited manner of the British bard, as to strike us with an air of originality. In the mean time it is to be remarked, that as Chaucer in some places has thrown in strokes of his own, so in others he has contracted the uninteresting and tedious prolixity of narrative, which he found in the Italian poet. And that he might avoid a servile imitation, and indulge himself as he pleased in an arbitrary departure from the original, it appears that he neglected the embarrassment of Boccacio's stanza, and preferred the English heroic couplet, of which this poem affords the first conspicuous example extant in our language.

The situation and structure of the temple of Mars are thus described.

> A forest
> In which ther wonneth neyther man ne best:
> With knotty knarry barrein trees old,
> Of stubbes sharpe, and hidous to behold,
> In which ther ran a romble and a swough.
> As though a storme shuld bersten every bough.
> And dounward from an hill, under a bent,
> Ther stood the temple of Mars armipotent,
> Wrought all of burned stele: of which th'entree
> Was longe, and streite, and gastly for to see:
> And therout came a rage and swiche a vise
> That it made all the gates for to rise.
> The northern light in at the dore shone,
> For window on the wall ne was ther none,
> Thurgh which men mighten any light discerne.

The dore was all of athamant eterne,
Yelenched overthwart and endelong,
With yren tough, and for to make it strong.
Every piler the temple to sustene
Was tonnè-grete of yren bright and shene.

The gloomy sanctuary of this tremendous fane was adorned with these characteristical imageries.

Ther saw I first the derke imagining
Of Felonie, and alle the compassing:
The cruel Irè, red as any glede.
The Pikepurse, and eke the pale Drede;
The Smiler with the knif under the cloke:
The shepen brenning with the blakè smoke;
The Treson of the mordring in the bedde,
The open Werre with woundes all bebledde;
Conteke with bloody knif, and sharp Manace,
All full of chirking was that sory place!
The sleer of himself yet saw I there,
His herte-blood hath bathed all his here,
The naile ydriven in the shode on hight,
The colde deth, with mouth gaping upright.
Amiddes of the temple sate Mischance,
With discomfort, and sory countenance.
Yet saw I Woodnesse laughing in his rage.
Armed complaint, outhees, and fiers Outrage;
The carraine in the bush, with throte ycorven,
A thousand slain, and not of qualme ystorven.
The tirant, with the prey by force yraft,
The toun destroied, there was nothing laft,
Yet saw I brent the shippes hoppesteres,
The hunte ystrangled with the wilde beres,
The sow freting the child right in the cradel,
The cokee yscalled, for all his long ladel.
Nought was foryete by th'infortune of Marte;
The carter overridden by his carte,
Under the wheel full low he lay adoun.
Ther were also of Martes division,
The Armerer, and the Bowyer, and the Smith
That forgeth sharpè swerdes on his stith.

> And all above, depeinted in a tour,
> Saw I Conquest sitting in gret honour,
> With thilke sharpe swerd over his hed,
> Y-hanging by a subtil twined thred.

This groupe is the effort of a strong imagination, unacquainted with selection and arrangement of images. It is rudely thrown on the canvas without order or art. In the Italian poets, who describe every thing, and who cannot, even in the most serious representations, easily suppress their natural predilection for burlesque and familiar imagery, nothing is more common than this mixture of sublime and comic ideas. The form of Mars follows, touched with the impetuous dashes of a savage and spirited pencil.

> The statue of Mars upon a carte stood,
> Armed, and loked grim as he were wood.
> A wolf ther stood beforne him at his fete
> With eyen red, and of a man he ete.
> With subtil pensil peinted was this storie,
> In redouting of Mars and of his glorie.

But the ground-work of this whole description is in the *Thebaid* of Statius. . . .

Statius was a favourite writer with the poets of the middle ages. His bloated magnificence of description, gigantic images, and pompous diction, suited their taste, and were somewhat of a piece with the romances they so much admired. They neglected the gentler and genuine graces of Virgil, which they could not relish. His pictures were too correctly and chastely drawn to take their fancies: and truth of design, elegance of expression, and the arts of composition were not their objects. In the mean time we must observe, that in Chaucer's Temple of Mars many personages are added; and that those which existed before in Statius have been retouched, enlarged, and rendered more distinct and picturesque by Boccacio and Chaucer. Arcite's address to Mars, at entering the temple, has great dignity, and is not copied from Statius.

> O strongè god, that in the regnes cold
> Of Trace honoured art, and lord yhold!
> And hast in every regne, and every lond,
> Of armes al the bride! in thin hond;
> And hem fortunist, as thee list devise,
> Accept of me my pitous sacrifise.

The following portrait of Lycurgus, an imaginary king of Thrace, is highly charged, and very great in the gothic style of painting.

> Ther maist thou se, coming with Palamon,
> Lycurge himself, the grete king of Trace;
> Blake was his berde, and manly was his face:
> The cercles of his eyen in his hed
> They gloweden betwixten yalwe and red:
> And like a griffon loked he about,
> With kemped heres on his browes stout:
> His limmes gret, his braunes hard and stronge,
> His shouldres brode, his armes round and longe.
> And as the guise was in his contree
> Ful highe upon a char of gold stood he:
> With foure white bolles in the trais.
> Instead of cote-armure, on his harnais
> With nayles yelwe, and bright as any gold,
> He hadde a beres skin cole-blake for old.
> His longe here was kempt behind his bak,
> As any ravenes fetherit shone for blake.
> A wreth of gold armgrete, of huge weight,
> Upon his hed sate full of stones bright,
> Of fine rubins, and of diamants.
> About his char ther wenten white alauns,
> Twenty and mo, as gret as any stere,
> To hunten at the leon or the dere;
> And folwed him with mosel fast ybound,
> Colered with gold and torretes filed round.
> A hundred lordes had he in his route,

> Armed full wel, with hertes sterne and stoute.

The figure of Emetrius king of India, who comes to the aid of Arcite, is not inferior in the same style, with a mixture of grace.

> With Arcita, in stories as men find,
> The gret Emetrius, the king of Inde,
> Upon a stedè bay, trapped in stele,
> Covered with cloth of gold diapred wele,
> Came riding like the god of armes Mars:
> His cote-armure was of a cloth of Tars,
> Couched with perles, white, and round and grete;

His sadel was of brent gold new ybete,
A mantelet upon his shouldres hanging,
Bretfull of rubies red, as fire sparkling.
His crispè here like ringes was yronne,
And that was yelwe, and glitered as the sonne.
His nose was high, his eyen bright citrin,
His lippes round, his colour was sanguin.
And a fewe fraknes in his face ysprent,
Betwixen yelwe and blake somdele ymeint.
And as a leon he his loking caste.
Of five and twenty yere his age I caste.
His berd was well begonnen for to spring,
His vois was as a trompe thondiring.
Upon his hed he wered, of laurer grene
A gerlond freshe, and lusty for to sene.
Upon his hond he bare for his deduit
An egle tame, as any lily white.
An hundred lordes had he with him there,
All armed, save hir hedes, in all hir gere.
About this king ther ran on every part
Full many a tame leon, and leopart.

The banner of Mars displayed by Theseus, is sublimely conceived.

The red statue of Mars, with spere and targe,
So shineth in his white banner large
That al the feldes gliteren up and doun.

This poem has many strokes of pathetic description, of which these specimens may be selected.

Upon that other side Palamon
Whan that he wist Arcita was ygon,
Swiche sorwe he maketh, that the grete tour
Resouned of his yelling and clamour:
The pure fetters on his shinnes grete
Were of his bitter salte teres wete.

Arcite is thus described, after his return to Thebes, where he despairs of seeing Emilia again.

His slepe, his mete, his drinke, is him byraft;
That lene he wex, and drie as is a shaft:

His eyen holwe, and grisly to behold
His hewe falwe, and pale as ashen cold:
And solitary he was, and ever alone,
And wailing all the night, making his mone.
And if he herdè song or instrument,
Than wold he wepe, he mighte not be stent.
So feble were his spirites and so low,
And changed so, that no man coude know
His speche, ne his vois, though men it herd.

Palamon is thus introduced in the procession of his rival Arcite's funeral:

Tho came this woful Theban Palamon
With flotery berd, and ruggy ashy heres,
In clothes blake ydropped all with teres,
And, (passing over of weping Emelie,)
Was reufullest of all the compagnie.

To which may be added the surprise of Palamon, concealed in the forest, at hearing the disguised Arcite, whom he supposes to be the squire of Theseus, discover himself at the mention of the name of Emilia.

Thrughout his herte
He felt a colde swerd sodenly glide:
For ire he quoke, no lenger wolde he hide,
And whan that he had herd Arcites tale,
As he were wood, with face ded and pale,
He sterte him up out of the bushes thikke, &c.

A description of the morning must not be omitted; which vies, both in sentiment and expression, with the most finished modern poetical landscape, and finely displays our author's talent at delineating the beauties of nature.

The besy larke, messager of day,
Saleweth in hire song the morwe gray;
And firy Phebus riseth up so bright,
That all the orient laugheth of the sight:
And with his stremes drieth in the greves
The silver dropes hanging on the leves.

Nor must the figure of the blooming Emilia, the most beautiful object of this vernal picture, pass unnoticed.

> Emelie, that fayrer was to sene
> Than is the lilie upon his stalke grene;
> And fresher than the May with floures newe,
> (For with the rose colour strof hire hewe).

In other parts of his works he has painted morning scenes *con amore:* and his imagination seems to have been peculiarly struck with the charms of a rural prospect at sun-rising.

We are surprised to find, in a poet of such antiquity, numbers so nervous and flowing: a circumstance which greatly contributed to render Dryden's paraphrase of this poem the most animated and harmonious piece of versification in the English language. I cannot leave the *Knight's Tale* without remarking, that the inventor of this poem appears to have possessed considerable talents for the artificial construction of a story. It exhibits unexpected and striking turns of fortune; and abounds in those incidents which are calculated to strike the fancy by opening resources to sublime description, or interest the heart by pathetic situations. On this account, even without considering the poetical and exterior ornaments of the piece, we are hardly disgusted with the mixture of manners, the confusion of times, and the like violations of propriety, which this poem, in common with all others of its age, presents in almost every page. . . .

Whatever were Chaucer's materials, he has on this subject constructed a poem of considerable merit, in which the vicissitudes of love are depicted in a strain of true poetry, with much pathos and simplicity of sentiment. He calls it, "a litill tragedie." Troilus is supposed to have seen Cresside in a temple; and retiring to his chamber, is thus naturally described, in the critical situation of a lover examining his own mind after the first impression of love.

And whan that he in chambre was alone, He down upon his beddis fete him sette, And first he gan to sike, and efte to grone, And thought aie on her so withoutin lette: That as he satte and woke, his spirit mette That he her saugh, and temple, and all the wise Right of her loke, and gan it newe avise. There is not so much nature in the sonnet to Love, which follows. It is translated from Petrarch; and had Chaucer followed his own genius, he would not have disgusted us with the affected gallantry and exaggerated compliments which it extends through five tedious stanzas. The doubts and delicacies of a young girl disclosing her heart to her lover, are exquisitely touched in this comparison.

> And as the newe abashid nightingale
> That stintith first, when she beginith sing,
> When that she herith any herdis tale,

Or in the hedgis anie wight stirring,
And after sikir doth her voice outring;
Right so Creseidè when that her drede stent
Opened her herte and told him her intent.

The following pathetic scene may be selected from many others. Troilus seeing Cresside in a swoon, imagines her to be dead. He unsheaths his sword with an intent to kill himself, and utters these exclamations.

And thou, cite, in which I live in wo,
And thou Priam, and brethren al ifere,
And thou, my mother, farwel, for I go:
And, Atropos, make ready thou my bere:
And thou Creseidè, O sweet hertè dere,
Receive thou now my spirit, would he say,
With swerd at hert all redy for to dey.
But as god would, of swough she tho abraide,
And gan to sighe, and TROILUS she cride:
And he answerid, Lady mine Creseide,
Livin ye yet? And let his sword doune glide,
Yes, hertè mine, that thankid be Cupide,
Quoth she: and therwithall she sorè sight
And he began to glad her as he might.
Toke her in armis two, and kist her oft,
And her to glad he did all his entent:
For which her ghost, that flickered aie alofte
Into her woefull breast aien it went:
But at the last, as that her eyin glent
Aside, anon she gan his swerde aspie,
As it lay bere, and gan for fere to crie:
And askid him why he had it outdrawe?
And Troilus anon the cause hir tolde,
And how therwith himself he would have slawe:
For which Creseide upon him gan behold,
And gan him in her armis fast to fold;
And said, O mercy, God, lo whiche a dede
Alas! how nere we werin bothè dede!

Pathetic description is one of Chaucer's peculiar excellencies.

In this poem are various imitations from Ovid, which are of too particular and minute a nature to be pointed out here, and belong to the province of a professed and formal commentator on the piece. The Platonic notion in the third book about universal love, and the doctrine that this principle acts with equal and uniform influence both in the natural and moral world, are a translation from Boethius. And in the *Knight's Tale* he mentions, from the same favourite system of philosophy, the *Faire Chaine of Love*. It is worth observing, that the reader is referred to Dares Phrygius, instead of Homer, for a display of the achievements of Troilus.

> His worthi dedis who so list him here,
> Rede Dares, he can tel hem all ifere.

Our author, from his excessive fondness for Statius, has been guilty of a very diverting and what may be called a double anachronism. He represents Cresside, with two of her female companions, sitting in a *pavid parlour,* and reading the *Thebaid* of Statius, which is called *the Geste of the Siege of Thebes,* and *the Romance of Thebis.* In another place, Cassandra translates the Arguments of the twelve books of the *Thebaid.* In the fourth book of this poem, Pandarus endeavours to comfort Troilus with arguments concerning the doctrine of predestination, taken from Bradwardine, a learned archbishop and theologist, and nearly Chaucer's cotemporary.

This poem, although almost as long as the *Eneid,* was intended to be sung to the harp, as well as read.

> And redde where so thou be, or ellis *songe.* . . .

Nothing can be more ingeniously contrived than the occasion on which Chaucer's *Canterbury Tales* are supposed to be recited. A company of pilgrims, on their journey to visit the shrine of Thomas Becket at Canterbury, lodge at the Tabarde-inn in Southwark. Although strangers to each other, they are assembled in one room at supper, as was then the custom; and agree, not only to travel together the next morning, but to relieve the fatigue of the journey by telling each a story. Chaucer undoubtedly intended to imitate Boccacio, whose *Decameron* was then the most popular of books, in writing a set of tales. But the circumstance invented by Boccacio, as the cause which gave rise to his *Decameron,* or the relation of his hundred stories, is by no means so happily conceived as that of Chaucer for a similar purpose. Boccacio supposes, that when the plague began to abate at Florence, ten young persons of both sexes retired to a country house, two miles from the city, with a design of enjoying fresh air, and passing ten days agreeably. Their principal and established amusement, instead of playing at chess after dinner, was for each to tell a tale. One superiority, which, among others, Chaucer's plan afforded above that of Boccacio, was the opportunity of displaying a variety of striking and dramatic characters, which would not have easily met but on such an expedition;—a circumstance which also contributed to give a variety to the stories. And for a number of persons in their situation, so natural, so practicable, so pleasant, I add so rational, a mode of entertainment, could not have been imagined.

The *Canterbury Tales* are unequal, and of various merit. Few, if any, of the stories are perhaps the invention of Chaucer. I have already spoken at large of the *Knight's Tale*, one of our author's noblest compositions. That of the *Canterbury Tales*, which deserves the next place, as written in the higher strain of poetry, and the poem by which Milton describes and characterises Chaucer, is the *Squier's Tale*. The imagination of this story consists in Arabian fiction engrafted on Gothic chivalry. Nor is this Arabian fiction purely the sport of arbitrary fancy: it is in great measure founded on Arabian learning.

Every reader of taste and imagination must regret, that instead of our author's tedious detail of the quaint effects of Canace's ring, in which a falcon relates her amours, and talks familiarly of Troilus, Paris, and Jason, the notable achievements we may suppose to have been performed by the assistance of the horse of brass, are either lost, or that this part of the story, by far the most interesting, was never written. After the strange knight has explained to Cambuscan the management of this magical courser, he vanishes on a sudden, and we hear no more of him.

> At after souper goth this noble king
> To seen this Hors of Bras, with all a route
> Of lordes and of ladies him aboute:
> Swiche wondring was ther on this Hors of Bras,
> That sin the gret assege of Troyè was,
> Ther as men wondred on an hors also,
> Ne was ther swiche a wondring as was tho.
> But finally the king asketh the knight
> The vertue of his courser and the might;
> And praied him to tell his govemaunce:
> The hors anon gan for to trip and daunce,
> Whan that the knight laid hond upon his reine.—
> Enfourmed whan the king was of the knight,
> And hath conceived in his wit aright,
> The maner and the forme of all this thing,
> Ful glad and blith, this noble doughty king
> Repaireth to his revel as beforne:
> The brydel is into the Toure yborne,

And kept among his jewels lefe and dere:
The horse vanisht: I n'ot in what manere.

By such inventions we are willing to be deceived. These are the triumphs
of deception over truth.

Magnanima mensogna, hor quando è al vero.
Si bello, che si possa à te preporre?

The *Clerke of Oxenfordes Tale,* or the story of Patient Grisilde, is the next
of Chaucer's Tales in the serious style which deserves mention. . . .

The pathos of this poem, which is indeed exquisite, chiefly consists
in invention of incidents, and the contrivance of the story, which cannot
conveniently be developed in this place: and it will be impossible to give any
idea of its essential excellence by exhibiting detached parts. The versification
is equal to the rest of our author's poetry. . . .

Dryden and Pope have modernised the two last-mentioned poems;
Dryden the tale of the *Nonnes Priest,* and Pope that of *January* and *May;*
intending perhaps to give patterns of the best of Chaucer's Tales in the comic
species. But I am of opinion that the *Miller's Tale* has more true humour than
either. Not that I mean to palliate the levity of the story, which was most
probably chosen by Chaucer in compliance with the prevailing manners of
an unpolished age, and agreeable to ideas of festivity not always the most
delicate and refined. Chaucer abounds in liberties of this kind, and this
must be his apology. So does Boccacio, and perhaps much more, but from a
different cause. The licentiousness of Boccacio's tales, which he composed *per
cacciar le malincolia delle femine,* to amuse the ladies, is to be vindicated, at
least accounted for, on other principles: it was not so much the consequence
of popular incivility, as it was owing to a particular event of the writer's age.
Just before Boccacio wrote, the plague at Florence had totally changed the
customs and manners of the people. . . .

But to return to the *Miller's Tale.* The character of the Clerke of Oxford,
who studied astrology, a science then in high repute, but under the specious
appearance of decorum, and the mask of the serious philosopher, carried on
intrigues, is painted with these lively circumstances.

This clerk was cleped hendy Nicholas,
Of dernè love he coude and of solas:
And therto he was slie, and ful prive,
And like a maiden meke for to se.
A chambre had he in that hostelrie
Alone, withouten any compagnie,

Ful fetisly ydight with herbes sote;
And he himself was swete as is the rote
Of licoris, or any setewale.
His almageste, and bokes grete and smale,
His astrelabre longing for his art,
His augrim stones layen faire apart,
On shelves, couched at his beddes hed;
His presse ycovered with a falding red:
And all above there lay a gay sautrie,
On which he made on nightes melodie
So swetely that al the chambre rong,
And *Angelus ad Virginem* he song.

In the description of the young wife of our philosopher's host, there is great elegance, with a mixture of burlesque allusions. Not to mention the curiosity of a female portrait, drawn with so much exactness at such a distance of time.

Fayre was this yongè wife, and therwithal
As any wesel hire body gent and smal.
A seint she wered, barred all of silk,
A barmecloth eke, as white as morwe milk,
Upon hire lendes, ful of many a gore.
White was hire smok, and brouded all before,
And eke behind, on hire colere aboute,
Of coleblak silk, within, and eke withoute.
The tapes of hire white volipere
Were of the same suit of hire colere.
Hire fillet brode of silk, and set full hye,
And sikerly she had a likerous eye.
Ful smal ypulled were hire browes two,
And thy were bent and black as any slo.
And she was wel more blisful on to see
Than is the newe perienet tree;
And softer than the wolle is of a wether:
And by hire girdle heng a purse of lether,
Tasseled with silk, and perlid with latoun.
In all this world to seken up and doun,
There nis no man so wise that coude thenche
So gay a popelot or swiche a wenche.
Full brighter was the shining of hire hewe

> Than in the Tour the noble yforged newe.
> But of hire song, it was as loud and yerne,
> As any swalow sitting on a berne.
> Therto she coude skip, and make a game,
> As any kid or calf folowing his dame.
> Hire mouth was swete as braket or the meth,
> Or hord of appels laid in hay or heth.
> Winsing she was as is a joly colt,
> Long as a mast, and upright as a bolt.
> A broche she bare upon hire low colere
> As brode as is the bosse of a bokelere.
> Hire shoon were laced on hire legges hie, &c.

Nicholas, as we may suppose, was not proof against the charms of his blooming hostess. He has frequent opportunities of conversing with her; for her husband is the carpenter of Oseney Abbey near Oxford, and often absent in the woods belonging to the monastery. His rival is Absalom, a parish-clerk, the gaiest of his calling, who being amorously inclined, very naturally avails himself of a circumstance belonging to his profession: on holidays it was his business to carry the censer about the church, and he takes this opportunity of casting unlawful glances on the handsomest dames of the parish. His gallantry, agility, affectation of dress and personal elegance, skill in shaving and surgery, smattering in the law, taste for music, and many other accomplishments, are thus inimitably represented by Chaucer, who must have much relished so ridiculous a character.

> Now was ther of that chirche a parish clerke,
> The which that was ycleped Absalon,
> Crulle was his here, and as the golde it shone,
> And strouted as a fannè large and brode,
> Ful streight and even lay his joly shode.
> His rode was red, his eyen grey as goos,
> With Poules windowes corven on his shoos.
> In hosen red he went ful fetisly:
> Yclad he was ful smal and properly
> All in a kirtel of a light waget,
> Ful faire, and thickè ben the pointes set:
> And therupon he had a gay surplise
> As white as is the blosme upon the rise.
> A mery child he was, so god me save,
> Wei coud he leten blod, and clippe, and shave.

And make a chartre of lond and a quitance;
In twenty manere coud he trip and dance,
After the scole of Oxenforde tho,
And with his legges casten to and fro.
And playen songes on a smal ribible,
Therto he song sometime a loud quinible.

. . . (O)ur carpenter, reflecting on the danger of being wise, and exulting in the security of his own ignorance, exclaims,

A man wote litel what shal him betide!
This man is fallen with his astronomie
In som woodnesse, or in som agonie.
I thought ay wel how that it shulde be:
Men shulde not know of goddes privetee.
Ya blessed be alway the lewed-man,
That nought but only his beleve can.
So ferd another clerke with astronomie;
He walked in the feldes for to prie
Upon the sterres what there shuld befalle
Till he was in a marlèpit yfalle;
He saw not that. But yet, by seint Thomas,
Me reweth sore of hendy Nicholas:
He shall be rated for his studying.

But the scholar has ample gratification for this ridicule. The carpenter is at length admitted; and the scholar continuing the farce, gravely acquaints the former that he has been all this while making a most important discovery by means of astrological calculations. He is soon persuaded to believe the prediction: and in the sequel, which cannot be repeated here, this humorous contrivance crowns the scholar's schemes with success, and proves the cause of the carpenter's disgrace. In this piece the reader observes that the humour of the characters is made subservient to the plot.

I have before hinted, that Chaucer's obscenity is in great measure to be imputed to his age. We are apt to form romantic and exaggerated notions about the moral innocence of our ancestors. Ages of ignorance and simplicity are thought to be ages of purity. The direct contrary, I believe, is the case. Rude periods have that grossness of manners which is not less friendly to virtue than luxury itself. In the middle ages, not only the most flagrant violations of modesty were frequently practised and permitted, but the most infamous vices. Men are less ashamed as they are less polished. Great refinement multiplies criminal pleasures, but at the same time prevents the actual commission of many enormities: at least it preserves public decency, and suppresses public licentiousness.

The *Reve's Tale,* or the *Miller of Trompington,* is much in the same style, but with less humour. This story was enlarged by Chaucer from Boccacio. There is an old English poem on the same plan, entitled, A *ryght pleasant and merye history of the Mylner ofAbington, with his Wife and faire Daughter, and two poore Scholars of Cambridge.* It begins with these lines.

> Faire lordinges, if you list to heere
> A mery jest your minds to cheere.

This piece is supposed by Wood to have been written by Andrew Borde, a physician, a wit, and a poet, in the reign of Henry the Eighth. It was at least evidently written after the time of Chaucer. It is the work of some tasteless imitator, who has sufficiently disguised his original, by retaining none of its spirit. I mention these circumstances, lest it should be thought that this frigid abridgement was the ground-work of Chaucer's poem on the same subject. In the class of humorous or satirical tales, the *Sompnour's Tale,* which exposes the tricks and extortions of the Mendicant friars, has also distinguished merit. This piece has incidentally been mentioned above with the *Plowman's Tale,* and Pierce Plowman.

Genuine humour, the concomitant of true taste, consists in discerning improprieties in books as well as characters. We therefore must remark under this class another tale of Chaucer, which till lately has been looked upon as a grave heroic narrative. I mean the *Rime of Sir Thopas.* Chaucer, at a period which almost realized the manners of romantic chivalry, discerned the leading absurdities of the old romances: and in this poem, which may be justly called a prelude to *Don Quixote,* has burlesqued them with exquisite ridicule. That this was the poet's aim, appears from many passages. But, to put the matter beyond a doubt, take the words of an ingenious critic. "We are to observe," says he, "that this was Chaucer's own Tale: and that, when in the progress of it, the good sense of the host is made to break in upon him, and interrupt him, Chaucer approves his disgust, and changing his note, tells the simple instructive *Tale of Meliboeus,* a *moral tale vertuous,* as he terms it; to show what sort of fictions were most expressive of real life, and most proper to be put into the hands of the people. It is further to be noted, that the *Boke* of *The Giant Olyphant, and Chylde Thopas,* was not a fiction of his own, but a story of antique fame, and very celebrated in the days of chivalry; so that nothing could better suit the poet's design of discrediting the old romances, than the choice of this venerable legend for the vehicle of his ridicule upon them." But it is to be remembered, that Chaucer's design was intended to ridicule the frivolous descriptions, and other tedious impertinencies, so common in the volumes of chivalry with which his age was overwhelmed, not to degrade in general or expose a mode of fabling, whose sublime extravagances constitute the marvellous grace of his own *Cambuscan;* a composition which at the same time abundantly demonstrates, that the manners of romance are better calculated to answer the purposes of pure poetry, to captivate the imagination, and to produce surprise, than the fictions of classical antiquity.

But Chaucer's vein of humour, although conspicuous in the *Canterbury Tales,* is chiefly displayed in the Characters with which they are introduced. In these his knowledge of the world availed him in a peculiar degree, and enabled him to give such an accurate picture of antient manners, as no cotemporary nation has transmitted to posterity. It is here that we view the pursuits and employments, the customs and diversions, of our ancestors, copied from the life, and represented with equal truth and spirit, by a judge of mankind, whose penetration qualified him to discern their foibles or discriminating peculiarities; and by an artist, who understood that proper selection of circumstances, and those predominant characteristics, which form a finished portrait. We are surprised to find, in so gross and ignorant an age, such talents for satire, and for observation on life; qualities which usually exert themselves at more civilised periods, when the improved state of society, by subtilising our speculations, and establishing uniform modes of behaviour, disposes mankind to study themselves, and renders deviations of conduct, and singularities of character, more immediately and necessarily the objects of censure and ridicule. These curious and valuable remains are specimens of Chaucer's native genius, unassisted and unalloyed. The figures are all British, and bear no suspicious signatures of Classical, Italian, or French imitation. The characters of Theophrastus are not so lively, particular, and appropriated. A few traits from this celebrated part of our author, yet too little tasted and understood, may be sufficient to prove and illustrate what is here advanced.

The character of the Prioresse is chiefly distinguished by an excess of delicacy and decorum, and an affectation of courtly accomplishments. But we are informed, that she was educated at the school of Stratford at Bow near London, perhaps a fashionable seminary for breeding nuns.

> There was also a nonne a Prioresse
> That of hire smiling was ful simple and coy;
> Hire gretest othe n'as but by seint Eloy, &c.
> And Frenche she spake full fayre and fetisly,
> After the scole of Stratford atte Bowe,

For Frenche of Paris was to hire unknowe,
At metè was she wel ytaughte withalle;
She lette no morsel from hire lippes falle,
Ne wette hire fingres in hire saucè depe;
Wel coude she carie a morsel, and wel kepe,
Thatte no drope ne fell upon hire brest;
In curtesie was sette ful moche hire lest.
Hire overlippè wiped she so clene,
That in hire cuppe was no ferthing sene
Of gresè, whan she dronken hadde hire draught,
Ful semely after hire mete she raught.—
And peined hire to contrefeten chere
Of court, and bene statelich of manere.

She has even the false pity and sentimentality of many modern ladies.

She was so charitable and so pitous,
She woldè wepe if that she saw a mous
Caughte in a trappe, if it were ded or bledde.
Of smalè houndes hadde she that she fed
With rosted flesh, and milk, and wastel brede:
But sore wept she if on of hem were dede,
Or if men smote it with a yerdè smert:
And all was conscience and tendre herte.

The Wife of Bath is more amiable for her plain and useful qualifications. She is a respectable dame, and her chief pride consists in being a conspicuous and significant character at church on a Sunday.

Of clothmaking she haddè swiche an haunt
She passed hem of Ipres and of Gaunt.
In all the parish, wif ne was there non
That to the offring bifore hire shulde gon;
And if ther did, certain so wroth was she,
That she was out of alle charite.
Hire coverchiefs weren ful fine of ground,
I dorste swere they weyeden a pound,
That on the sonday were upon hire hede:
Her hosen weren of fine scarlet rede,
Full streite iteyed, and shoon ful moist and newe:
Bold was hire face, and fayre and rede of hew.
She was a worthy woman all hire live:
Housbondes at the chirche dore had she had five.

The Frankelein is a country gentleman, whose estate consisted in free land, and was not subject to feudal services or payments. He is ambitious of showing his riches by the plenty of his table: but his hospitality, a virtue much more practicable among our ancestors than at present, often degenerates into luxurious excess. His impatience if his sauces were not sufficiently poignant, and every article of his dinner in due form and readiness, is touched with the hand of Pope or Boileau. He had been a president at the sessions, knight of the shire, a sheriff, and a coroner.

> An housholder, and that a grete, was he:
> Seint Julian he was in his contree.
> His brede, his ale, was alway after on;
> A better envyned man was no wher non.
> Withouten bake mete never was his hous
> Of fish and flesh, and that so plenteous,
> It snewed in his hous of mete and drinke,
> Of alle deintees that men coud of thinke.
> After the sondry sesons of the yere,
> So changed he his mete, and his soupere.
> Ful many a fat partrich hadde he in mewe,
> And many a breme, and many a luce, in stewe.
> Wo was his coke, but if his saucè were
> Poinant and sharpe, and ready all his gere!
> His table dormant in his halle alway,
> Stole redy covered, all the longe day.

The character of the Doctor of Phisicke preserves to us the state of medical knowledge, and the course of medical erudition then in fashion. He treats his patients according to rules of astronomy: a science which the Arabians engrafted on medicine.

> For he was grounded in astronomie:
> He kept his patient a ful gret dele
> In houres by his magike naturel. . . .

The Sompnour, whose office it was to summon uncanonical offenders into the archdeacon's court, where they were very rigorously punished, is humorously drawn as counteracting his profession by his example: he is libidinous and voluptuous, and his rosy countenance belies his occupation. This is an indirect satire on the ecclesiastical proceedings of those times. His affectation of Latin terms, which he had picked up from the decrees and pleadings of the court, must have formed a character highly ridiculous.

> And whan that he wel dronken had the win,
> Than wold he speken no word but Latine.
> A fewe termes coude he two or three,
> That he had lerned out of som decree.
> No wonder is, he herd it all the day:
> And eke ye knowen wel, how that a jay
> Can clepen watte as wel as can the pope:
> But whoso wolde in other thing him grope,
> Than hadde he spent all his philosophic,
> Ay *questio quid juris* wolde he crie.

He is with great propriety made the friend and companion of the Pardonere, or dispenser of indulgences, who is just arrived from the pope, "brimful of pardons come from Rome al hote;" and who carries in his wallet, among other holy curiosities, the virgin Mary's veil, and part of the sail of Saint Peter's ship.

The Monke is represented as more attentive to horses and hounds than to the rigorous and obsolete ordinances of Saint Benedict. Such are his ideas of secular pomp and pleasure, that he is even qualified to be an abbot.

> An outrider that loved venerie,
> A manly man, to ben an abbot able:
> Ful many a deinte hors hadde he in stable.—
> This ilkè monk lette old thinges pace,
> And held after the new world the trace.
> He yave not of the text a pulled hen
> That saith, that hunters ben not holy men.

He is ambitious of appearing a conspicuous and stately figure on horseback. A circumstance represented with great elegance.

> And whan he rode, men mighte his bridel here
> Gingeling in a whistling wind, as clere
> And eke as loude, as doth the chapel bell.

The gallantry of his riding dress, and his genial aspect, is painted in lively colours.

> I saw his sieves purfiled at the hond,
> With gris, and that the finest of the lond.
> And for to fasten his hode under his chinne
> He hadde of gold ywrought a curious pinne,
> A love-knotte in the greter end ther was.

His hed was balled, and shone as any glas,
And eke his face as it hadde ben anoint:
He was a lord ful fat, and in good point.
His eyen stepe, and rolling in his hed,
That stemed as a forneis of a led.
His botes souple, his hors in gret estat,
Now certainly he was a fayre prelat!
He was not pale as a forpined gost;
A fat swan loved he best of any rost.
His palfrey was as broune as is a berry.

The Frere, or friar, is equally fond of diversion and good living; but the poverty of his establishment obliges him to travel about the country, and to practise various artifices to provide money for his convent, under the sacred character of a confessor.

A frere there was, a wanton and a mery;
A limitour, a ful solempne man:
In all the ordres foure is non that can
So moche of daliance, and fayre langage.—
Ful swetely herde he confession:
Ful plesant was his absolution.
His tippet was ay farsed ful of knives
And pinnes for to given fayre wives.
And certainly he had a mery note:
Wei coude he singe and plaien on a rote.
Of yeddinges he bare utterly the pris.—
Ther n'as no man no wher so vertuous;
He was the beste begger in all his hous.—
Somewhat he lisped for his wantonnesse,
To make his English swete upon his tongue;
And in his harping, whan that he hadde songe,
His eyen twinkeled in his hed aright
As don the sterres in a frosty night.

With these unhallowed and untrue sons of the church is contrasted the Parsoune, or parish-priest: in describing whose sanctity, simplicity, sincerity, patience, industry, courage, and conscientious impartiality, Chaucer shows his good sense and good heart. Dryden imitated this character of the Good Parson, and is said to have applied it to bishop Ken.

The character of the Squire teaches us the education and requisite accomplishments of young gentlemen in the gallant reign of Edward the Third. But it is to be remembered, that our squire is the son of a knight, who has performed feats of chivalry in every part of the world; which the poet thus enumerates with great dignity and simplicity.

> At Alisandre' he was whan it was wonne,
> Ful often time he hadde the bord begonne,
> Aboven allè nations in Pruce.
> In Lettowe hadde he reysed and in Ruce:
> No cristen man so ofte of his degre
> In Gernade, at the siege eke hadde he be
> Of Algesir, and ridden in Belmarie.
> At Leyes was he, and at Satalie,
> Whan they were wonne: and in the gretè see:
> At many a noble armee hadde he be:
> At mortal batailles had he ben fiftene,
> And foughten for our faith at Tramissene
> In lystes thries, and ay slain his fo.
> This ilkè worthy Knight hadde ben also
> Sometime with the lord of Palatie:
> Agen another hethen in Turkic
> And evermore he hadde a sovereine pris,
> And though that he was worthy he was wise. . . .

The character of the Reve, an officer of much greater trust and authority during the feudal constitution than at present, is happily pictured. His attention to the care and custody of the manors, the produce of which was then kept in hand for furnishing his lord's table, perpetually employs his time, preys upon his thoughts, and makes him lean and choleric. He is the terror of bailiffs and hinds; and is remarkable for his circumspection, vigilance, and subtlety. He is never in arrears, and no auditor is able to over-reach or detect him in his accounts: yet he makes more commodious purchases for himself than for his master, without forfeiting the good will or bounty of the latter. Amidst these strokes of satire, Chaucer's genius for descriptive painting breaks forth in this simple and beautiful description of the Reve's rural habitation.

> His wonning was ful fayre upon an heth,
> With grene trees yshadewed was his place.

In the Clerke of Oxenforde our author glances at the inattention paid to literature, and the unprofitableness of philosophy. He is emaciated with study, clad in a thread-bare cloak, and rides a steed lean as a rake.

> For he hadde geten him yet no benefice,
> Ne was nought worldly to have an office:
> For him was lever han at his beddes hed
> A twenty bokes, clothed in black or red,
> Of Aristotle and his philosophie,
> Then robes riche, or fidel, or sautrie:
> But allbe that he was a philosophre,
> Yet hadde he but litel gold in cofre.

His unwearied attention to logic had tinctured his conversation with much pedantic formality, and taught him to speak on all subjects in a precise and sententious style. Yet his conversation was instructive: and he was no less willing to submit than to communicate his opinion to others.

> Souning in moral vertue was his speche,
> And gladly wolde he lerne, and gladly teche.

The perpetual importance of the Serjeant of Lawe, who by habit or by affectation has the faculty of appearing busy when he has nothing to do, is sketched with the spirit and conciseness of Horace.

> No wher so besy a man as he ther n'as,
> And yet he semed besier than he was.

There is some humour in making our lawyer introduce the language of his pleadings into common conversation. He addresses the hoste,

> Hoste, quoth he, *de pardeux jeo assent.*

The affectation of talking French was indeed general, but it is here appropriated and in character.

Among the rest, the character of the Hoste, or master of the Tabarde inn where the pilgrims are assembled, is conspicuous. He has much good sense, and discovers great talents for managing and regulating a large company; and to him we are indebted for the happy proposal of obliging every pilgrim to tell a story during their journey to Canterbury. His interpositions between the tales are very useful and enlivening; and he is something like the chorus on the Grecian stage. He is of great service in encouraging each person to begin his part, in conducting the scheme with spirit, in making proper observations on the merit or tendency of the several stories, in settling disputes which must naturally arise in the course of such an entertainment, and in connecting all the narratives into one continued system. His love of good cheer, experience in marshalling guests, address, authoritative deportment, and facetious disposition, are thus expressively displayed by Chaucer.

> Gret chere made our Hoste everich on,
> And to the souper sette he us anon;
> And served us with vitaille of the beste:
> Strong was his win, and wel to drinke us leste.
> A semely man our Hostè was with alle
> For to han ben a marshal in a halle.
> A largè man he was, with eyen stepe,
> A fairer burgeis is ther non in Chepe.
> Bold of his speche, and wise, and wel ytaught,
> And of manhood him lacked righte naught.
> Eke therto was he right a mery man, &c.

Chaucer's scheme of the *Canterbury Tales* was evidently left unfinished. It was intended by our author, that every pilgrim should likewise tell a Tale on their return from Canterbury. A poet who lived soon after the *Canterbury Tales* made their appearance, seems to have designed a supplement to this deficiency, and with this view to have written a Tale called the *Marchaunt's Second Tale,* or the *History of Beryn.* It was first printed by Urry, who supposed it to be Chaucer's. In the Prologue, which is of considerable length, there is some humour and contrivance; in which the author, happily enough, continues to characterise the pilgrims, by imagining what each did, and how each behaved, when they all arrived at Canterbury. After dinner was ordered at their inn, they all proceed to the cathedral. At entering the church one of the monks sprinkles them with holy water. The Knight with the better sort of the company goes in great order to the shrine of Thomas a Becket. The Miller and his companions run staring about the church: they pretend to blazon the arms painted in the glass windows, and enter into a dispute in heraldry: but the Hoste of the Tabarde reproves them for their improper behaviour and impertinent discourse, and directs them to the martyr's shrine. When all had finished their devotions, they return to the inn. In the way thither they purchase toys for which that city was famous, called *Canterbury brochis,* and here much facetiousness passes betwixt the Frere and the Sompnour, in which the latter vows revenge on the former, for telling a Tale so palpably levelled at his profession, and protests he will retaliate on their return by a more severe story. When dinner is ended, the Hoste of the Tabarde thanks all the company in form for their several Tales. The party then separate till supper-time by agreement. The Knight goes to survey the walls and bulwarks of the city, and explains to his son the Squier the nature and strength of them. Mention is here made of great guns. The Wife of Bath is too weary to walk far; she proposes to the Prioresse to divert themselves in the garden, which abounds with herbs proper for making salves. Others wander about the streets. The Pardoner has a low adventure, which ends much to his disgrace. The next morning they proceed on their return to Southwark: and our genial master of the Tabarde, just as they leave Canterbury, by way of putting the company into good humour, begins a panegyric on the morning and the month of April, some lines of which I shall quote, as a specimen of our author's abilities in poetical description.

> Lo! how the seson of the yere, and Averell shouris,
> Doith the bushis burgyn out blossomes and flouris.
> Lo! the prymerosys of the yere, how fresh they bene to
>   sene,
> And many othir flouris among the grassis grene.
> Lo! how they springe and sprede, and of divers hue,
> Beholdith and seith, both white, red, and blue.
> That lusty bin and comfortabyll for mannis sight,
> For I say for myself it makith my hert to light.

On casting lots, it falls to the Marchaunt to tell the first tale, which then follows. I cannot allow that this Prologue and Tale were written by Chaucer. Yet I believe them to be nearly coeval.

It is not my intention to dedicate a volume to Chaucer, how much soever he may deserve it; nor can it be expected, that, in a work of this general nature, I should enter into a critical examination of all Chaucer's pieces. Enough has been said to prove, that in elevation and elegance, in harmony and perspicuity of versification, he surpasses his predecessors in an infinite proportion; that his genius was universal, and adapted to themes of unbounded variety; that his merit was not less in painting familiar manners with humour and propriety, than in moving the passions, and in representing the beautiful or the grand objects of nature with grace and sublimity; in a word, that he appeared with all the lustre and dignity of a true poet, in an age which compelled him to struggle with a barbarous language, and a national want of taste; and when to write verses at all, was regarded as a singular qualification. It is true, indeed, that he lived at a time when the French and Italians had made considerable advances and improvements in poetry: and although proofs have already been occasionally given of his imitations from these sources, I shall close my account of him with a distinct and comprehensive view of the nature of the poetry which subsisted in France and Italy when he wrote; pointing out, in the mean time, how far and in what manner the popular models of those nations contributed to form his taste, and influence his genius. . . .

—Thomas Warton, *The History of English Poetry* (1778–81), ed. Richard Price Volume 2, 1840, pp. 129–216

Joseph Warton (1756–82)

Joseph Warton (1722–1800) was a noted eighteenth-century English scholar, critic, and author, who is best remembered today for his work on the poet and essayist Alexander Pope and his book *Essay on the Genius and Writings of Pope*. Pope had himself translated and adapted several of Chaucer's works, and here Warton discusses Pope's versions of *The House of Fame* and "The Wife of Bath's Tale" from *The Canterbury Tales*. Students who are working with Pope's adaptations of Chaucer will no doubt find Warton's comments useful; however, they are also indicative of how Chaucer was received in general by many in eighteenth-century English literary circles.

Warton considers that, in Pope's version of *The House of Fame*, "Pope's alterations of Chaucer are introduced with judgment and art; that these alterations are more in number, and more important in conduct, than any Dryden has made" (John Dryden likewise published adaptations of some of Chaucer's works.) Warton criticizes Chaucer for taking "every opportunity of satirizing the follies of his age" and questions the "very sudden transitions from the sublime to the ridiculous" that Warton believes characterizes the writing of the Middle Ages. Warton praises the abridgements and alterations Pope has levied on Chaucer as prudent in content and superior in style.

Conversely, Warton criticizes Pope for tackling "The Wife of Bath's Tale," a work Warton considers vulgar and crude, though Warton does point out that Pope "has omitted or softened the grosser and more offensive passages." Warton laments that Chaucer offers more worthy topics for Pope to have considered, and concludes that "the common notion seems to have arisen, that Chaucer's vein of poetry was chiefly turned to the light and the ridiculous. But they who look into Chaucer, will soon be convinced of this prevailing prejudice; and will find his comic vein . . . to be only like one of mercury, imperceptibly mingled with a mine of gold." Warton concludes by praising Chaucer, though students will likely find his criticisms of the man and his work more interesting.

On the revival of literature, the first writers seemed not to have observed any SELECTION in their thoughts and images. Dante, Petrarch, Boccace, Ariosto, make very sudden transitions from the sublime to the ridiculous. Chaucer, in his Temple of Mars, among many pathetic pictures, has brought in a strange line,

> The coke is scalded for all his long ladell.

No writer has more religiously observed the decorum here recommended than Virgil.

> This having heard and seen, some pow'r unknown,
> Strait chang'd the scene, and snatch'd me from the
>   throne;
> Before my view appear'd a structure fair,
> Its site uncertain, if in earth or air.

> (1. 417).

The scene here changes from the TEMPLE of FAME to that of Rumour. Such a change is not methinks judicious, as it destroys the unity of the subject, and distracts the view of the reader; not to mention, that the difference between Rumour and Fame is not sufficiently distinct and perceptible. POPE has, however, the merit of compressing the sense of a great number of Chaucer's lines into a small compass. As Chaucer takes every opportunity of satyrizing the follies of his age, he has in this part introduced many circumstances, which it was prudent in POPE to omit, as they would not have been either relished or understood in the present times.

> While thus I stood intent to see and hear,
> One came, methought, and whisper'd in my ear,
> What could thus high thy rash ambition raise?
> Art thou, fond youth, a candidate for praise?
> 'Tis true, (said I,) not void of hopes I came,
> For who so fond as youthful bards, of Fame?

This conclusion is not copied from Chaucer, and is judicious. Chaucer has finished his story inartificially, by saying he was surprised at the sight of a man of great authority, and awoke in a fright. The succeeding lines give a pleasing moral to the allegory; and the two last shew the man of honour and virtue, as well as the poet:

> Unblemish'd let me live, or die unknown:
> Oh grant an honest fame, or grant me none!

In finishing this Section, we may observe, that POPE's alterations of
Chaucer are introduced with judgment and art; that these alterations are
more in number, and more important in conduct, than any Dryden has made
of the same author. This piece was communicated to Steele, who entertained
a high opinion of its beauties, and who conveyed it to Addison. POPE had
ornamented the poem with the machinery of guardian angels, which he
afterwards omitted. . . .

The WIFE OF BATH is the other piece of Chaucer which POPE selected to
imitate. One cannot but wonder at his choice, which, perhaps, nothing but
his youth could excuse. Dryden, who is known not to be nicely scrupulous,
informs us, that he would not versify it on account of its indecency. POPE,
however, has omitted or softened the grosser and more offensive passages.
Chaucer afforded him many subjects of a more serious and sublime species;
and it were to be wished. POPE had exercised his pencil on the pathetic story
of the Patience of Grisilda, or Troilus and Cressida, or the Complaint of the
Black Knight; or, above all, on Cambuscan and Canace. From the accidental
circumstance of Dryden and POPE's having copied the gay and ludicrous
parts of Chaucer, the common notion seems to have arisen, that Chaucer's
vein of poetry was chiefly turned to the light and the ridiculous. But they
who look into Chaucer, will soon be convinced of this prevailing prejudice;
and will find his comic vein, like that of Shakespeare, to be only like one of
mercury, imperceptibly mingled with a mine of gold.

CHAUCER is highly extolled by Dryden, in the spirited and pleasing preface
to his fables; for his prefaces, after all, are very pleasing, notwithstanding the
opposite opinions they contain, because his prose is the most numerous and
sweet, the most *mellow* and *generous,* of any our language has yet produced.

—Joseph Warton, *Essay on the Genius and*
Writings of Pope, 1756–82

THE NINTEENTH CENTURY

WILLIAM GODWIN (1803–04)

The husband of English feminist pioneer Mary Wollstonecraft and the father of *Frankenstein* author Mary Shelley, William Godwin (1756–1836) was a renowned journalist and author in his day, and is sometimes considered the father of philosophical anarchism. The following excerpt, from the *Life of Chaucer*, describes several of Chaucer's works from an early-nineteenth-century perspective, and are particularly useful because of both Godwin's often critical perspective and his work with Chaucer's *Parliament of Fowls*, one of Chaucer's more minor works that has little representation elsewhere in this text.

Godwin begins his piece by declaring that Shakespeare and Chaucer are the two masters of English poetry, a construct that was becoming authoritative in Godwin's day. Godwin even declares that Chaucer surpasses Shakespeare in one respect, in that his ability to create what he did in "times of barbarism" far outweighs Shakespeare's working in a time of "uncommon refinement." Godwin then turns to Chaucer's *Troilus and Criseyde*, his work, along with "The Knight's Tale" in particular and *The Canterbury Tales* in general, that had been most admired in the previous century. Godwin, though he finds much to appreciate in *Troilus*, heaps criticism on the text, calling it at times rude in sentiment and "considerably barren of incident," an aspect of the work that leads part of it to become "tedious." Godwin also criticizes Criseyde as being "a false unconstant whore," a phrase he borrows from another writer, but one he supports. Godwin finds Chaucer's heroine not as sympathetic as he would like her to be, and he believes this portrayal affects the work. Godwin's perspective is not uncommon among readers of Chaucer's work, and students may wish to use Godwin's arguments as a springboard to examine why Chaucer created his Criseyde as he did.

Godwin next examines Chaucer's *Parliament of Fowls*, which Godwin calls the author's first court poem. *Parliament of Fowls* is a dream vision that demonstrates the great love of nature Chaucer possessed that so many critics in this book have described. The selections from Godwin's work finish with part of his discussion of *The Canterbury Tales*, which Godwin calls "one of the most extraordinary monuments of human genius." Nonetheless, Godwin dwells on many of the tales he deems "filthy, vulgar, and licentious," including "The Merchant's Tale," "The Wife of Bath's Prologue" and subsequent tale, "The Miller's Tale," and "The Reeve's Tale." Godwin considers these works part of the "natural" school of medieval poetry, a genre that was reactionary to the "romantic" tales of knight and ladies, courts and dragons, magical creatures and unending quests, a genre Chaucer himself satirizes in "The Tale of Sir Thopas."

Godwin notes, "The reader of the more correct taste, though offended with Chaucer for the choice of his topics, will peruse these divisions of his work again and again, for the sake of the eloquence and imagination they display." Godwin is one of the first critics to make a case for these tales, which now rank among the most popular, most read, and most studied of all *The Canterbury Tales*.

—〰— —〰— —〰—

I

The two names which perhaps do the greatest honour to the annals of English literature, are those of Chaucer and of Shakespear. Shakespear we have long and justly been accustomed to regard as the first in the catalogue of poetical and creative minds; and after the dramas of Shakespear, there is no production of man that displays more various and vigorous talent than the *Canterbury Tales*. Splendour of narrative, richness of fancy, pathetic simplicity of incident and feeling, a powerful style in delineating character and manners, and an animated vein of comic humour, each takes its turn in this wonderful performance, and each in turn appears to be that in which the author was most qualified to excel.

There is one respect at least in which the works of Chaucer are better fitted to excite our astonishment than those of Shakespear. Ordinary readers are inclined to regard the times of Shakespear as barbarous, because they are remote. But in reality the age of queen Elizabeth was a period of uncommon refinement. We have since that time enlarged our theatres; we have made some improvements in the mechanism of dramatical exhibition; and we have studied, with advantage or otherwise, the laws of the Grecian stage. But we have never produced any thing that will enter into comparison with the plays of Shakespear, or even of some of his contemporaries. What age can be less barbarous than that which, beside the dramatic productions of Shakespear[1], Fletcher, Massinger and Jonson, is illustrated with the names of Raleigh, of Hooker, of Bacon, and of Spenser?

But the times of Chaucer were in a much more obvious and unquestionable sense, so far as poetry is concerned, times of barbarism. The history of the revival of literature in the twelfth and thirteenth centuries will be treated in these volumes. The sole efforts in the art of verse which had been made in Western Europe previously to Chaucer, were romances of prodigious and supernatural adventure, prolix volumes of unvaried allegory, and the rhapsodies of the vagrant minstrel. These productions, though not unrelieved by admirable flights of imagination, were for the most part rugged in versification, prosaic in language, and diffusive and rambling in their story and conduct. What had been achieved in English, was little better than a jejune table of events with the addition of rhyme. Chaucer fixed and naturalised the genuine art of poetry in our island. But what is most memorable in his eulogy, is that he is the father of our language, the idiom of which was by the Norman conquest banished from courts and civilised life, and which Chaucer was the first to restore to literature, and the muses. No one man in the history of human intellect ever did more, than was effected by the single mind of Chaucer.

These are abundant reasons why Englishmen should regard Chaucer with peculiar veneration, should cherish his memory, and eagerly desire to be acquainted with whatever may illustrate his character, or explain the wonders he performed. The first and direct object of this work, is to erect a monument to his name, and, as far as the writer was capable of doing it, to produce an interesting and amusing book in modern English, enabling the reader, who might shrink from the labour of mastering the phraseology of Chaucer, to do justice to his illustrious countryman. It seemed probable also that, if the author were successful in making a popular work, many might by its means be induced to study the language of our ancestors, and the elements and history of our vernacular speech; a study at least as improving as that of the language of Greece and Rome.

A further idea, which was continually present to the mind of the author while writing, obviously contributed to give animation to his labours, and importance to his undertaking. The full and complete life of a poet would include an extensive survey of the manners, the opinions, the arts and the literature, of the age in which the poet lived. This is the only way in which we can become truly acquainted with the history of his mind, and the causes which made him what he was. We must observe what Chaucer felt and saw, how he was educated, what species of learning he pursued, and what were the objects, the events and the persons, successively presented to his view, before we can strictly and philosophically understand his biography. To delineate the state of England, such as Chaucer saw it, in every point of view in which it can be delineated, is the subject of this book.

But, while engaged in this study, the reader may expect to gain an additional advantage, beside that of understanding the poet. If the knowledge of contemporary objects is the biography of Chaucer, the converse of the proposition will also be true, and the biography of Chaucer will be the picture of a certain portion of the literary, political and domestic history of our country. The person of Chaucer may in this view be considered as the central figure in a miscellaneous painting, giving unity and individual application to the otherwise disjointed particulars with which the canvas is diversified. No man of moral sentiment or of taste will affirm, that a more becoming central figure to the delineation of England in the fourteenth century can be found, than the Englishman who gives name to these volumes. . . .

XV

(Concerning *Troilus and Creseide*) . . . , it is not difficult to infer the degree of applause to which its author is entitled. It has already been observed by one of the critics upon English Poetry[2], that it is "'almost as long as the Æneid." Considered in this point of view, the *Troilus and Creseide* will not appear to advantage. It is not an epic poem. It is not that species of composition which Milton[3] so admirably describes, as "the most consummat act of its authour's fidelity and ripeness;" the fruit of "years and industry;" the reservoir into which are poured the results of "all his considerat diligence, all his midnight watchings, and expence of Palladian oyl." The *Æneid* is a little code of politics and religion. It describes men and manners and cities and countries. It embraces an outline of the arts of peace and of war. It travels through the whole circumference of the universe; and brings together heaven and hell, and all that is natural and all that is divine, to aid the poet in the completion of his design. It is at once historical and prophetic. It comprises the sublime horrors of a great city captured and in flames, and the pathetic anguish of an ardent, disappointed and abandoned love. It comprehends a cycle of sciences and arts, as far as they could be connected with the principal subject; and if all other books were destroyed, the various elements of many sciences and arts might be drawn from an attentive perusal of this poem.

The plan of the *Æneid* in these respects, is precisely what the plan of an epic poem should be. The *Troilus and Creseide* can advance no pretensions to enter into this class of composition. It is merely a love-tale. It is not the labour of a man's life; but a poem which, with some previous knowledge of human sentiments and character, and a very slight preparation of science, the writer might perhaps be expected to complete in about as many months, as the work is divided into books. It is certainly much greater in extent of stanzas and pages, than the substratum and basis of the story can authorise.

It is also considerably barren of incident. There is not enough in it of matter generating visible images in the reader, and exciting his imagination with pictures of nature and life. There is not enough in it of vicissitudes of fortune, awakening curiosity and holding expectation in suspense.

Add to which, the catastrophe is unsatisfactory and offensive. The poet who would interest us with a love-tale, should soothe our minds with the fidelity and disinterestedness of the mutual attachment of the parties, and, if he presents us with a tragical conclusion, it should not be one which arises out of the total unworthiness of either. Creseide (as Mr. Urry, in his introduction to Henryson's epilogue to the *Troilus,* has very truly observed), however prepossessing may be the manner in which she appears in the early part of the poem, is "a false unconstant whore," and of a class which the mind of the reader almost demands to have exhibited, if not as "terminating in extream misery," at least as filled with penitence and remorse. Virgil indeed has drawn the catastrophe of his tale of Dido from the desertion of the lover. But the habits of European society teach us to apprehend less ugliness and loathsome deformity in the falshood of the lover, than of his mistress; and we repose with a tenderer and more powerful sympathy upon the abandoned and despairing state of the female. Besides, Virgil did not write a poem expressly upon the tale of Dido, but only employed it for an episode. The story of Romeo and Juliet is the most perfect model of a love-tale in the series of human invention. Dryden thoroughly felt this defect in the poem of Chaucer, and has therefore changed the catastrophe when he fitted the story for the stage, and represented the two lovers as faithful, but unfortunate.

But, when all these deductions have been made from the claims of the *Troilus and Creseide* upon our approbation, it will still remain a work interspersed with many beautiful passages, passages of exquisite tenderness, of great delicacy, and of a nice and refined observation of the workings of human sensibility. Nothing can be more beautiful, genuine, and unspoiled by the corrupt suggestions of a selfish spirit, than the sentiments of Chaucer's lovers. While conversing with them, we seem transported into ages of primeval innocence. Even Creseide is so good, so ingenuous and affectionate, that we feel ourselves as incapable as Troilus, of believing her false. Nor are the scenes of Chaucer's narrative, like the insipid tales of a pretended pastoral life, drawn with that vagueness of manner, and ignorance of the actual emotions of the heart, which, while we read them, we nauseate and despise. On the contrary, his personages always feel, and we confess the truth of their feelings; what passes in their minds, or falls from their tongues, has the clear and decisive character which proclaims it human, together with the vividness, subtleness and delicacy, which few authors in the most enlightened ages have been equally fortunate in seizing. Pandarus himself comes elevated and refined from the pen of Chaucer: his occupation loses its grossness, in the disinterestedness of his motive, and the sincerity of his friendship. In a word, such is the *Troilus and Creseide,* that no competent judge can rise from its perusal, without a strong impression of the integrity and excellence of the author's disposition, and of the natural relish he entertained for whatever is honourable, beautiful and just.

There is a great difference between the merits of any work of human genius considered abstractedly, taken as it belongs to the general stock of literary production and tried severely on its intrinsic and unchangeable pretensions, and the merits of the same work considered in the place which it occupies in the scale and series of literary history, and compared with the productions of its author's predecessors and contemporaries. In the former case the question we have to ask is, Is it good? In the latter we have to enquire, Was it good? To both these questions, when applied to Chaucer's poem of *Troilus and Creseide,* the fair answer will be an affirmative.

But it is in the latter point of view that the work we are considering shows to infinitely the greatest advantage. The poem will appear to be little less than a miracle, when we combine our examination of it, with a recollection of the times and circumstances in which it was produced. When Chaucer wrote it, the English tongue had long remained in a languid and almost perishing state, overlaid and suffocated by the insolent disdain and remorseless tyranny of the Norman ravagers and dividers of our soil. Previously to the eleventh century it had no cultivation and refinement from the cowardly and superstitious Saxons, and during that century and the following one it appeared in danger of being absolutely extinguished. With Chaucer it seemed to spring like Minerva from the head of Jove, at once accoutered and complete. Mandeville, Wicliffe and Gower, whom we may style the other three evangelists of our tongue, though all older in birth than Chaucer, did not begin too early to work upon the ore of their native language. He surprised his countrymen with a poem, eminently idiomatic, clear and perspicuous in its style, as well as rich and harmonious in its versification. His *Court of Love,* an earlier production, is not less excellent in both these respects. But it was too slight and short to awaken general attention. The *Troilus and Creseide* was of respectable magnitude, and forms an epoch in our literature.

Chaucer presented to the judgment of his countrymen a long poem, perfectly regular in its structure, and uninterrupted with episodes. It contained nothing but what was natural. Its author disdained to have recourse to what was bloated in sentiment, or romantic and miraculous in incident, for the purpose of fixing or keeping alive the attention. He presents real life and human sentiments, and suffers the reader to dwell upon and expand the operations of feeling and passion. Accordingly the love he describes is neither frantic, nor brutal, nor artificial, nor absurd. His hero conducts himself in all respects with the most perfect loyalty and honour; and his heroine, however she deserts her character in the sequel, is in the commencement modest, decorous, affectionate, and prepossessing. The loves of the *Troilus and Creseide* scarcely retain any traces of the preposterous and rude manners of the age in which they were delineated.

This poem therefore, as might have been expected, long fixed upon itself the admiration of the English nation. Chaucer, by his *Court of Love,* and the ditties and songs which had preceded it, had gratified the partiality of his friends, and given them no mean or equivocal promise of what he should hereafter be able to perform. But these, we may easily conceive, were of little general notoriety. The *Troilus and Creseide* was probably, more than any of his other works, the basis of his fame, and the foundation of his fortune. He wrote nothing very eminently superior to this, till his *Canterbury Tales,* which were the production of his declining age. Owing perhaps to the confusion and sanguinary spirit of the wars of York and Lancaster, English literature rather decayed than improved during the following century; and we had consequently no poem of magnitude, and of a compressed and continued plan, qualified to enter into competition with the *Troilus and Creseide,* from the earliest periods of our poetry to the appearance of the *Fairy Queen.* Accordingly, among many examples of its praises which might be produced, sir Philip Sidney in his *Defense of Poesy* has selected this performance, as the memorial of the talents of our poet, and the work in which he "undoubtedly did excellently well."

There are some particular defects belonging to this production beside those already mentioned, which are the more entitled to our notice, as they are adapted to characterise the stage of refinement to which our literature was advanced in the fourteenth century. In the first place, the poem is interspersed with many bases and vulgar lines, which are not only unworthy of the poet, but would be a deformity in any prose composition, and would even dishonour and debase the tone of familiar conversation. The following specimens will afford a sufficient illustration of this fact. Cupid is provoked at the ease and lightness of heart of the hero, and prepares to avenge himself of the contempt.

> —Sodainly he hitte him at the full,
> And yet as proude a pecocke can he pul
> > (B. I, ver. 210.)

> Thus wol she saine, and al the toune at ones,
> The wretch is dead, the divel have his bones.
> > (ver. 806.)

> Withouten jelousie, and soche debate,
> Shall no husbonde saine unto me checkemate.
> > (B. II, ver. 754.)

For him demeth men hote, that seeth him swete.
                    (ver. 1533.)

Now loketh than, if thei be nat to blame,
That hem avaunt of women, and by name,
That yet behight hem never this ne that,
Ne knowen hem more than mine oldé hat.
                    (B. III, ver. 321.)

I am, til God me better mindé sende,
At Dulcarnon, right at my wittés ende.
                    (ver. 933.)

For peril is with dretching in ydrawe,
Nay suche abodés ben nat worthe an hawe.
                    (ver. 856.)

Soche arguments ne be nat worthe a bene.
                    (ver. 1173.)

But soche an ese therwith thei in her wrought,
Right as a man is esed for to fele
For ache of hedde, to clawen him on his hele.
                    (B. IV, ver. 728)

I have herd saie eke, timés twisé twelve. (B. V, ver. 97.)

There are also lines interspersed in the poem, which are not more degraded by the meanness of the expression, than by the rudeness, not to say the brutality, of the sentiment. We may well be surprised, after considering the delicacy and decorum with which Chaucer has drawn his heroine, to find him polluting the portrait of her virgin character in the beginning of the poem with so low and pitiful a joke as this,

But whether that she children had or none,
I rede it nat, therfore I let it gone.
                    (B. I, ver. 132.)

The following sentiment must also be deeply disgustful to a just and well ordered mind. Calchas, the father of Creseide, languishes in the Grecian army for the restoration of his only child, and at length effects to his great joy the means of obtaining her in exchange for Antenor, a prisoner in the Grecian camp.

The whiché tale anon right as Creseide
Had herd, she (whiche that of her father rought,

As in this case, right naught, ne whan he deide)
Full busily, &c.

(B. IV, ver. 668.)

Another defect in this poem of Chaucer, of the same nature, and that is not less conspicuous, is the tediousness into which he continually runs, seemingly without the least apprehension that any one will construe this feature of his composition as a fault. He appears to have had no idea that his readers could possibly deem it too much to peruse any number of verses which he should think proper to pour out on any branch of his subject. To judge from the poem of *Troilus and Creseide,* we should be tempted to say, that compression, the strengthening a sentiment by brevity, and the adding to the weight and power of a work by cutting away from it all useless and cumbersome excrescences, was a means of attaining to excellence which never entered into our author's mind. A remarkable instance of this occurs in the fourth book, where upward of one hundred verses upon predestination are put into the mouth of Troilus, the materials of which are supposed to have been extracted from a treatise *De Causa Dei,* written by Thomas Bradwardine archbishop of Canterbury, a contemporary of our author. Other examples, scarcely less offensive to true taste, might be cited.

It is particularly deserving of notice that scarcely any one of the instances which might be produced under either of these heads of impropriety, has a parallel in the version made by Boccaccio of the same story, probably from the same author, and nearly at the same time. Few instances can be given in which the Italian writer has degenerated into any thing mean and vulgar, and he never suspends his narrative with idle and incoherent digressions. He seems to have been perfectly aware, that one of the methods to render a literary production commendable is to admit into it nothing which is altogether superfluous. The inference is, that, whatever may be the comparative degrees of imagination and originality between England and Italy in the fourteenth century, what is commonly called taste had made a much greater progress in the latter country than among us. . . .

XXI

The first poem which Chaucer wrote, so far as can now be ascertained, after he entered into the service of the court, is variously styled in different manuscripts, *The Assembly of Fowls,* and the *Parliament of Birds.* The subject of this poem is the suit or courtship of John of Gaunt just mentioned, and appears to have been written before the lady had accepted the addresses of her illustrious suitor. The natural construction therefore to be put upon such a performance is, that it implies a considerable degree of familiarity and confidence between the poet and the persons who are the subject of it: and indeed it is not improbable that it was penned at the request of the lover, for the purpose of softening the obduracy of his mistress's resistance. As the lady is represented in the course of the poem as deferring the suit of her admirer for a twelvemonth, a circumstance which occurs again in the Book of the Duchess above quoted, and as the marriage was solemnised in May 1359, the date of the poem obviously falls upon the year 1358.

This first courtly composition of Chaucer we may believe was written by the young poet with great care, and no ordinary degree of anxiety to produce something worthy of the masters into whose service he had entered. It was a new field that he was to occupy; and it was with very different feelings that he sat down to write. Hitherto he had been a poet in the purest and most unmingled sense of that word. He gave himself up to the impressions of nature, and to the sensations he experienced. He studied the writings of his contemporaries, and of certain of the ancients. He was learned, according to the learning of his day. He wrote, because he felt himself impelled to write. He analysed the models which were before him. He sought to please his friends and fellow-scholars in the two universities. He aspired to an extensive and lasting reputation. He formed the gigantic and arduous plan of giving poetry to a language, which could as yet scarcely be said to have any poetry to boast.

Now he was placed in a different scene. Without bearing the title of the court-poet, he was the court-poet in reality. He had no competitor. His superiority was universally acknowledged. He had been borne along on the tide of his acknowledged reputation to the eminence he at present occupied. He had the character of his country to sustain; and the literature of a nation rested upon his shoulders.

To every man a scene presented to the eye is impressive, much beyond the effect of any abstraction appealing to the understanding. This is still more the case with a poet, than with any other man. Chaucer had hitherto written for such as were lovers and discerners of true poetry, without well knowing, except perhaps within a limited circle, where they were to be found. He now wrote for the court of England, a court which at this moment was higher in lustre and character than any other in the world. He wrote for the conquerors of Cressy and Poitiers. He had before him sir John Chandos, sir Walter Manny, and the other heroes who had won immortal note on those plains. John king of France, and several of the first personages of that country, were now prisoners in London. Edward III was, it may be, no profound scholar, nor eminent judge of poetical composition. But the ardent imagination of Chaucer was not to be stopped by such impediments. He knew that a piece in which he celebrated the loves of a favourite son of the king, would be often mentioned in the highest circles, and the name of its author often repeated. He aspired, it may be, to that fame which the writer himself may hear, which brings strangers and scholars and persons of eminence to desire the happiness of knowing him, and which surrounds him with grateful whispers whenever he appears, as well as to that fame which breathes incense from the venerable tomb a thousand years after the poet is no more.

The *Parliament of Birds* is a poem marked with pregnancy of fancy and felicity of language. It is written in Rhythm Royal, the same species of stanza as that of the *Court of Love* and the *Troilus and Creseide*. It begins with an extract, beautifully expressed, of Cicero's *Somnium Scipionis* from the commentaries of Macrobius. The following stanzas will remind every reader of the manner of Spenser, mellifluous, soothing and animated.

> Then asked[4] he, if folke that here ben dede
> Have life and dwellyng in an other place?
> And[5] Affrican saied, Ye, withouten drede,
> And how our present worldly livés space
> N'is but a maner deth, what waie we trace,
> And rightfull folke shull gon, after thei die.
> To hev'n, and shewed him the galaxie.
> Then shew'd he him the little yerth that here is
> To regarde of the heven's quantité,
> And after shewed he hym the nine speris,
> And after that the melodie herd he,
> That cometh of thilke sperés thrisé thre,
> That welles of musike ben and melodie
> In this worlde here, and cause of harmonic
> Then saied he him, Sens that yerth was so lite,
> And full of torment, and of hardé grace,
> That he ne shuld hym in this world delite;
> Then told he him, in certain yerés space
> That ev'ry sterre should come into his place
> There it was first, and all should out of mind
> That in this worlde is doen of all mankynd.
>   (ver. 50.)

The poet had spent, as he says, a whole day in the study of the *Somnium Scipionis*. He informs us that he was extremely fond of reading; and illustrates this by an apposite simile.

For out of the olde feldés, as men saieth,
Cometh all this newe come fro yere to yere;
And out of oldé bokés, in gode faieth,
Cometh all this newe science that men lere.
(ver. 22.)

At length the sun sets, the light by which he was reading is gone, and Chaucer betakes himself to bed. He dreams; and imagines himself, like the hero of the *Somnium Scipionis,* attended by the vanquisher of Hannibal. The passage with which he introduces his dream, forcibly brings to mind a similar passage in Shakespear, though it must be admitted in this instance that the imitator has greatly surpassed his original.

The werie hunter sleping in his bedde,
The wodde ayen his minde goeth anone;
The judgé dremeth how his plees be spedde;
The carter dremeth how his cartés gone;
The riche of golde; the knight fight with his fone,
The sicke ymette he drinketh of the tonne;
The lover mette he hath his ladie wonne.[6]
(ver. 99.)

Under the conduct of the venerable Africanus, Chaucer arrives at a park and a temple, which prove to be consecrated to the God of Love. Considerable effort and vigour of mind are employed in a description of the scenery. The principal particulars which Chaucer has introduced in his account of the temple and the grounds immediately adjacent, are to be found indeed in the seventh book of Boccaccio's *Teseide.* Chaucer's imitation however, which is by no means a close one, contains many nice and beautiful touches, as well as some trivial and mean expressions, which are not to be found in Boccaccio. Among the former may be cited his description of the breeze which blows in the Garden of Love, while the birds carol aloft.

Therewith a winde, unneth it might be lesse,
Made in the levés grene a noisé soft,
Accordant to the foulés' song on loft.
(ver. 201.)

The circumstance is also subtly imagined, and purely his own, with which he describes Venus, who had retired to an obscure corner in her temple; though it has the defect of repeating one clause of the passage last quoted.

> Darke was that place, but afterward lightnesse
> I saw a lite, unnethes it might be lesse.
>   (ver. 263.)

It may be regarded as a singular circumstance, and characteristic of the imperfect refinement of the times in which Chaucer lived, that a somewhat licentious description of Priapus and Venus is introduced into a poem certainly designed for the perusal of a virgin princess, of great youth, and unimpeachable modesty. These are also among the passages which are without a counterpart in Boccaccio.

Meanwhile it is by no means clear . . . whether Chaucer took the story of Palamon and Arcite from Boccaccio, or from the Latin author from whom Boccaccio confesses that he drew his materials. From the circumstance that the description of the Garden and Temple of Love, introduced by Chaucer in this place, and which he has borrowed from the Teseide, or story of Palamon and Arcite, is not to be found in the *Knightes Tale,* the abridgment of that story in Chaucer's collections *of Canterbury Tales,* Mr. Tyrwhit thinks himself entitled to infer, "that the Poem of Palamon and Arcite must have been composed at a later period," than the *Parliament of Birds.* This proof however is by no means complete. It would follow indeed that the *Parliament of Birds* was written prior to the *Canterbury Tales;* but to establish that fact no indirect evidence is necessary. What passages might have existed in Chaucer's original unsuccessful poem of Palamon and Arcite, no trace of which is now to be discovered in his abridgment of it entitled the *Knightes Tale,* a reader of the present age is by no means competent to determine.

The most glaring fault imputable to the poem we are here considering, is that the earlier and the latter half of the composition are by no means of similar substance, or well accord with each other. The first three hundred verses are of lofty port and elevated character. Nothing can be of graver meaning, more interesting to the fancy, or more delicately expressed, than Chaucer's abstract of the *Somnium Scipionis.* To this succeed the *Garden* and *Temple of Love,* which, if they are not subjects of altogether so imposing a nature as the former, are yet fanciful, elevated, and full of poetical representation. The description of these being complete, what remains is that part of the poem which most properly answers to the title; the parliament, or assembly, of birds on St. Valentine's day to choose their mates. Chaucer here quits the Temple, and goes again into the garden, where, in a lawn, seated on a hill of flowers, and overcanopied with halls and bowers composed of the branches of trees, he finds the "quene, the noble goddesse, Nature," with the fowls of every different species assembled round her.

This part of the poem is executed with a very active fancy, and the characters of the various birds are excellently sustained. Chaucer divides his fowls into four classes; the birds of prey, the water-fowl, those which live upon insects and reptiles, and those which are nourished with seeds: and each of these classes has its representative; the falcon for the birds of prey, the goose for the water-fowl, the cuckow for the worm-eaters, and the turtle for the eaters of seed. The epithets applied to these personages are well chosen, not discovering the lazy and insignificant character often imputable to the epithets of inferior poets, but being all appropriate and expressive: and there is considerable humour in the vulgarity of the goose, the base selfishness of the cuckow, and the characteristic attributes of various other fowls which are successively introduced.

But, after all, there is something meagre and unnatural in this sort of allegory, where Chaucer introduces the lovers he means to compliment, under the personage of birds. We feel no sympathies for the amours of his male and female eagles. If the poet who attempts a plan of this sort, introduces any refined and animated sentiments, he violates the propriety of his allegory; and, if he adheres to the decorum of the fiction he has to sustain, he becomes insupportably frigid and tedious. There are indeed a ridiculous inequality and unconnectedness conspicuous through the whole of this poem. Scipio Africanus is introduced with no propriety as Chaucer's conductor to the Temple of Love; and it would have been a still greater absurdity if he had been shown among the nightingales and thrushes stung with the passion of the spring on St. Valentine's day. Accordingly he is conveniently dropped. He is just shown in the commencement of the narrative, and is heard of no more. We do not know that he even enters the Garden of Love, at the door of which he serves the poet in the capacity of a gentleman-usher.

The heroine of the poem, according to Chaucer's arrangement of it, is represented as a female eagle perched upon the hand of the goddess Nature. Three pretenders to her favour are introduced. Who these are it is impossible for us at this distance of time to determine; but it is probable that the number, and some other circumstances which are related respecting them, are founded in fact. The first is plainly the earl of Richmond, who presents himself

> With hed enclin'd, and with ful humble chere.
> (ver. 414.)

The second eagle founds his pretensions upon the length of his attachment. The third, like the first, builds his hope of success only upon the fervour of his passion. They are all treated with considerable respect by Chaucer. They are all eagles; and he adds in summing up their addresses,

> Of al my life, syth that day I was borne,
> So gentle pie, in love or other thinge,
> Ne herden never no man me beforne.
>
> (ver. 484.)

The balance however is forcibly made to lean in favour of the first, or royal eagle; and his suit, though not accepted, is only deferred for a year, with every omen of final success.

This subject being dispatched, the assembly of birds, who had been exceedingly eager for their dismission, is dissolved.

> And lorde the blisse and joye which that they make!
> For ech gan other in his wingés take,
> And with her neckés eche gan other winde,
> Thankinge alway the noble' goddesse of kinde.
>
> (ver. 669.)

At length, the shouting that "the foules made at her flight away" rouses the poet from his dream.

> I woke, and other bokés took me to
> To rede upon, and yet I rede alway.
>
> (ver. 690.)

This couplet deserved to be quoted as an evidence of the poet's habits. We have here Chaucer's own testimony, that he was a man of incessant reading and literary curiosity, and that, even at thirty years of age, and amidst the allurements of a triumphant and ostentatious court, one of the first and most insatiable passions of his mind was the love of books. . . .

LV

The *Canterbury Tales* is the great basis of the fame of Chaucer and indolent men have generally expressed themselves with contempt of the rest of his works as unworthy of attention. The enquiries in which we have been engaged have led us frequently to refer to his smaller pieces, nor has our love of poetry come away from the pursuit unrewarded. Many passages of exquisite thinking and fancy have been recited. He indeed who wishes to become personally acquainted with Chaucer, must of necessity have recourse to his minor pieces. The *Canterbury Tales* are too full of business, variety, character and action, to permit the writer in any great degree to show himself. It is in Chaucer's minor pieces that we discover his love of rural scenery, his fondness for study, the cheerfulness of his temper, his weaknesses and his strength, and the anecdotes of his life. The *Troilus and Creseide* in particular, that poem of which sir Philip Sidney speaks with so much delight, though deficient in action, cannot be too much admired for the suavity and gentleness of nature which it displays. There is nothing in it to move the rougher passions of our nature, no hatred, nor contempt, nor indignation, nor revenge. If its personages are unstudied in the refinements of artificial and systematic virtue, even their vices (if such we denominate them) are loving and gentle and undesigning and kind. All the milder and more delicate feelings of the soul are displayed in their history, and displayed in a manner which none but a poet of the purest and sweetest dispositions, and at the same time of the greatest discrimination, could have attained.

The *Canterbury Tales* is certainly one of the most extraordinary monuments of human genius. The splendour of the *Knightes Tale,* and the various fancy exhibited in that of the Squier, have never been surpassed. The history of *Patient Grisildis* is the most pathetic that ever was written; and he who compares Chaucer's manner of relating it, with that of the various authors who have treated the same materials, must be dead to all the characteristic beauties of this history, if he does not perceive how much Chaucer has outstripped all his competitors.

What infinite variety of character is presented to us in the *Prologue* to the *Canterbury Tales!* It is a copious and extensive review of the private life of the fourteenth century in England.

This has usually, and perhaps justly, been thought the most conspicuous excellence of Chaucer; his power of humour, of delineating characters, and of giving vivacity and richness to comic incidents.

Unhappily the age in which he lived was deficient in that nicety of moral apprehension and taste, upon which is built the no contemptible science of elegant manners and decorum. It has been said that men must have become debauched and consummate in their vices, before they can be masters in this science. This however is not true. There are no doubt various modes of expression, which will excite a prurient sport in the minds of the dissolute, and yet will be uttered with the most unapprehensive simplicity by the inexperienced and innocent; discrimination respecting these can only be the result of a certain familiarity with vice. But neither will these by the virtuous mind be regarded as almost any fault, even when discovered. But the licentiousness and coarseness of the tales of the twelfth and thirteenth centuries, copied by Boccaccio and Chaucer, are of a different sort; they are absolute corruption and depravity. The progress of refinement does not merely make men fastidious in their vices; it makes them in many respects more virtuous and innocent: it not only prompts us to conceal some vices, but also induces us peremptorily and resolutely to abjure many.

The *Milleres Tale* and the Reves *Tale* in Chaucer are filthy, vulgar and licentious. The *Tale of the Marchant,* and the *Wif of Bathes Prologue,* are in an eminent degree liable to the last of these accusations. Yet it has been truly observed that Chaucer never appears more natural, his style never flows more easily, and his vein is never more unaffected and copious, than on these occasions. No writer, either ancient or modern, can be cited, who excels our poet in the talent for comic narrative. The reader of the more correct taste, though offended with Chaucer for the choice of his topics, will peruse these divisions of his work again and again, for the sake of the eloquence and imagination they display. The story of the Cock and the Fox, called the *Nonnes Preestes Tale,* is the most admirable fable that ever was written, if the excellence of a fable consists in liveliness of painting, in the comic demureness with which human sentiments are made to fall from the lips of animals, or in the art of framing a consummate structure from the slightest materials. The *Sompnoures Tale,* though exceedingly offensive for the clownish joke with which it is terminated, is equal in its opening and preparatory circumstances to any satirical narrative that ever was penned. The entrance of the friar into the house of the sick man, his driving away the sleeping cat from the bench he thought proper to occupy, the manner in which he lays down his walking-stick, his scrip and his hat, and the conversation which follows, are all in the most exquisite stile of comic delineation.

To understand more precisely the degree of applause which is due to Chaucer, it is proper that we should distinguish between two principal schools in the poetry of modern European nations, the romantic, and the natural. On the first revival of poetry, the minds of men perhaps universally took a bent toward the former; we had nothing but Rowlands and Arthurs, sir Guys and sir Tristrams, and Paynim and Christian knights. There was danger that nature would be altogether cut out from the courts of Apollo. The senses of barbarians are rude, and require a strong and forcible impulse to put them in motion. The first authors of the humorous and burlesque tales of modern times were perhaps sensible of this error in the romance writers, and desirous to remedy it. But they frequently fell into an opposite extreme, and that from the same cause. They deliver us indeed from the monotony produced by the perpetual rattling of armour, the formality of processions and tapestry and cloth of gold, and the eternal straining after supernatural adventures. But they lead us into squalid scenes, the coarse buffoonery of the ale-house, and the offensive manners engendered by dishonesty and intemperance. Between the one and the other of these classes of poetry, we may find things analogous to the wild and desperate toys of Salvator Rosa, and to the boors of Teniers, but nothing that should remind us of the grace of Guido, or of the soft and simple repose of Claude Lorraine.

The *Decamerone* of Boccaccio seems to be the first work of modern times, which was written entirely on the principle of a style, simple, unaffected and pure. Chaucer, who wrote precisely at the same period, was the fellow-labourer of Boccaccio. He has declared open war against the romance manner in his Rime *of Sire Thopas.* His *Canterbury Tales* are written with an almost perpetual homage to nature. The *Troilus and Creseide,* though a tale of ancient times, treats almost solely of the simple and genuine emotions of the human heart.

Many however of the works of Chaucer must be confessed to be written in a bad taste, fashionable in the times in which he lived, but which the better judgment of later ages has rejected. The poem called *Chaucer's Dreme* is in the idlest and weakest style of Romance. Nothing can be more frivolous than the courtship of his male and female eagles in the *Parliament of Birds.* The idea of the worship of the daisy must be acknowledged to be full of affectation. A continued vein of allegory is always effeminate, strained and unnatural. This error, so far as relates to the *Romaunt of the Rose,* is only indirectly imputable to Chaucer. But, in the *Testament of Love,* and elsewhere, he has made it the express object of his choice.

Boccaccio and Chaucer, it might be supposed, would have succeeded in banishing the swelling and romantic style from the realms of poetry. We might have imagined that as knowledge and civilisation grew, the empire of nature would have continually become more firmly established. But this was not the case. These eminent writers rose too high beyond their contemporaries, and reached to refinements that their successors could not understand. . . .

What comes nearest to the preeminence of Shakespear is the Don Quixote of Cervantes, the Sir Roger de Coverley of Addison, the Lovelace of Richardson, the Parson Adams of Fielding, the Walter Shandy of Sterne, and the Hugh Strap of Smollet. Fletcher also, though perhaps his most conspicuous merits are of another sort, has great excellence in the animating of character, as will readily be discerned, particularly in his *Wit without Money,* and his *Little French Lawyer.*

The successive description of the several pilgrims in the *Prologue* to the *Canterbury Tales,* is worthy to class with these. No writer has ever exhibited so great a variety of talent in so short a compass, as Chaucer has done in this instance. . . .

His best works, his *Canterbury Tales* in particular, have an absolute merit, which stands in need of no extrinsic accident to show it to advantage, and no apology to atone for its concomitant defects. They class with whatever is best in the poetry of any country or any age. Yet when we further recollect that they were written in a remote and semi-barbarous age, that Chaucer had to a certain degree to create a language, or to restore to credit a language which had been sunk into vulgarity and contempt by being considered as a language of slaves, that history and the knowledge of past ages existed only in unconnected fragments, and that his writings, stupendous as we find them, are associated, as to the period of their production, with the first half-assured lispings of civilisation and the muse, the astonishment and awe with which we regard the great father of English poetry must be exceedingly increased, and the lover of human nature and of intellectual power will deem no time misspent that adds to his familiar acquaintance with the history of such a man, or with writings so produced.

Notes

1. A frivolous dispute has been raised respecting the proper way of spelling the name of our great dramatic poet. His own orthography in this point seems to have been unsettled. Perhaps, when the etymology of a proper name is obvious, it becomes right in us to supersede the fancy of the individual, and to follow a less capricious and more infallible guide.
2. Thomas Warton, *The History of English Poetry,* 1840, Vol. 1, Section 14.
3. *Areopagitica;* a Speech for the Liberty of Unlicenced Printing.
4. Scipio the younger, the destroyer of Numantia and Carthage.
5. Scipio the elder, the conqueror of Hannibal, whom the younger sees in his dream.
6.   She gallops night by night
    Through lovers' brains, and then they dream of love;
    O'er courtiers' knees, that dream on curtsies straight;
    O'er lawyers' fingers, who straight dream on fees;
    . . .
    Sometimes she driveth o'er a soldier's neck,
    And then dreams he of cutting foreign throats,
    Of breaches, ambuscadoes, Spanish blades,
    Of healths five fathoms deep; and then anon
    Drums in his ear; at which he starts, and wakes;
    And, being thus frighted, swears a prayer or two,
    And sleeps again.
                     (*Romeo and Juliet,* act II, scene i)

—William Godwin, *Life of Chaucer,* 1803–04, Vol. 1, pp. i–viii,
470–85; Vol. 2, pp. 168–84; Vol. 4, pp. 184–201

WILLIAM BLAKE (1809)

William Blake (1757–1827) was an English poet known for his poem "The Tiger," which features the immortal lines, "Tiger, tiger, burning bright / In the forests of the night." In addition to being a wordsmith, Blake was also an engraver and painter, and his "Catalogue Description" from 1809 was written for a one-man exhibition that featured an engraving of the pilgrims from *The Canterbury Tales*. In the description, Blake provides colorful and rich descriptions of Chaucer's pilgrims that anyone writing on the *Tales* may find useful.

Blake considers Chaucer "the great poetical observer of men who in every age is born to record and eternize its acts. This he does as a master, as a father, and superior . . . sometimes with severity, oftener with joke and sport." Blake writes that the Canterbury pilgrims "are the characters which compose all ages and nations . . . for we see the same characters repeated again and again." Blake considers Chaucer's characters to be universal, figures that would be recognizable to readers in any age; their titles and occupations would change, but their essential characteristics have become part of a timeless literary experience.

Blake's insights into specific members of the pilgrimage, discussed as he explains where he placed the pilgrims in his own depiction of them and why he designed them as he did, can be useful to any student writing on a particular Canterbury tale or character. For example, Blake describes the host, Harry Bailey, as "a leader of the age." The figure of the Plowman "is simplicity itself, with wisdom and strength for stamina." The Parson is "beloved and venerated by all, and neglected by all . . . [he] sends us such a burning and shining light!" Readers may find themselves disagreeing with some of Blake's character assessments; for example, he considers the Wife of Bath "a scourge and a blight." Many modern critics find the Wife of Bath earthy and zealous, an ardent defender of women in her day. Students writing on this character in particular may take issue with Blake's description.

Blake also discusses another engraving done of the Canterbury pilgrims completed just before his own. This engraving, by Thomas Stothard (whom Blake refers to as "Mr. S———"), was completed at the behest of Robert Cromek, a publisher who had previously worked with Blake. This competing depiction infuriated Blake, who claimed that Cromek and Stothard had stolen the idea from him. In comparing the two engravings, Blake unsurprisingly finds his own depiction superior, and students reading this section are well advised to examine Blake's criticism in a critical light as well. Rather, students might compare the two engravings for themselves.

Ultimately, Blake concludes that "Chaucer has been misunderstood in his sublime work" in how some of the pilgrims have traditionally been depicted or illustrated over the centuries. It should be remembered that Blake's own depictions of Chaucer's pilgrims, while often insightful and interesting, are still his own interpretations; nonetheless, students writing on artistic representations of Chaucer or on any of the individual pilgrims themselves might find Blake's descriptions and depictions particularly useful.

⚜ ⚜ ⚜

III

Sir Jeffery Chaucer and the nine and twenty Pilgrims on their journey to Canterbury.

The time chosen is early morning, before sunrise, when the jolly company are just quitting the Tabarde Inn. The Knight and Squire with the Squire's Yeoman lead the Procession; next follow the youthful Abbess, her nun and three priests; her greyhounds attend her—

> Of small hounds had she, that she fed
> With roast flesh, milk and wastel bread.

Next follow the Friar and Monk; then the Tapiser, the Pardoner, and the Somner and Manciple. After these 'Our Host,' who occupies the center of the cavalcade, directs them to the Knight as the person who would be likely to commence their task of each telling a tale in their order. After the Host follows the Shipman, the Haberdasher, the Dyer, the Franklin, the Physician, the Plowman, the Lawyer, the poor Parson, the Merchant, the Wife of Bath, the Miller, the Cook, the Oxford Scholar, Chaucer himself, and the Reeve comes as Chaucer has described:

> And ever he rode hinderest of the rout.

These last are issuing from the gateway of the Inn; the Cook and the Wife of Bath are both taking their morning's draught of comfort. Spectators stand at the gateway of the Inn, and are composed of an old Man, a Woman, and Children.

The Landscape is an eastward view of the country, from the Tabarde Inn, in Southwark, as it may be supposed to have appeared in Chaucer's time, interspersed with cottages and villages; the first beams of the Sun are seen above the horizon; some buildings and spires indicate the situation of the great City; the Inn is a gothic building, which Thynne in his Glossary says was the lodging of the Abbot of Hyde, by Winchester. On the Inn is inscribed its title, and a proper advantage is taken of this circumstance to describe the subject of the Picture. The words written over the gateway of the Inn are as follow: 'The Tabarde Inn, by Henry Baillie, the lodgynge-house for Pilgrims, who journey to Saint Thomas's Shrine at Canterbury.'

The characters of Chaucer's Pilgrims are the characters which compose all ages and nations: as one age falls, another rises, different to mortal sight, but to immortals only the same; for we see the same characters repeated again and again, in animals, vegetables, minerals, and in men; nothing new occurs in identical existence; Accident ever varies, Substance can never suffer change nor decay.

Of Chaucer's characters, as described in his *Canterbury Tales,* some of the names or titles are altered by time, but the characters themselves for ever remain unaltered, and consequently they are the physiognomies or lineaments of universal human life, beyond which Nature never steps. Names alter, things never alter. I have known multitudes of those who could have been monks in the age of monkery, who in this deistical age are deists. As Newton numbered the stars, and as Linneus numbered the plants, so Chaucer numbered the classes of men.

The Painter has consequently varied the heads and forms of his personages into all Nature's varieties; the Horses he has also varied to accord to their Riders; the costume is correct according to authentic monuments.

The Knight and Squire with the Squire's Yeoman lead the procession, as Chaucer has also placed them first in his prologue. The Knight is a true Hero, a good, great, and wise man; his whole length portrait on horseback, as written by Chaucer, cannot be surpassed. He has spent his life in the field; has ever been a conqueror, and is that species of character which in every age stands as the guardian of man against the oppressor. His son is like him with the germ of perhaps greater perfection still, as he blends literature and the arts with his warlike studies. Their dress and their horses are of the first rate, without ostentation, and with all the true grandeur that unaffected simplicity when in high rank always displays. The Squire's Yeoman is also a great character, a man perfectly knowing in his profession:

> And in his hand he bare a mighty bow.

Chaucer describes here a mighty man; one who in war is the worthy attendant on noble heroes.

The Prioress follows these with her female chaplain:

> Another Nonne also with her had she,
> That was her Chaplaine, and Priests three.

This Lady is described also as of the first rank, rich and honoured. She has certain peculiarities and little delicate affectations, not unbecoming in her, being accompanied with what is truly grand and really polite; her person and face Chaucer has described with minuteness; it is very elegant, and was the beauty of our ancestors, till after Elizabeth's time, when voluptuousness and folly began to be accounted beautiful.

Her companion and her three priests were no doubt all perfectly delineated in those parts of Chaucer's work which are now lost; we ought to suppose them suitable attendants on rank and fashion.

The Monk follows these with the Friar. The Painter has also grouped with these the Pardoner and the Sompnour and the Manciple, and has here also introduced one of the rich citizens of London: Characters likely to ride in company, all being above the common rank in life or attendants on those who were so.

For the Monk is described by Chaucer, as a man of the first rank in society, noble, rich, and expensively attended; he is a leader of the age, with certain humorous accompaniments in his character, that do not degrade, but render him an object of dignified mirth, but also with other accompaniments not so respectable.

The Friar is a character also of a mixed kind:

A friar there was, a wanton and a merry.

but in his office he is said to be a 'full solemn man': eloquent, amorous, witty, and satyrical; young, handsome, and rich; he is a complete rogue, with constitutional gaiety enough to make him a master of all the pleasures of the world.

His neck was white as the flour de lis,
Thereto strong he was as a champioun.

It is necessary here to speak of Chaucer's own character, that I may set certain mistaken critics right in their conception of the humour and fun that occurs on the journey. Chaucer is himself the great poetical observer of men, who in every age is born to record and eternize its acts. This he does as a master, as a father, and superior, who looks down on their little follies from the Emperor to the Miller; sometimes with severity, oftener with joke and sport.

Accordingly Chaucer has made his Monk a great tragedian, one who studied poetical art. So much so, that the generous Knight is, in the compassionate dictates of his soul, compelled to cry out:

'Ho, quoth the Knyght,—'good Sir, no more of this;
That ye have said is right ynough I wis;
And mokell more, for little heaviness
Is right enough for much folk, as I guesse.
I say, for me, it is a great disease,
Whereas men have been in wealth and ease,
To heare of their sudden fall, alas,
And the contrary is joy and solas.'

The Monk's definition of tragedy in the proem to his tale is worth
repeating:

Tragedie is to tell a certain story,
As old books us maken memory,
Of hem that stood in great prosperity,
And be fallen out of high degree,
Into miserie, and ended wretchedly.

Though a man of luxury, pride and pleasure, he is a master of art and learning,
though affecting to despise it. Those who can think that the proud Huntsman
and Noble Housekeeper, Chaucer's Monk, is intended for a buffoon or
burlesque character, know little of Chaucer.

For the Host who follows this group, and holds the center of the cavalcade,
is a first rate character, and his jokes are no trifles; they are always, though
uttered with audacity, and equally free with the Lord and the Peasant, they are
always substantially and weightily expressive of knowledge and experience;
Henry Baillie, the keeper of the greatest Inn of the greatest City; for such was
the Tabarde Inn in Southwark, near London: our Host was also a leader of
the age.

By way of illustration, I instance Shakspeare's Witches in *Macbeth*. Those
who dress them for the stage, consider them as wretched old women, and not
as Shakspeare intended, the Goddesses of Destiny; this shews how Chaucer
has been misunderstood in his sublime work. Shakspeare's Fairies also are the
rulers of the vegetable world, and so are Chaucer's; let them be so considered,
and then the poet will be understood, and not else.

But I have omitted to speak of a very prominent character, the Pardoner,
the Age's Knave, who always commands and domineers over the high and
low vulgar. This man is sent in every age for a rod and scourge, and for a
blight, for a trial of men, to divide the classes of men; he is in the most holy
sanctuary, and he is suffered by Providence for wise ends, and has also his
great use, and his grand leading destiny.

His companion, the Sompnour, is also a Devil of the first magnitude, grand, terrific, rich and honoured in the rank of which he holds the destiny. The uses to Society are perhaps equal of the Devil and of the Angel, their sublimity, who can dispute.

> In daunger had he at his own gise,
> The young girls of his diocese,
> And he knew well their counsel, &c.

The principal figure in the next groupe is the Good Parson; an Apostle, a real Messenger of Heaven, sent in every age for its light and its warmth. This man is beloved and venerated by all, and neglected by all: He serves all, and is served by none; he is, according to Christ's definition, the greatest of his age. Yet he is a Poor Parson of a town. Read Chaucer's description of the Good Parson, and bow the head and the knee to him, who, in every age, sends us such a burning and a shining light. Search, O ye rich and powerful, for these men and obey their counsel, then shall the golden age return: But alas! you will not easily distinguish him from the Friar or the Pardoner; they, also, are 'full solemn men,' and their counsel you will continue to follow.

I have placed by his side the Sergeant at Lawe, who appears delighted to ride in his company, and between him and his brother, the Plowman; as I wish men of Law would always ride with them, and take their counsel, especially in all difficult points. Chaucer's Lawyer is a character of great venerableness, a Judge, and a real master of the jurisprudence of his age.

The Doctor of Physic is in this groupe, and the Franklin, the voluptuous country gentleman, contrasted with the Physician, and on his other hand, with two Citizens of London. Chaucer's characters live age after age. Every age is a Canterbury Pilgrimage; we all pass on, each sustaining one or other of these characters; nor can a child be born, who is not one of these characters of Chaucer. The Doctor of Physic is described as the first of his profession; perfect, learned, completely Master and Doctor in his art. Thus the reader will observe, that Chaucer makes every one of his characters perfect in his kind; every one is an Antique Statue; the image of a class, and not of an imperfect individual.

This groupe also would furnish substantial matter, on which volumes might be written. The Franklin is one who keeps open table, who is the genius of eating and drinking, the Bacchus; as the Doctor of Physic is the Esculapius, the Host is the Silenus, the Squire is the Apollo, the Miller is the Hercules, &c. Chaucer's characters are a description of the eternal Principles that exist in all ages. The Franklin is voluptuousness itself, most nobly pourtrayed:

It snewed in his house of meat and drink.

The Plowman is simplicity itself, with wisdom and strength for its stamina. Chaucer has divided the ancient character of Hercules between his Miller and his Plowman. Benevolence is the plowman's great characteristic; he is thin with excessive labour, and not with old age, as some have supposed:

> He would thresh, and thereto dike and delve
> For Christe's sake, for every poore wight,
> Withouten hire, if it lay in his might.

Visions of these eternal principles or characters of human life appear to poets, in all ages; the Grecian gods were the ancient Cherubim of Phoenicia; but the Greeks, and since them the Moderns, have neglected to subdue the gods of Priam. These gods are visions of the eternal attributes, or divine names, which, when erected into gods, become destructive to humanity. They ought to be the servants, and not the masters of man, or of society. They ought to be made to sacrifice to Man, and not man compelled to sacrifice to them; for when separated from man or humanity, who is Jesus the Saviour, the vine of eternity, they are thieves and rebels, they are destroyers.

The Plowman of Chaucer is Hercules in his supreme eternal state, divested of his spectrous shadow; which is the Miller, a terrible fellow, such as exists in all times and places for the trial of men, to astonish every neighbourhood with brutal strength and courage, to get rich and powerful to curb the pride of Man.

The Reeve and the Manciple are two characters of the most consummate worldly wisdom. The Shipman, or Sailor, is a similar genius of Ulyssean art; but with the highest courage superadded.

The Citizens and their Cook are each leaders of a class. Chaucer has been somehow made to number four citizens, which would make his whole company, himself included, thirty-one. But he says there was but nine and twenty in his company:

> Full nine and twenty in a company.

The Webbe, or Weaver, and the Tapiser, or Tapestry Weaver, appear to me to be the same person; but this is only an opinion, for full nine and twenty may signify one more or less. But I dare say that Chaucer wrote 'A Webbe Dyer,' that is, a Cloth Dyer:

> A Webbe Dyer, and a Tapiser.

The Merchant cannot be one of the Three Citizens, as his dress is different, and his character is more marked, whereas Chaucer says of his rich citizens:

> All were yclothed in o liverie.

The characters of Women Chaucer has divided into two classes, the Lady Prioress and the Wife of Bath. Are not these leaders of the ages of men? The lady prioress, in some ages, predominates; and in some the wife of Bath, in whose character Chaucer has been equally minute and exact, because she is also a scourge and a blight. I shall say no more of her, nor expose what Chaucer has left hidden; let the young reader study what he has said of her: it is useful as a scarecrow. There are of such characters born too many for the peace of the world.

I come at length to the Clerk of Oxenford. This character varies from that of Chaucer, as the contemplative philosopher varies from the poetical genius. There are always these two classes of learned sages, the poetical and the philosophical. The painter has put them side by side, as if the youthful clerk had put himself under the tuition of the mature poet. Let the Philosopher always be the servant and scholar of inspiration and all will be happy.

Such are the characters that compose this Picture, which was painted in self-defence against the insolent and envious imputation of unfitness for finished and scientific art; and this imputation, most artfully and industriously endeavoured to be propagated among the public by ignorant hirelings. The painter courts comparison with his competitors, who, having received fourteen hundred guineas and more, from the profits of his designs in that well-known work, *Designs for Blair's Grave,* have left him to shift for himself, while others, more obedient to an employer's opinions and directions, are employed, at a great expence, to produce works, in succession to his, by which they acquired public patronage. This has hitherto been his lot—to get patronage for others and then to be left and neglected, and his work, which gained that patronage, cried down as eccentricity and madness; as unfinished and neglected by the artist's violent temper; he is sure the works now exhibited will give the lie to such aspersions.

Those who say that men are led by interest are knaves. A knavish character will often say, 'of what interest is it to me to do so and so?' I answer, 'of none at all, but the contrary, as you well know. It is of malice and envy that you have done this; hence I am aware of you, because I know that you act, not from interest, but from malice, even to your own destruction.' It is therefore become a duty which Mr. B. owes to the Public, who have always recognized him, and patronized him, however hidden by artifices, that he should not suffer such things to be done, or be hindered from the public Exhibition of his finished productions by any calumnies in future.

The character and expression in this picture could never have been produced with Rubens' light and shadow, or with Rembrandt's, or anything Venetian or Flemish. The Venetian and Flemish practice is broken lines, broken masses, and unbroken colours. Their art is to lose form; his art is to find form, and to keep it. His arts are opposite to theirs in all things.

As there is a class of men whose whole delight is the destruction of men, so there is a class of artists, whose whole art and science is fabricated for the purpose of destroying art. Who these are is soon known: 'by their works ye shall know them.' All who endeavour to raise up a style against Rafael, Mich. Angelo, and the Antique; those who separate Painting from Drawing; who look if a picture is well Drawn, and, if it is, immediately cry out, that it cannot be well Coloured—those are the men.

But to shew the stupidity of this class of men nothing need be done but to examine my rival's prospectus.

The two first characters in Chaucer, the Knight and the Squire, he has put among his rabble; and indeed his prospectus calls the Squire the fop of Chaucer's age. Now hear Chaucer:

> Of his Stature, he was of even length,
> And wonderly deliver, and of great strength;
> And he had be sometime in Chivauchy,
> In Flanders, in Artois, and in Picardy,
> And borne him well, as of so litele space.

Was this a fop?

> Well could he sit a horse, and faire ride,
> He could songs make, and eke well indite
> Just, and eke dance, pourtray, and well write.

Was this a fop?

> Curteis he was, and meek, and serviceable;
> And kerft before his fader at the table

Was this a fop?

It is the same with all his characters; he has done all by chance, or perhaps his fortune,—money, money. According to his prospectus he has Three Monks; these he cannot find in Chaucer, who has only One Monk, and that no vulgar character, as he has endeavoured to make him. When men cannot read they should not pretend to paint. To be sure Chaucer is a little difficult to him who has only blundered over novels, and catchpenny trifles of booksellers. Yet a little pains ought to be taken even by the ignorant and weak. He has put The Reeve, a vulgar fellow, between his Knight and Squire, as if he was resolved to go contrary in everything to Chaucer, who says of the Reeve:

And ever he rode hinderest of the rout.

In this manner he has jumbled his dumb dollies together and is praised by his equals for it; for both himself and his friend are equally masters of Chaucer's language. They both think that the Wife of Bath is a young, beautiful, blooming damsel, and H——— says, that she is the Fair Wife of Bath, and that the Spring appears in her Cheeks. Now hear what Chaucer has made her say of herself, who is no modest one:

> But Lord when it remembereth me
> Upon my youth and on my jollity
> It tickleth me about the heart root,
> Unto this day it doth my heart boot,
> That I have had my world as in my time;
> But age, alas, that all will envenime
> Hath bireft my beauty and my pith
> Let go; farewell: the Devil go therewith,
> The flower is gone; there is no more to tell
> The bran, as best I can, I now mote sell;
> And yet to be right merry will I fond,—
> Now forth to tell of my fourth husband.

She has had four husbands, a fit subject for this painter; yet the painter ought to be very much offended with his friend H———, who has called his 'a common scene,' 'and very ordinary forms,' which is the truest part of all, for it is so, and very wretchedly so indeed. What merit can there be in a picture of which such words are spoken with truth?

But the prospectus says that the Painter has represented Chaucer himself as a knave, who thrusts himself among honest people, to make game of and laugh at them; though I must do justice to the painter, and say that he has made him look more like a fool than a knave. But it appears in all the writings of Chaucer, and particularly in his *Canterbury Tales,* that he was very devout, and paid respect to true enthusiastic superstition. He has laughed at his knaves and fools, as I do now. But he has respected his True Pilgrims, who are a majority of his company, and are not thrown together in the random manner that Mr. S——— has done. Chaucer has no where called the Plowman old, worn out with age and labour, as the prospectus has represented him, and says that the picture has done so too. He is worn down with labour, but not with age. How spots of brown and yellow, smeared about at random, can be either young or old, I cannot see. It may be an old man; it may be a young one; it may be any thing that a prospectus pleases. But I know that where there are no lineaments there can be no character. And what connoisseurs call touch, I know by experience, must be the destruction of all character and expression, as it is of every lineament.

The scene of Mr. S———'s Picture is by Dulwich Hills, which was not the way to Canterbury; but perhaps the painter thought he would give them a ride round about, because they were a burlesque set of scare-crows, not worth any man's respect or care.

But the painter's thoughts being always upon gold, he has introduced a character that Chaucer has not; namely, a Goldsmith; for so the prospectus tells us. Why he has introduced a Goldsmith, and what is the wit of it, the prospectus does not explain. But it takes care to mention the reserve and modesty of the Painter; this makes a good epigram enough:

> The fox, the owl, the spider, and the mole,
> By sweet reserve and modesty get fat.

But the prospectus tells us, that the painter has introduced a Sea Captain; Chaucer has a Ship-man a Sailor, a Trading Master of a Vessel, called by courtesy Captain, as every master of a boat is; but this does not make him a Sea Captain. Chaucer has purposely omitted such a personage, as it only exists in certain periods: it is the soldier by sea. He who would be a Soldier in inland nations is a sea captain in commercial nations.

All is misconceived, and its mis-execution is equal to its misconception. I have no objection to Rubens and Rembrandt being employed, or even to their living in a palace; but it shall not be at the expence of Rafael and Michael Angelo living in a cottage, and in contempt and derision. I have been scorned long enough by these fellows, who owe to me all that they have; it shall be so no longer.

> I found them blind, I taught them how to see;
> And, now, they know me not, nor yet themselves.

—William Blake, *Descriptive Catalogue* (1809),
Blake: Complete Writings, 1966, ed. Keynes, pp. 556–75

GEORGE CRABBE (1812)

George Crabbe (1754–1832) was an English poet and naturalist. In the following excerpt, Crabbe, contemplating the genre Chaucer utilizes in his most famous work, discusses the framing device of *The Canterbury Tales*, considering it too complicated an example to use for his own *Tales in Verse*. Crabbe believes that "it is difficult to conceive that on any occasion" such a diverse group of people would travel together, stretching reason beyond what is sensible or credible for sustaining or justifying the use of such a device.

―――⚜―――   ―――⚜―――   ―――⚜―――

That the appearance of the present Volume before the Public is occasioned by a favourable reception of the former two, I hesitate not to acknowledge; because, while the confession may be regarded as some proof of gratitude, or at least of attention from an Author to his Readers, it ought not to be considered as an indication of vanity. It is unquestionably very pleasant to be assured that our labours are well received; but, nevertheless, this must not be taken for a just and full criterion of their merit: publications of great intrinsic value have been met with so much coolness, that a writer who succeeds in obtaining some degree of notice, should look upon himself rather as one favoured than meritorious, as gaining a prize from Fortune, and not a recompense for desert; and, on the contrary, as it is well known that books of very inferior kind have been at once pushed into the strong current of popularity, and are there kept buoyant by the force of the stream, the writer who acquires not this adventitious help, may be reckoned rather as unfortunate than undeserving; and from these opposite considerations it follows, that a man may speak of his success without incurring justly the odium of conceit, and may likewise acknowledge a disappointment without an adequate cause for humiliation or self-reproach.

But were it true that something of the complacency of self-approbation would insinuate itself into an author's mind with the idea of success, the sensation would not be that of unalloyed pleasure: it would perhaps assist him to bear, but it would not enable him to escape the mortification he must encounter from censures, which, though he may be unwilling to admit, yet he finds himself unable to confute; as well as from advice, which at the same time that he cannot but approve, he is compelled to reject.

Reproof and advice, it is probable, every author will receive, if we except those who merit so much of the former, that the latter is contemptuously denied them; now of these, reproof, though it may cause more temporary uneasiness, will in many cases create less difficulty, since errors may be corrected when opportunity occurs: but advice, I repeat, may be of such nature, that it will be painful to reject, and yet impossible to follow it; and in this predicament I conceive myself to be placed. There has been recommended to me, and from authority which neither inclination or prudence leads me to resist, in any new work I might undertake, an unity of subject, and that arrangement of my materials which connects the whole and gives additional interest to every part; in fact, if not an Epic Poem, strictly so denominated, yet such composition as would possess a regular succession of events, and a catastrophe to which every incident should be subservient, and which every character, in a greater or less degree, should conspire to accomplish.

In a Poem of this nature, the principal and inferior characters in some degree resemble a General and his Army, where no one pursues his peculiar objects and adventures, or pursues them in unison with the movements and grand purposes of the whole body; where there is a community of interests and a subordination of actors: and it was upon this view of the subject, and of the necessity for such distribution of persons and events, that I found myself obliged to relinquish an undertaking, for which the characters I could command, and the adventures I could describe, were altogether unfitted.

But if these characters which seemed to be at my disposal were not such as would coalesce into one body, nor were of a nature to be commanded by one mind, so neither on examination did they appear as an unconnected multitude, accidentally collected, to be suddenly dispersed; but rather beings of whom might be formed groups and smaller societies, the relations of whose adventures and pursuits might bear the kind of similitude to an Heroic Poem, which these minor associations of men (as pilgrims on the way to their saint, or parties in search of amusement, travellers excited by curiosity, or adventurers in pursuit of gain) have in points of connection and importance with a regular and disciplined Army.

Allowing this comparison, it is manifest that while much is lost for want of unity of subject and grandeur of design, something is gained by greater variety of incident and more minute display of character, by accuracy of description, and diversity of scene: in these narratives we pass from gay to grave, from lively to severe, not only without impropriety, but with manifest advantage. In one continued and connected Poem, the Reader is, in general, highly gratified or severely disappointed; by many independent narratives, he has the renovation of hope, although he has been dissatisfied, and a prospect of reiterated pleasure should he find himself entertained.

I mean not, however, to compare these different modes of writing as if I were balancing their advantages and defects before I could give preference to either; with me the way I take is not a matter of choice, but of necessity: I present not my Tales to the Reader as if I had chosen the best method of ensuring his approbation, but as using the only means I possessed of engaging his attention.

It may probably be remarked that Tales, however dissimilar, might have been connected by some associating circumstance to which the whole number might bear equal affinity, and that examples of such union are to be found in *Chaucer*, in *Boccace*, and other collectors and inventors of Tales, which considered in themselves are altogether independent; and to this idea I gave so much consideration as convinced me that I could not avail myself of the benefit of such artificial mode of affinity. To imitate the English Poet, characters must be found adapted to their several relations, and this is a point of great difficulty and hazard: much allowance seems to be required even for *Chaucer* himself, since it is difficult to conceive that on any occasion the devout and delicate *Prioress*, the courtly and valiant *Knight*, and 'the poure good Man the persone of a Towne,' would be the voluntary companions of the drunken *Miller*, the licentious *Sompnour*, and 'the Wanton Wife of Bath,' and enter into that colloquial and travelling intimacy which, if a common pilgrimage to the shrine of *St. Thomas* may be said to excuse, I know nothing beside (and certainly nothing in these times) that would produce such effect. *Boccace*, it is true, avoids all difficulty of this kind, by not assigning to the ten relators of his hundred Tales any marked or peculiar characters; nor, though there are male and female in company, can the sex of the narrator be distinguished in the narration. To have followed the method of *Chaucer*, might have been of use, but could scarcely be adopted, from its difficulty; and to have taken that of the Italian writer, would have been perfectly easy, but could be of no service: the attempt at union therefore has been relinquished, and these relations are submitted to the Public, connected by no other circumstances than their being the productions of the same Author, and devoted to the same purpose, the entertainment of his Readers.

It has been already acknowledged, that these compositions have no pretensions to be estimated with the more lofty and heroic kind of Poems, but I feel great reluctance in admitting that they have not a fair and legitimate claim to the poetic character: in vulgar estimation, indeed, all that is not prose, passes for poetry; but I have not ambition of so humble a kind as to be satisfied with a concession which requires nothing in the Poet, except his ability for counting syllables; and I trust something more of the poetic character will be allowed to the succeeding pages, than what the heroes of the *Dunciad* might share with the Author: nor was I aware that by describing, as faithfully as I could, men, manners, and things, I was forfeiting a just title to a name which has been freely granted to many whom to equal and even to excel is but very stinted commendation.

In this case it appears that the usual comparison between Poetry and Painting entirely fails: the Artist who takes an accurate likeness of individuals, or a faithful representation of scenery, may not rank so high in the public estimation, as one who paints an historical event, or an heroic action; but he is nevertheless a painter, and his accuracy is so far from diminishing his reputation, that it procures for him in general both fame and emolument: nor is it perhaps with strict justice determined that the credit and reputation of those verses which strongly and faithfully delineate character and manners, should be lessened in the opinion of the Public by the very accuracy, which gives value and distinction to the productions of the pencil.

Nevertheless, it must be granted that the pretensions of any composition to be regarded as Poetry, will depend upon that definition of the poetic character which he who undertakes to determine the question has considered as decisive; and it is confessed also that one of great authority may be adopted, by which the verses now before the Reader, and many others which have probably amused, and delighted him, must be excluded: a definition like this will be found in the words which the greatest of Poets, not divinely inspired, has given to the most noble and valiant Duke of Athens—

> The Poet's eye, in a fine frenzy rolling,
> Doth glance from Heaven to Earth, from Earth to Heaven;
> And, as Imagination bodies forth
> The forms of things unknown, the Poet's pen
> Turns them to shapes, and gives to airy nothing
> A local habitation, and a name.
> (*Midsummer Night's Dream,* Act V, Scene 1.)

Hence we observe the poet is one who, in the excursions of his fancy between heaven and earth, lights upon a kind of fairy-land in which he places a creation of his own, where he embodies shapes, and gives action and adventure to his ideal offspring; taking captive the imagination of his readers, he elevates them above the grossness of actual being, into the soothing and pleasant atmosphere of supra-mundane existence: there he obtains for his visionary inhabitants the interest that engages a reader's attention without ruffling his feelings, and excites that moderate kind of sympathy which the realities of nature oftentimes fail to produce, either because they are so familiar and insignificant that they excite no determinate emotion, or are so harsh and powerful that the feelings excited are grating and distasteful.

Be it then granted that (as *Duke Theseus* observes) '*such tricks hath strong Imagination,*' and that such Poets '*are of imagination all compact;*' let it be further conceded, that theirs is a higher and more dignified kind of composition, nay, the only kind that has pretensions to inspiration; still, that these Poets should so entirely engross the title as to exclude those who address their productions to the plain sense and sober judgment of their Readers, rather than to their fancy and imagination, I must repeat that I am unwilling to admit,—because I conceive that, by granting such right of exclusion, a vast deal of what has been hitherto received as genuine poetry would no longer be entitled to that appellation.

All that kind of satire wherein character is skilfully delineated, must (this criterion being allowed) no longer be esteemed as genuine Poetry; and for the same reason many affecting narratives which are founded on real events, and borrow no aid whatever from the imagination of the writer, must likewise be rejected: a considerable part of the Poems, as they have hitherto been denominated, of *Chaucer,* are of this naked and unveiled character; and there are in his Tales many pages of coarse, accurate, and minute, but very striking description. Many small Poems in a subsequent age of most impressive kind are adapted and addressed to the common sense of the Reader, and prevail by the strong language of truth and nature: they amused our ancestors, and they continue to engage our interest, and excite our feelings by the same powerful appeals to the heart and affections. In times less remote, *Dryden* has given us much of this Poetry, in which the force of expression and accuracy of description have neither needed nor obtained assistance from the fancy of the writer; the characters in his *Absalom and Achitophel* are instances of this, and more especially those of *Doeg* and *Ogg* in the second part: these, with all their grossness, and almost offensive accuracy, are found to possess that strength and spirit which has preserved from utter annihilation the dead bodies of *Tate* to whom they were inhumanly bound, happily with a fate the reverse of that caused by the cruelty of *Mezentius;* for there the living perished in the putrefaction of the dead, and here the dead are preserved by the vitality of the living. And, to bring forward one other example, it will be found that *Pope* himself has no small portion of this actuality of relation, this nudity of description, and poetry without an atmosphere; the lines beginning 'In *the worst inn's worst room,'* are an example, and many others may be seen in his Satires, Imitations, and above all in his Dunciad: the frequent absence of those '*Sports of Fancy,'* and '*Tricks of strong Imagination,'* have been so much observed, that some have ventured to question whether even this writer were a Poet; and though, as *Dr. Johnson* has remarked, it would be difficult to form a definition of one in which *Pope* should not be admitted, yet they who doubted his claim, had, it is likely, provided for his exclusion by forming that kind of character for their Poet, in which this elegant versifier, for so he must be then named, should not be comprehended.

These things considered, an Author will find comfort in his expulsion from the rank and society of Poets, by reflecting that men much his superiors were likewise shut out, and more especially when he finds also that men not much his superiors are entitled to admission.

But in whatever degree I may venture to differ from any others in my notions of the qualifications and character of the true Poet, I most cordially assent to their opinion who assert that his principal exertions must be made to engage the attention of his Readers; and further, I must allow that the effect of Poetry should be to lift the mind from the painful realities of actual existence, from its every-day concerns, and its perpetually-occurring vexations, and to give it repose by substituting objects in their place which it may contemplate with some degree of interest and satisfaction: but what is there in all this, which may not be effected by a fair representation of existing character? nay, by a faithful delineation of those painful realities, those every-day concerns, and those perpetually-occurring vexations themselves, provided they be not (which is hardly to be supposed) the very concerns and distresses of the Reader? for when it is admitted that they have no particular relation to him, but are the troubles and anxieties of other men, they excite and interest his feelings as the imaginary exploits, adventures, and perils of romance;—they soothe his mind, and keep his curiosity pleasantly awake; they appear to have enough of reality to engage his sympathy, but possess not interest sufficient to create painful sensations. Fiction itself, we know, and every work of fancy, must for a time have the effect of realities; nay, the very enchanters, spirits, and monsters of *Ariosto* and *Spenser* must be present in the mind of the Reader while he is engaged by their operations, or they would be as the objects and incidents of a Nursery Tale to a rational understanding, altogether despised and neglected: in truth, I can but consider this pleasant effect upon the mind of a Reader, as depending neither upon the events related (whether they be actual or imaginary), nor upon the characters introduced (whether taken from life or fancy), but upon the manner in which the Poem itself is conducted; let that be judiciously managed, and the occurrences actually copied from life will have the same happy effect as the inventions of a creative fancy;—while, on the other hand, the imaginary persons and incidents to which the Poet has given 'a local habitation, and a name,' will make upon the concurring feelings of the Reader, the same impressions with those taken from truth and nature, because they will appear to be derived from that source, and therefore of necessity will have a similar effect.

Having thus far presumed to claim for the ensuing pages the rank and title of Poetry, I attempt no more, nor venture to class or compare them with any other kinds of poetical composition; their place will doubtless be found for them.

A principal view and wish of the Poet must be to engage the mind of his Readers, as, failing in that point, he will scarcely succeed in any other: I therefore willingly confess that much of my time and assiduity has been devoted to this purpose; but, to the ambition of pleasing, no other sacrifices have, I trust, been made, than of my own labour and care. Nothing will be found that militates against the rules of propriety and good manners, nothing that offends against the more important precepts of morality and religion; and with this negative kind of merit, I commit my Book to the judgment and taste of the Reader,—not being willing to provoke his vigilance by professions of accuracy, nor to solicit his indulgence by apologies for mistakes.

—George Crabbe, *Preface to the Canterbury Tales,* 1812

WILLIAM HAZLITT
"TROILUS AND CRESSIDA" (1817)

One of the greatest English literary critics of the nineteenth century, William Hazlitt (1778–1830) wrote often on Chaucer, whom he considered "the most literal of poets." In the first excerpt, Hazlitt compares Chaucer to Shakespeare, and, in the second, he compares Chaucer to Spenser. Both pieces are of enormous value to students comparing either of those two authors to Chaucer.

In this excerpt, from a work on Shakespeare's plays, Hazlitt examines the versions of *Troilus and Criseyde* that these two writers penned. Noting differences in how each author approached his subject, Hazlitt writes that, "Chaucer attended chiefly to the real and natural, that is, to the involuntary and inevitable impressions on the mind in given circumstances." Shakespeare, Hazlitt believes, was more imaginative and passionate, and Hazlitt seemingly concludes that while both writers have their merits, Shakespeare is the superior of the two. Though these authors are frequently considered the two best writers in English, they are not often directly compared, so Hazlitt's work here is of value to anyone studying these two versions of *Troilus* or the two writers themselves.

※ ※ ※

In Chaucer, Cressida is represented as a grave, sober, considerate personage (a widow—he cannot tell her age, nor whether she has children or no) who has an alternate eye to her character, her interest, and her pleasure: Shakespear's Cressida is a giddy girl, an unpractised jilt, who falls in love with Troilus, as she afterwards deserts him, from mere levity and thoughtlessness of temper. She may be wooed and won to any thing and from any thing, at a moment's warning: the other knows very well what she would be at, and sticks to it, and is more governed by substantial reasons than by caprice or vanity. Pandarus again, in Chaucer's story, is a friendly sort of go-between, tolerably busy, officious, and forward in bringing matters to bear: but in Shakespear he has 'a stamp exclusive and professional:' he wears the badge of his trade; he is a regular knight of the game. The difference of the manner in which the subject is treated arises perhaps less from intention, than from the different genius of the two poets. There is no *double entendre* in the characters of Chaucer: they are either quite serious or quite comic. In Shakespear the ludicrous and ironical are constantly blended with the stately and the impassioned. We see Chaucer's characters as they saw themselves, not as they appeared to others or might have appeared to the poet. He is as deeply implicated in the affairs of his personages as they could be themselves. He had to go a long journey with each of them, and became a kind of necessary confidant. There is little relief, or light and shade in his pictures. The conscious smile is not seen lurking under the brow of grief or impatience. Every thing with him is intense and continuous— a working out of what went before.—Shakespear never committed himself to his characters. He trifled, laughed, or wept with them as he chose. He has no prejudices for or against them; and it seems a matter of perfect indifference whether he shall be in jest or earnest. According to him 'the web of our lives is of a mingled yarn, good and ill together.' His genius was dramatic, as Chaucer's was historical. He saw both sides of a question, the different views taken of it according to the different interests of the parties concerned, and he was at once an actor and spectator in the scene. If any thing, he is too various and flexible; too full of transitions, of glancing lights, of salient points. If Chaucer followed up his subject too doggedly, perhaps Shakespear was too volatile and heedless. The Muse's wing too often lifted him off his feet. He made infinite excursions to the right and the left.

> He hath done
> Mad and fantastic execution,
> Engaging and redeeming of himself
> With such a careless force and forceless care,
> As if that luck in very spite of cunning
> Bad him win all.

Chaucer attended chiefly to the real and natural, that is, to the involuntary and inevitable impressions on the mind in given circumstances: Shakespear exhibited also the possible and the fantastical,—not only what things are in themselves, but whatever they might seem to be, their different reflections, their endless combinations. He lent his fancy, wit, invention, to others, and borrowed their feelings in return. Chaucer excelled in the force of habitual sentiment; Shakespear added to it every variety of passion, every suggestion of thought or accident. Chaucer described external objects with the eye of a painter, or he might be said to have embodied them with the hand of a sculptor, every part is so thoroughly made out, and tangible:—Shakespear's imagination threw over them a lustre

Prouder than when blue Iris bends.

We must conclude this criticism; and we will do it with a quotation or two. One of the most beautiful passages in Chaucer's tale is the description of Cresseide's first avowal of her love.

> And as the new abashed nightingale,
> That stinteth first when she beginneth sing,
> When that she heareth any herde's tale,
> Or in the hedges any wight stirring,
> And, after, sicker doth her voice outring;
> Right so Cresseide, when that her dread stent,
> Opened her heart, and told him her intent.

See also the two next stanzas, and particularly that divine one beginning

Her armes small, her back both straight and soft, &c.

Compare this with the following speech of Troilus to Cressida in the play.

> O, that I thought it could be in a woman;
> And if it can, I will presume in you,
> To feed for aye her lamp and flame of love,
> To keep her constancy in plight and youth,
> Out-living beauties out-ward, with a mind
> That doth renew swifter than blood decays.
> Or, that persuasion could but thus convince me,
> That my integrity and truth to you
> Might be affronted with the match and weight
> Of such a winnow'd purity in love;
> How were I then uplifted! But alas,
> I am as true as Truth's simplicity,
> And simpler than the infancy of Truth.

These passages may not seem very characteristic at first sight, though we think they are so. We will give two, that cannot be mistaken. Patroclus says to Achilles,

> Rouse yourself; and the weak wanton Cupid
> Shall from your neck unloose his amorous fold,

And like a dew-drop from the lion's mane,
Be shook to air.

Troilus, addressing the God of Day on the approach of the morning that parts him from Cressida, says with much scorn,

What! proffer'st thou thy light here for to sell?
Go, sell it them that smalle seles grave.

If nobody but Shakespear could have written the former, nobody but Chaucer would have thought of the latter.— Chaucer was the most literal of poets, as Richardson was of prose-writers.

Every thing in Chaucer has a downright reality. A simile or a sentiment is as if it were given in upon evidence. In Shakespear the commonest matter-of-fact has a romantic grace about it; or seems to float with the breath of imagination in a freer element. No one could have more depth of feeling or observation than Chaucer, but he wanted resources of invention to lay open the stores of nature or the human heart with the same radiant light, that Shakespear has done. However fine or profound the thought, we know what was coming, whereas the effect of reading Shakespear is 'like the eye of vassalage encountering majesty.' Chaucer's mind was consecutive, rather than discursive. He arrived at truth through a certain process; Shakespear saw every thing by intuition. Chaucer had great variety of power, but he could do only one thing at once. He set himself to work on a particular subject. His ideas were kept separate, labelled, ticketed and parcelled out in a set form, in pews and compartments by themselves. They did not play into one another's hands. They did not re-act upon one another, as the blower's breath moulds the yielding glass. There is something hard and dry in them. What is the most wonderful thing in Shakespear's faculties is their excessive sociability, and how they gossipped and compared notes together.

—William Hazlitt, "Troilus and Cressida,"
Characters of Shakespeare's Plays 1817, pp. 89–92

WILLIAM HAZLITT
"ON CHAUCER AND SPENSER" (1818)

In this excerpt, from *Lectures on English Poetry*, Hazlitt strikes a more common comparison between Chaucer and Spenser. Calling them "two out of four of the greatest names in [English] poetry," Hazlitt writes that, "Spenser delighted in luxurious enjoyment; Chaucer, in severe activity of mind. As Spenser was the most romantic and visionary, Chaucer was the most practical of all the great poets, the most a man of business and the world." Hazlitt also notes that Spenser's "poetical temperament was as effeminate as Chaucer's was stern and masculine." This is an interesting contrast between these two writers, and students may find it worthwhile to examine the writings of each man to uncover where Hazlitt's conclusions manifest themselves in each poet's work.

The excerpt continues with a discussion of several of the pilgrims in *The Canterbury Tales*, including an effective but brief consideration of the Summoner. Hazlitt then examines Chaucer's ability to draw unique and fascinating characters and Chaucer's excellence at describing nature, characteristics of the poet noted by several other authors excerpted in this volume. Finally, Hazlitt concludes that, "Chaucer has more of this deep, internal, sustained sentiment, than any other writer, except Boccaccio. In depth of simple pathos, and intensity of conception, never swerving from his subject, I think no other writer comes near him, not even the Greek tragedians."

Having, in the former lecture, given some account of the nature of poetry in general, I shall proceed, in the next place, to a more particular consideration of the genius and history of English poetry. I shall take, as the subject of the present lecture, Chaucer and Spenser, two out of four of the greatest names in poetry, which this country has to boast. Both of them, however, were much indebted to the early poets of Italy, and may be considered as belonging, in a certain degree, to the same school. The freedom and copiousness with which our most original writers, in former periods, availed themselves of the productions of their predecessors, frequently transcribing whole passages, without scruple or acknowledgement, may appear contrary to the etiquette of modern literature, when the whole stock of poetical common-places has become public property, and no one is compelled to trade upon any particular author. But it is not so much a subject of wonder, at a time when to read and write was of itself an honorary distinction, when learning was almost as great a rarity as genius, and when in fact those who first transplanted the beauties of other languages into their own, might be considered as public benefactors, and the founders of a national literature.—There are poets older than Chaucer, and in the interval between him and Spenser; but their genius was not such as to place them in any point of comparison with either of these celebrated men; and an inquiry into their particular merits or defects might seem rather to belong to the province of the antiquary, than be thought generally interesting to the lovers of poetry in the present day.

Chaucer (who has been very properly considered as the father of English poetry) preceded Spenser by two centuries. He is supposed to have been born in London, in the year 1328, during the reign of Edward III, and to have died in 1400, at the age of seventy-two. He received a learned education at one, or at both of the universities, and travelled early into Italy, where he became thoroughly imbued with the spirit and excellences of the great Italian poets and prose-writers, Dante, Petrarch, and Boccace; and is said to have had a personal interview with one of these, Petrarch. He was connected, by marriage, with the famous John of Gaunt, through whose interest he was introduced into several public employments. Chaucer was an active partisan, a religious reformer, and from the the share he took in some disturbances, on one occasion, he was obliged to fly the country. On his return, he was imprisoned, and made his peace with government, as it is said, by a discovery of his associates. Fortitude does not appear, at any time, to have been the distinguishing virtue of poets.—There is, however, an obvious similarity between the practical turn of Chaucer's mind and restless impatience of his character, and the tone of his writings. Yet it would be too much to attribute the one to the other as cause and effect: for Spenser, whose poetical temperament was as effeminate as Chaucer's was stern and masculine, was equally engaged in public affairs, and had mixed equally in the great world. So much does native disposition predominate over accidental circumstances, moulding them to its previous bent and purposes! For while Chaucer's intercourse with the busy world, and collision with the actual passions and conflicting interests of others, seemed to brace the sinews of his understanding, and gave to his writings the air of a man who describes persons and things that he had known and been intimately concerned in; the same opportunities, operating on a differently constituted frame, only served to alienate Spenser's mind the more from the 'close-pent up' scenes of ordinary life, and to make him 'rive their concealing continents', to give himself up to the unrestrained indulgence of 'flowery tenderness'.

It is not possible for any two writers to be more opposite in this respect. Spenser delighted in luxurious enjoyment; Chaucer, in severe activity of mind. As Spenser was the most romantic and visionary, Chaucer was the most practical of all the great poets, the most a man of business and the world. His poetry reads like history. Everything has a downright reality; at least in the relator's mind. A simile, or a sentiment, is as if it were given in upon evidence. Thus he describes Cressid's first avowal of her love.

And as the new abashed nightingale,
That stinteth first when she beginneth sing,
When that she heareth any herde's tale,
Or in the hedges any wight stirring,
And after, sicker, doth her voice outring;
Right so Cresseide, when that her dread stent,
Open'd her heart, and told him her intent.

This is so true and natural, and beautifully simple, that the two things seem identified with each other. Again, it is said in the Knight's Tale—

Thus passeth yere by yere, and day by day,
Till it felle ones in a morwe of May,
That Emelie that fayrer was to sene
Than is the lilie upon his stalke grene;
And fresher than the May with floures newe,
For with the rose-colour strof hire hewe:
I n'ot which was the finer of hem two.

This scrupulousness about the literal preference, as if some question of matter of fact was at issue, is remarkable. I might mention that other, where he compares the meeting between Palamon and Arcite to a hunter waiting for a lion in a gap;—

That stondeth at a gap with a spere,
Whan hunted is the lion or the bere,
And hereth him come rushing in the greves,
And breking bothe the boughes and the leves:—
or that still finer one of Constance, when she is condemned to death:—
Have ye not seen somtime a pale face
(Among a prees) of him that hath been lad
Toward his deth, wheras he geteth no grace,
And swiche a colour in his face hath had,
Men mighten know him that was so bestad,
Amonges all the faces in that route;
So stant Custance, and loketh hire aboute.

The beauty, the pathos here does not seem to be of the poet's seeking, but a part of the necessary texture of the fable. He speaks of what he wishes to describe with the accuracy, the discrimination of one who relates what has happened to himself, or has had the best information from those who have been eye-witnesses of it. The strokes of his pencil always tell. He dwells only on the essential, on that which would be interesting to the persons really concerned: yet as he never omits any material circumstance, he is prolix from the number of points on which he touches, without being diffuse on any one; and is sometimes tedious from the fidelity with which he adheres to his subject, as other writers are from the frequency of their digressions from it. The chain of his story is composed of a number of fine links, closely connected together, and rivetted by a single blow. There is an instance of the minuteness which he introduces into his most serious descriptions in his account of Palamon when left alone in his cell:

> Swiche sorrow he maketh that the grete tour
> Resouned of his yelling and clamour:
> The pure fetters on his shinnes grete
> Were of his bitter salte teres wete.

The mention of this last circumstance looks like a part of the instructions he had to follow, which he had no discretionary power to leave out or introduce at pleasure. He is contented to find grace and beauty in truth. He exhibits for the most part the naked object, with little drapery thrown over it. His metaphors, which are few, are not for ornament, but use, and as like as possible to the things themselves. He does not affect to show his power over the reader's mind, but the power which his subject has over his own. The readers of Chaucer's poetry feel more nearly what the persons he describes must have felt, than perhaps those of any other poet. His sentiments are not voluntary effusions of the poet's fancy, but founded on the natural impulses and habitual prejudices of the characters he has to represent. There is an inveteracy of purpose, a sincerity of feeling, which never relaxes or grows vapid, in whatever they do or say. There is no artificial, pompous display, but a strict parsimony of the poet's materials, like the rude simplicity of the age in which he lived. His poetry resembles the root just springing from the ground, rather than the full-blown flower. His muse is no 'babbling gossip of the air', fluent and redundant; but, like a stammerer, or a dumb person, that has just found the use of speech, crowds many things together with eager haste, with anxious pauses, and fond repetitions to prevent mistake. His words point as an index to the objects, like the eye or finger. There were none of the common-places of poetic diction in our author's time, no reflected lights of fancy, no borrowed roseate tints; he was obliged to inspect things for himself, to look narrowly, and almost to handle the object, as in the obscurity of morning we partly see and partly grope our way; so that his descriptions have a sort of tangible character belonging to them, and produce the effect of sculpture on the mind. Chaucer had an equal eye for truth of nature and discrimination of character; and his interest in what he saw gave new distinctness and force to his power of observation. The picturesque and the dramatic are in him closely blended together, and hardly distinguishable; for he principally describes external appearances as indicating character, as symbols of internal sentiment. There is a meaning in what he sees; and it is this which catches his eye by sympathy. Thus the costume and dress of the Canterbury Pilgrims—of the Knight—the Squire—the Oxford Scholar—the Gap-toothed Wife of Bath, and the rest, speak for themselves. . . .

The Serjeant at Law is the same identical individual as Lawyer Dowling in *Tom Jones,* who wished to divide himself into a hundred pieces, to be in a hundred places at once.

> No wher so besy a man as he ther n'as,
> And yet he semed besier than he was.

The Frankelein, in 'whose hous it snewed of mete and drinke'; the Shipman, 'who rode upon a rouncie, as he couthe'; the Doctour of Phisike, 'whose studie was but litel of the Bible'; the Wife of Bath, in

> All whose parish ther was non,
> That to the offring before hire shulde gon,
> And if ther did, certain so wroth was she,
> That she was out of alle charitee;

—the poure Persone of a toun, 'whose parish was wide, and houses fer asonder'; the Miller, and the Reve, 'a slendre colerike man', are all of the same stamp. They are every one samples of a kind; abstract definitions of a species. Chaucer, it has been said, numbered the classes of men, as Linnaeus numbered the plants. Most of them remain to this day: others that are obsolete, and may well be dispensed with, still live in his descriptions of them. Such is the Sompnoure:

> A Sompnoure was ther with us in that place,
> That hadde a fire-red cherubinnes face,
> For sausefleme he was, with eyen narwe,
> As hote he was, and likerous as a sparwe,
> With scalled browes blake, and pilled berd:
> Of his visage children were sore aferd.
> Ther n'as quicksilver, litarge, ne brimston,
> Boras, ceruse, ne oile of tartre non,
> Ne oinement that wolde dense or bite,

That him might helpen of his whelkes white,
Ne of the knobbes sitting on his chekes.
Wei loved he garlike, onions, and lekes,
And for to drinke strong win as rede as blood.
Than wolde he speke, and crie as he were wood.
And whan that he wel dronken had the win,
Than wold he speken no word but Latin.
A fewe termes coude he, two or three,
That he had lerned out of som decree;
No wonder is, he heard it all the day.—
    In danger hadde he at his owen gise
The yonge girles of the diocise,
And knew hir conseil, and was of hir rede.
A gerlond hadde he sette upon his hede
As gret as it were for an alestake:
A bokeler hadde he made him of a cake.
With him ther rode a gentil Pardonere—
That hadde a vois as smale as hath a gote.

It would be a curious speculation (at least for those who think that the characters of men never change, though manners, opinions, and institutions may) to know what has become of this character of the Sompnoure in the present day; whether or not it has any technical representative in existing professions; into what channels and conduits it has withdrawn itself, where it lurks unseen in cunning obscurity, or else shows its face boldly, pampered into all the insolence of office, in some other shape, as it is deterred or encouraged by circumstances. *Chaucer's characters modernized,* upon this principle of historic derivation, would be an useful addition to our knowledge of human nature. But who is there to undertake it?

The descriptions of the equipage, and accoutrements of the two kings of Thrace and Inde, in the Knight's Tale, are as striking and grand, as the others are lively and natural. The imagination of a poet brings such objects before us, as when we look at wild beasts in a menagerie; their claws are pared, their eyes glitter like harmless lightning; but we gaze at them with a pleasing awe, clothed in beauty, formidable in the sense of abstract power.

Chaucer's descriptions of natural scenery possess the same sort of characteristic excellence, or what might be termed *gusto.* They have a local truth and freshness, which gives the very feeling of the air, the coolness or moisture of the ground. Inanimate objects are thus made to have a fellow-feeling in the interest of the story; and render back the sentiment of the speaker's mind. One of the finest parts of Chaucer is of this mixed kind. It is the beginning of the *Flower and the Leaf,* where he describes the delight of that young beauty, shrouded in her bower, and listening, in the morning of the year, to the singing of the nightingale; while her joy rises with the rising song, and gushes out afresh at every pause, and is borne along with the full tide of pleasure, and still increases, and repeats, and prolongs itself, and knows no ebb. The coolness of the arbour, its retirement, the early time of the day, the sudden starting up of the birds in the neighbouring bushes, the eager delight with which they devour and rend the opening buds and flowers, are expressed with a truth and feeling, which make the whole appear like the recollection of an actual scene:

> Which as me thought was right a pleasing sight,
> And eke the briddes song for to here,
> Would haue rejoyced any earthly wight,
> And I that couth not yet in no manere
> Heare the nightingale of all the yeare,
> Ful busily herkened with herte and with eare,
> If I her voice perceiue coud any where.
> And I that all this pleasaunt sight sie,
> Thought sodainly I felt so sweet an aire
> Of the eglentere, that certainely
> There is no herte I deme in such dispaire,
> Ne with thoughts froward and contraire,
> So ouerlaid, but it should soone haue bote,
> If it had ones felt this savour sote.
> And as I stood and cast aside mine eie,
> I was ware of the fairest medler tree
> That ever yet in all my life I sie
> As full of blossomes as it might be,
> Therein a goldfinch leaping pretile
> Fro bough to bough, and as him list he eet
> Here and there of buds and floures sweet.
> And to the herber side was joyning
> This faire tree, of which I haue you told,
> And at the last the brid began to sing,
> Whan he had eaten what he eat wold,
> So passing sweetly, that by manifold
> It was more pleasaunt than I coud deuise,
> And whan his song was ended in this wise,

The nightingale with so merry a note
Answered him, that all the wood rong
So sodainly, that as it were a sote,
I stood astonied, so was I with the song
Thorow rauished, that till late and long,
I ne wist in what place I was, ne where,
And ayen me thought she song euen by mine ere.
Wherefore I waited about busily
On euery side, if I her might see,
And at the last I gan full well aspie
Where she sat in a fresh grene laurer tree,
On the further side euen right by me,
That gaue so passing a delicious smell,
According to the eglentere full well.
Whereof I had so inly great pleasure,
That as me thought I surely rauished was
Into Paradice, where my desire
Was for to be, and no ferther passe
As for that day, and on the sote grasse,
I sat me downe, for as for mine entent,
The birds song was more conuenient,
And more pleasaunt to me by manifold,
Than meat or drinke, or any other thing,
Thereto the herber was so fresh and cold,
The wholesome sauours eke so comforting,
That as I demed, sith the beginning
Of the world was neur seene or than
So pleasaunt a ground of none earthly man.
And as I sat the birds harkening thus,
Me thought that I heard voices sodainly,
The most sweetest and most delicious
That euer any wight I trow truly
Heard in their life, for the armony
And sweet accord was in so good musike,
That the uoice to angels was most like.

There is here no affected rapture, no flowery sentiment: the whole is an ebullition of natural delight 'welling out of the heart', like water from a crystal spring. Nature is the soul of art: there is a strength as well as a simplicity in the imagination that reposes entirely on nature, that nothing else can supply.

It was the same trust in nature, and reliance on his subject, which enabled Chaucer to describe the grief and patience of Griselda; the faith of Constance; and the heroic perseverance of the little child, who, going to school through the streets of Jewry,

> Oh *Alma Redemptoris mater,* loudly sung,

and who after his death still triumphed in his song. Chaucer has more of this deep, internal, sustained sentiment, than any other writer, except Boccaccio. In depth of simple pathos, and intensity of conception, never swerving from his subject, I think no other writer comes near him, not even the Greek tragedians. I wish to be allowed to give one or two instances of what I mean. I will take the following from the *Knight's Tale.* The distress of Arcite, in consequence of his banishment from his love, is thus described:

> Whan that Arcite to Thebes comen was,
> Ful oft a day he swelt and said Alas,
> For sene his lady shall he never mo.
> And shortly to concluden all his wo,
> So mochel sorwe hadde never creature,
> That is or shall be, while the world may dure.
> His slepe, his mete, his drinke is him byraft.
> That lene he wex, and drie as is a shaft.
> His eyen holwe, and grisly to behold,
> His hewe salwe, and pale as ashen cold,
> And solitary he was, and ever alone,
> And wailing all the night, making his mone.
> And if he herde song or instrument,
> Than wold he wepe, he mighte not be stent.
> So feble were his spirites, and so low,
> And changed so, that no man coude know
> His speche ne his vois, though men it herd.

This picture of the sinking of the heart, of the wasting away of the body and mind, of the gradual failure of all the faculties under the contagion of a rankling sorrow, cannot be surpassed. Of the same kind is his farewell to his mistress, after he has gained her hand and lost his life in the combat:

> 'Alas the wo! alas the peines stronge,
> That I for you have suffered, and so longe!
> Alas the deth! alas min Emilie!
> Alas departing of our compagnie;

> Alas min hertes quene! alas my wif!
> Min hertes ladie, ender of my lif!
> What is this world? what axen men to have?
> Now with his love, now in his colde grave
> Alone withouten any compagnie.'

The death of Arcite is the more affecting, as it comes after triumph and victory, after the pomp of sacrifice, the solemnities of prayer, the celebration of the gorgeous rites of chivalry. The descriptions of the three temples of Mars, of Venus, and Diana, of the ornaments and ceremonies used in each, with the reception given to the offerings of the lovers, have a beauty and grandeur, much of which is lost in Dryden's version. For instance, such lines as the following are not rendered with their true feeling:

> Why shulde I not as well eke tell you all
> The purtreiture that was upon the wall
> Within the temple of mighty Mars the rede—
> That highte the gret temple of Mars in Trace
> In thilke colde and frosty region,
> Ther as Mars hath his sovereine mansion.
> First on the wall was peinted a forest,
> In which ther wonneth neyther man ne best,
> With knotty knarry barrein trees old
> Of stubbes sharp and hidous to behold;
> In which ther ran a romble and a swough,
> As though a storme shuld bresten every bough.

And again, among innumerable terrific images of death and slaughter painted on the wall, is this one:

> The statue of Mars upon a carte stood
> Armed, and looked grim as he were wood.
> A wolf ther stood beforne him at his fete
> With eyen red, and of a man he ete.

The story of Griselda is in Boccaccio; but the Clerk of Oxenforde, who tells it, professes to have learned it from Petrarch. This story has gone all over Europe, and has passed into a proverb. In spite of the barbarity of the circumstances, which are abominable, the sentiment remains unimpaired and unalterable. It is of that kind, 'that heaves no sigh, that sheds no tear'; but it hangs upon the beatings of the heart; it is a part of the very being; it is as inseparable from it as the breath we draw. It is still and calm as the face of death. Nothing can touch it in its ethereal purity: tender as the yielding flower, it is fixed as the marble firmament. The only remonstrance she makes, the only complaint she utters against all the ill-treatment she receives, is that single line where, when turned back naked to her father's house, she says,

> Let me not like a worm go by the way.

. . . The story of the little child slain in Jewry (which is told by the Prioress, and worthy to be told by her who was 'all conscience and tender heart') is not less touching than that of Griselda. It is simple and heroic to the last degree. The poetry of Chaucer has a religious sanctity about it, connected with the manners and superstitions of the age. It has all the spirit of martyrdom.

It has also all the extravagance and the utmost licentiousness of comic humour, equally arising out of the manners of the time. In this too Chaucer resembled Boccaccio that he excelled in both styles, and could pass at will 'from grave to gay, from lively to severe'; but he never confounded the two styles together (except from that involuntary and unconscious mixture of the pathetic and humorous, which is almost always to be found in nature), and was exclusively taken up with what he set about, whether it was jest or earnest. The *Wife of Bath's Prologue* (which Pope has very admirably modernized) is, perhaps, unequalled as a comic story. The *Cock and the Fox* is also excellent for lively strokes of character and satire. *January and May* is not so good as some of the others. Chaucer's versification, considering the time at which he wrote, and that versification is a thing in a great degree mechanical, is not one of his least merits. It has considerable strength and harmony, and its apparent deficiency in the latter respect arises chiefly from the alterations which have since taken place in the pronunciation or mode of accenting the words of the language. The best general rule for reading him is to pronounce the final *e,* as in reading Italian.

It was observed in the last Lecture that painting describes what the object is in itself, poetry what it implies or suggests. Chaucer's poetry is not, in general, the best confirmation of the truth of this distinction, for his poetry is more picturesque and historical than almost any other. But there is one instance in point which I cannot help giving in this place. It is the story of the three thieves who go in search of Death to kill him, and who meeting with him, are entangled in their fate by his words, without knowing him. In the printed catalogue to Mr. West's (in some respects very admirable) picture of Death on the Pale Horse, it is observed, that 'In poetry the same effect is produced by a few abrupt and rapid gleams of description, touching, as it were with fire, the features and edges of a general mass of awful obscurity; but in painting, such indistinctness would be a defect, and imply that the artist wanted the power to portray the conceptions of his fancy. Mr. West was of opinion that to delineate a physical form, which in its moral impression would approximate to that of the visionary Death of Milton, it was necessary to endow it, if possible, with the appearance of superhuman strength and energy. He has therefore exerted the utmost force and perspicuity of his pencil on the central figure. '—One might suppose from this, that the way to represent a shadow was to make it as substantial as possible. Oh, no! Painting has its prerogatives (and high ones they are), but they lie in representing the visible, not the invisible. The moral attributes of Death are powers and effects of an infinitely wide and general description, which no individual or physical form can possibly represent, but by a courtesy of speech, or by a distant analogy. The moral impression of Death is essentially visionary; its reality is in the mind's eye. Words are here the only *things;* and things, physical forms, the mere mockeries of the understanding. The less definite, the less bodily the conception, the more vast, unformed, and unsubstantial, the nearer does it approach to some resemblance of that omnipresent, lasting, universal, irresistible principle, which everywhere, and at some time or other, exerts its power over all things. Death is a mighty abstraction, like Night, or Space, or Time. He is an ugly customer, who will not be invited to supper, or to sit for his picture. He is with us and about us, but we do not see him. He stalks on before us, and we do not mind him: he follows us close behind, and we do not turn to look back at him. We do not see him making faces at us in our lifetime, nor perceive him afterwards sitting in mock-majesty, a twin-skeleton, beside us, tickling our bare ribs, and staring into our hollow eye-balls! Chaucer knew this. He makes three riotous companions go in search of Death to kill him, they meet with an old man whom they reproach with his age, and ask why he does not die, to which he answers thus:

> Ne Deth, alas! ne will not han my lif.
> Thus walke I like a restless caitiff,
> And on the ground, which is my modres gate,
> I knocke with my staf, erlich and late,
> And say to hire, 'Leve, mother, let me in.
> Lo, how I vanish, flesh and blood and skin,
> Alas! when shall my bones ben at reste?
> Mother, with you wolde I changen my cheste,
> That in my chambre longe time hath be,
> Ye, for an heren cloute to wrap in me.'
> But yet to me she will not don that grace,
> For which ful pale and welked is my face.

They then ask the old man where they shall find out Death to kill him, and he sends them on an errand which ends in the death of all three. We hear no more of him, but it is Death that they have encountered!

—William Hazlitt, "On Chaucer and Spenser," (1818),
Lectures on English Poetry, 1933, pp. 30–51

WILLIAM WORDSWORTH
"SONNET XXIII: EDWARD VI" (1822)

'Sweet is the holiness of Youth'—so felt
Time-honoured Chaucer when he framed the Lay
By which the Prioress beguiled the way,
And many a Pilgrim's rugged heart did melt.
Hadst thou, loved Bard! whose spirit often dwelt
In the clear land of vision, but foreseen
King, Child, and Seraph, blended in the mien
Of pious Edward kneeling as he knelt
In meek and simple Infancy, what joy
For universal Christendom had thrilled
Thy heart! what hopes inspired thy genius, skilled
(O great Precursor, genuine morning Star)
The lucid shafts of reason to employ,
Piercing the Papal darkness from afar!

—William Wordsworth, "Sonnet XXIII: Edward VI,"
Ecclesiastical Sonnets, 1822, p. 65

GEORGE GORDON, LORD BYRON (1830)

Chaucer, notwithstanding the praises bestowed on him, I think obscene and contemptible:—he owes his celebrity merely to his antiquity, which he does not deserve so well as Pierce Plowman, or Thomas of Ercildoune. English living poets I have avoided mentioning:—we have none who will survive their productions. Taste is over with us.

—George Gordon, Lord Byron, "Memorandum Book, 30
November 1807," *The Life, Letters and Journals of Lord Byron,*
1830, ed. Moore, Ch. 5, p. 49

Ralph Waldo Emerson (1837)

It is remarkable, the character of the pleasure we derive from the best books. They impress us with the conviction, that one nature wrote and the same reads. We read the verses of one of the great English poets, of Chaucer, of Marvell, of Dryden, with the most modern joy,—with a pleasure, I mean, which is in great part caused by the abstraction of all *time* from their verses. There is some awe mixed with the joy of our surprise, when this poet, who lived in some past world, two or three hundred years ago, says that which lies close to my own soul, that which I also had well-nigh thought and said. But for the evidence thence afforded to the philosophical doctrine of the identity of all minds, we should suppose some pre-established harmony, some foresight of souls that were to be, and some preparation of stores for their future wants, like the fact observed in insects, who lay up food before death for the young grub they shall never see.

—Ralph Waldo Emerson, "The American Scholar," 1837

Elizabeth Barrett Browning
"Mrs. Browning on Chaucer" (1842)

The English poet Elizabeth Barrett Browning (1806–1861) is perhaps as famous for her works *Sonnets from the Portuguese* and *Aurora Leigh* as she is for her storied marriage to fellow poet Robert Browning. Often considered the greatest female poet in the English language, Barrett Browning demonstrated her great fondness for Chaucer in the 1842 essay "Mrs. Browning on Chaucer."

Barrett Browning begins her essay by declaring that "it is in Chaucer we touch the true height, and look abroad into the kingdoms and glories of our poetical literature,—it is with Chaucer that we begin our 'Books of the Poets,' our collections and selections, our pride of place and names"— high praise, indeed. And while students may find her rapturous acclaim of Chaucer appealing, it is her response to two prominent scholarly discussions of Chaucer from her day that students will likely find more useful in their own critical examinations of the poet.

The first discussion involves Chaucer's meter, a topic of several of the excerpts in this text. Barrett Browning criticizes what she considers to be an odd obsession with Chaucer's rhythms: "Critics, indeed, have set up a system based upon the crushed atoms of first principles, maintaining that poor Chaucer wrote by accent only! Grant to them that he counted no verses on his fingers; grant that he never disciplined his highest thoughts to walk up and down in a paddock—ten paces and a turn; grant that his singing is not after the likeness of their singsong; but there end your admissions." Dismissing these arguments, she concludes that, "Chaucer wrote by quantity, just as Homer did before him, as Goethe did after him, just as all poets must. Rules differ, principles are identical. All rhythm presupposes quantity. Organ-pipe or harp, the musician plays by time. Greek or English, Chaucer or Pope, the poet sings by time."

Perhaps the more interesting scholarly debate Barrett Browning engages in also references the work of Samuel Johnson (1755). In comparing Gower to Chaucer, Barrett Browning notes, as Johnson did, that Gower, through the voice of Venus, calls Chaucer "mi disciple." Johnson assumes that Gower means quite literally that he, Gower, is Chaucer's master, and not the narrator Venus (most contemporary critics do not accuse Gower of such hubris.) This causes Johnson to conclude that Gower is the true founder of English poetry. Barrett Browning, while disagreeing with Johnson, believes that Gower's line also suggests that he was Chaucer's mentor, and that this suggestion was not wholly accurate. She argues that Gower's declaration likely spurred Chaucer on to his greatest work, as a response to the challenge Gower issued in his *Confessio Amantis*.

Barrett Browning concludes her essay by comparing Chaucer and Spenser, noting interestingly that "Chaucer has a cheerful humanity: Spenser, a cheerful ideality." Her comparison of the two might prove beneficial to students who are likewise comparing this pair of great English writers.

⸙ ⸙ ⸙

But it is in Chaucer we touch the true height, and look abroad into the kingdoms and glories of our poetical literature,—it is with Chaucer that we begin our 'Books of the Poets,' our collections and selections, our pride of place and names. And the genius of the poet shares the character of his position: he was made for an early poet, and the metaphors of dawn and spring doubly become him. A morning star, a lark's exultation, cannot usher in a glory better. The 'cheerful morning face,' 'the breezy call of incense-breathing morn,' you recognise in his countenance and voice: it is a voice full of promise and prophecy. He is the good omen of our poetry, the 'good bird,' according to the Romans, 'the best good angel of the spring,' the nightingale, according to his own creed of good luck heard before the cuckoo,

> Up rose the sunne, and uprose Emilie,

and uprose her poet, the first of a line of kings, conscious of futurity in his smile. He is a king, and inherits the earth, and expands his great soul smilingly to embrace his great heritage. Nothing is too high for him to touch with a thought, nothing too low to dower with an affection. As a complete creature cognate of life and death, he cries upon God,—as a sympathetic creature he singles out a daisy from the universe ('si douce est la marguerite'), to lie down by half a summer's day[1], and bless it for fellowship. His senses are open and delicate, like a young child's—his sensibilities capacious of supersensual relations, like an experienced thinker's. Child-like, too, his tears and smiles lie at the edge of his eyes, and he is one proof more among the many, that the deepest pathos and the quickest gaieties hide together in the same nature. He is too wakeful and curious to lose the stirring of a leaf, yet not too wide awake to see visions of green and white ladies[2] between the branches; and a fair House of Fame and a noble Court of Love[3] are built and holden in the winking of his eyelash. And because his imagination is neither too 'high fantastical' to refuse proudly the gravitation of the earth, nor too 'light of love' to lose it carelessly, he can create as well as dream, and work with clay as well as cloud; and when his men and women stand by the actual ones, your stop-watch shall reckon no difference in the beating of their hearts. He knew the secret of nature and art,—that truth is beauty,—and saying 'I will make "A Wife of Bath" as well as Emilie, and you shall remember her as long,' we do remember her as long. And he sent us a train of pilgrims, each with a distinct individuality apart from the pilgrimage, all the way from Southwark, and the Tabard Inn, to Canterbury and Becket's shrine: and their laughter comes never to an end, and their talk goes on with the stars, and all the railroads which may intersect the spoilt earth for ever, cannot hush the 'tramp tramp' of their horses' feet.

Controversy is provocative. We cannot help observing, because certain critics observe otherwise, that Chaucer utters as true music as ever came from poet or musician; that some of the sweetest cadences in all our English are extant in his— 'swete upon his tongue' in completest modulation. Let 'Den-ham's strength and Waller's sweetness join' the Io paean of a later age, the *'eurekamen'* of Pope and his generation. Not one of the 'Queen Anne's men' measuring out tuneful breath upon their fingers, like ribbons for topknots, did know the art of versification as the old rude Chaucer knew it. Call him rude for the picturesqueness of the epithet; but his verse has, at least, as much regularity in the sense of true art, and more manifestly in proportion to our increasing acquaintance with his dialect and pronunciation, as can be discovered or dreamed in the French school. Critics, indeed, have set up a system based upon the crushed atoms of first principles, maintaining that poor Chaucer wrote by accent only! Grant to them that he counted no verses on his fingers; grant that he never disciplined his highest thoughts to walk up and down in a paddock—ten paces and a turn; grant that his singing is not after the likeness of their singsong; but there end your admissions. It is our ineffaceable impression, in fact, that the whole theory of accent and quantity held in relation to ancient and modern poetry stands upon a fallacy, totters rather than stands; and that, when considered in connection with such old moderns as our Chaucer, the fallaciousness is especially apparent. Chaucer wrote by quantity, just as Homer did before him, as Goethe did after him, just as all poets must. Rules differ, principles are identical. All rhythm presupposes quantity. Organ-pipe or harp, the musician plays by time. Greek or English, Chaucer or Pope, the poet sings by time. What is this accent but a stroke, an emphasis with a successive pause to make complete the time? And what is the difference between this accent and quantity, but the difference between a harp-note and an organ-note? otherwise, quantity expressed in different ways? It is as easy for matter to subsist out of space, as music out of time.

Side by side with Chaucer comes Gower, who is ungratefully disregarded too often, because side by side with Chaucer. He who rides in the king's chariot will miss the people's 'hie est.' Could Gower be considered apart, there might be found signs in him of an independent royalty, however his fate may seem to lie in waiting for ever in his brother's ante-chamber, like Napoleon's tame kings. To speak our mind, he has been much undervalued. He is nailed to a comparative degree; and everybody seems to make it a condition of speaking of him, that something be called inferior within him, and something superior out of him. He is laid down flat, as a dark background for 'throwing out' Chaucer's light; he is used as a *pou sto* for leaping up into the empyrean of Chaucer's praise. This is not just nor worthy. His principal poem, the *Confessio Amantis,* preceded the *Canterbury Tales,* and proves an abundant fancy, a full head and full heart, and neither ineloquent.[4] We do not praise its design,—in which the father confessor is set up as a story-teller, like the bishop of Tricca, 'avec l'ame,' like the Cardinal de Retz, 'le moins ecclesiastique du monde,' —while we admit that he tells his stories as if born to the manner of it, and that they are not much the graver, nor, peradventure, the holier either, for the circumstance of the confessorship. They are, indeed, told gracefully and pleasantly enough, and if with no superfluous life and gesture, with an active sense of beauty in some sort, and as flowing a rhythm as may bear comparison with many octosyllabics of our day; Chaucer himself having done more honour to their worth as stories than we can do in our praise, by adopting and crowning several of their number for king's sons within his own palaces.[5] And this recalls that, at the opening of one glorious felony, the *Man of Lawes Tale,* he has written, a little unlawfully and ungratefully considering the connection, some lines of harsh significance upon poor Gower,[6] whence has been conjectured by the grey gossips of criticism, a literary jealousy, an unholy enmity, nothing less than a soul-chasm between the contemporary poets. We believe nothing of it; no nor of the Shakespeare and jonson feud after it:

'To alle such cursed stories we saie fy.'

That Chaucer wrote in irritation is clear[7]: that he was angry seriously and lastingly, or beyond the pastime of passion spent in a verse as provoked by a verse, there appears to us no reason for crediting. But our idea of the nature of the irritation will expound itself in our idea of the offence, which is here in Dan Gower's proper words, as extracted from the Ladie Venus's speech in the *Confessio Amantis:*

'And grete well Chaucer whan ye mete,
As my disciple and poete! . . .
Forthy now in his daies old,
Thou shalt him telle this message,
That he upon his latter age,
To sette an ende of alle his werke
As he who is mine owne clerke,
Do make his testament of love.'

We would not slander Chaucer's temper,—we believe, on the contrary, that he had the sweetest temper in the world,—and still it is our conviction, none the weaker, that he was far from being entirely pleased by this 'message.' We are sure he did not like the message, and not many poets would. His 'elvish countenance' might well grow dark, and 'his sugred mouth' speak somewhat sourly, in response to such a message. Decidedly, in our own opinion, it was an impertinent message, a provocative message, a most inexcusable and odious message! Waxing hotter ourselves the longer we think of it, there is the more excuse for Chaucer. For, consider, gentle reader! this indecorous message preceded the appearance of the *Canterbury Tales*,[8] and proceeded from a rival poet in the act of completing his principal work,—its plain significance being 'I have done my poem, and you cannot do yours because you are superannuated.' And this, while the great poet addressed was looking farther forward than the visible horizon, his eyes dilated with a mighty purpose. And to be counselled by this, to shut them forsooth, and take his crook and dog and place in the valleys like a grey shepherd of the Pyrenees—he, who felt his foot strong upon the heights! he, with no wrinkle on his forehead deep enough to touch the outermost of inward smooth dreams—he, in the divine youth of his healthy soul, in the quenchless love of his embracing sympathies, in the untired working of his perpetual energies,—to 'make an ende of alle his werke' and be old, as if he were not a poet! 'Go to, O vain man,'—we do not reckon the age of the poet's soul by the shadow on the dial! Enough that it falls upon his grave.

But this Sackville stands too low for admeasurement with Spenser, and we must look back, if covetous of comparisons, to some one of a loftier and more kingly stature. We must look back far, and stop at Chaucer. Spenser and Chaucer do naturally remind us of each other, they two being the most cheerful-hearted of the poets—with whom cheerfulness, as an attribute of poetry, is scarcely a common gift.

Chaucer and Spenser fulfilled their destiny, and grew to their mutual likeness as cheerful poets, by certain of the former processes [glorifying sensual things with the inward sense, &c.]. They two are alike in their cheerfulness, yet are their cheerfulnesses most unlike. Each poet laughs: yet their laughters ring with as far a difference as the sheep-bell on the hill, and the joy-bell in the city. Each is earnest in his gladness: each active in persuading you of it. You are persuaded, and hold each for a cheerful man. The whole difference is, that Chaucer has a cheerful humanity: Spenser, a cheerful ideality. One, rejoices walking on the sunny side of the street; the other, walking out of the street in a way of his own, kept green by a blessed vision. One, uses the adroitness of his fancy by distilling out of the visible universe her occult smiles; the other, by fleeing beyond the possible frown, the occasions of natural ills, to that 'cave of cloud' where he may smile safely to himself. One, holds festival with men—seldom so coarse and loud, indeed, as to startle the deer from their green covert at Woodstock[9]—or with homely Nature and her 'dame Marguerite' low in the grasses:[10] the other adopts, for his playfellows, imaginary or spiritual existences, and will not say a word to Nature herself, unless it please her to dress for his masque, and speak daintily sweet, and rare like a spirit. The human heart of one utters oracles; the imagination of the other speaks for his heart, and we miss no prophecy. For music, we praised Chaucer's, and not only as Dryden did, for 'a Scotch tune.' But never issued there from lip or instrument, or the tuned causes of nature, more lovely sound than we gather from our Spenser's Art. His rhythm is the continuity of melody. It is the singing of an angel in a dream.

Shirley is the last dramatist, *Valete et plaudite, o posteri*. Standing in his traces, and looking backward and before, we became aware of the distinct demarcations of five eras of English poetry: the first, the Chaucerian, although we might call it *Chaucer*, the second, the Elizabethan; the third, which culminates in Cowley; the fourth, in Dryden and the French school; the fifth, the return to nature of Cowper and his successors of our day. These five rings mark the age of the fair and stingless serpent we are impelled, like the Ancient Mariner, to bless—but not 'unaware.' *'Ah benedicite!'* we bless her so, out of our Chaucer's rubric, softly, but with a plaintiveness of pleasure.

Notes

1. *Prologue* to the *Legende of Good Women*, 1. 179–182 of the 2nd cast of the Prologue.—Furnivall

> 2. And by the hande he helde this noble quene,
>
> Corowned with white, and clothed al in grene.
>
> *(Prologue to the Legende,* 2nd cast, 1. 241–2.)

But the allusion is doubtless to the Ladies of *The Flower & Leaf,* which certainly Chaucer never wrote. It must be more than 50 years after his date.—F.

3. This poem cannot be proved to be Chaucer's.—F.

4. Apply here what Mrs Browning (that is, Miss Barrett) says at p. 163–4 on the difference between the Elizabethan period and the Cowley one. "The voices are eloquent enough, thoughtful enough, fanciful enough; but something is defective. Can any one suffer, as an experimental reader, the transition between the second and third periods, without feeling that something is defective? What is so? And who dares to guess that it may be INSPIRATION?" Gower, of course, writes most respectable verse; but he is a *bore.* It's just like him, to patronise Chaucer!—F.

5. I do not believe for a moment that Chaucer adapted his stories from Gower, as he had probably written his Constance, &c, long before Gower's *Confessio* appeared. The stories were common enough; and both writers went to the same original. But out of that they made very different poems.—F.

6. 1. 78–88. Where he says that he wouldn't write of such cursed stories as Canace's (who loved her own brother sinfully), or such unnatural abominations as Tyro Apollonius, who ravisht his own daughter, and of whom Gower had written the story in his *Confessio.* Why shouldn't Chaucer have been chaffing the "moral Gower," that most respectable man, for his gross impropriety? It's just the kind of thing Chaucer would have enjoyed, especially when he had himself just finisht his free-and-easy *Miller's* and *Reeve's Tales,* and broken off the *Cook's,* because the flavour was getting a little too strong. He, in fact, said to his readers, "You may perhaps think my stories a little naughty; but really they're not half so bad as that moral and proper old gentleman's who's Poet Lawreate. Mine are only fun, whereas that old respectable's are about incest! Bad I may be; but as bad as that proper old Gower who writes about unnatural crimes!! God forbid!!!" It's something like Swinburne reproaching Tupper for the immoral tendency of his productions. And who wouldn't enjoy that joke?—F.

7. Not to me.—F.

8. Did the *Canterbury Tales* ever *appear* at all, in our sense of the word? Separate Tales, or fragments or groups of them, may have been circulated during Chaucer's life; but assuredly they never "appeared" as a whole, like Gower's *Confessio* did.—F.

9. There is no foundation for the late legend that connects Chaucer with Woodstock.—F.

10. *Prologue* to the *Legende*.—F.

> —Elizabeth Barrett Browning, "Mrs. Browning on Chaucer,"
> (1842), *Essays on Chaucer*, ed. Frederick J. Furnivall,
> 1868–94, pp. 157–64

JAMES RUSSELL LOWELL (1846)

An important American literary critic, James Russell Lowell (1819–91) was also a noted poet and abolitionist. *Conversations on Some of the Old Poets* was Lowell's first work of book-length criticism, and it proved to be a commercial and critical hit. The book contains a series of dialogues between two young narrators, Philip and John, who may represent the more conservative and free-thinking sides of Lowell's own personality. The two narrators hold conversations on numerous authors, including Chaucer, George Chapman, John Ford, Philip Massinger, and John Webster, though Lowell also included opinions on topics ranging from the abolition movement to the church to public manners as part of the literary discussion.

In the following excerpt, Philip and John's discussion is largely focused on "The Nun's Priest's Tale," though they also spend time examining "The Knight's Tale." In the context of those discussions, Lowell first notes, "You must put no faith at all in any idea you may have got of Chaucer from Dryden or Pope." Though Lowell admires the work of Chaucer's most prominent translators/adaptors, he feels that neither ultimately does justice to the medieval writer's oeuvre. Philip also notes Chaucer's great merits as a writer, which includes his sincerity, his minute observation of nature, and his humor. Speaking of his humor, John notes to Philip, "After all, your Chaucer was a satirist, and you should, in justice, test him with the same acid which you applied so remorselessly to Pope," to which Philip responds, "Chaucer's satire is of quite another complexion. A hearty laugh and a thrust in the ribs are his weapons. He makes fun of you to your face, and, even if you wince a little, you cannot help joining in his mirth."

Lowell also makes an interesting observation on the tendency to modernize Chaucer's language, lamenting "how much our Chaucer loses by the process," though Lowell himself does this throughout the text. Lowell also notes that "Chaucer reminds me oftenest of Crabbe," though he concludes that Crabbe is ultimately not quite at Chaucer's level. In articulating the quality of Chaucer that makes him such a remarkable poet, Lowell writes succinctly, "When Chaucer describes his Shipman, we seem to smell tar." Students will find many useful observations about Chaucer sprinkled throughout Lowell's dialogue, and may even find it helpful to imitate Lowell's critical conversational method in their own explorations of Chaucer's work.

Philip: You must put no faith at all in any idea you may have got of Chaucer from Dryden or Pope. Dryden appreciated his original better than Pope; but neither of them had a particle of his humor, nor of the simplicity of his pathos. The strong point in Pope's displays of sentiment is in the graceful management of a cambric handkerchief. You do not believe a word that Heloise says, and feel all the while that she is squeezing out her tears as if from a half-dry sponge. Pope was not a man to understand the quiet tenderness of Chaucer, where you almost seem to hear the hot tears fall, and the simple, choking words sobbed out. I know no author so tender as he; Shakspeare himself was hardly so. There is no declamation in his grief. Dante is scarcely more downright and plain. To show you how little justice Dryden has done him, I will first read you a few lines from his version of "The Knight's Tale," and then the corresponding ones of the original. It is the death-scene of Arcite.

> Conscience (that of all physic works the last)
> Caused him to send for Emily in haste;
> With her, at his desire, came Palamon.
> Then, on his pillow raised, he thus begun:
> 'No language can express the smallest part
> Of what I feel and suffer in my heart
> For you, whom best I love and value most.
> But to your service I bequeath my ghost;
> *Which, from this mortal body when untied,*
> Unseen, unheard, shall hover at your side,
> Nor fright you waking, nor your sleep offend,
> But wait officious, and your steps attend.
> *How I have loved! Excuse my faltering tongue;*
> *My spirit's feeble and my pains are strong;*
> This I may say: I only grieve to die,
> Because I lose *my charming Emily.'*

John: I am quite losing my patience. The sentiment of Giles Scroggins, and the verse of Blackmore! Surely, nothing but the meanest servility to his original could excuse such slovenly workmanship as this.

Philip: There is worse to come. Of its fidelity as a translation you can judge for yourself, when you hear Chaucer.

> 'To die when Heaven had put you in my power,
> Fate could not choose a more malicious hour!
> What greater curse could envious Fortune give
> Than just to die when I began to live?
> *Vain men, how vanishing a bliss we crave!*
> *Now warm in love, now withering in the grave!*
> *Never, O, never more to see the sun!*
> *Still dark in a damp vault, and still alone!*
> This fate is common.'

I wish you especially to bear in mind the lines I have emphasized. Notice, too, how the rhyme is impertinently forced upon the attention throughout. We can hardly help wondering if a nuncupatory testament were ever spoken in verse before. There is none of this French-lustre in Chaucer.

> Arcite must die;
> For which he sendeth after Emily,
> And Palamon, that was his cousin dear;
> Then spake he thus, as ye shall after hear:
> 'Ne'er may the woful spirit in my heart
> Declare one point of all my sorrow's smart
> To you, my lady, that I love the most;
> But I bequeath the service of my ghost
> To you aboven any cre-a-ture,
> Since that my life may now no longer dure.
> Alas, the woe! alas, the pains so strong,
> That I for you have suffered,—and so long!
> Alas, the death! alas, mine Emily!
> Alas, the parting of our company!
> Alas, my heart's true queen! alas, my wife!
> My heart's dear lady, ender of my life!
> What is this world? What asketh man to have?
> Now with his love,—now in his cold, cold grave,
> Alone, withouten any company!
> Farewell, my sweet! farewell, mine Emily!

And softly take me in your armes twey (two arms),
For love of God, and hearken what I say.'

John: Perfect! I would not have a word changed, except the second "cold" before "grave." It takes away from the simplicity, and injures the effect accordingly. In the lines just before that, I could fancy that I heard the dying man gasp for breath. After hearing this, Dryden's exclamation-marks savor of the playbills, where one sees them drawn up in platoons, as a bodyguard to the name of an indifferent player,—their number being increased in proportion as the attraction diminishes. And in that seemingly redundant line,

Alone, withouten any company,

how does the repetition and amplification give force and bitterness to the thought, as if Arcite must need dwell on his expected loneliness, in order to feel it fully! There is nothing here about *"charming* Emily," *"envious* Fortune,"—no bandying of compliments. Death shows to Arcite, as he does mostly to those who are cut off suddenly in the May-time and blossom of the senses, as a bleak, bony skeleton, and nothing more. Dryden, I remember, in his "Art of Poetry," says,

Chaucer alone, fixed on this solid base,
In his old style conserve's a modern grace;
Too happy, if the freedom of his rhymes
Offended not the method of our times.

But if what you have read (unless you have softened it greatly) be a specimen of his rudeness, save us from such "method" as that of Dryden!

Philip: I hardly changed a syllable. The word to which you objected, as redundant, was an addition of my own to eke out the measure; "colde" being pronounced as two syllables in Chaucer's time. The language of the heart never grows obsolete or antiquated, but falls as musically from the tongue now as when it was first uttered. Such lustiness and health of thought and expression seldom fail of leaving issue behind them. One may trace a family-likeness to these in many of Spenser's lines, and I please myself sometimes with imagining pencil-marks of Shakspeare's against some of my favorite passages in Chaucer. At least, the relationship may be traced through Spenser, who calls Chaucer his master, and to whom Shakspeare pays nearly as high a compliment. . . .

John: After all, your Chaucer was a satirist, and you should, in justice, test him with the same acid which you applied so remorselessly to Pope.

Philip: Chaucer's satire is of quite another complexion. A hearty laugh and a thrust in the ribs are his weapons. He makes fun of you to your face,

and, even if you wince a little, you cannot help joining in his mirth. He does not hate a vice because he has a spite against the man who is guilty of it. He does not cry, "A rat i' the arras!" and run his sword through a defenceless old man behind it. But it is not for his humor, nor, indeed, for any one quality, that our old Chaucer is dear and sacred to me. I love to call him *old* Chaucer. The farther I can throw him back into the past, the dearer he grows; so sweet is it to mark how his plainness and sincerity outlive all changes of the outward world. Antiquity has always something reverend in it. Even its most material and perishable form, which we see in pyramids, cairns, and the like, is brooded over by a mysterious presence which strangely awes us. Whatever has been hallowed by the love and pity, by the smiles and tears of men, becomes something more to us than the moss-covered epitaph of a buried age. There was a meaning in the hieroglyphics, which Champollion could not make plainer. It is only from association with Man that any thing seems old. The quarries of the Nile may be coeval with the planet itself, yet it is only the still fresh dints of the Coptic chisel that gift them with the spell of ancientness. Let but the skeleton of a man be found among the remains of those extinct antediluvian monsters, and straightway that which now claimed our homage as a triumph of comparative anatomy, shall become full of awe and mystery, and dim with the gray dawnlight of time. Once, from those shapeless holes, a human soul looked forth upon its huge empire of past and future. Once, beneath those crumbling ribs, beat a human heart, that seeming narrow isthmus between time and eternity, wherein there was yet room for hope and fear, and love and sorrow, to dwell, with all their wondrous glooms and splendors. Before, we could have gone no farther back than Cuvier. Those mighty bones of ichthyosauri and plesiosauri seemed rather a record of his energy and patience, than of a living epoch in earth's history. Now, how modern and of to-day seem Memnon and Elephanta! If there be a vener-ableness in any outward symbols, in which rude and dumb fashion the soul of man first strove to utter itself, how much more is there in the clearer and more inspired sentences of ancient lawgivers and poets!

John: You have contrived very adroitly to get the Deluge between us. I shall not attempt the perilous navigation to your side, and can only wish you a safe return to mine. Camoens swam ashore from a shipwreck, with the Lusiad in his teeth; and I hope you will do as much for Chaucer. I long to hear more of him.

Philip: It would be easier for me to emulate Waterton's ride on the alligator's back, and make an extempore steed of the most tractable-looking ichthyosaurus I can lay hands on. However, here I am safely back again. But before I read you any thing else from Chaucer, I must please myself by praising him a little more. His simplicity often reminds me of Homer; but, except in the single quality of *invention,* I prefer him to the Ionian. Yet we must remember that he shares this deficiency with Shakspeare, who scarcely ever scrupled to run in debt for his plots. . . .

Philip: But we must come back to Chaucer. There is in him the exuberant freshness and greenness of spring. Every thing he touches leaps into full blossom. His gladness and humor and pathos are irrepressible as a fountain. Dam them with a prosaic subject, and they overleap it in a sparkling cascade that turns even the hindrance to a beauty. Choke them with a tedious theological disquisition, and they bubble up forthwith, all around it, with a delighted gurgle. There is no cabalistic Undine stone or seal-of-Solomon that can shut them up for ever. Reading him is like brushing through the dewy grass at sunrise. Every thing is new and sparkling and fragrant. He is of kin to Belphoebe, whose

> Birth was of the womb of morning dew,
> And her conception of the joyous prime.

I speak now of what was truly Chaucer. I strip away from him all that belonged to the time in which he lived, and judge him only by what belongs equally to all times. For it is only in as far as a poet advances into the universal, that he approaches immortality. There is no nebulosity of sentiment about him, no insipid vagueness in his sympathies. His first merit, the chief one in all art, is sincerity. He does not strive to body forth something which shall have a meaning; but, having a clear meaning in his heart, he gives it as clear a shape. Sir Philip Sydney was of his mind, when he bade poets look into their own hearts and write. He is the most unconventional of poets, and the frankest. If his story be dull, he rids his hearers of all uncomfortable qualms by being himself the first to yawn. He would have fared but ill in our day, when the naked feelings are made liable to the penalties of an act for the punishment of indecent exposure. Very little care had he for the mere decencies of life. Were he alive now, I can conceive him sending a shudder through St. James's Coffee-house, by thrusting his knife into his mouth; or making all Regent Street shriek for harts-horn, by giving a cab-driver as good as he sent, in a style that would have pleased old Burton. The highest merit of a poem is, that it reflects alike the subject and the poet. It should be neither objective nor subjective exclusively. Reason should stand at the helm, though the wayward breezes of feeling must puff the sails. Nature has hinted at this, by setting the eyes higher than the heart. Chaucer's poems can claim more of the former than of the latter of these excellencies. Observation of outward nature and life is more apparent in them than a deep inward experience, and it is the observation of a cheerful, unwearied spirit. His innocent self-forgetfulness gives us the truest glimpses into his own nature, and, at the same time, makes his pictures of outward objects wonderfully clear and vivid. Though many of his poems are written in the first person, yet there is not a shade of egoism in them. It is but the simple art of the story-teller, to give more reality to what he tells.

John: Yes, it was not till our own day that the poets discovered what mystical significance had been lying dormant for ages in a capital I. It seems strange that a letter of such powerful bewitchment had not made part of the juggling wares of the Cabalists and Theurgists. Yet we find no mention of it in Rabbi Akiba or Cornelius Agrippa. Byron wrought miracles with it. I fear that the noble Stylites of modern song, who, from his lonely pillar of self, drew crowds of admiring votaries to listen to the groans of his self-inflicted misery, would have been left only to feel the cold and hunger of his shelterless pinnacle in Chaucer's simpler day.

Philip: Yes, Byron always reminds me of that criminal who was shut in a dungeon, the walls of which grew every day narrower and narrower, till they crushed him at last. His selfishness walled him in, from the first; so that he was never open to the sweet influences of nature, and those sweeter ones which the true heart finds in life. The sides of his jail were semi-transparent, giving him a muddy view of things immediately about him; but selfishness always builds a thick roof overhead, to cut off the heavenward gaze of the spirit. And how did it press the very life out of him, in the end!

John: Byron's spirit was more halt than his body. It had been well for him, had he been as ashamed, or at least as conscious, of one as of the other. He should have been banished, like Philoctetes, to some Isle of Lemnos, where his lameness should not have been offensive and contagious. As it was, the world fell in love with the defect. Some malicious Puck had dropped the juice of love-in-idleness upon its eyes, and limping came quite into fashion. We have never yet had a true likeness of Byron. Leigh Hunt's, I think, is more faithful than Moore's. Moore never forgot that his friend was a lord, and seemed to feel that he was paying himself a side-compliment in writing a life of him. I always imagine Moore's portrait of Byron with an "I am, my dear Moore, yours, &c." written under it, as a specimen of his autography. But to our poet. You have given me a touch of his pathos; let me hear some of the humor which you have commended so highly.

Philip: Praise beforehand deadens the flavor of the wine; so that, if you are disappointed, the blame must be laid upon me. I will read you a few passages from his "Nun's Priest's Tale." It has been modernized by Dryden, under the title of "The Cock and the Fox"; but he has lost much of the raciness of the original. I have chosen this tale, because it will, at the same time, give you an idea of his minute observation of nature. I shall modernize it as I read, preserving as much as possible the language, and, above all, the spirit of the original. But you must never forget how much our Chaucer loses by the process. The story begins with a description of the poor widow who owns the hero of the story, Sir Chaunticlere. Then we have a glimpse of the hero himself. The widow has

> A yard enclosed all about
> With sticks, and also a dry ditch without,
> In which she had a cock night Chaunticlere;
> In all the land for voice was not his peer;
> Not merrier notes the merry organ plays
> Within the churches, upon holydays;
> And surer was his crowing in his lodge
> Than is a clock, or abbey horologe:
> He knew by nature every step to trace
> Of the equinoctial in his native place,
> And, when fifteen degrees it had ascended,
> Then crew he so as might not be amended.
> His comb was redder than the fine coral,
> Embattled as it were a castle-wall;
> His bill was black, and like the jet it shone;
> Like azure were his legs and toes each one;
> His nails were white as lilies in the grass,
> And like the burned gold his color was.

John: What gusto! If he had been painting Arthur or Charlemagne, he would not have selected his colors with more care. Without pulling out a feather from his hero's cockhood, he contrives to give him a human interest. How admirable is the little humorous thrust at the astronomers, too, in restricting Sir Chaunticlere's knowledge of the heavenly motions to his own village!

Philip: Yes, Chaucer has the true poet's heart. One thing is as precious to him in point of beauty as another. He would have described his lady's cheek by the same flower to which he has here likened the nails of Chaunticlere. To go on with our story.

> This gentle cock had in his governance
> Seven wifely hens to do him all pleasaunce,
> Of whom the fairest-colored in the throat
> Was known as the fair damsel Partelote;

Courteous she was, discreet and debonair,
Companionable, and bore herself so fair,
Sithence the hour she was a seven-night old,
That truly she the royal heart did hold
Of Chaunticlere bound fast in every limb;
He loved her so, that it was well with him:
But such a joy it was to hear them sing,
When that the bright sun in the east 'gan spring,
In sweet accord!

Chaunticlere, one morning, awakens his fair wife Partelote by a dreadful groaning; and, on her asking the cause, informs her that it must have been the effect of a bad dream he had been haunted by.

I dreamed, that, as I roamed up and down,
Within our yard, I there beheld a beast,
Like to a hound, that would have made arrest
Upon my body, and have had me dead.
His color twixt a yellow was and red,
And tipped were his tail and both his ears
With black, unlike the remnant of his hairs.
His snout was small, and glowing were his eyes:
Still, for his look, the heart within me dies.
Partelote treats his fears with scorn. She asks, indignantly,
How durst you now for shame say to your love
That any thing could make you feel afeard?
Have you no manly heart, yet have a beard?

She then gives him a lecture on the physiological causes of dreams, hints at a superfluity of bile, and recommends some simple remedy which her own housewifely skill can concoct from herbs that grow within the limits of his own manor. She also quotes Cato's opinion of the small faith to be put in dreams. Her lord, who does not seem superior to the common prejudice against having his wife make too liberal a display of her learning, replies by overwhelming her with an avalanche of weighty authorities, each one of which, he tells her, is worth more than ever Cato was. He concludes with a contemptuous defiance of all manner of doses, softening it toward his lady by an adroit compliment.

But let us speak of mirth, and stint of this:
Dame Partelote, as I have hope of bliss,
Of one thing God hath sent me largest grace;

For, when I see the beauty of your face,
You are so scarlet red about your eyes,
That, when I look on you, my terror dies;
For just so sure as *in principio*
Mulier est hominis confusio,
(Madam, the meaning of this Latin is,
Woman is man's chief joy and sovereign bliss,)
Whene'er I feel at night your downy side,
I am so full of solace and of pride,
That I defy the threatenings of my dream.
And, with that word, he flew down from the
        beam,—
For it was day,—and eke his spouses all;
And with a chuck he 'gan them for to call,
For he had found a corn lay in the yard:
Royal he was, and felt no more afeard;
He looketh as a lion eyes his foes,
And roameth up and down upon his toes;
Scarcely he deigneth set his feet to ground;
He chucketh when a kernel he hath found,
And all his wives run to him at his call.

John: What an admirable barn-yard picture! The very chanticleer of our childhood, whose parallel Bucks county and Dorking have striven in vain to satisfy our maturer vision with! A chanticleer whose memory writes *Ichabod* upon the most populous and palatial fowl-houses of manhood! Chaucer's Pegasus ambles along as easily, and crops the grass and daisies of the roadside as contentedly, as if he had forgotten his wings.

Philip: Yes, the work in hand is, for the time, noblest in the estimation of our poet. His eye never looks beyond it, or cheats it of its due regard by pining for something fairer and more worthy. The royalty is where he is, whether in hovel or palace. Nothing that God has not thought it beneath him to make does he deem it beneath him to study and prove worthy of all admiration. Wordsworth is like him in this. . . .

Chaucer reminds me oftenest of Crabbe, in the unstudied plainness of his sentiment, and the minuteness of his descriptions. But, in Crabbe's poetry, Tyburn-tree is seen looming up in the distance, and the bell of the parish workhouse is heard jangling. It had been better for Crabbe, if he had studied Chaucer more and Pope less. The frigid artificiality of his verse often contrasts almost ludicrously with the rudeness of his theme. It is Captain Kidd in a starched cambric neckcloth and white gloves. When Chaucer describes his Shipman, we seem to smell tar.

> There also was a shipman from far west;
> For aught I know, in Dartmouth he abode;
> Well as he could upon a hack he rode,
> All in a shirt of tow-cloth to the knee;
> A dagger hanging by a lace had he,
> About his neck, under his arm adown;
> The summer's heat had made his hue all brown.
> He was a right good fellow certainly,
> And many a cargo of good wine had he
> Run from Bordeaux while the tidewaiter slept;
> Of a nice conscience no great care he kept,
> If that he fought and had the upperhand,
> By water he sent them home to every land;
> But in his craft to reckon well the tides,
> The deep sea currents, and the shoals besides,
> The sun's height and the moon's, and pilotage,—
> There was none such from Hull unto Carthage;
> Hardy he was and wise, I undertake;
> His beard had felt full many a tempest's shake;
> He knew well all the havens as they were
> From Gothland to the Cape de Finisterre,
> And every creek in Brittany and Spain;
> His trusty bark was named the Magdelaine.

John: The "savage Rosa" never dashed the lights and shades upon one of his bandits with more bold and picturesque effect. How that storm-grizzled beard stands out from the canvass! The effect is so real, that it seems as if the brown old sea-king had sat for his portrait, and that every stroke of the brush had been laid on within reach of the dagger hanging at his side. Witness the amiable tints thrown in here and there, to palliate a grim wrinkle or a shaggy eyebrow. The poet takes care to tell us that

> He was a right good fellow certainly,

lest his sitter take umbrage at the recital of his smuggling exploits in the next verse. And then with what a rough kind of humor he lets us into the secret of his murderous propensities, by hinting that he gave a passage home by water to those of whom he got the upperhand! In spite of the would-be good-humored leer, the cut-throat look shows through. It may be very pleasant riding with him as far as Canterbury, and we might even laugh at his clumsiness in the saddle, but we feel all the while that we had rather not be overhauled by him upon the high seas. His short and easy method of sending acquaintances thus casually made to their respective homes, by water, we should not be inclined to admire so much as he himself would; especially if, as a preliminary step, he should attempt to add to the convenience of our respiratory organs with that ugly dagger of his, by opening a larger aperture somewhere nearer to the lungs. We should be inclined to distrust those extraordinary powers of natation for which he would give us credit. Even Lord Byron, I imagine, would dislike to mount that steed that "knew its rider" so well, or even to "lay his hand upon its mane," if our friend, the Shipman, held the stirrup.

Philip: The whole prologue to the Canterbury Tales is equally admirable, but there is not time for me to read the whole. You must do that for yourself. I only give you a bunch or two of grapes. To enjoy the fruit in its perfection, you must go into the vineyard yourself, and pluck it with the bloom on, before the flavor of the sunshine has yet faded out of it; enjoying the play of light upon the leaves also, and the apt disposition of the clusters, each lending a grace to the other.

John: Your metaphor pleases me. I like the grapes better than the wine which is pressed out of them, and they seem to me a fitting emblem of Chaucer's natural innocence. Elizabeth Barrett, a woman whose genius I admire, says very beautifully of Chaucer,

> Old Chaucer, with his infantine,
> Familiar clasp of things divine,—
> *That stain upon his lips is wine.*

I had rather think it pure grape-juice. The first two lines take hold of my heart so that I believe them intuitively, and doubt not but my larger acquaintance with Chaucer will prove them to be true.

Philip: I admire them as much as you do, and to me they seem to condense all that can be said of Chaucer. But one must know him thoroughly to feel their truth and fitness fully. At the first glimpse you get of his face, you are struck with the merry twinkle of his eye, and the suppressed smile upon his lips, which betrays itself as surely as a child in playing hide-and-seek. It is hard to believe that so happy a spirit can have ever felt the galling of that

> Chain wherewith we are darkly bound,

or have beaten its vain wings against the insensible gates of that awful mystery whose key can never be enticed from the hand of the warder,

Death. But presently the broad, quiet forehead, the look of patient earnestness, and the benignant reverence of the slightly bowed head, make us quite forget the lightsome impression of our first look. Yet in the next moment it comes back upon us again more strongly than ever. Humor is always a main ingredient in highly poetical natures. It is almost always the superficial indication of a rich vein of pathos, nay, of tragic feeling, below. Wordsworth seems to be an exception. Yet there is a gleam of it in his sketch of that philosopher

> Who could peep and botanize
> Upon his mother's grave,

and of a grim, reluctant sort in some parts of Peter Bell and the Wagoner. But he was glad to sink a shaft beneath the surface, where he could gather the more precious ore, and dwell retired from the jeers of a boorish world. In Chaucer's poetry, the humor is playing all the time round the horizon, like heat-lightning. It is unexpected and unpredictable; but, as soon as you turn away from watching for it, behold, it flashes again as innocently and softly as ever. It mingles even with his pathos, sometimes. The laughing eyes of Thalia gleam through the tragic mask she holds before her face. In spite of your cold-water prejudices, I must confess that I like Miss Barrett's third line as well as the others. But while we are wandering so far from the poor old widow's yard, that fox, "full of iniquity,"

> That new Iscariot, new Ganelon,
> That false dissimulator, Greek Sinon,

as Chaucer calls him, may have made clean away with our noble friend Sir Chaunticlere.

John: Now, Esculapius defend thy bird! The Romans believed that the lion himself would strike his colors at the crowing of a cock,—a piece of natural history to which the national emblems of England and France have figuratively given the lie. But cunning is often more serviceable than bravery, and Sir Russel the fox may achieve by diplomacy the victory to which the lion was not equal.

Philip: We shall see. Diplomatists are like the two Yankees who swapped jacknives together till each had cleared five dollars. Such a Sir Philip Sydney among cocks, at least, could not fall without a burst of melodious tears from every civilized barn-yard. The poet, after lamenting that Sir Chaunticlere had not heeded better the boding of his dream, warns us of the danger of woman's counsel, from Eve's time downward; but takes care to add,

> These speeches are the cock's, and none of mine;
> For I no harm of woman can divine.

He then returns to his main argument; and no one, who has not had poultry for bosom-friends from childhood, can appreciate the accurate grace and pastoral humor of his descriptions. The fox, meanwhile, has crept into the yard and hidden himself.

> Fair in the sand, to bathe her merrily,
> Lies Partelote, and all her sisters by,
> Against the sun, and Chaunticlere so free
> Sang merrier than the mermaid in the sea
> (For Physiologus saith certainly
> How that they sing both well and merrily),
> And so befell, that, as he cast his eye
> Among the worts upon a butterfly,
> 'Ware was he of the fox that lay full low;
> Nothing it lists him now to strut or crow,
> But cries anon, Cuk! cuk! and up doth start,
> As one that is affrayed in his heart.

The knight would have fled, as there are examples enough in Froissart to prove it would not have disgraced his spurs to do, considering the greatness of the odds against him, but the fox plies him with courteous flattery. He appeals to Sir Chaunticlere's pride of birth, pretends to have a taste in music, and is desirous of hearing him sing, hoping all the while to put his tuneful throat to quite other uses. A more bitter fate than that of Orpheus seems to be in store for our feathered son of Apollo; since his spirit, instead of hastening to join that of his Eurydice, must rake for corn in Elysian fields, with the bitter thought, that not one but seven Eurydices are cackling for him "*superis in auris.*" The fox

> Says, 'Gentle Sir, alas! what will you do?
> Are you afraid of him that is your friend?
> Now, certes, I were worse than any fiend,
> If I to you wished harm or villany;
> I am not come your counsel to espy,
> But truly all that me did hither bring
> Was only for to hearken how you sing;
> For, on my word, your voice is merrier even
> Than any angel hath that is in heaven,

And you beside a truer feeling show, Sir,
Than did Boece, or any great composer.
My Lord, your father (God his spirit bless!
And eke your mother, for her gentleness)
Hath honored my poor house to my great ease,
And, certes, Sir, full fain would I you please.
But, since men talk of singing, I will say
(Else may I lose my eyes this very day),
Save you, I never heard a mortal sing
As did your father at the daybreaking;
Certes, it was with all his heart he sung,
And, for to make his voice more full and strong,
He would so pain him, that with either eye
He needs must wink, so loud he strove to cry,
And stand upon his tiptoes therewithal,
And stretch his comely neck forth long and small.
Discretion, too, in him went hand in hand
With music, and no man in any land
In wisdom or in song did him surpass.'

John: I thought Chaucer's portrait of the son perfect, till Sir Russel hung up his of the father beside it. Why, Vandyke himself would look chalky beside such flesh and blood as this. Such a cock, one would think, might have served a score of Israelites for a sacrifice at their feast of atonement, or have been a sufficient thank-offering to the gods for twenty Spartan victories. Stripped of his feathers, Plato would have taken him for something more than human. It must have been such a one as this that the Stoics esteemed it as bad as parricide to slay.

Philip: The fox continues,
'Let's see, can you your father counterfeit?'
This Chaunticlere his wings began to beat,
As one that could not his foul treason spy,
So he was ravished by his flattery. . . .
Sir Chaunticlere stood high upon his toes,
Streached forth his neck and held his eyes shut close,
And gan to crow full loudly for the nonce,
When Dan Russel, the fox, sprang up at once,
And by the gorget seized Sir Chaunticlere,
And on his back toward the wood him bare.

Forthwith the seven wives begin a sorrowful ululation; Dame Partelote, in her capacity as favorite, shrieking more sovereignly than the rest. Another Andromache, she sees her Hector dragged barbarously from the walls of his native Illium, whose defence and prop he had ever been. Then follows a picture which surpasses even Hogarth.

> The luckless widow and her daughters two,
> Hearing the hens cry out and make their woe,
> Out at the door together rushed anon,
> And saw how toward the wood the fox is gone,
> Bearing upon his back the cock away;
> They cried 'Out, out, alas! and welaway!
> Aha, the fox!' and after him they ran,
> And, snatching up their staves, ran many a man;
> Ran Col the dog, ran Talbot and Gerland,
> And Malkin, with her distaff in her hand;
> Ran cow and calf, and even the very hogs,
> So frighted with the barking of the dogs,
> And shouting of the men and women eke,
> Ran till they thought their very hearts would break,
> And yelled as never fiends in hell have done;
> The dicks screamed, thinking that their sand was run;
> The geese, for fear, flew cackling o'er the trees;
> Out of their hive buzzed forth a swarm of bees;
> So hideous was the noise, ah, *benedicite!*
> Certes, not Jack Straw and his varletry
> Raised ever any outcry half so shrill,
> When they some Fleming were about to kill,
> As that same day was made about the fox:
> Vessels of brass they brought forth and of box,
> And horns and bones, on which they banged and
>   blew;
> It seemed the very sky would split in two. . . .
> The cock, who lay upon the fox's back,
> In all his dread unto his captor spake,
> And said: 'Most noble Sir, if I were you,
> I would (as surely as God's help I sue)
> Cry, "Turn again, ye haughty villains all!
> A very pestilence upon you fall!
> Now I am come unto the forest's side,

Maugre your heads, the cock shall here abide;
I will him eat, i' faith, and that anon."'
Answered the fox, 'Good sooth, it shall be done!'
And, as he spake the word, all suddenly,
The cock broke from his jaws deliverly,
And high upon a tree he flew anon.
And when the fox saw that the cock was gone,
Alas! O Chaunticlere, alas!' quoth he,
'I have, 'tis true, done you some injury,
In that I made you for a while afeard,
By seizing you from forth your native yard;
But, Sir, I did it with no ill intent;
Come down, and I will tell you what I meant,
God help me as I speak the truth to you!'
'Nay,' quoth the other, 'then, beshrew us two,
But first beshrew myself both blood and bones,
If thou beguile me oftener than once;
Never again shalt thou by flattery
Make me to sing and wink the while mine eye;
For he that winketh, when he most should see,
Deserves no help from Providence, pardie.'

John: So our friend Sir Chaunticlere escapes, after all. The humorous moral of the story is heightened by the cunning Reynard's being foiled with his own weapons. The bare fact of induing animals with speech and other human properties is, in itself, highly ludicrous. Fables always inculcate magnanimity. To see our weaknesses thus palpably bodied forth in their appropriate animal costume brings them down from the false elevation to which their association with ourselves had raised them. The next time we meet them in life, their human disguise drops off, and the ape or the owl takes our own place or that of our friend. That treatise of Baptista Porta's, in which he traces the likeness between men's faces and those of animals, is painful and shocking; but when we casually note a human expression in the countenance of a brute, it is merely laughable. In the former instance, the mind is carried downward, and in the latter upward. To children there is nothing humorous in Æsop. They read his fables as soberly as they afterwards read Scott's novels. The moral is always skipped, as tedious. The honey-bag is all they seek; the sting is of no use, save to the bee. Yet, afterwards, we find that Lucian and Rabelais are dull beside Æsop; and the greater the seeming incongruity, the greater the mirth.

Philip: Chaucer was aware of this, when he put so much pedantry into the mouth of Chaunticlere; and the fox's allusion to Boethius makes me laugh in spite of myself. Chaunticlere's compliment to Dame Partelote, too, where he expresses the intense satisfaction which he feels in observing that

> She is so scarlet red about her eyes,

is the keenest of satires upon those lovers who have sung the bodily perfections of their mistresses, and who have set their affections, as it were, upon this year's leaves, to fall off with them at the bidding of the first November blast of fortune. It was a Platonic notion, to which Spenser gave in his allegiance, that a fair spirit always chose a fair dwelling, and beautified it the more by its abiding. It is the sweetest apology ever invented for a physical passion. But I do not like this filching of arrows from heavenly love, to furnish forth the quiver of earthly love withal. Love is the most hospitable of spirits, and adorns the interior of his home for the nobler welcome, not the exterior for the more lordly show. It is not the outside of his dwelling that invites, but the soft domestic murmur stealing out at the door, and the warm, homely light gushing from the windows. No matter into what hovel of clay he enters, that is straightway the palace, and beauty holds her court in vain. I doubt if Chaucer were conscious of his sarcasm, but I can conceive of no more cutting parody than a sonnet of Chaunticlere's upon his mistress's comb or beak, or other gallinaceous excellency. Imagine him enthusiastic over her sagacity in the hunting of earthworms, and her grace in scratching for them with those toes

> White as lilies in the grass,

standing upon one leg as he composed a quatrain upon her tail-feathers, and finally losing himself in the melodious ecstasy of her cackle!

There is certainly, as you have said, something ludicrous in the bare idea of animals indued with human propensities and feelings, and the farther away we get from any physical resemblance, the more keenly moved is our sense of humor. That king-making jelly of the bees strips Nicholas and Victoria of their crowns and ermine, and makes them merely forked radishes, like the rest of us. And when I learned that there was domestic slavery among certain species of the ants, I could not but laugh, as I imagined some hexapodal McDuffie mounted upon a cherry-stone, and convincing a caucus of chivalrous listeners of their immense superiority to some neighbouring hill, whose inhabitants got in their own harvest of bread-crumbs and dead beetles, unaided by that patriarchal machinery.

John: The passage you first read me from the death-scene of Arcite moved me so much, that I cannot help wishing you would read me something more in the same kind.

—James Russell Lowell, *Conversations on Some of the Old Poets*, 1846, pp. 16–49

LEIGH HUNT (1848)

A prolific author of the Romantic movement, Leigh Hunt (1784–1859) is best known today for *The Story of Rimini* as well as several smaller works. In the excerpt below, Hunt calls Chaucer a "companion of princes" and a "reformer . . . a stirrer out in the world," referring perhaps to Chaucer's penchant for satire or his on-again off-again reputation as a medieval political activist. Like other critics of his era, Hunt also notes Chaucer's fondness for nature imagery in his work, noting that "[i]t is as hard to get him out of a grove as his friend Boccaccio."

Chaucer was a courtier, and a companion of princes; nay, a reformer also, and a stirrer out in the world. He understood that world, too, thoroughly, in the ordinary sense of such understanding; yet, as he was a true great poet in everything, so in nothing more was he so than in loving the country, and the trees and fields. It is as hard to get him out of a grove as his friend Boccaccio; and he tells us, that, in May, he would often go out into the meadows to "abide" there, solely in order to "look upon the daisy." Milton seems to have made a point of never living in a house that had not a garden to it.

—Leigh Hunt, A *Jar of Honey from Mount Hybla*, 1848, p. 122

HENRY DAVID THOREAU "FRIDAY" (1849)

Henry David Thoreau (1817–62) was an American author, naturalist, transcendentalist, and abolitionist known for his nature reflection *Walden* and *Civil Disobedience*, his essay on individual resistance to an unjust state. An exceptionally well-read individual and a talented writer, Thoreau muses on Chaucer's place in the pantheon of English literature in the following excerpt, taken from his work *A Week on the Concord and Merrimack Rivers.* Thoreau begins the piece by placing Chaucer in his historical context, with an emphasis on examining the works that preceded the medieval author. While many of the essays in this text have also examined Chaucer's place in the history of English literature, none has previously considered Chaucer's relationship to the Anglo-Saxon and early Middle English works that were composed before Chaucer's time, so students will find Thoreau's comments here particularly important.

Writing of Chaucer's work, Thoreau notes, "There is no wisdom that can take place of humanity, and we find *that* in Chaucer." Echoing many of the medieval writers in this text, Thoreau observes that Chaucer "was as simple as Wordsworth in preferring his homely but vigorous Saxon tongue when it was neglected by the court and had not yet attained to the dignity of a literature." Thoreau here demonstrates that one of Chaucer's great contributions to English was popularizing the use of the tongue for the literature of the land, echoing the words of Lydgate and Caxton, among others. A strong admirer of Chaucer's, Thoreau stirringly concludes that, "He is not heroic, as Raleigh, nor pious, as Herbert, nor philosophical, as Shakespeare; but he is the child of the English muse, that child which is the father of the man." In writing this, Thoreau recognizes that while there was an English literary tradition that preceded Chaucer, the author of *The Canterbury Tales* had an impact on the literature of England that far surpassed anyone who had come before him, and thus still deserves to be considered "the father of English poetry."

What a contrast between the stern and desolate poetry of Ossian and that of Chaucer, and even of Shakespeare and Milton, much more of Dryden, and Pope, and Gray! Our summer of English poetry, like the Greek and Latin before it, seems well advanced toward its fall, and laden with the fruit and foliage of the season, with bright autumnal tints; but soon the winter will scatter its myriad clustering and shading leaves, and leave only a few desolate and fibrous boughs to sustain the snow and rime, and creak in the blasts of ages. We cannot escape the impression that the Muse has stooped a little in her flight when we come to the literature of civilised eras. Now first we hear of various ages and styles of poetry; it is pastoral, and lyric, and narrative, and didactic; but the poetry of runic monuments is of one style, and for every age. The bard has in a great measure lost the dignity and sacredness of his office. Formerly he was called a *seer*, but now it is thought that one man sees as much as another. He has no longer the bardic rage, and only conceives the deed, which he formerly stood ready to perform. Hosts of warriors earnest for battle could not mistake nor dispense with the ancient bard. His lays were heard in the pauses of the fight. There was no danger of his being overlooked by his contemporaries. But now the hero and the bard are of different professions. When we come to the pleasant English verse, the storms have all cleared away and it will never thunder and lighten more. The poet has come within doors, and exchanged the forest and crag for the fireside, the hut of the Gael, and Stonehenge with its circles of stones, for the house of the Englishman. No hero stands at the door prepared to break forth into song of heroic action, but a homely Englishman, who cultivates the art of poetry. We see the comfortable fireside, and hear the crackling fagots in all the verse.

Notwithstanding the broad humanity of Chaucer, and the many social and domestic comforts which we meet with in his verse, we have to narrow our vision somewhat to consider him, as if he occupied less space in the landscape, and did not stretch over hill and valley as Ossian does. Yet, seen from the side of posterity, as the father of English poetry, preceded by a long silence or confusion in history, unenlivened by any strain of pure melody, we easily come to reverence him. Passing over the earlier continental poets, since we are bound to the pleasant archipelago of English poetry, Chaucer's is the first name after that misty weather in which Ossian lived which can detain us long. Indeed, though he represents so different a culture and society, he may be regarded as in many respects the Homer of the English poets. Perhaps he is the youthfullest of them all. We return to him as to the purest well, the fountain farthest removed from the highway of desultory life. He is so natural and cheerful, compared with later poets, that we might almost regard him as a personification of spring. To the faithful reader his muse has even given an aspect to his times, and when he is fresh from perusing him they seem related to the golden age. It is still the poetry of youth and life rather than of thought; and though the moral vein is obvious and constant, it has not yet banished the sun and daylight from his verse. The loftiest strains of the muse are, for the most part, sublimely plaintive, and not a carol as free as nature's. The content which the sun shines to celebrate from morning to evening is unsung. The muse solaces herself, and is not ravished but consoled. There is a catastrophe implied, and a tragic element in all our verse, and less of the lark and morning dews than of the nightingale and evening shades. But in Homer and Chaucer there is more of the innocence and serenity of youth than in the more modern and moral poets. The *Iliad* is not Sabbath but morning reading, and men cling to this old song because they still have moments of unbaptised and uncommitted life, which give them an appetite for more. To the innocent there are neither cherubim nor angels. At rare intervals we rise above the necessity of virtue into an unchangeable morning light, in which we have only to live right on and breathe the ambrosial air. The Iliad represents no creed nor opinion, and we read it with a rare sense of freedom and irresponsibility, as if we trod on native ground and were autochthones of the soil.

Chaucer had eminently the habits of a literary man and a scholar. There were never any times so stirring that there were not to be found some sedentary still. He was surrounded by the din of arms. The battles of Hallidon Hill and Neville's Cross, and the still more memorable battles of Cressy and Poictiers, were fought in his youth; but these did not concern our poet much, Wickliffe and his reform much more. He regarded himself always as one privileged to sit and converse with books. He helped to establish the literary class. His character as one of the fathers of the English language would alone make his works important, even those which have little poetical merit. He was as simple as Wordsworth in preferring his homely but vigorous Saxon tongue when it was neglected by the court and had not yet attained to the dignity of a literature, and rendered a similar service to his country to that which Dante rendered to Italy. If Greek sufficeth for Greek, and Arabic for Arabian, and Hebrew for Jew, and Latin for Latin, then English shall suffice for him, for any of these will serve to teach truth 'right as divers pathes leaden divers folke the right waye to Rome.' In the *Testament of Love* he writes, 'Let then clerkes enditen in Latin, for they have the propertie of science, and the knowinge in that facultie, and lette Frenchmen in their Frenche also enditen their queinte termes, for it is kyndely to their mouthes, and let us shewe our fantasies in soche wordes as we lemeden of our dames tonge.'

He will know how to appreciate Chaucer best who has come down to him the natural way, through the meagre pastures of Saxon and ante-Chaucerian poetry; and yet, so human and wise he appears after such diet, that we are liable to misjudge him still. In the Saxon poetry extant, in the earliest English, and the contemporary Scottish poetry, there is less to remind the reader of the rudeness and vigour of youth than of the feebleness of a declining age. It is for the most part translation of imitation merely, with only an occasional and slight tinge of poetry, oftentimes the falsehood and exaggeration of fable without its imagination to redeem it, and we look in vain to find antiquity restored, humanised, and made blithe again by some natural sympathy between it and the present. But Chaucer is fresh and modern still, and no dust settles on his true passages. It lightens along the line, and we are reminded that flowers have bloomed, and birds sung, and hearts beaten in England. Before the earnest gaze of the reader the rust and moss of time gradually drop off, and the original green life is revealed. He was a homely and domestic man, and did breathe quite as modern men do.

There is no wisdom that can take place of humanity, and we find *that* in Chaucer. We can expand at last in his breadth, and we think that we could have been that man's acquaintance. He was worthy to be a citizen of England, while Petrarch and Boccacio lived in Italy, and Tell and Tamerlane in Switzerland and Asia, and Bruce in Scotland, and Wickliffe, and Gower, and Edward the Third, and John of Gaunt, and the Black Prince were his own countrymen as well as contemporaries; all stout and stirring names. The fame of Roger Bacon came down from the preceding century, and the name of Dante still possessed the influence of a living presence. On the whole, Chaucer impresses us as greater than his reputation, and not a little like Homer and Shakespeare, for he would have held up his head in their company. Among early English poets he is the landlord and host, and has the authority of such. The affectionate mention which succeeding early poets make of him, coupling him with Homer and Virgil, is to be taken into the account in estimating his character and influence. King James and Dunbar of Scotland speak of him with more love and reverence than any modern author of his predecessors of the last century. The same childlike relation is without a parallel now. For the most part we read him without criticism, for he does not plead his own cause, but speaks for his readers, and has that greatness of trust and reliance which compels popularity. He confides in the reader, and speaks privily with him, keeping nothing back. And in return the reader has great confidence in him, that he tells no lies, and reads his story with indulgence, as if it were the circumlocution of a child, but often discovers afterwards that he has spoken with more directness and economy of words than a sage. He is never heartless,

> For first the thing is thought within the hart,
> Er any word out from the mouth astart.

And so new was all his theme in those days, that he did not have to invent, but only to tell.

We admire Chaucer for his sturdy English wit. The easy height he speaks from in his Prologue to the *Canterbury Tales,* as if he were equal to any of the company there assembled, is as good as any particular excellence in it. But though it is full of good sense and humanity, it is not transcendent poetry. For picturesque description of persons it is, perhaps, without a parallel in English poetry; yet it is essentially humorous, as the loftiest genius never is. Humour, however broad and genial, takes a narrower view than enthusiasm. To his own finer vein he added all the common wit and wisdom of his time, and everywhere in his works his remarkable knowledge of the world, and nice perception of character, his rare common sense and proverbial wisdom, are apparent. His genius does not soar like Milton's, but is genial and familiar. It shows great tenderness and delicacy, but not the heroic sentiment. It is only a greater portion of humanity with all its weakness. He is not heroic, as Raleigh, nor pious, as Herbert, nor philosophical, as Shakespeare; but he is

the child of the English muse, that child which is the father of the man. The
charm of his poetry consists often only in an exceeding naturalness, perfect
sincerity, with the behaviour of a child rather than of a man.

Gentleness and delicacy of character are everywhere apparent in his
verse. The simplest and humblest words come readily to his lips. No one can
read the Prioress's tale, understanding the spirit in which it was written, and
in which the child sings *O alma redemptoris mater,* or the account of the
departure of Constance with her child upon the sea, in the Man of Lawe's tale,
without feeling the native innocence and refinement of the author. Nor can
we be mistaken respecting the essential purity of his character, disregarding
the apology of the manners of the age. A simple pathos and feminine
gentleness, which Wordsworth only occasionally approaches, but does not
equal, are peculiar to him. We are tempted to say that his genius was feminine
not masculine. It was such a feminineness, however, as is rarest to find in
woman, though not the appreciation of it; perhaps it is not to be found at all
in woman, but is only the feminine in man.

Such pure and genuine and childlike love of Nature is hardly to be found
in any poet.

Chaucer's remarkably trustful and affectionate character appears in his
familiar, yet innocent and reverent, manner of speaking of his God. He comes
into his thought without any false reverence, and with no more parade than
the zephyr to his ear. If Nature is our mother, then God is our father. There
is less love and simple, practical trust in Shakespeare and Milton. How rarely
in our English tongue do we find expressed any affection for God! Certainly,
there is no sentiment so rare, as the love of God. Herbert almost alone
expresses it, 'Ah, my dear God!' Our poet uses similar words with propriety;
and whenever he sees a beautiful person, or other object, prides himself on
the 'maistry' of his God. He even recommends Dido to be his bride—

> if that God that heaven and yearth made,
> Would have a love for beauty and goodness,
> And womanhede, trouth, and semeliness.

But in justification of our praise, we must refer to his works themselves,
to the Prologue to the *Canterbury Tales,* the account of Gentilesse, the Flower
and the Leaf, the stories of Griselda, Virginia, Ariadne, and Blanche the
Dutchesse, and much more of less distinguished merit. There are many poets
of more taste, and better manners, who knew how to leave out their dulness;
but such negative genius cannot detain us long; we shall return to Chaucer
still with love. Some natures, which are really rude and ill-developed, have
yet a higher standard of perfection than others which are refined and well

balanced. Even the clown has taste, whose dictates, though he disregards them, are higher and purer than those which the artist obeys. If we have to wander through many dull and prosaic passages in Chaucer, we have at least the satisfaction of knowing that it is not an artificial dulness, but too easily matched by many passages in life. We confess that we feel a disposition commonly to concentrate sweets, and accumulate pleasures; but the poet may be presumed always to speak as a traveller, who leads us through a varied scenery, from one eminence to another, and it is, perhaps, more pleasing, after all, to meet with a fine thought in its natural setting. Surely fate has enshrined it in these circumstances for some end. Nature strews her nuts and flowers broadcast, and never collects them into heaps. This was the soil it grew in, and this the hour it bloomed in; if sun, wind, and rain came here to cherish and expand the flower, shall not we come here to pluck it?

A true poem is distinguished not so much by a felicitous expression, or any thought it suggests, as by the atmosphere which surrounds it. Most have beauty of outline merely, and are striking as the form and bearing of a stranger; but true verses come toward us indistinctly, as the very breath of all friendliness, and envelop us in their spirit and fragrance. Much of our poetry has the very best manners, but no character. It is only an unusual precision and elasticity of speech, as if its author had taken, not an intoxicating draught, but an electuary. It has the distinct outline of sculpture, and chronicles an early hour. Under the influence of passion all men speak thus distinctly, but wrath is not always divine.

There are two classes of men called poets. The one cultivates life, the other art—one seeks food for nutriment, the other for flavour; one satisfies hunger, the other gratifies the palate. There are two kinds of writing, both great and rare: one that of genius, or the inspired, the other of intellect and taste, in the intervals of inspiration. The former is above criticism, always correct, giving the law to criticism. It vibrates and pulsates with life for ever. It is sacred, and to be read with reverence, as the works of nature are studied. There are few instances of a sustained style of this kind; perhaps every man has spoken words, but the speaker is then careless of the record. Such a style removes us out of personal relations with its author; we do not take his words on our lips, but his sense into our hearts. It is the stream of inspiration, which bubbles out, now here, now there, now in this man, now in that. It matters not through what ice-crystals it is seen, now a fountain, now the ocean stream running under ground. It is in Shakespeare, Alpheus, in Burns, Arethuse; but ever the same. The other is self-possessed and wise. It is reverent of genius and greedy of inspiration. It is conscious in the highest and the least degree. It consists with the most perfect command of the faculties. It dwells in a repose as of the desert, and objects are as distinct in it as oases or palms in the horizon of sand. The train of thought moves with subdued and measured step, like a caravan. But the pen is only an instrument in its hand, and not instinct with life, like a longer arm. It leaves a thin varnish or glaze over all its work. The works of Goethe furnish remarkable instances of the latter.

There is no just and serene criticism as yet. Nothing is considered simply as it lies in the lap of eternal beauty, but our thoughts, as well as our bodies, must be dressed after the latest fashions. Our taste is too delicate and particular. It says nay to the poet's work, but never yea to his hope. It invites him to adorn his deformities, and not to cast them off by expansion, as the tree its bark. We are a people who live in a bright light, in houses of pearl and porcelain, and drink only light wines, whose teeth are easily set on edge by the least natural sour. If we had been consulted, the backbone of the earth would have been made, not of granite, but of Bristol spar. A modern author would have died in infancy in a ruder age. But the poet is something more than a scald, 'a smoother and polisher of language'; he is a Cincinnatus in literature, and occupies no west end of the world. Like the sun, he will indifferently select his rhymes, and with a liberal taste weave into his verse the planet and the stubble.

In these old books the stucco has long since crumbled away, and we read what was sculptured in the granite. They are rude and massive in their proportions, rather than smooth and delicate in their finish. The workers in stone polish only their chimney ornaments, but their pyramids are roughly done. There is a soberness in a rough aspect, as of unhewn granite, which addresses a depth in us, but a polished surface hits only the ball of the eye. The true finish is the work of time, and the use to which a thing is put. The elements are still polishing the pyramids. Art may varnish and gild, but it can do no more. A work of genius is rough-hewn from the first, because it anticipates the lapse of time, and has an ingrained polish, which still appears when fragments are broken off, and essential quality of its substance. Its beauty is at the same time its strength, and it breaks with a lustre.

The great poem must have the stamp of greatness as well as its essence. The reader easily goes within the shallowest contemporary poetry, and informs it with all the life and promise of the day, as the pilgrim goes within the temple, and hears the faintest strains of the worshippers; but it will have to speak to posterity, traversing these deserts, through the ruins of its outmost walls, by the grandeur and beauty of its proportions.

—Henry David Thoreau, "Friday,"
A Week on the Concord and Merrimack Rivers, 1849

LEIGH HUNT (1855)

In the following essay, Hunt considers "the analogies between musical and poetical composition," applying terminology normally reserved for describing music to several of Chaucer's lines and describing the "musical feeling" of the medieval writer's poetry. Hunt's approach may be appealing to many students, who may also wish to explore the musicality of Chaucer or even compare Chaucer's lines to the popular music of today.

Hunt begins his piece by declaring that Chaucer was his "great master in the art of poetry," a view echoed by many poets who lived in the generations after Chaucer, including Lydgate, Hoccleve, and even Spenser. Hunt explains that he studied "versification in the school of Dryden," but found something lacking in the "sentiment and imagination" of Dryden. Hunt adds: "Chaucer is the greatest narrative poet in the language; that is to say, the greatest and best teller of stories, in the understood sense of that term. He is greatest in every respect, and in the most opposite qualifications; greatest in pathos, greatest in pleasantry, greatest in character, greatest in plot, greatest even in versification." Hunt continues to compare Dryden and Chaucer for the remainder of the piece, and any student working on these two authors will find his insights helpful.

Hunt writes, "Of all the definitions which have been given of poetry, the best is that which pronounces it to be 'geniality, singing.'" His examination of the musical possibilities of English poetry, and of Chaucer in particular, is a highlight of the text, and students may wish to peruse Hunt's words carefully and adapt his method for themselves.

―◦◦◦― ―◦◦◦― ―◦◦◦―

PREFACE, Containing Remarks on the Father of English Narrative Poetry; On the Ill-Understood Nature of Heroic Verse; On the Necessity, Equally Ill-Understood, of the Musical Element in Poetry to Poetry in General; And on the Absurdity of Confining the Name of Poetry to Any One Species of It in Particular.

As this book, in issuing from the house of Messrs. Rout-ledge, acquires a special chance of coming under the cognizance of travellers by the railway, I have pleased myself with fancying, that it gives me a kind of new link, however remote like the rest, with my great master in the art of poetry; that is to say, with the great master of English narrative in verse, the Father of our Poetry itself, Chaucer.

Nay, it gives me two links, one general, and one particular; for as Chaucer's stories, in default of there being any printed books and travelling carriages in those days, were related by travellers to one another, and as these stories will be read, and (I hope) shown to one another, by travellers who are descendants of those travellers (see how the links thicken as we advance!), so one of Chaucer's stories concerned a wonderful Magic Horse; and now, one of the most wonderful of all such horses will be speeding my readers and me together to all parts of the kingdom, with a fire hitherto unknown to any horse whatsoever.

How would the great poet have been delighted to see the creature!—and what would he not have said of it!

I say 'creature,' because though your fiery Locomotive is a creation of man's, as that of the poet was, yet as the poet's 'wondrous Horse of Brass' was formed out of ideas furnished him by Nature, so, out of elements no less furnished by Nature, and the first secrets of which are no less amazing, has been formed this wonderful Magic Horse of Iron and Steam, which, with vitals of fire, clouds literally flowing from its nostrils, and a bulk, a rushing, and a panting like that of some huge antediluvian wild beast, is now heard and seen in all parts of the country, and in most parts of civilized Europe, breaking up the old grounds of alienation, and carrying with it the seeds of universal brotherhood.

Verily, something even of another, but most grating link, starts up out of that reflection upon the poet's miracle; for the hero who rode his horse of brass made war with Russia; and we Englishmen, the creators of the Horse of Iron, are warring with the despot of the same barbarous country, pitting the indignant genius of civilization against his ruffianly multitudes.

> At Sarra, in the land of Tartarie,
> There dwelt a king that warned Russie,
> Through which there died many a doughty man.

Many a doughty man, many a noble heart of captain and of common soldier, has perished in this new war against the old ignorance;—an ignorance, that by its sullen persistence in rejecting the kindly advice of governments brave and great enough to be peaceful, forced the very enthusiasts of peace (myself among the number) into the conviction, that out of hatred and loathing of war itself, war must be made upon him. . . .

Let me take this opportunity of recommending such readers as are not yet acquainted with Chaucer, to make up for their lost time. The advice is not to my benefit, but it is greatly to theirs, and loyalty to him forces me to speak. The poet's 'old English' is no difficulty, if they will but believe it. A little study would soon make them understand it as easily as that of most provincial dialects. Chaucer is the greatest narrative poet in the language; that is to say, the greatest and best teller of stories, in the understood sense of that term. He is greatest in every respect, and in the most opposite qualifications; greatest in pathos, greatest in pleasantry, greatest in character, greatest in plot, greatest even in versification, if the unsettled state of the language in his time, and the want of all native precursors in the art, be considered; for his verse is anything but the rugged and formless thing it has been supposed to be; and if Dryden surpassed him in it, not only was the superiority owing to the master's help, but there were delicate and noble turns and cadences in the old poet, which the poet of the age of Charles the Second wanted spirituality enough to appreciate.

There have been several Chaucers, and Helps to Chaucer, published of late years. Mr. Moxon has printed his entire works in one double-columned large octavo volume; Messrs. Rout-ledge have published the *Canterbury Tales* in a smaller volume, with delicate illustrations by Mr. Corbould, the best (as far as I am aware) that ever came from his pencil; and there is a set of the poet's works now going through the press, more abundant than has yet appeared in commentary and dissertation, in Robert Bell's *Annotated Edition of the English Poets,*—the only collection of the kind in the language, though it has so long been a desideratum. Chaucer's country disgraced itself for upwards of a century by considering the Father of its Poetry as nothing but an obsolete jester. Even poets thought so, in consequence of a prevailing ignorance of nine-tenths of his writings, originating in the gross tastes of the age of Charles the Second. There are passages, it is true, in Chaucer, which for the sake of all parties, persons of thorough delicacy will never read twice; for they were compliances with the licence of an age, in which the court itself, his sphere, was as clownish in some of its tastes as the unqualified admirers of Swift and Prior are now; and the great poet lamented that he had condescended to write them. But by far the greatest portion of his works is full of delicacies of every kind, of the noblest sentiment, of the purest, most various, and most profound entertainment.

Postponing, however, what I have to say further on the subject of Chaucer, it becomes, I am afraid, a little too obviously proper, as well as more politic, to return, in this Preface, to the book of the humblest of his followers. . . .

When I wrote the 'Story of Rimini' which was between the years 1812 and 1815, I was studying versification in the school of Dryden. Masterly as my teacher was, I felt, without knowing it, that there was a want in him, even in versification; and the supply of this want, later in life, I found in his far greater master, Chaucer; for though Dryden's versification is noble, beautiful, and so complete of its kind, that to an ear uninstructed in the metre of the old poet, all comparison between the two in this respect seems out of the question, and even ludicrous, yet the measure in which Dryden wrote not only originated, but attained to a considerable degree of its beauty, in Chaucer; and the old poet's immeasurable superiority in sentiment and imagination, not only to Dryden, but to all, up to a very late period, who have written in the same form of verse, left him in possession of beauties, even in versification, which it remains for some future poet to amalgamate with Dryden's in a manner worthy of both, and so carry England's noble heroic rhyme to its pitch of perfection.

Critics, and poets too, have greatly misconceived the rank and requirements of this form of verse, who have judged it from the smoothness and monotony which it died of towards the close of the last century, and from which nothing was thought necessary for its resuscitation but an opposite unsystematic extreme. A doubt, indeed, of a very curious and hitherto unsuspected, or at least unnoticed nature, may be entertained by inquirers into the musical portion of the art of poetry (for poetry is an art as well as a gift); namely, whether, since the time of Dryden, any poets whatsoever, up to the period above alluded to (and very few indeed have done otherwise since then), thought of versification as a thing necessary to be studied at all, with the exceptions of Gray and Coleridge.

The case remains the same at present; but such assuredly was not the case either with Dryden himself, or with any of the greater poets before him, the scholarly ones in particular, such as Spenser, Milton, and their father Chaucer, who was as learned as any of them for the time in which he lived, and well acquainted with metres, French, Latin, and Italian.

Poets less reverent to their art, out of a notion that the gift, in their instance, is of itself sufficient for all its purposes, (which is much as if a musician should think he could do without studying thorough-bass, or a painter without studying drawing and colours,) trust to an ear which is often not good enough to do justice to the amount of gift which they really possess; and hence comes a loss, for several generations together, of the whole musical portion of poetry, to the destruction of its beauty in tone and in movement, and the peril of much good vitality in new writers. For proportions, like all other good things, hold together; and he that is wanting in musical feeling where music is required, is in danger of being discordant and disproportionate in sentiment, of not perceiving the difference between thoughts worthy and unworthy of utterance. It is for this reason among others, that he pours forth "crotchets" in abundance, not in unison with his theme, and wanting in harmony with one another.

There is sometimes a kind of vague and (to the apprehension of the unmusical) senseless melody, which in lyrical compositions, the song in particular, really constitutes, in the genuine poetical sense of the beautiful, what the scorner of it says it falsely and foolishly constitutes—namely, a good half of its merit. It answers to variety and expression of tone in a beautiful voice, and to 'air,' grace, and freedom in the movements of a charming person. The Italians, in their various terms for the beautiful, have a word for it precisely answering to the first feeling one has in attempting to express it— *vago*,—vague; something wandering, fluctuating, undefinable, unde-tainable, moving hither and thither at its own sweet will and pleasure, in accordance with what it feels. It overdoes nothing and falls short of nothing; for itself is nothing but the outward expression of an inward grace. You perceive it in all genuine lyrical compositions, of whatever degree, and indeed in all compositions that sing or speak with true musical impulse, in whatsoever measure, in the effusions of Burns, of Ben Jonson, of Beaumont and Fletcher, of Allan Ramsay, of Metastasio, of Coleridge; and again in those of Dryden, of Spenser, of Chaucer, of Ariosto; in poems however long, and in passages however seemingly unlyrical; for it is one of the popular, and I am afraid, generally speaking, critical mistakes, in regard to rhymed verse, that in narrative and heroic poems there is nothing wanting to the music, provided the line or the couplet be flowing, and the general impression not rude or weak; whereas the best couplet, however admirable in itself and worthy of quotation, forms but one link in the chain of the music to which it belongs. Poems of any length must consist of whole strains of couplets, whole sections and successions of them, brief or prolonged, all as distinct from one another and complete in themselves, as the *adagios* and *andantes* of symphonies and sonatas, each commencing in the tone and obvious spirit of commencement, proceeding through as great a variety of accents, stops, and pauses, as the notes and phrases of any other musical composition, and coming at an equally fit moment to a close.

Enough stress has never yet been laid on the analogies between musical and poetical composition. All poetry used formerly to be sung; and poets still speak of 'singing' what they write. Petrarch used to 'try his sonnets on the lute'; that is to say, to examine them in their musical relations, in order to see how they and musical requirement went together; and a chapter of poetical narrative is called to this day a canto, or chant. Every distinct section or paragraph of a long poem ought to form a separate, interwoven, and varied melody; and every very short poem should, to a fine ear, be a still more obvious melody of the same sort, in order that its brevity may contain as much worth as is possible, and show that the poet never forgets the reverence due to his art.

I have sometimes thought that if Chaucer could have heard compositions like those of Coleridge's *Christabel,* he might have doubted whether theirs was not the best of all modes and measures for reducing a narrative to its most poetic element, and so producing the quintessence of a story. And for stories not very long, not very substantial in their adventures, and of a nature more imaginary than credible, so they might be. But for narrative poetry in general, for epic in particular, and for stories of any kind that are deeply to affect us as creatures of flesh and blood and human experience, there is nothing for a sustained and serious interest comparable with our old heroic measure, whether in blank verse or rhyme, in couplet or in stanza. An epic poem written in the *Christabel,* or any other brief lyrical measure, would acquire, in the course of perusal, a comparative tone of levity, an air of too great an airiness. The manner would turn to something like not being in earnest, and the matter resemble a diet made all of essences. We should miss *pieces de resistance,* and the homely, but sacred pabulum of 'our daily bread.' You could as soon fancy a guitar put in place of a church organ, as an *Iliad* or *Paradise Lost* written in that manner. You would associate with it no tone of Scripture, nothing of the religious solemnity which Chaucer has so justly been said to impart to his pathetic stories. When poor Griselda, repudiated by her husband, and about to return to her father's cottage, puts off the clothes which she had worn as the consort of a great noble, she says,—

> Thus with hir fader for a certain space
> Dwelleth this flowr of wifly pacience,
> That neither by hir wordes ne hir face,
> Biforn the folk, ne eek in hir absence,
> Ne shewed she that hire was doon offence,
> Ne of hir hye estaat no remembraunce
> Ne hadde she, as by hir countenaunce.
> No wonder is, for in hir grete estat
> Hir gost was evere in plein humilitee:
> No tendre mouth, noon herte delicat,
> No pompe, no semblant of royaltee.

This quotation from the Bible would have been injured by a shorter measure.

Griselda, in words most proper and affecting, but which cannot so well be quoted, apart from the entire story, goes on to say, that she must not deprive of every one of its clothes the body which had been made sacred by motherhood. She tells the father of her children, that it is not fit she should be seen by the people in that condition.

> —Wherefore I you pray,
> *Let me not like a worm go by the way.*

This is one of the most imploring and affecting lines that ever were written. It is also most beautifully modulated, though not at all after the fashion of the once all in all 'smooth' couplet. But the masterly accents throughout it, particularly the emphasis on 'worm,' would have wanted room, and could have made no such earnest appeal, in a measure of less length and solemnity.

Irony itself gains by this measure. There is no sarcasm in *Hudibras,* exquisite as its sarcasm is, comparable for energy of tone and manner with Dryden's denunciation (I do not say just denunciation) of every species of priest. . . .

I have dwelt more than is customary on this musical portion of the subject of poetry, for two reasons: first, because, as I have before intimated, it has a greater connexion than is commonly thought, both with the spiritual and with the substantial portions of the art; and second, because, as I have asserted, and am prepared to show, versification, or the various mode of uttering that music, has been neglected among us to a degree which is not a little remarkable, considering what an abundance of poets this country has produced.

England, it is true, is not a musical country; at any rate not yet, whatever its new trainers may do for it. But it is a very poetical country, *minus* this requisite of poetry; and it seems strange that the deficit should be corporately, as well as nationally characteristic. It might have been imagined, that superiority in the one respect would have been accompanied by superiority in the other;—that they who excelled the majority of their countrymen in poetical perception, would have excelled them in musical. Is the want the same as that which has made us inferior to other great nations in the art of painting? Are we geographically, commercially, statistically, or how is it, that we are less gifted than other nations with those perceptions of the pleasurable, which qualify people to excel as painters and musicians? It is observable, that our poetry, compared with that of other countries, is deficient in animal spirits.

At all events, it is this ignorance of the necessity of the whole round of the elements of poetry for the production of a perfect poetical work, and the non-perception, at the same time, of the two-fold fact, that there is no such work in existence, and that the absence of no single element of poetry hinders the other elements from compounding a work truly poetical of its kind, which at different periods of literature produce so many defective and peremptory judgments respecting the exclusive right of this or that species of poetry to be called poetry. In Chaucer's time, there were probably Chaucerophilists who would see no poetry in any other man's writing. Sir Walter Raleigh, nevertheless, who, it might be supposed, would have been an enthusiastic admirer of the Knight's and Squire's Tales, openly said, that he counted no English poetry of any value but that of Spenser. In Cowley's time, 'thinking' was held to be the all in all of poetry: poems were to be crammed full of thoughts, otherwise intellectual activity was wanting; and hence, nothing was considered poetry, in the highest sense of the term, that did not resemble the metaphysics of Cowley. His 'language of the heart,' which has survived them, went comparatively for nothing. When the Puritans brought sentiment into discredit, nothing was considered comparable, in any species of poetry, with the noble music and robust sensuous perception of Dryden. Admirable poet as he was, he was thought then, and long afterwards, to be far more admirable,—indeed, the sole

> Great high-priest of all the Nine.

Then 'sense' became the all in all; and because Pope wrote a great deal of exquisite sense, adorned with wit and fancy, he was pronounced, and long considered, literally, the greatest poet that England had seen. A healthy breeze from the un-sophisticate region of the Old English Ballads suddenly roused the whole poetical elements into play, restoring a sense of the combined requisites of imagination, of passion, of simple speaking, of music, of animal spirits, &c, not omitting, of course, the true thinking which all sound feeling implies; and though, with the prevailing grave tendency of the English muse, some portions of these poetical requisites came more into play than others, and none of our poets, either since or before, have combined them all as Chaucer and Shakspeare did, yet it would as ill become poets or critics to ignore any one of them in favour of exclusive pretensions on the part of any others, as it would to say, that all the music, and animal spirits, and comprehensiveness might be taken out of those two wonderful men, and they remain just what they were.

To think that there can be no poetry, properly so called, where there is anything 'artificial,' where there are conventionalisms of style, where facts are simply related without obviously imaginative treatment, or where manner, for its own sake, is held to be a thing of any account in its presentation of matter, is showing as limited a state of critical perception as that of the opposite conventional faction, who can see no poetry out of the pale of received forms, classical associations, or total subjections of spiritual to material treatment. It is a case of imperfect sympathy on both sides;—of incompetency to discern and enjoy in another what they have no corresponding tendency to in themselves. It is often a complexional case; perhaps always so, more or less: for writers and critics, like all other human creatures, are physically as well as morally disposed to be what they become.

It is the entire man that writes and thinks, and not merely the head. His leg has often as much to do with it as his head;—the state of his calves, his vitals, and his nerves.

There is a charming line in Chaucer:—

Uprose the sun, and uprose Emily.

Now here are two simple matters of fact, which happen to occur simultaneously. The sun rises, and the lady rises at the same time. Well, what is there in that, some demanders of imaginative illustration will say? Nothing, answers one, but an hyperbole. Nothing, says another, but a conceit. It is a mere commonplace turn of gallantry, says a third. On the contrary, it is the reverse of all this. It is pure morning freshness, enthusiasm, and music. Writers, no doubt, may repeat it till it becomes a commonplace, but that is another matter. Its first sayer, the great poet, sees the brightest of material creatures, and the beautifulest of human creatures, rising at dawn at the same time. He feels the impulse strong upon him to do justice to the appearance of both; and with gladness in his face, and music on his tongue, repeating the accent on a repeated syllable, and dividing the *rhythm* into two equal parts, in order to leave nothing undone to show the merit on both sides, and the rapture of his impartiality, he utters, for all time, his enchanting record.

Now it requires animal spirits, or a thoroughly loving nature, to enjoy that line completely; and yet, on looking well into it, it will be found to contain (by implication) simile, analogy, and, indeed, every other form of imaginative expression, apart from that of direct illustrative words; which, in such cases, may be called needless commentary. The poet lets nature speak for herself. He points to the two beautiful objects before us, and is content with simply hailing them in their combination.

In all cases where Nature should thus be left to speak for herself (and they are neither mean nor few cases, but many and great) the imaginative faculty, which some think to be totally suspended at such times, is, on the contrary, in full activity, keeping aloof all irrelevancies and impertinence, and thus showing how well it understands its great mistress. When Lady Macbeth says she should have murdered Duncan herself,

Had he not resembled
Her father as he slept,

she said neither more nor less than what a poor criminal said long afterwards, and quite unaware of the passage, when brought before a magistrate from a midnight scuffle in a barge on the Thames;—'I should have killed him, if he had not looked so like my father while he was sleeping.' Shakspeare made poetry of the thought by putting it into verse,—into modulation; but he would not touch it otherwise. He reverenced Nature's own simple, awful, and sufficing suggestion too much, to add a syllable to it for the purpose of showing off his subtle powers of imaginative illustration. And with no want of due reverence to Shakspeare be it said, that it is a pity he did not act invariably with the like judgment;—that he suffered thought to crowd upon thought, where the first feeling was enough. So, what can possibly be imagined simpler, finer, completer, less wanting anything beyond itself, than the line in which poor old Lear, unable to relieve himself with his own trembling fingers, asks the byestander to open his waistcoat for him,—not forgetting, in the midst of his anguish, to return him thanks for so doing, like a gentleman:

> Pray you undo this button—Thank you, Sir.

The poet here presents us with two matters of fact, in their simplest and apparently most prosaical form; yet, when did ever passion or imagination speak more intensely? and this, purely because he has let them alone?

There is another line in Chaucer, which seems to be still plainer matter of fact, with no imagination in it of any kind, apart from the simple necessity of imagining the fact itself. It is in the story of the Tartar king, which Milton wished to have had completed. The king has been feasting, and is moving from the feast to a ballroom:

> Before him goeth the loud minstrelsy.

Now, what is there in this line (it might be asked) which might not have been said in plain prose? which indeed is not prose? The king is preceded by his musicians, playing loudly. What is there in that?

Well, there is something even in that, if the prosers who demand so much help to their perceptions could but see it. But verse fetches it out and puts it in its proper state of movement. The line itself, being a line of verse, and therefore a musical movement, becomes processional, and represents the royal train in action. The word 'goeth,' which a less imaginative writer would have rejected in favour of something which he took to be more spiritual and uncommon, is the soul of the continuity of the movement. It is put, accordingly, in its most emphatic place. And the word 'loud' is suggestive at once of royal power, and of the mute and dignified serenity, superior to that manifestation of it, with which the king follows.

> *Before* him goeth the loud minstrelsy.

Any reader who does not recognise the stately "go," and altogether noble sufficingness of that line, may rest assured that thousands of the beauties of poetry will remain for ever undiscovered by him, let him be helped by as many thoughts and images as he may.

So in a preceding passage where the same musicians are mentioned.

> And so befell, that after the third course,
> While that this King sat thus in his nobley,—
>   [nobleness]
> Hearing his minstrallés their thingés play
> Before him at his board deliciously,
> In at the hallé-door all suddenly
> There came a knight upon a steed of brass,
> And in his hand a broad mirror of glass;
> Upon his thumb he had of gold a ring,
> And by his side a naked sword hanging,
> And up he rideth to the highé board.—
> In all the hallé n'as there spoke a word *[was not]*
> For marvel of this knight—Him to behold
> Full busily they waited, young and old.

In some of these lines, what would otherwise be prose, becomes, by the musical feeling, poetry. The king, 'sitting in his nobleness,' is an imaginative picture. The word 'deliciously' is a venture of animal spirits, which, in a modern writer, some critics would pronounce to be affected, or too familiar; but the enjoyment, and even incidental appropriateness and *relish* of it, will be obvious to finer senses. And in the pause in the middle of the last couplet but one, and that in the course of the first line of its successor, examples were given by this supposed unmusical old poet, of some of the highest refinements of versification.

The secret of musical, as of all other feeling, lies in the depths of the harmonious adjustments of our nature; and a chord touched in any one of them, vibrates with the rest. In the Queen's beautiful letter to Mr. Sidney Herbert, about the sufferers in the Crimea, the touching words, 'those poor noble wounded and sick men,' would easily, and with perfectly poetical sufficiency, flow into verse. Chaucer, with his old English dissyllable, *poore*, (more piteous, because lingering in the sound) would have found in them a verse ready made to his hand—

> Those poorĕ noble wounded and sick men.

The passage is in fact just like one of his own verses, sensitive, earnest, strong, simple, full of truth, full of harmonious sympathy. Many a manly eye will it moisten; many a poor soldier, thus acknowledged to be a 'noble,' will it pay for many a pang. What, if transferred to verse, would it need from any other kind of imaginative treatment? What, indeed, could it receive but injury? And yet, to see what is said by the demanders, on every possible poetical occasion, of perpetual commentating thoughts and imaginative analogies, one must conclude that they would pronounce it to be wholly unfit for poetry, unless something very fine were added about 'poor,' something very fine about 'noble,' something very fine about 'wounded,' and something very fine about 'sick;' a process by which our sympathy with the suffering heroes would come to nothing, in comparison with our astonishment at the rhetoric of the eulogizers,—which, indeed, is a 'consummation' that writers of this description would seem to desire.

Of all the definitions which have been given of poetry, the best is that which pronounces it to be 'geniality, singing.' I think, but am not sure, that it is Lamb's; perhaps it is Coleridge's. I had not seen it, or, if I had, had lost all recollection of it, when I wrote the book called 'Imagination and Fancy'; otherwise I would have substituted it for the definition given in that book; for it comprehends, by implication, all which is there said respecting the different classes and degrees of poetry, and excludes, at the same time, whatsoever does not properly come within the limits of the thing defined.

Geniality, thus considered, is not to be understood in its common limited acceptation of a warm and flowing spirit of companionship. It includes that and every other motive to poetic utterance; but it resumes its great primal meaning of the power of productiveness; that power from which the word Genius is derived, and which falls in so completely with the meaning of the word Poet itself, which is Maker. The poet makes, or produces, because he has a desire to do so; and what he produces is found to be worthy, in proportion as time shows a desire to retain it. As all trees are trees, whatever be the different degrees of their importance, so all poets are poets whose productions have a character of their own, and take root in the ground of national acceptance. The poet sings, because he is excited, and because whatsoever he does must be moulded into a shape of beauty. If imagination predominates in him, and it is of the true kind, and he loves the exercise of it better than the fame, he stands a chance of being a poet of the highest order, but not of the only order. If fancy predominates, and the fancy is of the true kind, he is no less a poet in kind, though inferior in degree. If thought predominate, he is a contemplative poet: if a variety of these faculties in combination, he is various accordingly; less great, perhaps, in each individually, owing to the divided interest which he takes in the claim upon his attention; but far greater, if equally great in all. Nevertheless, he does not hinder his less accomplished brethren from being poets. There is a talk of confining the appellation poet, to the inspired poet. But who and what is the inspired poet? Inspired means 'breathed into;' that is to say, by some superior influence. But how is not Dryden breathed into as well as Chaucer? Milton as well as Shakspeare? or Pope as well as Milton? The flute, though out of all comparison with the organ, is still an instrument 'breathed into.' The only question is, whether it is breathed into finely, and so as to render it a flute extraordinary; whether the player is a man of genius after his kind, not to be mechanically made. You can no more make a Burns than a Homer; no more the author of a *Rape of the Lock* than the author of *Paradise Lost.* If you could, you would have Burnses as plentiful as blackberries and as many *Rapes of the Lock* as books of mightier pretension, that are for ever coming out and going into oblivion. Meantime, the *Rape of the Lock* remains, and why? Because it is an inspired poem; a poem as truly inspired by the genius of wit and fancy, as the gravest and grandest that ever was written was inspired by passion and imagination.

This is the secret of a great, national, book-reading fact, the existence of which has long puzzled exclusives in poetry; to wit, the never-failing demand in all civilized countries for successive publications of bodies of collected verse, called English or British Poets, Italian Poets, French Poets, Spanish Poets, &c.—collections which stand upon no ceremony whatever with exclusive predilections, but tend to include every thing that has attained poetical repute, and are generally considered to be what they ought to be in proportion as they are copious. Poetasters are sometimes admitted for poets; and poets are sometimes missed, because they have been taken for poetasters. But, upon the whole, the chance of excess is preferred: and the preference is well founded; for the whole system is founded on a judicious instinct. Feelings are nature's reasons; communities often feel better than individuals reason; and they feel better in this instance.

—Leigh Hunt, Stories in Verse, 1855, pp. 1–19

RALPH WALDO EMERSON (1856)

A taste for plain strong speech, what is called a biblical style, marks the English. . . . It is not less seen in poetry. Chaucer's hard painting of his Canterbury pilgrims satisfies the senses. . . . This mental materialism makes the value of English transcendental genius.

The marriage of the two qualities (materialism and intellectuality) is in their speech.

—Ralph Waldo Emerson, English Traits,
1856, Vol. 5, Centenary ed., pp. 233–34

WALTER SAVAGE LANDOR "TO CHAUCER" (1863)

Chaucer, O how I wish thou wert
Alive and, as of yore, alert!
Then, after bandied tales, what fun
Would we two have with monk and nun.
Ah, surely verse was never meant
To render mortals somnolent.
In Spenser's labyrinthine rhymes
I throw my arms o'erhead at times,
Opening sonorous mouth as wide
As oystershells at ebb of tide.
Mistake me not: I honour him
Whose magic made the Muses dream
Of things they never knew before,
And scenes they never wandered o'er.
I dare not follow, nor again
Be wafted with the wizard train.
No bodyless and soulless elves
I seek, but creatures like ourselves.
If any poet now runs after
The Faeries, they will split with laughter,
Leaving him in the desert, where
Dry grass is emblematic fare.
Thou wast content to act the squire
Becomingly, and mount no higher,
Nay, at fit season to descend
Into the poet with a friend,
Then ride with him about thy land
In lithesome nutbrown boots well-tann'd,
With lordly greyhound, who would dare
Course against law the summer hare.
Nor takes to heart the frequent crack
Of whip, with curse that calls him back.
The lesser Angels now have smiled
To see thee frolic like a child,
And hear thee, innocent as they.
Provoke them to come down and play.

—Walter Savage Landor,
"To Chaucer," *Heroic Idylls,* 1863, pp. 142–43

Frederick Denison Maurice "On Books" (1865)

A theologian and prolific author in nineteenth-century England, Frederick
Denison Maurice (1805–72) was a keen admirer of Chaucer. Maurice notes
that while Chaucer was not a political or religious reformer like his contemporary John Wycliffe, Chaucer "helped forward the Reformation by
making men acquainted with themselves and their fellows." Maurice's
commentary is especially useful for those writing about Chaucer's connec-
tions to and influence on the religious culture of his day.

⸻

The earliest poetry belongs to the same age with Wycliffe's Bible. Chaucer
was possibly the friend of Wycliffe—certainly shared many of his sympathies
and antipathies. He loved the priest, or, as he was called, the secular priest,
who went among the people, and cared for them as his fellow countrymen;
he intensely disliked the friars, who flattered them and cursed them, and
in both ways governed them and degraded them. His education had been
different from Wycliffe's, his early poetical powers had been called forth by
the ladies and gentlemen of the court. He mingled much French with his
speech, as they did; he acquired from them a kind of acquaintance with life
which Wycliffe could not obtain in the Oxford schools. Had he remained
under their influence he might have been merely a very musical court singer;
but he entered into fellowship with common citizens. He became a keen
observer of all the different forms of life and society in his time—a keen
observer, and, as all such are, genial, friendly, humorous, able to understand
men about him by sympathising with them, able to understand the stories
of the past by his experience of the present. Without being a reformer like
Wycliffe, he helped forward the Reformation by making men acquainted with
themselves and their fellows, by stripping off disguises, and by teaching them
to open their eyes to the beautiful world which lay about them. Chaucer is the
genuine specimen of an English poet—a type of the best who were to come
after him; with cordial affection for men and for nature; often tempted to
coarseness, often yielding to his baser nature in his desire to enter into all the
different experiences of men; apt through this desire, and through his hatred
of what was insincere, to say many things of which he had need to repent,
and of which he did repent; but never losing his loyalty to what was pure, his
reverence for what was divine. He is an illustration of the text from which I
started. The English books which live through ages are those which connect
themselves with human life and action. His other poems, though graceful
and harmonious, are only remembered, because in his *Canterbury Tales* he
has come directly into contact with the hearts and thoughts, the sufferings

and sins, of men and women, and has given the clearest pictures we possess of all the distinctions and occupations in his own day.

—Frederick Denison Maurice, "On Books," 1865,
The Friendship of Books and Other Lectures, 1874, pp. 76–77

FRANCIS JAMES CHILD
"ELISION OF FINAL VOWELS" (1869)

Francis James Child (1825–1896) was a prominent American literary scholar and editor who wrote the influential *Observations on the Language of Chaucer*. An ardent admirer of Chaucer, whom Child calls "a master poet for any time," Child observes that whenever Chaucer's poetry becomes "awkward, halting, or even unharmonious . . . then we have not the verse that Chaucer wrote," especially when it concerns the pronunciation of the final "e" in Chaucerian Middle English, a construct that was part of a prominent nineteenth-century debate on the proper pronunciation of Chaucer's language. Child contends that later editors likely altered the Chaucerian text whenever the sound becomes too awkward, believing Chaucer too masterful a writer to create many ill-sounding lines of poetry.

Even if Chaucer followed invariable rules with regard to the pronouncing or suppressing of the final *e,* it cannot be expected that they should be entirely made out by examining one single text of the *Canterbury Tales,* which, though relatively a good one, is manifestly full of errors. A comparison of several of the better manuscripts would enable us to speak with much more accuracy and confidence. Tyrwhitt's arbitrary text may very frequently be used to clear up, both in this and in other particulars, the much superior manuscript published by Wright. Still the question whether an *e* was pronounced would often be one of much delicacy (as the previous question whether it actually existed is sometimes one of great difficulty), and not to be determined by counting syllables on the fingers. No supposition is indeed more absurd than that Chaucer, a master poet for any time, could write awkward, halting, or even unharmonious verses. It is to be held, therefore, that when a verse is bad, and cannot be made good anyway as it stands, then we have not the verse that Chaucer wrote. But with regard to the particular point upon which we are now engaged, it would often be indifferent, or nearly so, whether a final *e* is absolutely dropped, or lightly glided over. Then again, as not a few grammatical forms were most certainly written both with and without this termination, the fuller form would often slip in where the other would be preferable or necessary, much depending on the care, the intelligence, or the good ear of the scribe. Very often the concurrence of an initial vowel, justifying elision, with a doubtful final *e*, renders it possible to read a verse in two ways or more; and lastly, hundreds of verses are so mutilated or corrupted that no safe opinion can be based upon them. Such verses as these ought plainly not to be used either to support or impugn a conclusion; neither ought the general rules which seem to be authorized by the majority of instances be too rigorously applied to the emendation of verses that cannot be made, as they stand, to come under these rules.

—Francis James Child, "Elision of Final Vowels," *Early English Pronunciation*, 1869, Pt. 1, Ch. 4, ed. Ellis, p. 360

James Russell Lowell "Chaucer" (1870)

An American literary critic, James Russell Lowell (1819–1891) was also a noted poet and abolitionist. The lengthy excerpt below, though full of rich material, contains four sections that are of primary use to students writing about Chaucer. The first section enjoins the scholarly debate regarding Chaucer and his sources. Lowell identifies the four main groups that influenced Chaucer's work—the Latins (especially Ovid), the troubadours (medieval court poets of southern France), the *trouveres* (medieval poet/musicians located in northern France), and the Italians (particularly Dante, Petrarch, and Boccaccio). Though this aspect of Chaucer's work has been discussed by numerous other writers excerpted in this volume—including John Dryden, who also speaks of Ovid, and William Minto, who speaks of the trouveres—Lowell's work on the subject here is exceptionally clear and comprehensive, and is a good place for students working with Chaucer to begin understanding the issues behind the scholarly debate on his sources.

Lowell next compares Chaucer to Dante, the most thorough comparison of the two found in this text. Lowell declares Dante to be a "more universal poet" while Chaucer was a "more truly national one," a man who reflected the England of his day. While discussing these two great poets, Lowell refers to the oft-repeated maxim that Chaucer "did for English what Dante is supposed to have done for Italian," that Chaucer is largely responsible for sparking the English literary tradition. Lowell cautions against such strong statements, noting that "Languages are never made in any such fashion." His work here provides a strong counterpoint to the more enthusiastic critics in this text who refer to Chaucer as having practically "invented" English.

Lowell then considers Chaucer and his two great English contemporaries, John Gower, author of the *Confessio Amantis*, and William Langland, author of *Piers Ploughman*. Unlike Nashe and Barrett Browning, who praise Gower, or Samuel Johnson, who places Gower above Chaucer, Lowell dismisses Gower, suggesting, "His tediousness is omnipresent." Lowell finds a stronger connection between Chaucer and Langland, about whom Lowell writes, "Langland has as much tenderness, as much interest in the varied picture of life, as hearty a contempt for hypocrisy, and almost an equal sense of fun." Still, Lowell ultimately concludes that Chaucer had a "rare . . . genius" that places him above his fellow English medieval writers.

Lowell's last section may prove his most helpful to students studying Chaucer. His discussion of Chaucer and meter, and meter in poetry in general, acts as a strong primer to help in comprehending the other excerpts in this volume that also tackle the question of meter in Chaucer. Though Lowell believes that "A great deal of misapprehension would be avoided in discussing English metres," his work on the subject provides students with a clear if concise glimpse into the issues at the heart of this Chaucerian scholarly debate.

The first question we put to any poet, nay, to any so-called national literature, is that which Farinata addressed to Dante, *Chi fur li maggior tui?* Here is no question of plagiarism, for poems are not made of words and thoughts and images, but of that something in the poet himself which can compel them to obey him and move to the rhythm of his nature. Thus it is that the new poet, however late he come, can never be forestalled, and the ship-builder who built the pinnace of Columbus has as much claim to the discovery of America as he who suggests a thought by which some other man opens new worlds to us has to a share in that achievement by him unconceived and inconceivable. Chaucer undoubtedly began as an imitator, perhaps as mere translator, serving the needful apprenticeship in the use of his tools. Children learn to speak by watching the lips and catching the words of those who know how already, and poets learn in the same way from their elders. They import their raw material from any and everywhere, and the question at last comes down to this,—whether an author have original force enough to assimilate all he has acquired, or that be so overmastering as to assimilate *him*. If the poet turn out the stronger, we allow him to help himself from other people with wonderful equanimity. Should a man discover the art of transmuting metals and present us with a lump of gold as large as an ostrich-egg, would it be in human nature to inquire too nicely whether he had stolen the lead?

Nothing is more certain than that great poets are not sudden prodigies, but slow results. As an oak profits by the foregone lives of immemorial vegetable races that have worked-over the juices of earth and air into organic life out of whose dissolution a soil might gather fit to maintain that nobler birth of nature, so we may be sure that the genius of every remembered poet drew the forces that built it up out of the decay of a long succession of forgotten ones. Nay, in proportion as the genius is vigorous and original will its indebtedness be greater, will its roots strike deeper into the past and grope in remoter fields for the virtue that must sustain it. Indeed, if the works of the great poets teach anything, it is to hold mere invention somewhat cheap. It is not the finding of a thing, but the making something out of it after it is found, that is of consequence. Accordingly, Chaucer, like Shakespeare, invented almost nothing. Wherever he found anything directed to Geoffrey Chaucer, he took it and made the most of it. It was not the subject treated, but himself, that was the new thing. *Cela m'appartient de droit,* Moliere is reported to have said when accused of plagiarism. Chaucer pays that "usurious interest which genius," as Coleridge says, "always pays in borrowing." The characteristic touch is his own. In the famous passage about the caged bird, copied from the *Romaunt of the Rose,* the "gon eten wormes" was added by him. We must let him, if he will, eat the heart out of the literature that had preceded him, as we sacrifice the mulberry-leaves to the silkworm, because he knows how to convert them into something richer and more lasting. The question of originality is not one of form, but of substance, not of cleverness, but of imaginative power. Given your material, in other words the life in which you live, how much can you see in it? For on that depends how much you can make of it. Is it merely an arrangement of man's contrivance, a patchwork of expediencies for temporary comfort and convenience, good enough if it last your time, or is it so much of the surface of that ever-flowing deity which we call Time, wherein we catch such fleeting reflection as is possible for us, of our relation to perdurable things? This is what makes the difference between Æschylus and Euripides, between Shakespeare and Fletcher, between Goethe and Heine, between literature and rhetoric. Something of this depth of insight, if not in the fullest, yet in no inconsiderable measure, characterizes Chaucer. We must not let his playfulness, his delight in the world as mere spectacle, mislead us into thinking that he was incapable of serious purpose or insensible to the deeper meanings of life.

There are four principal sources from which Chaucer may be presumed to have drawn for poetical suggestion or literary culture,—the Latins, the Troubadours, the Trouveres, and the Italians. It is only the two latter who can fairly claim any immediate influence in the direction of his thought or the formation of his style. The only Latin poet who can be supposed to have influenced the spirit of mediæval literature is Ovid. . . .

Chaucer, to whom French must have been almost as truly a mother tongue as English, was familiar with all that had been done by Troubadour or Trouvere. In him we see the first result of the Norman yeast upon the home-baked Saxon loaf. The flour had been honest, the paste well kneaded, but the inspiring leaven was wanting till the Norman brought it over. Chaucer works still in the solid material of his race, but with what airy lightness has he not infused it? Without ceasing to be English, he has escaped from being insular. But he was something more than this; he was a scholar, a thinker, and a critic. He had studied the *Divina Commedia* of Dante, he had read Petrarca and Boccaccio, and some of the Latin poets. He calls Dante the great poet of Italy, and Petrarch a learned clerk. It is plain that he knew very well the truer purpose of poetry, and had even arrived at the higher wisdom of comprehending the aptitudes and limitations of his own genius. He saw clearly and felt keenly what were the faults and what the wants of the prevailing literature of his country. In the *Monk's Tale* he slyly satirizes the long-winded morality of Gower, as his prose antitype, Fielding, was to satirize the prolix sentimentality of Richardson. In the rhyme of Sir Thopas he gives the *coup de grace* to the romances of Chivalry, and in his own choice of a subject he heralds that new world in which the actual and the popular were to supplant the fantastic and the heroic.

Before Chaucer, modern Europe had given birth to one great poet, Dante; and contemporary with him was one supremely elegant one, Petrarch. Dante died only seven years before Chaucer was born, and, so far as culture is derived from books, the moral and intellectual influences to which they had been subjected, the speculative stimulus that may have given an impulse to their minds,—there could have been no essential difference between them. Yet there are certain points of resemblance and of contrast, and those not entirely fanciful, which seem to me of considerable interest. Both were of mixed race, Dante certainly, Chaucer presumably so. Dante seems to have inherited on the Teutonic side the strong moral sense, the almost nervous irritability of conscience, and the tendency to mysticism which made him the first of Christian poets,—first in point of time and first in point of greatness. From the other side he seems to have received almost in overplus a feeling of order and proportion, sometimes wellnigh hardening into mathematical precision and formalism,—a tendency which at last brought the poetry of the Romanic races to a dead-lock of artifice and decorum. Chaucer, on the other hand, drew from the South a certain airiness of sentiment and expression, a felicity of phrase and an elegance of turn, hitherto unprecedented and hardly yet matched in our literature, but all the while kept firm hold of his native soundness of understanding, and that genial humor which seems to be the proper element of worldly wisdom. With Dante life represented the passage of the soul from a state of nature to a state of grace; and there would have been almost an even chance whether (as Burns says) the *Divina Commedia* had turned out a song or a sermon, but for the wonderful genius of its author, which has compelled the sermon to sing and the song to preach, whether they would or no. With Chaucer, life is a pilgrimage, but only that his eye may be delighted with the varieties of costume and character. There are good morals to be found in Chaucer, but they are always incidental. With Dante the main question is the saving of the soul, with Chaucer it is the conduct of life. The distance between them is almost that between holiness and prudence. Dante applies himself to the realities, Chaucer to the scenery of life, and the former is consequently the more universal poet, as the latter is the more truly national one. Dante represents the justice of God, and Chaucer his loving-kindness. If there is anything that may properly be called satire in the one, it is like a blast of the divine wrath, before which the wretches cower and tremble, which rends away their cloaks of hypocrisy and their masks of worldly propriety, and leaves them shivering in the cruel nakedness of their shame. The satire of the other is genial with the broad sunshine of humor, into which the victims walk forth with a delightful unconcern, laying aside of themselves the disguises that seem to make them uncomfortably warm, till they have made a thorough betrayal of themselves so unconsciously that we almost pity while we laugh. Dante shows us the punishment of sins against God and one's neighbor, in order that we may shun them, and so escape the doom that awaits them in the other world. Chaucer exposes the cheats of the transmuter of metals, of the begging friars, and of the pedlers of indulgences, in order that we may be on our guard against them in this world. If we are to judge of what is national only by the highest and most characteristic types, surely we cannot fail to see in Chaucer the true forerunner and prototype of Shakespeare, who, with an imagination of far deeper grasp, a far wider reach of thought, yet took the same delight in the pageantry of the actual world, and whose moral is the moral of worldly wisdom only heightened to the level of his wide-viewing mind, and made typical by the dramatic energy of his plastic nature.

Yet of Chaucer had little of that organic force of life which so inspires the poem of Dante that, as he himself says of the heavens, part answers to part with mutual interchange of light, he had a structural faculty which distinguishes him from all other English poets, his contemporaries, and which indeed is the primary distinction of poets properly so called. There is, to be sure, only one other English writer coeval with himself who deserves in any way to be compared with him, and that rather for contrast than for likeness.

With the single exception of Langland, the English poets, his contemporaries, were little else than bad versifiers of legends classic or mediaeval, as it might happen, without selection and without art. Chaucer is the first who broke away from the dreary traditional style, and gave not merely stories, but lively *pictures* of real life as the ever-renewed substance of poetry. He was a reformer, too, not only in literature, but in morals. But as in the former his exquisite tact saved him from all eccentricity, so in the latter the pervading sweetness of his nature could never be betrayed into harshness and invective. He seems incapable of indignation. He mused good-naturedly over the vices and follies of men, and, never forgetting that he was fashioned of the same clay, is rather apt to pity than condemn. There is no touch of cynicism in all he wrote. Dante's brush seems sometimes to have been smeared with the burning pitch of his own fiery lake. Chaucer's pencil is dipped in the cheerful color-box of the old illuminators, and he has their patient delicacy of touch, with a freedom far beyond their somewhat mechanic brilliancy.

English narrative poetry, as Chaucer found it, though it had not altogether escaped from the primal curse of long-windedness so painfully characteristic of its prototype, the French Romance of Chivalry, had certainly shown a feeling for the picturesque, a sense of color, a directness of phrase, and a simplicity of treatment which give it graces of its own and a turn peculiar to itself. In the easy knack of story-telling, the popular minstrels cannot compare with Marie de France. The lightsomeness of fancy, that leaves a touch of sunshine and is gone, is painfully missed in them all. Their incidents enter dispersedly, as the old stage directions used to say, and they have not learned the art of concentrating their force on the key-point of their hearers' interest. They neither get fairly hold of their subject, nor, what is more important, does it get hold of them. But they sometimes yield to an instinctive hint of leaving-off at the right moment, and in their happy negligence achieve an effect only to be matched by the highest successes of art.

> That lady heard his mourning all
> Right under her chamber wall,
> In her oriel where she was,
> Closed well with royal glass;
> Fulfilled it was with imagery
> Every window, by and by;

On each side had there a gin
Sperred with many a divers pin;
Anon that lady fair and free
Undid a pin of ivory
And wide the window she open set,
The sun shone in at her closet.

It is true the old rhymer relapses a little into the habitual drone of his class, and shows half a mind to bolt into their common inventory style when he comes to his *gins* and *pins,* but he withstands the temptation manfully, and his sunshine fills our hearts with a gush as sudden as that which illumines the lady's oriel. Coleridge and Keats have each in his way felt the charm of this winsome picture, but have hardly equalled its hearty honesty, its economy of material, the supreme test of artistic skill. I admit that the phrase *"had there a gin"* is suspicious, and suggests a French original, but I remember nothing altogether so good in the romances from the other side of the Channel. One more passage occurs to me, almost incomparable in its simple straightforward force and choice of the right word.

Sir Graysteel to his death thus thraws,
He welters [wallows] and the grass updraws; . . .
A little while then lay he still,
(Friends that saw him liked full ill,)
And bled into his armor bright.

The last line, for suggestive reticence, almost deserves to be put beside the famous

Quel giorno più non vi leggemmo avante

of the great master of laconic narration. In the same poem[1] the growing love of the lady, in its maidenliness of unconscious betrayal, is touched with a delicacy and tact as surprising as they are delightful. But such passages, which are the despair of poets who have to work in a language that has faded into diction, are exceptional. They are to be set down rather to good luck than to art. Even the stereotyped similes of these fortunate illiterates, like "weary as water in a weir," or "glad as grass is of the rain," are new, like nature, at the thousandth repetition. Perhaps our palled taste overvalues the wild flavor of these wayside treasure-troves. They are wood-strawberries, prized in proportion as we must turn over more leaves ere we find one. This popular literature is of value in helping us towards a juster estimate of Chaucer by showing what the mere language was capable of, and that all it wanted was a poet to put it through its paces. For though the poems I have quoted be, in their present form, later than he, they are, after all, but modernized versions of older copies, which they doubtless reproduce with substantial fidelity.

It is commonly assumed that Chaucer did for English what Dante is supposed to have done for Italian and Luther for German, that he, in short, in some hitherto inexplicable way, created it. But this is to speak loosely and without book. Languages are never made in any such fashion, still less are they the achievement of any single man, however great his genius, however powerful his individuality. They shape themselves by laws as definite as those which guide and limit the growth of other living organisms. Dante, indeed, has told us that he chose to write in the tongue that might be learned of nurses and chafferers in the market. His practice shows that he knew perfectly well that poetry has needs which cannot be answered by the vehicle of vulgar commerce between man and man. What he instinctively felt was, that there was the living heart of all speech, without whose help the brain were powerless to send will, motion, meaning, to the limbs and extremities. But it is true that a language, as respects the uses of literature, is liable to a kind of syncope. No matter how complete its vocabulary may be, how thorough an outfit of inflections and case-endings it may have, it is a mere dead body without a soul till some man of genius set its arrested pulses once more athrob, and show what wealth of sweetness, scorn, persuasion, and passion lay there awaiting its liberator. In this sense it is hardly too much to say that Chaucer, like Dante, found his native tongue a dialect and left it a language. But it was not what he did with deliberate purpose of reform, it was his kindly and plastic genius that wrought this magic of renewal and inspiration. It was not the new words he introduced,[2] but his way of using the old ones, that surprised them into grace, ease, and dignity in their own despite. In order to feel fully how much he achieved, let any one subject himself to a penitential course of reading in his contemporary, Gower, who worked in a material to all intents and purposes the same, or listen for a moment to the barbarous jangle which Lydgate and Occleve contrive to draw from the instrument their master had tuned so deftly. Gower has positively raised tediousness to the precision of science, he has made dulness an heirloom for the students of our literary history. As you slip to and fro on the frozen levels of his verse, which give no foothold to the mind, as your nervous ear awaits the inevitable recurrence of his rhyme, regularly pertinacious as the tick of an eight-day clock and reminding you of Wordsworth's

> Once more the ass did lengthen out
> The hard, dry, seesaw of his horrible bray,

you learn to dread, almost to respect, the powers of this indefatigable man. He is the undertaker of the fair mediaeval legend, and his style has the hateful gloss, the seemingly unnatural length, of a coffin. Love, beauty, passion, nature, art, life, the natural and theological virtues,—there is nothing beyond his power to disenchant, nothing out of which the tremendous hydraulic press of his allegory (or whatever it is, for I am not sure if it be not something even worse) will not squeeze all feeling and freshness and leave it a juiceless pulp. It matters not where you try him, whether his story be Christian or pagan, borrowed from history or fable, you cannot escape him. Dip in at the middle or the end, dodge back to the beginning, the patient old man is there to take you by the button and go on with his imperturbable narrative. You may have left off with Clytemnestra, and you begin again with Samson; it makes no odds, for you cannot tell one from tother. His tediousness is omnipresent, and like Dogberry he could find in his heart to bestow it all (and more if he had it) on your worship. The word *lengthy* has been charged to our American account, but it must have been invented by the first reader of Gower's works, the only inspiration of which they were ever capable. Our literature had to lie by and recruit for more than four centuries ere it could give us an equal vacuity in Tupper, so persistent a uniformity of commonplace in the "Recreations of a Country Parson." Let us be thankful that the industrious Gower never found time for recreation!

But a fairer as well as more instructive comparison lies between Chaucer and the author of *Piers Ploughman.* Langland has as much tenderness, as much interest in the varied picture of life, as hearty a contempt for hypocrisy, and almost an equal sense of fun. He has the same easy abundance of matter. But what a difference! It is the difference between the poet and the man of poetic temperament. The abundance of the one is a continual fulness within the fixed limits of good taste; that of the other is squandered in overflow. The one can be profuse on occasion; the other is diffuse whether he will or no. The one is full of talk; the other is garrulous. What in one is the refined *bonhomie* of a man of the world, is a rustic shrewdness in the other. Both are kindly in their satire, and have not (like too many reformers) that vindictive love of virtue which spreads the stool of repentance with thistle-burrs before they invite the erring to seat themselves therein. But what in Piers *Ploughman* is sly fun, has the breadth and depth of humor in Chaucer; and it is plain that while the former was taken up by his moral purpose, the main interest of the latter turned to perfecting the form of his work. In short, Chaucer had that fine literary sense which is as rare as genius, and, united with it, as it was in him, assures an immortality of fame. It is not merely what he has to say, but even more the agreeable way he has of saying it, that captivates our attention and gives him an assured place in literature. Above all, it is not in detached passages that his charm lies, but in the entirety of expression and the cumulative effect of many particulars working toward a common end. Now though *ex ungue leonem* be a good rule in comparative anatomy, its application, except in a very limited way, in criticism is sure to mislead; for we should always bear in mind that the really great writer is great in the mass, and is to be tested less by his cleverness in the elaboration of parts than by that *reach* of mind which is incapable of random effort, which selects, arranges, combines, rejects, denies itself the cheap triumph of immediate effects, because it is absorbed by the controlling charm of proportion and unity. A careless good-luck of phrase is delightful; but criticism cleaves to the teleological argument, and distinguishes the creative intellect, not so much by any happiness of natural endowment as by the marks of design. It is true that one may sometimes discover by a single verse whether an author have imagination, or may make a shrewd guess whether he have style or no, just as by a few spoken words you may judge of a man's accent; but the true artist in language is never spotty, and needs no guide-boards of admiring italics, a critical method introduced by Leigh Hunt, whose feminine temperament gave him acute perceptions at the expense of judgment. This is the Boeotian method, which offers us a brick as a sample of the house, forgetting that it is not the goodness of the separate bricks, but the way in which they are put together, that brings them within the province of art, and makes the difference between a heap and a house. A great writer does not reveal himself here and there, but everywhere. Langland's verse runs mostly like a brook, with a beguiling and wellnigh slumberous prattle, but he, more often than any writer of his class, flashes into salient lines, gets inside our guard with the homethrust of a forthright word, and he gains if taken piecemeal. His imagery is naturally and vividly picturesque, as where he says of Old Age,—

> Eld the hoar
> That was in the vaunrward,
> And bare the banner before death,—

and he softens to a sweetness of sympathy beyond Chaucer when he speaks of the poor or tells us that Mercy is "sib of all sinful"; but to compare *Piers Ploughman* with the *Canterbury Tales* is to compare sermon with song.

Let us put a bit of Langland's satire beside one of Chaucer's. Some people in search of Truth meet a pilgrim and ask him whence he comes. He gives a long list of holy places, appealing for proof to the relics on his hat:—

'I have walked full wide in wet and in dry
And sought saints for my soul's health.'
'Know'st thou ever a relic that is called
Truth? Couldst thou show us the way where that wight
        dwelleth?'
'Nay, so God help me,' said the man then,
'I saw never palmer with staff nor with scrip
Ask after him ever till now in this place.'

This is a good hit, and the poet is satisfied; but, in what I am going to quote from Chaucer, everything becomes picture, over which lies broad and warm the sunshine of humorous fancy.

In olde dayes of the King Artour
Of which that Britouns speken gret honour,
All was this lond fulfilled of fayerie:
The elf-queen with her joly compaignie
Danced fill oft in many a grene mede:
This was the old opinion as I rede;
I speke of many hundrid yer ago:
But now can no man see none elves mo,
For now the grete charite and prayeres
Of lymytours and other holy freres
That sechen every lond and every streem,
As thick as motis in the sonnebeam,
Blessyng halles, chambres, kichenes, and boures,
Citees and burghes, castels hihe and toures,
Thorpes and bernes, shepnes and dayeries,
This makith that ther ben no fayeries.
For ther as wont to walken was an elf
There walkith none but the lymytour himself,
In undermeles and in morwenynges,
And sayth his matyns and his holy thinges,
As he goth in his lymytatioun.
Wommen may now go saufly up and doun;
In every bush or under every tre
There is none other incubus but he,
And he ne wol doon hem no dishonour.

How cunningly the contrast is suggested here between the Elf-queen's jolly company and the unsocial limiters, thick as motes in the sunbeam, yet each walking by himself! And with what an air of innocent unconsciousness is the deadly thrust of the last verse given, with its contemptuous emphasis on the *he* that seems so well-meaning! Even Shakespeare, who seems to come in after everybody has done his best with a "Let me take hold a minute and show you how to do it," could not have bettered this.

Piers Ploughman is the best example I know of what is called popular poetry,—of compositions, that is, which contain all the simpler elements of poetry, but still in solution, not crystallized around any thread of artistic purpose. In it appears at her best the Anglo-Saxon Muse, a first cousin of Poor Richard, full of proverbial wisdom, who always brings her knitting in her pocket, and seems most at home in the chimney-corner. It is genial; it plants itself firmly on human nature with its rights and wrongs; it has a surly honesty, prefers the downright to the gracious, and conceives of speech as a tool rather than a musical instrument. If we should seek for a single word that would define it most precisely, we should not choose simplicity, but homeliness. There is more or less of this in all early poetry, to be sure; but I think it especially proper to English poets, and to the most English among them, like Cowper, Crabbe, and one is tempted to add Wordsworth,—where he forgets Coleridge's private lectures. In reading such poets as Langland, also, we are not to forget a certain charm of distance in the very language they use, making it unhackneyed without being alien. As it is the chief function of the poet to make the familiar novel, these fortunate early risers of literature, who gather phrases with the dew still on them, have their poetry done for them, as it were, by their vocabulary. But in Chaucer, as in all great poets, the language gets its charm from him. The force and sweetness of his genius kneaded more kindly together the Latin and Teutonic elements of our mother tongue, and made something better than either. The necessity of writing poetry, and not mere verse, made him a reformer whether he would or no; and the instinct of his finer ear was a guide such as none before him or contemporary with him, nor indeed any that came after him, till Spenser, could command. Gower had no notion of the uses of rhyme except as a kind of crease at the end of every eighth syllable, where the verse was to be folded over again into another layer. He says, for example,

> This maiden Canacee was hight,
> Both in the day and eke by night,

as if people commonly changed their names at dark. And he could not even contrive to say this without the clumsy pleonasm of *both* and *eke*. Chaucer was put to no such shifts of piecing out his metre with loose-woven bits of baser stuff. He himself says, in the *Man of Law's Tale*,—

Me lists not of the chaff nor of the straw
To make so long a tale as of the corn.

One of the world's three or four great story-tellers, he was also one of
the best versifiers that ever made English trip and sing with a gayety that
seems careless, but where every foot beats time to the tune of the thought.
By the skilful arrangement of his pauses he evaded the monotony of the
couplet, and gave to the rhymed pentameter, which he made our heroic
measure, something of the architectural repose of blank verse. He found
our language lumpish, stiff, unwilling, too apt to speak Saxonly in grouty
monosyllables; he left it enriched with the longer measure of the Italian and
Provengal poets. He reconciled, in the harmony of his verse, the English
bluntness with the dignity and elegance of the less homely Southern speech.
Though he did not and could not create our language (for he who writes
to be read does not write for linguisters), yet it is true that he first made it
easy, and to that extent modern, so that Spenser, two hundred years later,
studied his method and called him master. He first wrote *English;* and it
was a feeling of this, I suspect, that made it fashionable in Elizabeth's day
to "talk pure Chaucer." Already we find in his works verses that might pass
without question in Milton or even Wordsworth, so mainly unchanged
have the language of poetry and the movement of verse remained from his
day to our own.

> Thou Polymnia
> On Pernaso, that, with[3] thy sisters glade,
> By Helicon, not far from Cirrea,
> Singest with voice memorial in the shade,
> Under the laurel which that may not fade.
> And downward from a hill under a bent
> There stood the temple of Mars omnipotent
> Wrought all of burned steel, of which th' entree
> Was long and strait and ghastly for to see:
> The northern light in at the doores shone
> For window in the wall ne was there none
> Through which men mighten any light discerne;
> The dore was all of adamant eterne.

And here are some lines that would not seem out of place in the "Paradise of
Dainty Devises":—

> Hide, Absolom, thy gilte [gilded] tresses clear,
> Esther lay thou thy meeknesses all adown. . . .

> Make of your wifehood no comparison;
> Hide ye your beauties Ysoude and Elaine,
> My lady cometh, that all this may distain.

When I remember Chaucer's malediction upon his scrivener, and consider that by far the larger proportion of his verses (allowing always for change of pronunciation) are perfectly accordant with our present accentual system, I cannot believe that he ever wrote an imperfect line. His ear would never have tolerated the verses of nine syllables, with a strong accent on the first, attributed to him by Mr. Skeat and Mr. Morris. Such verses seem to me simply impossible in the pentameter iambic as Chaucer wrote it. A great deal of misapprehension would be avoided in discussing English metres, if it were only understood that quantity in Latin and quantity in English mean very different things. Perhaps the best quantitative verses in our language (better even than Coleridge's) are to be found in Mother Goose, composed by nurses wholly by ear and beating time as they danced the baby on their knee. I suspect Chaucer and Shakespeare would be surprised into a smile by the learned arguments which supply their halting verses with every kind of excuse except that of being readable. When verses were written to be chanted, more license could be allowed, for the ear tolerates the widest deviations from habitual accent in words that are sung. *Segnius irritant demissa per aurem.* To some extent the same thing is true of anapaestic and other tripping measures, but we cannot admit it in marching tunes like those of Chaucer. He wrote for the eye more than for the voice, as poets had begun to do long before.[4] Some loose talk of Coleridge, loose in spite of its affectation of scientific precision, about "retardations" and the like, has misled many honest persons into believing that they can make good verse out of bad prose. Coleridge himself, from natural fineness of ear, was the best metrist among modern English poets, and, read with proper allowances, his remarks upon versification are always instructive to whoever is not rhythm-deaf. But one has no patience with the dyspondaeuses, the paeon primuses, and what not, with which he darkens verses that are to be explained only by the contemporary habits of pronunciation. Till after the time of Shakespeare we must always bear in mind that it is not a language of books but of living speech that we have to deal with. Of this language Coleridge had little knowledge, except what could be acquired through the ends of his fingers as they lazily turned the leaves of his haphazard reading. If his eye was caught by a single passage that gave him a chance to theorize he did not look farther. Speaking of Massinger, for example, he says, "When a speech is interrupted, or one of the characters speaks aside, the last syllable of the former speech and first of the succeeding Massinger counts for one, because both are supposed to be spoken at the same moment.

> 'And felt the sweetness *of't*
>   'How her mouth runs over.'

Now fifty instances may be cited from Massinger which tell against this fanciful notion, for one that seems, and only seems, in its favor. Any one tolerably familiar with the dramatists knows that in the passage quoted by Coleridge, the *how* being emphatic, *"how her"* was pronounced *how'r*. He tells us that "Massinger is fond of the anapaest in the first and third foot, as:—

> Tŏ yoŭr mōre | thăn mās | cŭlĭnĕ rēa | sŏn
>   thāt | cŏmmānds 'ĕm ||.

Likewise of the second paeon (ˇˉˇˇ) in the first foot, followed by four trochees (ˉˇ), as:—

> Sŏ grēēdĭlў̆ | lōng fŏr, | knōw theiˇr | tītĭll | ātĭŏns."

In truth, he was no fonder of them than his brother dramatists who, like him, wrote for the voice by the ear. "To your" is still one syllable in ordinary speech, and "masculine" and "greedily" were and are dissyllables or trisyllables according to their place in the verse. Coleridge was making pedantry of a very simple matter. Yet he has said with perfect truth of Chaucer's verse, "Let a few plain rules be given for sounding the final *e* of syllables, and for expressing the terminations of such words as *ocëan* and *natiön*, &c, as dissyllables,—or let the syllables to be sounded in such cases be marked by a competent metrist. This simple expedient would, with a very few trifling exceptions, where the errors are inveterate, enable any one to feel the perfect smoothness and harmony of Chaucer's verse." But let us keep widely clear of Latin and Greek terms of prosody! It is also more important here than even with the dramatists of Shakespeare's time to remember that we have to do with a language caught more from the ear than from books. The best school for learning to understand Chaucer's elisions, compressions, slurrings-over and runnings-together of syllables is to listen to the habitual speech of rustics with whom language is still plastic to meaning, and hurries or prolongs itself accordingly. Here is a contraction frequent in Chaucer, and still common in New England:—

> But me were lever than [lever'n] all this town,
>   quod he.

Let one example suffice for many. To Coleridge's rules another should be added by a wise editor; and that is to restore the final n in the infinitive and third person plural of verbs, and in such other cases as can be justified by the authority of Chaucer himself. Surely his ear could never have endured the sing-song of such verses as

> I couth*e* tell*e* for a gown*e*-cloth,

or

> Than ye to me schuld brek*e* your*e* trouth*e*.

Chaucer's measure is so uniform (making due allowances) that words should be transposed or even omitted where the verse manifestly demands it,—and with copyists so long and dull of ear this is often the case. Sometimes they leave out a needful word:—

> But er [the] thunder stynte, there cometh rain,
> When [that] we ben yflattered and ypraised,
> Tak [ye] him for the greatest gentleman.

Sometimes they thrust in a word or words that hobble the verse:—

> She trowed he were yfel in [some] maladie,
> Ye faren like a man [that] had lost his wit,
> Then have I got of you the maystrie, quod she,
> (Then have I got the maystery, quod she,)
> And quod the jugë [also] thou must lose thy head.

Sometimes they give a wrong word identical in meaning:—

> And therwithal he knew [couthe] mo proverbes.

Sometimes they change the true order of the words:—

> Therefore no woman of clerkës is [is of clerkes]
>   praised
> His felaw lo, here he stont [stont he] hool on live.
> He that covèteth is a porë wight
> For he wold have that is not in his might;
> But he that nought hath ne coveteth nought to have.

Here the "but" of the third verse belongs at the head of the first, and we get rid of the anomaly of "coveteth" differently accented within two lines. Nearly all the seemingly unmetrical verses may be righted in this way. I find a good example of this in the last stanza of *Troilus and Creseide*. As it stands, we read,—

Thou one, two, and three, eterne on live
That raignast aie in three, two and one.

It is plain that we should read "one *and* two" in the first verse, and "three *and* two" in the second. Remembering, then, that Chaucer was here translating Dante, I turned (after making the correction) to the original, and found as I expected

Quell' uno *e* due e tre che sempre vive
E regna sempre in tre *e* due ed uno.
							(Par. xiv. 28, 29)

In the stanza before this we have,—

To thee and to the philosophic*all* strode,
To vouchsafe [vouchësafe] there need is, to correct;

and further on,—

With all mine herte' of mercy ever I pray
And to the Lord aright thus I speake and say,

where we must either strike out the second "I" or put it after "speake." . . .

I will give one more example of Chaucer's verse, again making my selection from one of his less mature works. He is speaking of Tarquin:—

And ay the morë he was in despair
The more he coveted and thought her fair;
His blindë lust was all his coveting.
On morrow when the bird began to sing
Unto the siege he cometh full privily
And by himself he walketh soberly
The imáge of her recording alway new:
Thus lay her hair, and thus fresh was her hue,
Thus sate, thus spake, thus span, this was her cheer,
Thus fair she was, and this was her manére.
All this conceit his heart hath new ytake,
And as the sea, with tempest all toshake,
That after, when the storm is all ago,
Yet will the water quap a day or two,
Right so, though that her formë were absént,
The pleasance of her forme was presént.

And this passage leads me to say a few words of Chaucer as a descriptive poet; for I think it a great mistake to attribute to him any properly dramatic power, as some have done. Even Herr Hertzberg, in his remarkably intelligent essay, is led a little astray on this point by his enthusiasm. Chaucer is a great narrative poet; and, in this species of poetry, though the author's personality should never be obtruded, it yet unconsciously pervades the whole, and communicates an individual quality,—a kind of flavor of its own. This very quality, and it is one of the highest in its way and place, would be fatal to all dramatic force. The narrative poet is occupied with his characters as picture, with their grouping, even their costume, it may be, and he feels for and with them instead of being they for the moment, as the dramatist must always be. The story-teller must possess the situation perfectly in all its details, while the imagination of the dramatist must be possessed and mastered by it. The latter puts before us the very passion or emotion itself in its utmost intensity; the former gives them, not in their primary form, but in that derivative one which they have acquired by passing through his own mind and being modified by his reflection. The deepest pathos of the drama, like the quiet "no more but so?" with which Shakespeare tells us that Ophelia's heart is bursting, is sudden as a stab, while in narrative it is more or less suffused with pity,—a feeling capable of prolonged sustention. This presence of the author's own sympathy is noticeable in all Chaucer's pathetic passages, as, for instance, in the lamentation of Constance over her child in the *Man of Law's Tale*. When he comes to the sorrow of his story, he seems to croon over his thoughts, to soothe them and dwell upon them with a kind of pleased compassion, as a child treats a wounded bird which he fears to grasp too tightly, and yet cannot make up his heart wholly to let go. It is true also of his humor that it pervades his comic tales like sunshine, and never dazzles the attention by a sudden flash. Sometimes he brings it in parenthetically, and insinuates a sarcasm so slyly as almost to slip by without our notice, as where he satirizes provincialism by the cock who

> By nature knew ech ascensioun
> Of equinoxial in thilke toun.

Sometimes he turns round upon himself and smiles at a trip he has made into fine writing:—

> Till that the brighte sun had lost his hue,
> For th' orisont had reft the sun his light,
> (This is as much to sayen as 'it was night.')

Nay, sometimes it twinkles roguishly through his very tears, as in the

'Why wouldest thou be dead,' these women cry,
'Thou haddest gold enough—and Emily?'

that follows so close upon the profoundly tender despair of Arcite's
farewell:—

What is this world? What asken men to have?
Now with his love now in the coldë grave
Alone withouten any company!

The power of diffusion without being diffuse would seem to be the highest
merit of narration, giving it that easy flow which is so delightful. Chaucer's
descriptive style is remarkable for its lowness of tone,—for that combination
of energy with simplicity which is among the rarest gifts in literature. Perhaps
all is said in saying that he has style at all, for that consists mainly in the
absence of undue emphasis and exaggeration, in the clear uniform pitch
which penetrates our interest and retains it, where mere loudness would only
disturb and irritate.

Not that Chaucer cannot be intense, too, on occasion; but it is with a quiet
intensity of his own, that comes in as it were by accident.

Upon a thickë palfrey, paper-white,
With saddle red embroidered with delight,
Sits Dido:
And she is fair as is the brightë morrow
That healeth sickë folk of nightës sorrow.
Upon a courser startling as the fire,
Æneas sits.

Pandarus, looking at Troilus,

Took up a light and found his countenance
As for to look upon an old romance.

With Chaucer it is always the thing itself and not the description of it that
is the main object. His picturesque bits are incidental to the story, glimpsed
in passing; they never stop the way. His key is so low that his high lights are
never obtrusive. His imitators, like Leigh Hunt, and Keats in his *Endymion*,
missing the nice gradation with which the master toned everything down,
become streaky. Hogarth, who reminds one of him in the variety and natural
action of his figures, is like him also in the subdued brilliancy of his coloring.
When Chaucer condenses, it is because his conception is vivid. He does
not need to personify Revenge, for personification is but the subterfuge of

unimaginative and professional poets; but he embodies the very passion itself in a verse that makes us glance over our shoulder as if we heard a stealthy tread behind us:—

The smiler with the knife hid under the cloak.[5]

And yet how unlike is the operation of the imaginative faculty in him and Shakespeare! When the latter describes, his epithets imply always an impression on the moral sense (so to speak) of the person who hears or sees. The sun "flatters the mountain-tops with sovereign eye"; the bending "weeds lacquey the dull stream"; the shadow of the falcon "coucheth the fowl below"; the smoke is "helpless"; when Tarquin enters the chamber of Lucrece "the threshold grates the door to have him heard." His outward sense is merely a window through which the metaphysical eye looks forth, and his mind passes over at once from the simple sensation to the complex *meaning* of it,—feels *with* the object instead of merely feeling it. His imagination is forever dramatizing. Chaucer gives only the direct impression made on the eye or ear. He was the first great poet who really loved outward nature as the source of conscious pleasurable emotion. The Troubadour hailed the return of spring; but with him it was a piece of empty ritualism. Chaucer took a true delight in the new green of the leaves and the return of singing birds,—a delight as simple as that of Robin Hood:—

> In summer when the shaws be sheen,
> And leaves be large and long,
> It is full merry in fair forest
> To hear the small birds' song.

He has never so much as heard of the "burthen and the mystery of all this unintelligible world." His flowers and trees and birds have never bothered themselves with Spinoza. He himself sings more like a bird than any other poet, because it never occurred to him, as to Goethe, that he ought to do so. He pours himself out in sincere joy and thankfulness. When we compare Spenser's imitations of him with the original passages, we feel that the delight of the later poet was more in the expression than in the thing itself. Nature with him is only good to be transfigured by art. We walk among Chaucer's sights and sounds; we listen to Spenser's musical reproduction of them. In the same way, the pleasure which Chaucer takes in telling his stories has in itself the effect of consummate skill, and makes us follow all the windings of his fancy with sympathetic interest. His best tales run on like one of our inland rivers, sometimes hastening a little and turning upon themselves in eddies that dimple without retarding the current; sometimes loitering smoothly, while here and there a quiet thought, a tender feeling, a pleasant image, a golden-hearted verse, opens quietly as a water-lily, to float on the surface without breaking it into ripple. The vulgar intellectual palate hankers after the titillation of foaming phrase, and thinks nothing good for much that does not go off with a pop like a champagne cork. The mellow suavity of more precious vintages seems insipid: but the taste, in proportion as it refines, learns to appreciate the indefinable flavor, too subtle for analysis. A manner has prevailed of late in which every other word seems to be underscored as in a school-girl's letter. The poet seems intent on showing his sinew, as if the power of the slim Apollo lay in the girth of his biceps. Force for the mere sake of force ends like Milo, caught and held mockingly fast by the recoil of the log he undertook to rive. In the race of fame, there are a score capable of brilliant *spurts* for one who comes in winner after a steady pull with wind and muscle to spare. Chaucer never shows any signs of effort, and it is a main proof of his excellence that he can be so inadequately sampled by detached passages,—by single lines taken away from the connection in which they contribute to the general effect. He has that continuity of thought, that evenly prolonged power, and that delightful equanimity, which characterize the higher orders of mind. There is something in him of the disinterestedness that made the Greeks masters in art. His phrase is never importunate. His simplicity is that of elegance, not of poverty. The quiet unconcern with which he says his best things is peculiar to him among English poets, though Goldsmith, Addison, and Thackeray have approached it in prose. He prattles inadvertently away, and all the while, like the princess in the story, lets fall a pearl at every other word. It is such a piece of good luck to be natural! It is the good gift which the fairy godmother brings to her prime favorites in the cradle. If not genius, it alone is what makes genius amiable in the arts. If a man have it not, he will never find it, for when it is sought it is gone.

When Chaucer describes anything, it is commonly by one of those simple and obvious epithets or qualities that are so easy to miss. Is it a woman? He tells us she is *fresh;* that she has *glad* eyes; that "every day her beauty newed"; that

> Methought all fellowship as naked
> Withouten her that I saw once,
> As a corone without the stones.

Sometimes he describes amply by the merest hint, as where the Friar, before setting himself softly down, drives away the cat. We know without need of more words that he has chosen the snuggest corner. In some of his early poems he sometimes, it is true, falls into the catalogue style of his contemporaries; but after he had found his genius he never particularizes too much,— a process as deadly to all effect as an explanation to a pun. The first stanza of the *Clerk's Tale* gives us a landscape whose stately choice of objects shows a skill in composition worthy of Claude, the last artist who painted nature epically:—

> There is at the west endë of Itaile,
> Down at the foot of Vesulus the cold,
> A lusty plain abundant of vitaile,
> Where many a tower and town thou may'st behold
> That founded were in time of fathers old,
> And many another delitable sight;
> And Salucës this noble country hight.

The Pre-Raphaelite style of landscape entangles the eye among the obtrusive weeds and grass-blades of the foreground which, in looking at a real bit of scenery, we overlook; but what a sweep of vision is here! and what happy generalization in the sixth verse as the poet turns away to the business of his story! The whole is full of open air.

But it is in his characters, especially, that his manner is large and free; for he is painting history, though with the fidelity of portrait. He brings out strongly the essential traits, characteristic of the genus rather than of the individual. The Merchant who keeps so steady a countenance that

> There wist no wight that he was e'er in debt,

the Sergeant at Law, "who seemed busier than he was," the Doctor of Medicine, whose "study was but little on the Bible,"— in all these cases it is the type and not the personage that fixes his attention. William Blake says truly, though he expresses his meaning somewhat clumsily, "the characters of Chaucer's Pilgrims are the characters which compose all ages and nations. Some of the names and titles are altered by time, but the characters remain forever unaltered, and consequently they are the physiognomies and lineaments of universal human life, beyond which Nature never steps. Names alter, things never alter. As Newton numbered the stars, and as Linnaeus numbered the plants, so Chaucer numbered the classes of men." In his outside accessaries, it is true, he sometimes seems as minute as if he were illuminating a missal. Nothing escapes his sure eye for the picturesque,—the cut of the beard, the soil of armor on the buff jerkin, the rust on the sword, the expression of the eye. But in this he has an artistic purpose. It is here that he individualizes, and, while every touch harmonizes with and seems to complete the moral features of the character, makes us feel that we are among living men, and not the abstracted images of men. Crabbe adds particular to particular, scattering rather than deepening the impression of reality, and making us feel as if every man were a species by himself; but Chaucer, never forgetting the essential sameness of human nature, makes it possible, and even probable, that his motley characters should meet on a common footing, while he gives to each the *expression* that belongs to him, the result of special circumstance or training. Indeed, the absence of any suggestion of *caste* cannot fail to strike any reader familiar with the literature on which he is supposed to have formed himself. No characters are at once so broadly human and so definitely outlined as his. Belonging, some of them, to extinct types, they continue contemporary and familiar forever. So wide is the difference between knowing a great many men and that knowledge of human nature which comes of sympathetic insight and not of observation alone.

It is this power of sympathy which makes Chaucer's satire so kindly,— more so, one is tempted to say, than the panegyric of Pope. Intellectual satire gets its force from personal or moral antipathy, and measures offences by some rigid conventional standard. Its mouth waters over a galling word, and it loves to say *Thou,* pointing out its victim to public scorn. *Indignatio facit versus,* it boasts, though they might as often be fathered on envy or hatred. But imaginative satire, warmed through and through with the genial leaven of humor, smiles half sadly and murmurs *We.* Chaucer either makes one knave betray another, through a natural jealousy of competition, or else expose himself with a *naivete* of good-humored cynicism which amuses rather than disgusts. In the former case the butt has a kind of claim on our sympathy; in the latter, it seems nothing strange, as I have already said, if the sunny atmosphere which floods that road to Canterbury should tempt anybody to throw off one disguise after another without suspicion. With perfect tact, too, the Host is made the *choragus* in this diverse company, and the coarse jollity of his temperament explains, if it do not excuse, much that would otherwise seem out of keeping. Surely nobody need have any scruples with *him.*

Chaucer seems to me to have been one of the most purely original of poets, as much so in respect of the world that is about us as Dante in respect of that which is within us. There had been nothing like him before, there has been nothing since. He is original, not in the sense that he thinks and says what nobody ever thought and said before, and what nobody can ever think and say again, but because he is always natural, because, if not always absolutely new, he is always delightfully fresh, because he sets before us the world as it honestly appeared to Geoffrey Chaucer, and not a world as it seemed proper to certain people that it ought to appear. He found that the poetry which had preceded him had been first the expression of individual feeling, then of class feeling as the vehicle of legend and history, and at last had wellnigh lost itself in chasing the mirage of allegory. Literature seemed to have passed through the natural stages which at regular intervals bring it to decline. Even the lyrics of the *jongleurs* were all run in one mould, and the Pastourelles of Northern France had become as artificial as the Pastorals of Pope. The Romances of chivalry had been made over into prose, and the *Melusine* of his contemporary Jehan d'Arras is the forlorn hope of the modern novel. Arrived thus far in their decrepitude, the monks endeavored to give them a religious and moral turn by allegorizing them. Their process reminds one of something Ulloa tells us of the fashion in which the Spaniards converted the Mexicans: "Here we found an old man in a cavern so extremely aged as it was wonderful, which could neither see nor go because he was so lame and crooked. The Father, Friar Raimund, said it were good (seeing he was so aged) to make him a Christian; whereupon we baptized him." The monks found the Romances in the same stage of senility, and gave them a saving sprinkle with the holy water of allegory. Perhaps they were only trying to turn the enemy's own weapons against himself, for it was the free-thinking *Romance of the Rose* that more than anything else had made allegory fashionable. Plutarch tells us that an allegory is to say one thing where another is meant, and this might have been needful for the personal security of Jean de Meung, as afterwards for that of his successor, Rabelais. But, except as a means of evading the fagot, the method has few recommendations. It reverses the true office of poetry by making the real unreal. It is imagination endeavoring to recommend itself to the understanding by means of cuts. If an author be in such deadly earnest, or if his imagination be of such creative vigor as to project real figures when it meant to cast only a shadow upon vapor; if the true spirit come, at once obsequious and terrible, when the conjurer has drawn his circle and gone through with his incantations merely to produce a proper frame of mind in his audience, as was the case with Dante, there is no longer any question of allegory as the word and thing are commonly understood. But with all secondary poets, as with Spenser for example, the allegory does not become of one substance with the poetry, but is a kind of carven frame for it, whose figures lose their meaning, as they cease to be contemporary. It was not a style that could have much attraction for a nature so sensitive to the actual, so observant of it, so interested by it, as that of Chaucer. He seems to have tried his hand at all the forms in vogue, and to have arrived in his old age at the truth, essential to all really great poetry, that his own instincts were his safest guides, that there is nothing deeper in life than life itself, and that to conjure an allegorical significance into it was to lose sight of its real meaning. He of all men could not say one thing and mean another, unless by way of humorous contrast.

In thus turning frankly and gayly to the actual world, and drinking inspiration from sources open to all; in turning away from a colorless abstraction to the solid earth and to emotions common to every pulse; in discovering that to make the best of nature, and not to grope vaguely after something better than nature, was the true office of Art; in insisting on a definite purpose, on veracity, cheerfulness, and simplicity, Chaucer shows himself the true father and founder of what is characteristically *English* literature. He has a hatred of cant as hearty as Dr. Johnson's, though he has a slier way of showing it; he has the placid common-sense of Franklin, the sweet, grave humor of Addison, the exquisite taste of Gray; but the whole texture of his mind, though its substance seem plain and grave, shows itself at every turn iridescent with poetic feeling like shot silk. Above all, he has an eye for character that seems to have caught at once not only its mental and physical features, but even its expression in variety of costume,—an eye, indeed, second only, if it should be called second in some respects, to that of Shakespeare.

I know of nothing that may be compared with the prologue to the *Canterbury Tales,* and with that to the story of the *Canon's Yeoman* before Chaucer. Characters and portraits from real life had never been drawn with such discrimination, or with such variety, never with such bold precision of outline, and with such a lively sense of the picturesque. His Parson is still unmatched, though Dryden and Goldsmith have both tried their hands in emulation of him. And the humor also in its suavity, its perpetual presence and its shy unobtrusiveness, is something wholly new in literature. For anything that deserves to be called like it in English we must wait for Henry Fielding.

Chaucer is the first great poet who has treated To-day as if it were as good as Yesterday, the first who held up a mirror to contemporary life in its infinite variety of high and low, of humor and pathos. But he reflected life in its large sense as the life of *men,* from the knight to the ploughman,—the life of every day as it is made up of that curious compound of human nature with manners. The very form of the *Canterbury Tales* was imaginative. The garden of Boccaccio, the supper-party of Grazzini, and the voyage of Giraldi make a good enough thread for their stories, but exclude all save equals and friends, exclude consequently human nature in its wider meaning. But by choosing a pilgrimage, Chaucer puts us on a plane where all men are equal, with souls to be saved, and with another world in view that abolishes all distinctions. By this choice, and by making the Host of the Tabard always the central figure, he has happily united the two most familiar emblems of life,—the short journey and the inn. We find more and more as we study him that he rises quietly from the conventional to the universal, and may fairly take his place with Homer in virtue of the breadth of his humanity.

In spite of some external stains, which those who have studied the influence of manners will easily account for without imputing them to any moral depravity, we feel that we can join the pure-minded Spenser in calling him "most sacred, happy spirit." If character may be divined from works, he was a good man, genial, sincere, hearty, temperate of mind, more wise, perhaps, for this world than the next, but thoroughly humane, and friendly with God and men. I know not how to sum up what we feel about him better than by saying (what would have pleased most one who was indifferent to fame) that we love him more even than we admire. We are sure that here was a true brotherman so kindly that, in his *House of Fame,* after naming the great poets, he throws in a pleasant word for the oaten-pipes.

> Of the little herd-grooms
> That keepen beasts among the brooms.

No better inscription can be written on the first page of his works than that which he places over the gate in his *Assembly of Fowls,* and which contrasts so sweetly with the stern lines of Dante from which they were imitated:—

> Through me men go into the blissful place
> Of the heart's heal and deadly woundes' cure;
> Through me men go unto the well of Grace,
> Where green and lusty May doth ever endure;
> This is the way to all good aventure;
> Be glad, thou Reader, and thy sorrow offcast,
> All open am I, pass in, and speed thee fast!

Notes

1. Sir *Eger and Sir Grine* in the Percy Folio. The passage quoted is from Ellis.
2. I think he tried one now and then, like "eyen *columbine.*"
3. Commonly printed *hath.*
4. Froissart's description of the book of traités amoureux et de moralité, which he had had engrossed for presentation to Richard II. in 1394, is enough to bring tears to the eyes of a modern author. "Et lui plut très grandement; et plaire bien lui devoit car il était enluminé, écrit et historié et couvert de vermeil velours à dis cloux d'argent dorés d'or, et roses d'or au milieu, et à deux grands fremaulx dorés et richement ouvrés au milieu

de rosiers d'or." How lovingly he lingers over it, hooking it together with *et* after *et!* But two centuries earlier, while the *jongleurs* were still in full song, poems were also read aloud.

> Pur remembrer des ancessours
> Les faits et les dits et les mours,
> Deit Ten les livres et les gestes
> Et les estoires *lire a festes.*
> > (*Roman du Rou*)

But Chaucer wrote for the private reading of the closet.
5. Compare this with the Mumbo-Jumbo Revenge in Collins's Ode.

—James Russell Lowell, "Chaucer,"
Works, 1870, Volume 3, pp. 298–366

WILLIAM MINTO
"GEOFFREY CHAUCER" (1874)

William Minto (1845–93) was a Scottish critic and scholar, a professor at the University of Aberdeen, and author of the respected *Characteristics of English Poets from Chaucer to Shirley.* In the essay below, taken from his book, Minto labels what he considers to be the most significant qualities of Chaucer's poetry.

Minto begins by examining Chaucer's French influences. Many of the other excerpts in this volume have explored Chaucer's relationship to his Italian sources, especially Boccaccio and Petrarch, so Minto's work on Chaucer's connection to the French medieval literary tradition and to Guillaume de Lorris in particular is useful to students discussing Chaucer's potential influences. Minto then identifies six key aspects that he believes are the "chief qualities" of Chaucer's work. The first is Chaucer's "[a]rchaisms [old-fashioned expressions] of word and inflection." Minto writes that "[t]he natural effect of archaisms on pathetic passages is to make them sweeter and simpler by making them more childlike." Chaucer's second chief characteristic is his directness, which marks him as the "opposite of a dreamy poet." The third is his incredible animation. The fourth is his "tender sentiment," which Minto finds especially reflected when Chaucer writes about nature. The fifth characteristic is Chaucer's affinity for women and his female characters. The sixth, and last, is his buoyant sense of humor.

Minto describes each of these characteristics in some detail, and sharp-eyed readers should note that many of these qualities have been described in previous excerpts in this volume. Students working with any one of these specific characteristics are well advised to consult those other excerpts that discuss these same issues to compare what different authors had to say about a similar subject.

I. His Life, Character, and Works

To regard Chaucer as the first genial day in the spring of English poetry, is to take, perhaps, a somewhat insular view of his position. On a more comprehensive view, it would appear more apposite to call him a fine day, if not the last fine day, in the autumn of mediaeval European poetry. He may be described as the father of English poetry—the first great poet that used the English language; but it is more instructive to look upon him as the English son and heir of a great family of French and Italian poets. He was the great English master in a poetic movement that originated in the south of Europe, among the provinces of the Langue d'Oc, which had been going on with brilliant energy for more than two centuries before his birth, and had produced among its masterpieces the *Romance of the Rose,* and the poetry of Dante and Petrarch. . . .

Chaucer was the first writer for all time that used the English language. But viewed as a figure in European literature, he must be regarded as the last of the Trouveres. His works float on the surface of the same literary wave; a deep gulf lies between them and the next, on the crest of which are the works of our great Elizabethans. Some patriotic Englishmen have strongly resented the endeavour of M. Sandras[1] to consider Chaucer as an imitator of the Trouveres. They are justified in taking offence at the word "imitator." It is too much to say that Chaucer produced nothing but imitations of G. de Lorris or other Trouveres, till he conceived the plan of the *Canterbury Tales;* and that the *Canterbury Tales,* though so far original in form, are animated throughout by the spirit of Jean de Meun. To say this is to produce a totally false impression as regards the decided individuality and pronounced English characteristics of Chaucer. He undoubtedly belongs to the line of the Trouveres. He was a disciple of theirs; he studied in the school of Guillaume de Lorris and Jean de Meun, by the side of Guillaume de Machault and Eustache Deschamps. He adopted the same poetical machinery of vision and allegory. He made the same elaborate studies of colour and form. From French predecessors he received the stimulus to his minute observation of character. It was emulation of them that kindled his happy genius for story-telling. The relation between Chaucer and the Trouveres is much closer than the relation between Shakespeare and the foreign originals that supplied him with plots, or than the relation between Mr Tennyson and the

Arthurian legends. Making allowance for differences of national character, Chaucer owed as much to Guillaume de Lorris as Shakespeare to Marlowe, or Tennyson to Wordsworth; and in spite of national character, there was probably more affinity between pupil and master in the one case than in the others. At the same time, we should keep clear of such a word as imitation, which would imply that Chaucer had no character of his own. He received his impulse from the French: he made liberal use of their forms and their materials; yet his works bear the impress and breathe the spirit of a strong individuality; and this individuality, though most obvious in the *Canterbury Tales,* is throughout all his works distinctively English. Finally, to add one word on the comparative extent of Chaucer's obligations to Italian sources: while he translated largely from Boccaccio, and while it may be possible to trace an expansion of his poetic ideals coincident with the time when he may be supposed to have made his first acquaintance with Italian poetry, it is not to be questioned that he was most deeply indebted for general form, imagery, and characterization to the Trouveres, whose language and works he must have been familiar with from boyhood. . . .

It may almost be said to have been an accident that Chaucer did not write in French, as his contemporary Gower began by doing. But he had the sense to discern a capable literary instrument in the nascent English, which the king at this time was doing his utmost to encourage. A poet is not begotten by circumstances, but circumstances may do much to make or mar him, and a man of genius, able to make the new language move in verse, was sure of a warm welcome at the Court of Edward III. The atmosphere was most favourable to the development of a poet of genial pleasure-loving disposition. Edward's reign was the flowering period of chivalry in England. It was the midsummer, the July, of chivalry; the institution was then in full blossom. All that it is customary to say about the gladness of life in the England of Chaucer's time was true of the Court; if a whole nation could be gladdened by the beautiful life of a favoured few, then all England must have been happy and merry. Pageantry was never more gorgeous or more frequent, courtesy of manner never more refined. The Court was like the Garden of Mirth in the *Romance of the Rose;* there were hideous figures on the outside of the walls, but inside all was sunshine and merry-making, and now and then the doors were thrown open and gaily attired parties issued forth to hunt or tournament. These amusements were arranged on a scale of unparalleled splendour.

It was a most gladsome and picturesque life at the Court of Edward III., and in that life Chaucer's poetry was an incident. This is a key to its joyous character. Animated playing on the surface of passion without breaking the crust, humorous pretence of incapacity when dull or difficult subjects come in the way, an eye for the picturesque, abundant supply of incident, never-failing fertility of witty suggestion—these are some of the qualities that made Chaucer's poetry acceptable to the audience for which he wrote. He never ventured on dangerous ground. He kept as far as possible from disagreeable realities. We search in vain for the most covert allusion to the painful events of the time. Devastating pestilences, disaster abroad, discontent and insurrection at home—he took for granted that his audience did not care to hear about such things, and he passed such things by. They wished to be entertained, and he entertained them charmingly, with lively adventures in high and human life, pictures of the life chivalric with its hunts and tournaments, pictures of the life vulgar with its intervals of riotous mirth, sweet love-tales, comical intrigues, graphic and humorous sketches of character. . . .

When we look closely at the construction of his poems, trying to realise how they were built up in the poet's mind, we are comfirmed in our first impressions of the equability of his proceedings. We are not to suppose that he sang as the birds sing without effort—out of "the inborn kindly joyousness of his nature," as Coleridge says. His work is too solid for that. Those perfect touches of character in the Prologue to the *Canterbury Tales* were not put together with unpremeditated flow: we should as soon believe that a picture of Hogarth's was dashed off at a sitting. And, indeed, Chaucer tells us himself, in his *House of Fame,* that he wrote love-songs till his head ached, and pored over books till his eyes had a dazed look. Still, he worked equably, with patient elaboration. He is not carried away into incontinent fine frenzies of creation; his words and images do not flash together with lightning energy like the words and images of Shakespeare. His imagination is not overpowered by excited fecundity. Perhaps none of our poets combine such wealth of imagination with such perfect command over its resources: such power of expressing the incident or feeling in hand, with such ease in passing from it when it has received its just proportion; perhaps none of them can put so much into the mouth of a personage, and at the same time observe such orderly clearness, and such propriety of character. If you wish to understand his processes of construction, you cannot do better than study such passages as the elaborate self-disclosure of Januarius, when he consults with his friends about the expediency of marrying, or the imprudent candour of the Pardoner, or trie talk between Chanticleer and Pertelot in the tale of the *Nun's Priest.* We are there struck by another consideration, and that is, how much he must have owed to his predecessors the garrulous inventive Fableors of northern France; and with what clearness of eye, and freedom and firmness of hand, he gathered, sifted, and recombined their opulent details of action and character.

The *Canterbury Tales* could no more have grown out of the imagination and observation of one man than the *Iliad*, although one man had scope for the highest genius in adding to, taking from, kneading, and wholly recasting the materials furnished by many less distinguished labourers. . . .

II. His Language, Metres, and Imagery

Chaucer's similitudes are taken from such familiar sources, that M. Sandras charges him with giving a vulgar tone to his renderings of the chivalrous romances of Boccaccio. Whether it was that his English humour now and then broke out through his chivalrous sentiment, or whatever may be the explanation, there certainly is some ground for the charge. The comparison of Cressida to the "chief letter A," is so like our modern vulgar "A I," that we are not perhaps unbiassed judges in that particular case. But there are a few similitudes in the *Knight's Tale* expressed with a primitive simplicity that must have drawn a smile from the poet himself. Such is the comparison of Palamon and Arcite quarrelling about Emily to two dogs fighting for a bone, while a kite comes in and carries off the object of contention. And still more amusing and unworthy of the subject is the comparison of poor humanity struggling on through the dark world with uncertain footing, to a drunk man, drunk as a mouse, who knows that he has a house, but does not know how to reach it, and finds the way very slippery. These similitudes are undeniably vivid: but unless our judgment is biassed by modern feelings, they belonged even in Chaucer's age more to the quaint monk than the chivalrous knight.

Most of Chaucer's similitudes, however—and he uses comparatively few, either as extended similes or as metaphors—are simple without being quaint or humorously inadequate to the subject. In this respect he contented himself with commonplaces, and made no effort to embellish his style with far-fetched flowers. He gives his warriors the look of griffins and lions, and makes them fight like cruel tigers and wild boars. Occasionally he expands the comparison, and gives it a certain local colour after the Italian manner, as when he introduces the Thracian hunter, or the tiger of the Galgopley, or the lion of Belmarie, or the pale face of the criminal on his way to execution. In extolling the charms of his heroines, he describes for the most part directly; and when he wants a brief illumination, makes use of the immemorial comparisons from the simple beauties of inanimate nature, the rose and the lily, sunlight and moonlight, spring-time and morning.

We are accustomed to think that Chaucer was able to dispense with a richly loaded diction, because he wrote for a primitive audience, thankful for small poetical mercies. But they were not so unsophisticated that a poet could make a reputation for colour, or as they might have called it, flowers of rhetoric, "the blossoms fresh of Tullius' garden sweet," upon the strength of comparing lovely women to roses and lilies, sunshine and spring, perennial as is the charm in thinking of such a likeness. Chaucer might have had to bestir himself for less familiar "tropes" and figures, had it not been that the structure of his poems gave him the opportunity of flooding his pages with colour in direct description. Beautiful women, heroic men, gorgeous buildings, gay processions, splendid armour, gardens and fountains, woods and rivers, birds and beasts, come in his way as the poet of fables and allegories, love, character, and romantic adventure; and he describes them enthusiastically with the utmost opulence of detail. His pictorial imagination was not called upon for many fragmentary contributions, but every now and then it received steady employment. What need had his readers for isolated touches of colour when their poet gave them such accumulations to revel in as the Gardens of Venus, the Temple of Venus, the House of Fame, the Court of Love, the Tournament before Theseus, the rival troops of the knights and ladies of the *Flower and the Leaf?*

The *Parliament of Birds* is perhaps the richest of Chaucer's smaller poems—"imitations," as M. Sandras calls them,—but the *Book of the Duchess* is as good an example as need be of the poetical machinery that he inherited. The central aim of the poem is to commiserate the death of Blanche, Duchess of Lancaster, and to express the sorrow of her husband; but this object has grown into fold after fold of richly coloured and animated conception. . . .

III. The Chief Qualities of his Poetry

It is not unlikely that our impressions of the chief qualities of Chaucer's poetry are different in some respects from those felt by his contemporaries. In all probability we pass lightly over many things that fascinated them, and admire many things that they received with comparative indifference. Their captivating novelties have become our commonplaces, their impressive reflections have become trite; and, on the other hand, many passages that would doubtless have seemed tame and commonplace to them, strike us with all the freshness of reawakened nature, or with the strange interest of things exhumed after long ages of burial.

We cannot recover, with any assurance of certainty, the feelings of Richard II's courtiers when first they were charmed by the English language in the compositions of a great poet. We cannot imagine how his descriptions of fair women, fine buildings, flowers, trees, and bird-singing, were heard or read by those familiar with the *Romance of the Rose;* nor how his *Canterbury*

Tales affected minds that knew such plots and incidents by the hundred. We know what a master of language can do with the most familiar materials; we know how fervently Chaucer's power was acknowledged, not only among his countrymen, but also on the other side of the Channel: but how they felt his power, which of its elements appealed to them most irresistibly, must ever remain matter for speculation.

Archaisms of word and inflection cannot but be inseparable elements in the sum total of the effects of Chaucer's poetry on us. Single words have changed their associations very materially since the days of Chaucer; and there are many that signify nothing to the present generation, many that are empty sounds, whose meaning may be attained only by dim approximation through glossarial synonyms. Words faintly picked up from a glossary have not the same power as the words of our mother-tongue. Even if we have a literary familiarity with them, the matter is not altogether mended. In all cases we may be sure that a passage with obsolete words in it does not move us as it moved contemporary readers. What may have been the effect of the passage when its words were hung about with the associations of the time, we cannot realise either by patient study or impatient flash of imagination: it is a dead thing, that no intellectual alchemy can resuscitate. We only know that it must have been different from what we experience. A phrase in a modern poem, even, does not go with equal power to the heart of every reader. Chance associations are fruitful sources of colouring peculiar to the individual. But to none of us can an obsolete word of Chaucer's have the same associations that it bore to men in whose mouths and ears it was a familiar visitor.

The natural effect of archaisms on pathetic passages is to make them sweeter and simpler by making them more childlike. Such lines as—

> The newë green, of jolif ver the prime
> And sweetë smelling floweres white and red;

or—

> And as I could this freshë flower I grette,
> Kneeling alway, till it unclosed was
> Upon the smallë, softë, sweetë grass,
> That was with flowerës sweet embroided all—

come to us like the prattle of childhood, and fill us with the freshness of spring as no modern words could do. Even lines that are not so appropriate in the infantile mouth, are made prettier by their archaic garb. Take the following:—

> She was not brown ne dun of hue,
> But white as snow y-fallen new.
> Her nose was wrought at point devise,
> For it was gentle and tretis,
> With eyen glad and browës bent;
> Her hair down to her heelës went,
> And she was simple as dove of tree;
> Full debonaire of heart was she.

These lines, particularly the two about the lady's nose, are such as a modern reader would apply to a beautiful pet; they probably carried a more elevated sentiment when first written.

Look now at a passage that, apart from the quaintness of the language, should carry the sense of splendour—the march of Theseus upon Thebes.

> The red statue of Mars with spear and targe
> So shineth in his whitë banner large,
> That all the fieldës glitteren up and doun:
> And by his banner borne was his pennoun
> Of gold full rich, in which there was y-beat
> The Minotaur which that he wan in Crete.
> Thus rid this duke, thus rid this conquerour,
> And in his host of chivalry the flower,
> Till that he came to Thebës and alight
> Fair in a field there as he thought to fight.

The archaic inflections and turn of language give this a quaint unction, as if it were the imperfect utterance of an astonished child. The influence of the diction co-operates largely in reminding us that the splendour is a thing of bygone times, strange and wonderful in our imaginations. In the following astrological passage, matter and manner go together in the same way. It is the reflection of the Man of Law on the infatuated passion of the Soldan for Constance.

> Paraventure, in thilkë largë book
> Which that men clepe the Heaven, y-written was
> With starrës, when that he his birthë took,
> That he for love should have his death, alas!
> For in the starrës, clearer than is glass,
> Is written, God wot, whoso could it read
> The death of every man withouten dread.
> In starrës many a winter there beforn
> Was written the death of Hector, Achilles,

> Of Pompey, Julius, ere they were born;
> The strife of Thebës, and of Hercules,
> Of Sampson, Turnus, and of Socrates
> The death; but mennës wittës been so dull
> That no wight can well read it at the full.

Later on in the same tale, there is another astrological passage—an impassioned appeal to the starry destinies—when Constance is setting sail for the East to the marriage that proves so fatal.

> O firstë moving cruel firmament!
> With thy diurnal swough that crowdest aye
> And hurlest all fro East to Occident
> That naturally would hold another way!
> Thy crowding set the heaven in such array
> At the beginning of this fierce voyage,
> That cruel Mars hath slain this marriage.

In this passage the archaic trappings, and particularly the bit of dogma about the natural course of the firmament, are rather in the way—interfering with our perception of the dignity and passion of the apostrophe.

The archaic diction makes itself felt with peculiar harmony in the narrative of supernatural manifestations, such as were ascribed to devils and magicians. Sir Walter Scott might have envied the following account of the ritual of Arcite in the temple of Mars, and the answer to his prayer:—

> The prayer stint of Arcita the strong:
> The ringës on the temple door that hong,
> And eke the doorës clattereden full fast,
> Of which Arcita somewhat him aghast.
> The firës brende up on the altar bright
> That it gan all the temple for to light;
> A sweetë smell anon the ground up gave
> And Arcita anon his hand up have,
> And more incense into the fire he cast,
> With other ritës mo, and at the last
> The statue of Mars began his hauberk ring,
> And with that sound he heard a murmuring
> Full low and dim, and said thus, 'Victory!'

This is a more active and instantaneously impressive sorcery than the calm power of the stars, and the archaisms seem to go with it in readier harmony.

Take now another point. Chaucer sympathises deeply with the victims of deceitful love, and assails false lovers with cordial anger. If he were a dreamy poet like Spenser—a poet whose indignation assumed a wailful and regretful tone—the antique words and turns would be in perfect unison; they would help to translate the objects of our pity and anger farther and farther away from the living world—farther and farther back into a dim distance from indignant tears and frowns. But Chaucer is the opposite of a dreamy poet; his feelings are fresh and quick, his expression direct and demonstrative; he pities Dido, Ariadne, Phyllis, Medea, and flames out with fierce passion against Æneas, Theseus, Demophon, and Jason, as heartily as if they had all been his personal acquaintances. He cannot think of the treachery of the false lovers without getting into a passion.

> But welaway! the harm, the ruth,
> That hath betide for such untruth!
> As men may oft in bookës read,
> And all day see it yet in deed,
> That for to thinken it a teen is.

He utterly repudiates the pretence of Æneas that he was urged to leave Carthage by a destiny that he could not disobey; he treats this with scorn as a shallow and commonplace excuse for leaving a love that had become stale. He travels beyond his authorities to imagine the complainings of the forsaken queen; refers his readers for the whole of the touching story to Ovid; and cries with sudden energy—

> And were it not too long to endite,
> By God, I would it herë write!

He is no less furious at Theseus—

> How false eke was Duke Theseus,
> That as the story telleth us,
> How he betrayed Adriane;
> The Devil be his soulës bane!

Demophon, the son of Theseus, wicked son of a wicked sire, prone to deceit as the young of the fox, is treated with contemptuous scorn for his treachery to Phyllis—

> Me list not vouchesafe on him to swink,
> Dispenden on him a penful of ink,
> For false he was in love right as his sire;
> The Devil set their soulës both on fire!

Jason is held up to especial contempt; the poet proceeds to impeach him with especial zest—

> Thou root of falsë lovers, Duke Jason!
> Thou sly devourer and confusion
> Of gentle women, gentle crëatures!

Now there is no mistaking the genuineness of all this passion. But can we echo all these imprecations with true fervour? Do they not sound strange in our ears? Can we feel them as the poet's contemporaries did?

It was the opinion of De Quincey that, in the quality of animation, Chaucer is superior to Homer. The comparison is not, perhaps, altogether fair, because Chaucer's themes, as a rule, admit of lighter treatment than Homer's: but certainly no poet could well be more animated than Chaucer. All his works are full of bright colour, fresh feeling, and rapid ease and gaiety of movement. There is no tedious dulness in his descriptions; no lingering in the march of his narrative. With all his loquacity and vivacity, he knows when his readers have had enough of one thing, and passes easily on to something else. The ease of his transitions is very remarkable. Some writers drive so hard at the expression of what lies before them for the moment, that they cannot recover themselves quickly enough to make a graceful turn to what succeeds: they throw themselves off the track, and become confused and uncertain in their apprehension of the main subject. This Chaucer never seems to do; he always keeps his main subject clearly and firmly in view; and his well-marked digressions add to the general animation, by dispersing the feeling of rigid restraint without tending in the slightest to produce confusion.

It is in the *Knight's Tale* and the *Squire's Tale,* which deal to some extent with martial subjects, that Chaucer may most fairly be compared with Homer. The comparison is not unfavourable to our native poet. Even in conveying a vivid impression of the stir of an excited crowd, in which Homer is so excelling, we cannot allow that Chaucer is inferior. What could be more animated than Chaucer's account in the *Squire's Tale* of the bustling and buzzing multitude that assembled to stare at the magic horse, broad mirror of glass, and ring of gold, and to exchange speculations concerning the nature of these wonderful presents? Take, again, the gathering to the tournament before Theseus, in the *Knight's Tale.* What could be more inspiring, more alive with bright movement, splendid evolution, and fresh air than this? The herald has just proclaimed that the more deadly weapons are excluded from the lists; whereupon—

The voïce of the people toucheth heaven,
So loudë criedë they with merry steven:
'God savë such a lord that is so good:
He willeth no destruction of blood!'
Up goth the trumpës and the melody.
And to the listës ride the company
By ordinancë through the city large,
Hanging with cloth of gold and not with serge.
Full like a lord this noble Duke can ride;
These Two Thebanës upon either side:
And after rode the Queen, and Emily,
And of ladies another company,
And of communës after their degree.
And thus they passeden through that city,
And to the listës comen they by time.
It was not of the day yet fully prime,
When settë was Thesëus rich and high,
Hippolyta the Queen, and Emily,
And other ladies in their degrees about,
Unto the seatës presseth all the rout;
And westëward, thorough the gates of Mart,
Arcite, and eke the hundred of his part,
With banners red is entered right anon;
And in that selvë moment Palamon
Is under Venus, eastward in that place,
With banner white, and hardy cheer and face.

We should expect the courtier of Richard II., even when writing in his old age, to be more animated in his treatment of love than the blind old man of the rocky isle. And such he is. We shall see that Chaucer specially excels in depicting the tender aspects of the passion, but he was a master also of its cheering inspirations. Everybody has by heart his cheerful description of the youthful squire. That gay gentleman, however, was basking in the unbroken sunshine of love; you must take one who has known its dark eclipse, if you wish to see an example of its full power. Take Arcita of the *Knight's Tale,* who has been changed by his passion out of all recognition: he has become lean, hollow-eyed, and sallow, and his spirits have been so low that the sound of music brought tears into his eyes. Consider the change wrought on this woful lover when he has made some progress towards success, and his youthful energies return to their natural tone. Take him when he walks out of a May morning with his rising hopes, and drinks in the sympathy of nature, which also is rejoicing in its recovery from darkness and winter.

> The busy larkë, messenger of day,
> Salueth in her song the morrow gray;
> And fiery Phoebus riseth up so bright
> That all the orient laugheth of the light,
> And with his streamës dryeth in the greves
> The silver droppës, hanging on the leaves.
> And Arcita, that is in the court royal
> With Thesëus, his squiër principal,
> Is risen, and looketh on the merry day.
> And for to doon his observance to May,
> Remembering of the point of his desire,
> He on his courser, starting as the fire,
> Is ridden into the fieldës him to play,
> Out of the court, were it a mile or tway.
> And to the grove, of which that I you told,
> By aventure his way he gan to hold,
> To maken him a garland of the greves,
> Were it of woodëbind or hawthorn leaves,
> And loud he sung against the sunnë sheen:—
> 'May, with all thy flowrës and thy green,
> Welcome be thou, fairë freshë May!
> I hope that I some greenë getten may.'
> And fro his courser, with a lusty heart,
> Into the grove full lustily he start,
> And in a path he roamed up and down.

When we go for a feast of tender feeling to a poet possessing in large measure the quality of animation, we should not go in a languid mood. We need not, of course, follow his lead; we may choose our own pace. Instead of going with the surface of the lively brook, and seeing no more of its pebbles and the beauties of its banks and winding nooks than the rapid glance that its speed allows, we may fix on delicious spots, and feed there to our heart's content. It is this quality of animation that makes Chaucer so peculiarly the poet of outdoor summer weather, the most delightful of companions on the hillside, or by the running streams.

Chaucer's heart fitted him well to be the poet of tender sentiment. He seems to have dealt with fond observation on everything that was bright and pretty, from "the smallë fowlës that sleepen all the night with open eye,[1]" to the little herd-grooms playing on their pipes of green corn. He watched the little conies at their play, the little squirrels at their sylvan feasts; he looked into the "coldë wellë streamës, nothing dead," to admire

> The smallë fishes bright
> With finnës red, and scalës silver white.

He knew, too, the colour of every feather in Chanticleer, and had minutely studied his majesty's habits towards his subjects. But of all things of beauty in nature, the singing-birds were his most especial favourites. He often dwells on the ravishing sweetness of their melodies. His finest picture of their exuberance of joy in the spring—their tuneful defiance of the fowler, their billing and chirruping, their vows of eternal fidelity—occurs in the opening of the *Legend of Good Women*.

A man of the world himself, Chaucer still could enter into simple love-making among unsophisticated gentle creatures of a larger growth than the amorous little birds. Perhaps no passage shows the poet's exquisite tenderness better than the wooing of Thisbe by Pyramus, so well known in its ludicrous aspects from the caricature in *Midsummer Night's Dream;* and it is but an act of justice to these two faithful lovers to let them be seen as they were conceived by a sympathetic poet.

> This wall, which that betwix them bothë stood
> Was cloven atwo, right fro the top adoun,
> Of oldë time, of his foundatioun.
> But yet this clift was so narrow and lite. . . .
> But what is that that love cannot espy?
> Ye lovers two, if that I shall not lie,
> Ye founden first this little narrow clift!
> And with a sound as soft as any shrift,
> They let their wordës through the cliftë pace,
> And tolden while they stooden in the place,
> All their complaint of love and all their woe.
> At every timë when they durstë so,
> Upon the one side of the wall stood he,
> And on that other sidë stood Thisbe,
> The sweetë sound of other to receive.
> And thus their wardens wouldë they deceive,
> And every day this wall they wouldë threat,
> And wish to God that it were down y-beat.

> Thus would they sayn:—Alas, thou wicked
>   wall!
> Through thine envyë thou us lettest all!
> Why nilt thou cleave, or fallen all atwo?
> Or at the leastë, but thou wouldest so,
> Yet wouldest thou but onës let us meet,
> Or onës that we mightë kissen sweet,
> Then were we covered of our carës cold.
> But nathëless, yet be we to thee hold
> In as much as thou sufferest for to gone
> Our wordës through thy lime and eke thy stone,
> Yet oughtë we with thee been well apaid.'
> And when these idle wordës weren said,
> The coldë wall they wouldë kissen of stone,
> And take their leave, and forth they wouldë gone.

Thoroughly as his heart seems to go with this simple, earnest passion, almost infantile in its fondness, he can strike many another key in the infinitely varied art of love. Especially is he skilled in the chivalrous profession of entire submission to his lady's will, and humble adoration of her pre-eminent excellence. Take, for example, the opening stave of his humble prayer to Pity, which, without doubt, the cruel fair was at liberty to apply to herself.

> Humblest of heart, highest of reverence,
> Benignë flower, corown of virtues allë!
> Sheweth unto your royal excellence,
> Your servant, if I durstë me so callë,
> His mortal harm, in which he is y-fallë,
> And not all only for his evil fare,
> But for your renown, as I shall declare. . . .
> What needeth to show parcel of my pain,
> Sith every wo that hertë may bethink,
> I suffer; and yet I dare not to you plain,
> For well I wot, although I wake or wink,
> Ye reckë not whether I float or sink.
> Yet nathëless my truth I shall susteen,
> Unto my death, and that shall well be seen.

All forlorn lovers have his best services at their command. We may apply to him his own favourite line, many times repeated—

For pity runneth soon in gentle heart.

How feelingly he depicts the situation of Palamon—imprisoned and love-sick Palamon!

> In darkness and horrible and strong prison
> This seven year hath sitten Palamon,
> Forpined, what for wo and for distress.
> Who feeleth double sorrow and heaviness
> But Palamon? that love distraineth so,
> That wood out of his wit he goth for wo.

The woful pangs of sweet Aurelius too, his languor and furious torments, are followed with deep sympathy; and the heartbroken agony of forsaken Troilus is most intimately realised. In the expression of "deep heart's-sorrowing," Chaucer's words always flow with peculiar richness and intimate aptness of choice.

Naturally, however, it is womanhood in distress that enters his heart with the keenest stroke. He might well plead before the god and goddess of love that, if he had laughed at some of the foibles of the sex, he had not been indifferent to their virtues and their sufferings. His gallery of distressed heroines was as wide as the range of legend and history that was known to him: Constance, Griselda, Virginia, Cecilia, Alcyone, Alcestis, Cleopatra, Thisbe, Dido, Hypsipyle, Medea, Lucrece, Ariadne, Philomela, Phyllis, Hypermnestra. The thought of their suffering agitates him, destroys his composure; he cannot proceed without stopping to express his compassion, or to appeal to heaven against the caprice of Fortune or the wickedness of men. But he never dwells long on such scenes. It was not for him to harrow the feelings of his audience; when he has said enough to move them, he at once proceeds to effect a diversion. Lingering agonies were not to his taste. His representative the Host is almost choked with emotion at the Doctor's tale of Appius and Virginia; he relieves himself with furious denunciation of Appius, and tries to laugh the painful theme out of his memory. The legends of Constance (Man of Law's Tale) and Griselda (Clerk's Tale), have the happy termination of comedy; and the story of their prolonged sufferings is relieved by many a passing word of indignant blame against the guilty causes of their misery. Mediaeval readers liked long-drawn martyrdoms, but in the hands of such an artist as Chaucer, whether he dealt with the martyrs of religion or the martyrs of love, the pathos is never hard and overbearing; our pity is kept quick and fresh, and not allowed to stagnate in oppressive anguish. Such a poem as Wordsworth's 'Margaret' was impossible for him.

One of the most delightful of the *Canterbury Tales* is the *Franklin's Tale*. The incorruptible fidelity of the beautiful Dorigen, the equanimity and magnanimity of her brave husband Arviragus, the resolution of the Squire Aurelius not to be outdone in generosity by the Knight, capped by the resolution of the Knight not to be outdone by the Squire, make this tale a unique embodiment of the highest ideals of chivalry: scrupulous adherence to a rash promise on the one hand being met by renunciation of unfair advantage on the other. The chivalry of the tale is fantastic, but the poet's art makes it credible and beautiful.

Chaucer's humour is the most universally patent and easily recognised of his gifts. The smile or laugh that he raises, by refined irony or by broad rough jest and incident, is conspicuously genial. Mephistophelian mockery and Satanic grimness are not in his way. This had nothing to do with his being the bright morning star of English poetry—writing with the buoyancy of youth at a time when the struggle for existence was less fierce, when there was no bitter feeling between high and low, no envenomed warfare of civil or religious party. There never has been age nor country in which the fierce spirit has wanted fuel for its fierceness. It was simply the nature of the man to be genial,—"attempered and soft" as the climate of his gardens of Venus. He would have been so in whatever age he had lived.

The great criterion of good-nature, the indispensable basis of humour, is the power of making or sustaining a jest at one's own expense; and none of our humorists bear this test so well as Chaucer. He often harps on his own supposed imperfections, his ignorance of love, his want of rhetorical skill, his poverty. His poverty, real or pretended—and, unfortunately, it would seem to have been real—is the subject of several jokes in his poems, as it must have been in his private talk. In the *House of Fame,* when describing how the walls, roofs, and floors of the temple were plated with gold half a foot thick "as fine as ducat of Venice," he cannot resist the temptation to add—

Of which too little in my pouch is.

His "Complaint to his Purse" is conceived in a very gay spirit:—

Now voucheth safe this day, ere it be night,
That I of you the blissful sound may hear,
Or see your colour like the sunnë bright,
That of yellowness haddë never peer.
Ye be my life! ye be mine heartës steer!
Queen of comfort and goodë company!
Beth heavy again or ellës mote I die.

We must know this hobby of his to understand the full comic force of his comparing Alison to a newly forged noble, bright from the mint.

The freedom of his humour, as one would expect, was progressive. There are unequivocal touches of humour both in *Chaucer's Dream* and in the *Court of Love;* witness the sly treatment of Morpheus, and the poet's timid entry into the sacred court; but the humour, as became the subjects, is lurking and subordinate. It is worth noting, that in the *Court of Love,* though he could not profess entire ignorance of the passion as he did so often afterwards, he professes to have kept out of the service of Venus for a most unconscionable length of time; he was actually eighteen before he went to her court, and then he had to be summoned. But the humour is much less overt in the *Court of Love,* than in the more mature *House of Fame.* In that poem, as in the *Canterbury Tales,* he treats his own personality with reckless contempt. When the poet is caught up, at first he loses consciousness; but by-and-by the eagle wakes him up with comical remonstrances at his timidity. Half reassured, he begins to wonder vaguely what all this can mean:—

> O God, thought I, that madest kind,
> Shall I none other wayes die?
> Whe'r Jovës will me stellify,
> Or what thing may this signify?
> I neither am Enoch, ne Eli,
> Ne Romulus, ne Ganymede,
> That was y-bore up, as men read,
> To heaven with Dan Jupiter,
> And made the goddës botteler!
> Lo, this was then my fantasy!
> But he that bare me gan espy,
> That I so thought, and saidë this—
> 'Thou deemest of thyself amiss;
> For Jovës is not thereabout,
> I dare will put thee out of doubt,
> To make of thee as yet a star.'

The comparison between his own stout person and Ganymede, and the implied conception of himself as the butler[2] of the gods, are delicious. But, indeed, the passage throughout is so rich, that it is difficult to say which is its most comical touch.

The outcome of his broad humour is seen in the general plan of the *Canterbury Tales* as much as in some of the pronounced particulars. With the rougher sort of the pilgrims, and as we shall presently see, only with them, the pilgrimage is a tipsy revel, a hilarious holiday "outing." They are the merriest company that mine "Host of the Tabard" has had under his roof for many a day; and they are such jolly noisy good fellows that, at supper overnight, the host is tempted to propose that he should go with them and direct their merriment on the way. In the energy of his good-fellowship and confident sudden prospect of a hilarious journey, he cries for immediate decision on his plan—

> Now by my father's soulë that is dead,
> But ye be merry, smiteth off mine head.
> Hold up your hands withouten morë speech.

They agree; and the idea thus conceived is carried out with no less spirit. The pilgrims must have made a sensation as they rode out of town. The more respectable members of the company doubtless bore themselves with becoming gravity, but the wilder spirits put no restraint upon their mirth. The Miller brought them out of town to the music of his bagpipes—and a bagpipe in the hands of a drunk man is an instrument likely to attract some attention. The harum-scarum pimpled-faced bacchanalian Summoner had put on his head a garland large enough for an alehouse sign, and flourished a cake as a buckler. His friend and compeer the Pardoner had, "for jollity," trussed up his hood in his wallet, and let his yellow flaxen hair hang in disorder on his shoulders, saying that it was the new fashion.

> Full loud he sang 'Come hither, love, to me.'
> This Summoner bare to him a stiff burdoun,
> Was never trump of half so great a soun.

A company with spirits so uproarious in it tasked all the Host's powers of maintaining order, authoritative though he was. Of course they broke through. The Knight, who drew the lot for telling the first tale, was allowed to finish it; but as soon as he had done, the drunk Miller struck in and insisted on telling a noble tale that he knew. Though hardly able to keep his seat, he was not so drunk as not to know that he was drunk; he knew that, he said, "by his soun," and he besought them, if he said anything out of place, to lay the blame on the ale of South-wark. His tale does ample justice to his inspiration. The Host having once let the reins out of his hands was not able to resume them: the president of such a company must keep his authority by giving his subjects liberty to take their own way. The butt of the *Millers Tale* was a carpenter; and the Reeve being a carpenter thought himself aggrieved, and wanted to return the compliment by telling an equally coarse tale about the cuckolding of a miller. The Host, with the true instinct of a ruler, at once humoured him, and asserted his own dignity by cutting short his prologue, and commanding him to tell his tale. Then the gross Cook, chuckling over the discomfiture of the Miller, wanted to tell "a little jape that fell in our city," and the judicious Host granted permission. There was more intoxicated personality, wrangling, and peace-making, as they went on. The Friar enraged the Summoner by relating an awkward adventure that happened to one of his profession; and the Summoner gave a merciless Roland for his Oliver. After a long draught of ale, the Pardoner recklessly exposed all the tricks of his trade, and had the audacious assurance, after this full confession of his roguery, to try to work upon the feelings of his brother pilgrims, and extract money from them. It is to be feared, too, that the Host required a little too much of the "corny ale" to drown his pity for poor Virginia: one cannot otherwise account for his getting into a hot quarrel with the Pardoner, which required the intervention of the Knight to smooth it over. Towards the close of the pilgrimage the Cook showed symptoms of being overcome with sleep and ale, and seemed to be in danger of falling from his horse. The Host rebuked him, and the Manciple fell out upon him with such a torrent of abuse, that poor Robin overbalanced himself and tumbled to the ground in a furious futile effort to articulate a reply, and there was much shoving to and fro before they could set him in the saddle again. A pretty pilgrimage to the shrine of a saint! There is endless food for deep animal laughter in the humours of these riotous pilgrims—particularly that madcap pair of ecclesiastics—the Summoner and the Pardoner. One is constantly finding fresh points of comical view in that precious couple. It is a mistake, I may remark, to look in the *Canterbury Tales* for satire. If there is any, it is there by failure and imperfection; it is a flaw in the poet's design, which was to provide material for disinterested laughter, zealous and profound. To suppose that there is any satire in the candid revelation of the Pardoner's gross deceptions of the credulous vulgar, is to fail to rise to the height of the humour of that great character. There is no more ill-nature in the elaboration of his reckless freaks, than in the often-quoted and justly-praised delicate irony of the opening of the *Wife of Bath's Tale.*[3]

As regards any lurking satirical purpose in the *Canterbury Tales,* if we suppose that we discern any such purpose, we may take for granted that we are still on the outside of their riotous humour. It is true that a good many of the pilgrims are men of somewhat damaged reputation, or, at least, doubtful virtue. The Merchant is not beyond suspicion; the Miller steals corn; the Reeve has secured a comfortable feathering for his own nest; the Cook is a profligate sot; all the ecclesiastics, Monk, Friar, and Pardoner, exhibit a wide difference between their practice and their doctrine; and even the respectable professional men, the Lawyer and the Doctor, have a questionable liking for large fees. But these failings are not dwelt upon from the point of view of the satirist. With all their sinful taints, the pilgrims are represented as being on the whole jovial companions, satisfied with themselves and with each other; the taints, indeed, are not shown in the aspect of sins, but rather in the aspect of ludicrous peccadilloes or foibles. The sinners are elevated by the hilarity of the occasion above the sense of sin; and the poet does not hold them up to scorn or contempt, but enters genially into the spirit of their holiday revel. He does not join them to backbite and draw out their weaknesses for the bitter amusement or sharp dislike of his readers: he joins them to enjoy their company. Chaucer's humour in the *Canterbury Tales* is not in the spirit of Jean de Meun; it comes much nearer the spirit of Burns in the "Jolly Beggars."

IV. His Delineation of Character

It is somewhat startling to put together, as I have done in the preceding section, the buffoonery that went on throughout the Canterbury pilgrimage. We remember the tales of high chivalrous sentiment and exquisite pathos, and we ask how these were compatible with such noisy ribaldry. The explanation is, that the tales are suited to the characters and manners of the different pilgrims; and that while one set of them indulge largely in ale and inebriated freaks and loud animal mirth, the more respectable sort preserve a becoming dignity.

To a certain extent Professor Lowell is right in saying that there is no caste feeling among Chaucer's pilgrims. Knight and yeoman, monk and cook, lodge all night in the same inn, set out in a company on the same errand, and contribute to a common entertainment subject to the direction of one man, and that an inn-keeper. But we should greatly misunderstand the delicacy of Chaucer's sense of manners as well as of character, if we went away with the impression that in the *Canterbury Tales* there is no trace of the distinctions of rank, and that in the pilgrimage there is no respect paid to persons.

In the *Prologue,* the poet begs pardon for not setting the pilgrims in their degree—

> Also I pray you to forgive it me
> All have I not set folk in their degree
> Here in this tale, as that they shoulde stand.
> My wit is short, ye may well understand.

He had a livelier plan in view than to make them tell off their tales in the order of their rank. But though he did not adopt this palpable and unmistakable way of indicating caste, he does really show respect of persons in several less gross and obvious ways. A line is drawn, though unobtrusively and with delicate suggested art, between "the gentles" and the other pilgrims. If this had not been done, we should have been compelled to say that our poet had inaccurately portrayed the life of the time. But he has done it, and done it not by harsh angular forced assertion, but easily and naturally in his clearsighted shaping and working out of his materials. The careful reader gets the clue from such passages as that at the end of the *Knight's Tale,* where we are told that the whole company, young and old, praised it as a noble and memorable story, "and namely," that is, particularly, "the *gentles* every one." That was the sort of tale that the gentles felt themselves at liberty to approve of. When the Pardoner took up with animation the Host's request that he should tell a merry tale, forthwith the "gentles" began to cry that they must have no ribaldry: "Tell us," they said, "some moral thing that we may learn." It is very misleading to apologise, as some writers on Chaucer do, for the gross obscenity of certain of the tales, on the ground that this was the outspoken fashion of the time—that decorum then permitted greater freedom of language. The savour of particular words may have changed since the time of Chaucer; but then, as now, people with any pretensions to refinement were bound to abstain strictly in the presence of ladies from all ribaldry of speech and manner, on pain of being classed with "churls" and "villains." In the *Court of Love,* the gentle lover is warned emphatically that he must not be

> Ribald in speech, or out of measure pass,
> Thy bound exceeding; think on this alway:
> For women been of tender heartes aye.

And in the *Canterbury Tales,* Chaucer carefully guards himself against being supposed to be ignorant of this law. The ribald tales are introduced as the humours of the lower orders, persons ignorant or defiant of the rules of refined society, and moreover, as we have seen, excited, intoxicated, out for a pilgrimage as riotous and wild as our pilgrimage to the Derby.[4] Such riotous mirth was very far indeed from being the fashion of the time among fashionable people. Mark how careful Chaucer is to shield himself from the responsibility of it. In the *Prologue* (1. 725), he prays his readers of their courtesy not to set down his plainness of speech as his "villany": he is bound to record faithfully every word that was said, though it had been said by his own brother. He does, indeed, whether seriously or jocularly, allege the example of Christ and Plato as authorities for plainness of speech; but he does not repeat this when he returns to the matter before the first of his freespoken tales. In the prologue to the *Miller's Tale,* he is most explicit. He says that the obstinate Miller would not forbear for any man, "but told his churlish tale in his manner." And then he makes this clear and elaborate apology for rehearsing it,—

And, therefore, every *gentle* wight I pray,
For, Goddës love, deemeth not that I say
Of evil intent; but for I must rehearse
Their talës all, be they better or worse,
Or ellës falsen some of my matter.
And, therefore, whoso list it not to hear,
Turn over the leaf and chose another tale;
For he shall find enowë great and small,
Of *storial thing that toucheth gentilesse,*
And eke morality and holiness.
Blameth not me, if that ye chose amiss.
The Miller is a churl, ye know well this,
So was the Reeve and other many mo,
And harlotry they tolden bothë two.
Aviseth you, and put me out of blame;
And eke men shall not maken earnest of game.

Observe, accordingly, how the tales are distributed. Nothing ribald is put into the mouth of the gentles, and nothing ribald is told concerning their order. The "very perfect gentle knight," who never said any villany to any manner of man, recites the tale of Palamon and Arcite, with its chivalrous love and rivalry, its sense of high womanly beauty, its gorgeous descriptions of temple, ritual, procession, and tournament. His son, the gallant, well-mannered, well-dressed squire, embroidered like a mead, with his head full of love, romance, song, and music, gives a fragment of a romance about King Cambuscan and his daughter Canace, and the wonderful exploits of a magic horse, a magic mirror, and a magic ring. The professional men—the busy lawyer, the studious clerk, the irreligious but good-hearted doctor—give the pathetic stories of Constance, Griselda, and Virginia: the two first of which may be justly described as tales of morality. The Franklin tells the old Breton lay of Dorigen and Arviragus, models of chivalrous virtue. The Prioress and the Second Nun relate holy legends of martrydom. These are "the gentles," and such are their tales. The tales of vulgar merriment are told by the Miller, the Reeve, the Wife of Bath, the Friar, the Summoner, the Merchant, the Shipman. And as regard is had to the condition of the narrator in the character of the tale ascribed to him, so the persons engaged in degrading adventure are below the rank of the gentles. Januarius, indeed, in the *Merchant's Tale,* is called a worthy knight; but he is a blind dotard, long past knightly exercise and knightly feeling: and his May, who is so easily won to play him false, is represented as a maiden of small degree. The rank of all the other befooled heroes is plain: they are a carpenter, a miller, a summoner, a friar, and a merchant.[5] The gentle order is respected. They join the company, and enjoy the ribald speech and behaviour of their riotous, inebriated, vulgar companions; but they do not forfeit their self-respect, by contributing a share to the noisy merriment. When they have had enough of it, or when the tales threaten to become too boisterous, they use their influence to give a more sober tone to the proceedings. They do not break rough jests on each other as the vulgar do. And mine host knows his place sufficiently well to be less familiar and imperious with them than with the Miller and the Cook; he is courteous to the Knight, and ludicrously over-polite to the Prioress.

I may seem to have insisted too much on this distinction between the "gentles" and the "roughs" in the Canterbury pilgrimage; but the truth is, that we cannot have too vivid a hold of this distinction if we wish to understand either the *Canterbury Tales*, or Chaucer's poetry generally. Unless we realise this, we cannot feel how thoroughly and intimately his poems are transfused with chivalrous sentiment. What is more, we cannot appreciate the perfect skill with which he has maintained this sentiment in the *Canterbury Tales*, and at the same time transferred to his pages a faithful representation of vulgar manners in their wildest luxuriance.

Waiving all questions as to whether Chaucer was most of Norman or of Saxon, of Celt or of Teuton, we cannot escape from admitting that he was deeply impressed with the wide difference between chivalrous sentiments and the sentiments and manners prevalent among the dependants of chivalry. The difference may not have in reality been so profound as it was in ideal; but Chaucer felt it deeply. How deeply, we see most clearly in the "Cuckoo and Nightingale," and the *Parliament of Birds*, where the antagonistic sentiments are placed in express contrast. The Cuckoo is a vulgar bird, and takes gross ridiculous views of love: the Nightingale is a gentle bird, and regards love with delicate seriousness. Similar types are represented, with greater epic variety, in the *Parliament of Birds*. There is no mistaking the contrast in these allegorical fables; the vulgar birds, the Water Fowls, the Seed Fowls, and the Worm Fowls, are sharply snubbed for their chuckling vulgarity by the haughty and refined Birds of Prey. But in the *Canterbury Tales* the poet has achieved the triumph of making the antagonistic sentiments work smoothly side by side, and that is really their main triumph as a broad picture of manners and character. There, with dignified carriage, are seen the type of men and women whose sensibilities were trained to appreciate the tender refinement of Chaucer, and who allowed themselves more boisterous entertainments only under decorous pretexts, listening without participating. Side by side, following their own humours with noisy independence, are their vulgar associates, stopping at every ale-stake to eat and drink, half choked with ribald laughter, finding in the contrast between themselves and the reserved gentles an additional incentive to their gross open mirth. The *Canterbury Tales* embody two veins of feeling that powerfully influenced the literature of the fifteenth century—the sentiment that fed on chivalrous romances, and the appetite for animal laughter that received among other gratifications the grotesque literature of miracle-plays.

If we fail to perceive this contrast between the serious and the ludicrous side of the Canterbury pilgrimage, if we miss the poet's reconciliation of the two without repression of either, Chaucer's genius, in so far as regards manners and character, has laboured for us in vain. A dead weight flattens his figures into the page. The exquisite delicacy of his delineation is confused. We drag down the Knight and the Prioress by involving them in the responsibility of the *Miller's Tale:* we crush the life out of the Miller and the Summoner, and reduce them to wretched tameness by supposing them to fraternise with the Knight in a certain amount of decorous restraint. The pilgrimage becomes a muddled, jumbled, incoherent, unintelligible thing.

We must not, however, allow our attention to two large divisions, however much that may be the key to a right understanding of the *Canterbury Tales,* to make us overlook the varied types that lie within these divisions. Every character, indeed, is typical—Knight, Squire, Yeoman, Prioress, Monk, Friar, Merchant, Clerk, Sergeant of Law, Franklin, Cheapside Burgess, Cook, Shipman, Doctor of Physic, Wife of Bath, Parson, Ploughman, Miller, Manciple, Reeve, Summoner, Pardoner: and the characteristics of their various lines of life are drawn as no other generation has been in equal space. I shall not attempt to pick out supreme examples of Chaucer's skill. The compression of masterly touches in that *Prologue* can hardly be spoken of in sane language: there is not one of the seven or eight hundred lines but contains something to admire.

Apart from the skill of the delineation, one typical individual is specially interesting from his relations to the time, and that is the poor Parson. He cannot be said to belong, in rank at least, to the gentle class: he is of poor extraction, the brother of the Ploughman. He represents the serious element among the lower classes. During the riot of the pilgrimage, he is put down and silenced. He ventures to rebuke the Host for his profane language, and is jeered at and extinguished by that worthy as a Lollard. But when the ribald intoxication of the road has exhausted itself, his grave voice is heard and respected: and he brings the pilgrims into Canterbury with a tale more in harmony with the ostensible object of their journey.

Notes

1. *Étude sur G. Chaucer, considéré comme imitateur des Trouvères*, 1859. See, in particular, Mr Furnivall's *Trial-Forewords, Chaucer Society*, 1871.

2. This, however, is one of those cases where Time has lent an additional touch to the humour. The butler was a higher functionary than we should understand now by the name.

3. If M. Sandras has understood English humour, which seems to baffle Frenchmen as Scotch "wut" baffles Englishmen, he would hardly have said that in the *Canterbury Tales* Chaucer's natural affinity with the spirit of Jean de Meun is made conspicuous. In the following section I shall show how Chaucer maintains his agreement with the spirit of chivalry.

4. That the behaviour of the more uproarious of Chaucer's pilgrims was based on real life we may see from one of Thorpe's indignant accounts of the actual pilgrimages to the shrine of St. Thomas (quoted in Morley's *English Writers*, 1890, ii. 291): "They will ordain with them before to have with them both men and women that can sing wanton songs, and some other pilgrims will have with them bagpipes; so that every town they come through, what with the noise of their singing, and with the sound of their piping, and with the jangling of their Canterbury bells, and with the barking out of dogs after them, that they make more noise than if the king came there away with all his clarions, and many other minstrels. And if these men and women be a month in their pilgrimage, many of them shall be a half-year after great janglers, tale-tellers, and liars." In saying that in Chaucer's company "each fellow-traveller carried his wit for bagpipe," Professor Morley seems to have overlooked the Miller's instrument, and generally he seems inclined to make the pilgrimage a much tamer affair than it would appear to have been. I have endeavoured to show how the poet's decorous self-respect is reconciled with fidelity to the manners of the time.

5. Observe, in passing, another evidence of Chaucer's sense of courtly propriety in his *Troilus and Cressida*. The knights and ladies that heard his poems read would not have tolerated Shakespeare's representation of Pandarus, one of the knights of Troy, as a gross procurer, or of Cressida, a lady of rank, as an incontinent wanton. Chaucer's Pandarus is an accomplished knight, moved to his questionable service by pity for the despair of his friend; Cressida the loveliest, most refined, and most discreet of widows, overcome by passionate love, dexterous intrigue, and favouring accidents.

—William Minto, "Geoffrey Chaucer,"
Characteristics of English Poets, 1874, pp. 1–44

Felix Lindner "The Alliteration in Chaucer's *Canterbury Tales*" (1876)

Felix Lindner (1849–1917) was a prominent German scholar of medieval literature and letters. In the following excerpt, students will find Lindner's discussion of Chaucer's use of alliteration in his texts helpful, especially if writing about the various poetic devices Chaucer employed.

Alliteration is the repetition of a particular consonant sound at the beginning of words clustered closely together in a line or several lines of poetry. Alliteration was a defining characteristic of the Anglo-Saxon poetry that had established itself prominently in England during the years 600–1100. Many critics theorized that while alliteration never went out of style as a poetic device, its use as a hallmark in poetry ended with the Anglo-Saxons. Lindner suggests, however, that alliteration survived much later into the Middle Ages than anyone had previously supposed, and that Chaucer himself used alliteration in many of his works.

Lindner believes Chaucer did so for three reasons. The first is that alliteration allowed Chaucer to reflect and imitate the spoken language of his day, especially the language of the middle and lower classes, which are represented by numerous characters in *The Canterbury Tales* especially. Lindner suggests that the second reason Chaucer used alliteration is "his sympathy with old customs and manners; this is visible in all his tales. The character of the Anglo-Saxon seems not to be quite lost in Chaucer's poems." The third reason was ornamental; alliteration made Chaucer's verses stand out among his peers. Though Lindner provides several examples of alliteration in Chaucer, students may wish to examine Chaucer's texts and find their own examples if they are pursuing research in this area.

I was induced to undertake the following investigation by J. reading an article by Professor K. Regel, 'Die Alliteration im Layamon,' which is published in the first volume of *Germanistische Studien*, p. 171, ff. In this he shows to what a surprising extent alliteration, the original German manner of versifying, is retained in Layamon, long after the law of rhyme had been in use among the German nations. I will in this essay attempt to show that alliteration reaches to a later date,[1] that it is to be found in the poems of Chaucer, and to a greater extent than we should have expected.

I believe an investigation like this has not been undertaken till now, since the oft-quoted statement of Chaucer in the prologue to the *Persones Tale* seemed opposed to it.[2] This statement in which Chaucer says that alliterative metre was not within the range of a southern man (comp. verse 17353, ff.) runs thus:

But trusteth wel, I am a sotherne man,
I cannot geste rom, ram, ruf by letter,
And God wote, rime hold I but litel better.

Now, if we did not know that Chaucer was possessed of the gift of humour, and that he was also continually chaffing his own poetry, we should plead that he, in these verses, is not speaking himself, but that these words are only the 'Persones,' who says that, being unacquainted with either alliteration or rhyme, he therefore intends to tell his tale in prose. And we should argue that if the poet said, referring to himself, that he 'holds rime but litel better,' all his poems prove the contrary; while there is no objection whatever to attributing these words to the Parson, who indeed at that time may not have been able to write verses. But knowing Chaucer's sly humour as we do, and recollecting some of the other places in which like statements are made about himself and his poetry and knowledge,[3] we cannot get out of the conclusion, that Chaucer, in the lines above, while he meant to make an excuse for giving the Parson a prose tale, also meant to chaff the old stiff alliterative poetry, as well as his own rymes (whose ease and grace were such a contrast to the former's roughness and clumsiness), just as in the *Rime of Sire Thopas,* which is intentionally so bad,[4] he was parodying the balderdash into which the minstrels and rymers of his day had degraded the old Romances, those Romances which even Shakspere praised.[5]

But because Chaucer made fun of the *rom-ram-ruf* poetry, that was no reason why he should not make use, judicious use, of the power, the gratefulness to the ear, the old-friend's-voice tones, that alliteration lends to verse. And we shall see that Chaucer has indeed made frequent use of alliterative combinations, not only of such as are found in the old English language, but also of others made up of words of French origin. In Shakspere it is the same. He endeavours to make the use of alliterative rhyme ridiculous by usually placing it in the mouths of his comic characters; for instance, *Mids. Night's Dream,* V. i.:

Whereat with blade, with bloody blameful blade,
He bravely broached his boiling bloody breast.

Or in Love's L. L., IV. ii. 58: "I will something affect the letter, for it argues facility: The preyful princess pierced and prickt a pretty pleasing pricket."

And yet how many alliterative verses and combinations are to be found in Shakspere. See a very interesting article on this subject, 'Die Alliteration im Englischen vor und bei Shakspere,' by Rector Dr K. Seitz in the programme of the 'Marne Hoheren Biirgerschule,' Easter, 1875, to whom I am indebted for most of the parallels I quote from Shakspere.

I will now endeavour to point out the reasons which made Chaucer often revert to alliteration. Our poet was a man who, from his manner of life, had sufficient opportunities of observing people of all classes. With what avidity he seized these opportunities, and borrowed from every condition its especial peculiarities, is shown in his *Canterbury Tales*. Every character of them is a type of its class. Not only does he depict their outward appearance, their thoughts and feelings, but makes them speak the language of their class. I do not mean, of course, that Chaucer produces examples of the peculiar dialects then spoken in England; only rarely do we find proofs of dialect; for example, in the *Reeves Tale*, where Chaucer puts the forms 'makes,' 'fares,' 4021; 'findes,' 'bringes,' 'says,' 'Tis,' 4084, 4200, 4237; 'thou is,' 4087, etc., into the mouths of persons from Cambridge. But the tales of the lower classes are composed in a popular tone and in the popular language, and the stories of higher situated persons are written in a loftier style and nobler language. Certainly at that time the feeling for and the pleasure in alliteration was preserved by the people to a far greater extent than at the present, when many of the old forms then in common use are lost. If Chaucer endeavoured to imitate the people's style he was almost compelled to admit into his poems alliterative forms and combinations. In the tales of persons of higher rank this was not in the same degree necessary, as they, being for the most part either of Norman descent, or brought up in the use of Norman customs and opinions, paid but little heed to the form and contents of the old English poems; while the lower classes, for the most part of Saxon descent, preserved faithfully the songs which told of the great deeds of their forefathers, and with them the tendency to alliteration. Compare Geoffrey Chaucer's *Canterbury Tales*, translated into German by Wilhelm Hertzberg, Hildburghausen, 1866, p. 45: "But just at Chaucer's time the original form of the Anglo-Saxon verse with alliteration became popular again amongst the lower classes through *Piers Ploughman's Vision*, and other similar poems of a religious tendency."

Now, Chaucer held for many years the post of Controller of the Customs in the port of London—a duty which, as his appointment testifies, he was obliged to fulfil personally, and which he might not perform by deputy. The poet was called to this office on the 8th of June, 1374, and only on the 17th of February, 1386, did he receive permission to exercise his control of customs by deputy. During this long time he certainly had daily opportunities of studying and observing the language of the people. Being a man of unusually quick observation, he made use of his varied experience. The fruit of his study of the world and of men is exhibited in his *Canterbury Tales*.

The imitation of the language of the people was therefore one reason for the poet to revive alliteration. To this may be added a second,—his sympathy

with old customs and manners; this is visible in all his tales. The character of
the Anglo-Saxon seems not to be quite lost in Chaucer's poems. See Hertzberg,
p. 53: "It is almost as if his Anglo-Saxon nature (which we recognize in his
preference for the hard-handed son of the people) wished to avenge itself
on the French culture in him, by mixing blunt, peasant wit with the refined
character of the court." So we may conclude, with tolerable certainty, that
he had a strong natural inclination for the old alliterative forms, which was
perhaps unknown to himself. We observe how he reverts to alliteration in
depicting camp scenes and strong emotions, and often produces the most
glorious effects by this mixture of alliteration and rhyme.

The third reason for Chaucer's use of alliterative forms is to ornament his
verses, and to make them more striking. The national character at this time
was rather inclined to find peculiar pleasure in artificial verses, and therefore
the poet frequently made use of alliteration for rhythmical painting, which
was highly prized by the art-poets of that time. This is also shown by the
many onomatopoetic verses in the *Canterbury Tales,* of which I am going to
quote a few. In the verses 170 and 171 we can clearly hear the sound of the
bells on the bridle of the monk's horse:

> men might his bridel here
> Gingling in a whistling wind as clere
> And eke as loud as doth a chapel belle.

The description of the sound of church bells, comp. ver. 3655:

> Till that the belles of laudes gan to ringe.

In the verses 2339–2340—

> And as it queinte it made a whisteling
> As don these brondes wet in hir brenning,

we can plainly hear the hissing of the burning wood.

Similar to the well-known onomatopoetical verse in the beginning of
the *Iliad,* the rattling of the arrows in the quiver of Apollo is described, ver.
2360:

> the armes in the cas
> Of the goddesse clatteren fast and ring.

Other verses of this kind are:

> 2434: And with that sound he heard a murmuring
> Ful low and dim
> 2602: Now ringen trompes loud and clarioun.

4099:   With kepe kepe; stand stand; jossa warderers.

2607:   Ther shiveren shaftes upon sheldes thicke.

2693:   His brest tobrosten with his sadel bon.

These few hastily-selected examples are sufficient for our purpose. The two last verses are especially important, as they are both onomatopoetic and alliterative.

These are the reasons which probably induced Chaucer to employ alliterative forms and combinations. The same was the case with Chaucer's contemporaries on the continent. In Middle High German the poets also made frequent use of alliteration; compare Ignaz von Zingerle: *Die Alliteration bei mittelhochdeutschen Dichtern,* Wien, 1864; and Ferdinand Vetter: *Zum Muspilli und zur germanischen Alliterations Poesie,* Wien, 1872.

What Regel says of Layamon, that he shows his pleasure in similar sounds by his tendency to repeat several words at the beginning of successive verses, is true of Chaucer also. Here, too, I will limit myself to a few out of the great number of examples which at once strike one when reading—

404:    His stremes and his dangers him besides
         His herbergh and his mone, his lodemenage.

983:    Thus ryt this duke, thus ryt this conquerour.

1872:   Who looketh lightly now but Palamon?
         Who springeth up for joye but Arcite?
         Who coud it tell, or who coud it endite

2275:   Up roos the sonne and up roos Emelye.

2573:   And after rood the queen and Emelye,
         And after hem of ladyes another companye,
         And after hem of comunes after her degre.

2775:   Alas the deth! alas min Emelye!
         Alas departing of our companye!
         Alas min hertes quene! alas my wif!

We may compare with this vers. 590–592, 2927–60, 11458–61, etc. To the poet's lively joy in similar sounds his plays upon words also bear testimony:

7289:   God *save* you alle *save* this cursed frere.

10419:   Al be it that I can nat sowne his *style,*
          Ne can nat clymben over so heigh a *style.*

10569:   And yit is glas nought like aisshen or *feme*
          But for they han yknowen it so *feme.*

11035:   *Colours* ne know I none withouten drede
          But swiche *colours* as growen in the mede.

To these may be added the repetition of certain forms of sentences which the poet frequently uses with epic skill: 'Still as eny stoon,' 3472, 7997, 10485 (compare Shakspere, *King John*, IV. i., 'I will not struggle, I will stand stone-still;' *Lucretia*: 'Stone-still astonished'); 'domb as eny stoon,' 776; (and) 'deed as eny stoon, 10788; 'wel I wot.'

Notes

1. It of course exists, more or less, in the whole range of English poetry, and is freely used by Gower, and Chaucer's other contemporaries and successors. "Alliteration's artful aid" has always been too great a help to the charms of poetry, to allow of its being neglected by writers of verse.
2. See an essay on alliterative poetry by the Rev. W. W. Skeat, in vol. iii. of Bishop Percy's Folio MS., Ballads and Romances.
3. Compare in the *Man of Lawes Prologue*:

    > I can right now no thrifty tale sain, 4466
    > But Chaucer (though he can but lewedly
    > On metres and on riming craftily)
    > Hath said them, in swiche English as he can
    > Of olde time," etc.
    > But natheles.
    > I speke in prose and let him rimes make.   4516

    We know that in spite of the last verse the *Man of Lawes Tale* is not told in prose, but in verse.

    In another place, ver. 11578 in the *Frankeleines Tale,* he says, as almost in the *Hous of Fame*:

    > I can no termes of Astrologie.

    But not only this tale, but many others contain such a multitude of astrological expressions, and show such a knowledge of the science, that they prove just the contrary.
4. The host exclaims, ver. 13858:

    > Thy drasty riming is not worth a tord;
    > Thou doest nought elles but dispendest time.
    > Sire, at o word, thou shalt no lenger rime.
5. (Sonnet CVI.)

    > When in the chronicle of wasted time
    >   I see descriptions of the fairest wights,
    > And beauty making beautiful old rhyme,
    >   In praise of ladies dead, and lovely knights,
    > Then, in the blazon of sweet beauty's best,

Of hand, of foot, of lip, of eye, of brow,
I see their antique pen would have express'd
    Even such a beauty as you master now.
So all their praises are but prophecies
    Of this our time, all you prefiguring;
And for they look'd but with divining eyes,
    They had not skill enough your worth to sing:
For we, which now behold these present days,
Have eyes to wonder, but lack tongues to praise.

—Felix Lindner, "The Alliteration in Chaucer's
Canterbury Tales," (1876), *Essays on Chaucer*
1868–94, pp. 199–205

JOHN RUSKIN "LETTER 61" (1876)

And for the standard theological writings which are ultimately to be the foundation of this body of secular literature (the projected St. George's library), I have chosen seven authors, whose lives and works, so far as the one can be traced or the other certified, shall be, with the best help I can obtain from the good scholars of Oxford, prepared one by one in perfect editions for the St. George's schools. These seven books will contain, in as many volumes as may be needful, the lives and writings of the men who have taught the purest theological truth hitherto known to the Jews, Greeks, Latins, Italians, and English; namely, Moses, David, Hesiod, Virgil, Dante, Chaucer, and, for seventh, summing the whole with vision of judgment, St. John the Divine.

The Hesiod I purpose, if my life is spared, to translate myself (into prose), and to give in complete form. Of Virgil I shall only take the two first Georgics, and the sixth book of the Aeneid, but with the Douglas translation; adding the two first books of Livy, for completion of the image of Roman life. Of Chaucer, I take the authentic poems, except the Canterbury Tales; together with, be they authentic or not, the Dream, and the fragment of the translation of the Romance of the Rose, adding some French chivalrous literature of the same date. I shall so order this work, that, in such measure as it may be possible to me, it shall be in a constantly progressive relation to the granted years of my life. The plan of it I give now, and will explain in full detail, that my scholars may carry it out, if I cannot.

And now let my general readers observe, finally, about all reading,—You must read, for the nourishment of your mind, precisely under the moral laws which regulate your eating for the nourishment of the body. That is to say, you must not eat for the pleasure of eating, nor read for the pleasure of reading. But, if you manage yourself rightly, you will intensely enjoy your dinner, and your book. If you have any sense, you can easily follow out this analogy: I have not time at present to do it for you; only be sure it holds, to the minutest particular, with this difference only, that the vices and virtues of reading are more harmful on the one side, and higher on the other, as the soul is more precious than the body. Gluttonous reading is a worse vice than gluttonous eating; filthy and foul reading, a much more loathsome habit than filthy eating. Epicurism in books is much more difficult of attainment than epicurism in meat, but plain and virtuous feeding the most entirely pleasurable.

And now, one step of farther thought will enable you to settle a great many questions with one answer.

As you may neither eat, nor read, for the pleasure of eating or reading, so you may do *nothing else* for the pleasure of it, but for the use. The moral difference between a man and a beast is, that the one acts primarily for use, the other for pleasure. And all acting for pleasure before use, or instead of use, is, in one word, 'Fornication.'

—John Ruskin, "Letter 61," Fors Clavigera, 1876, pp. 21–22

Adolphus William Ward "Characteristics of Chaucer and His Poetry" (1879)

Ward (1837–1924) was an English historian most noted for his *History of the English Dramatic Literature to the Age of Queen Anne*. In this essay, Ward considers "Chaucer's inner nature" and examines how those personal characteristics that reveal themselves in Chaucer's writing are reflected in "his poetical characteristics." Students may find it interesting to mimic Ward's approach in their own writing about Chaucer, or to debate what Ward believes he has uncovered about Chaucer from clues found within his texts.

Ward begins his essay by noting the lack of solid biographical information about Chaucer's life, instead relying on Chaucer's texts themselves to provide clues about his character. Ward believes that Chaucer was "indifferent to the lack of brilliant success in life." This reflects Chaucer's "contented faith." Ward adds, "[p]ersonal inspection, in [Chaucer's] opinion, was not necessary for a faith which at some times may, and at others must, take the place of knowledge." Ward believes that Chaucer holds no "strong personal views on questions either of ecclesiastical or of religious policy," and if he did, the writer did not "use his poetry, allegorical or otherwise, as a vehicle of his wishes, hopes, or fears on these heads." Most contemporary scholars disagree with this, believing that *The Canterbury Tales* in particular satirizes the Church and other social institutions. Ward's arguments about Chaucer and religion can be used as a springboard for a student's own perspective on the issue.

Chaucer's supposed ambivalence toward the Church was not reflected in his attitudes toward women, however; Ward writes that "the irony, sarcasm, and fun lavished by Chaucer" on women may have been because Chaucer himself was "unhappy as a husband." Many current critics disagree with this view; though Ward's explorations of Chaucer's "attacks on women" were not uncommon in his time, students today may find his perspective out of date and use these arguments as a counterpoint in discussing the issue themselves.

Ward addresses these aspects of Chaucer's characters as "principles [that] affected" his writing. While Chaucer "is mediaeval in tricks of style and turns of phrase," Ward believes that Chaucer himself is timeless. Ward argues that Chaucer's great gifts to English literature include the "vividness" of his "descriptive power, [his] brightness and variety of imagery, and [his] flow of diction," "his keen sense of the ridiculous and [his] power of satire," and his "penetrating insight into the minds of men." Because of these aspects of his work, Ward argues that Chaucer is in many ways the predecessor of both the Elizabethan dramatic poets of the Renaissance and the great English novelists of the eighteenth and nineteenth centuries. Any student writing about Chaucer's poetical style or comparing Chaucer to later English poets would do well to start here.

Ultimately, Ward does not conclude that Chaucer is the greatest poet in the English language, nor does he believe that Chaucer's work is without its flaws; but Ward does assert that Chaucer is one of the most important writers of all time, because "in his poetry there is *life*." Ward's essay thus suggests to readers avenues for their own explorations of Chaucer by examining his works for possible clues to the author's beliefs and values.

One very pleasing quality in Chaucer must have been his modesty. In the course of his life this may have helped to recommend him to patrons so many and so various, and to make him the useful and trustworthy agent that he evidently became for confidential missions abroad. Physically, as has been seen, he represents himself as prone to the habit of casting his eyes on the ground; and we may feel tolerably sure that to this external manner corresponded a quiet, observant disposition, such as that which may be held to have distinguished the greatest of Chaucer's successors among English poets. To us, of course, this quality of modesty in Chaucer makes itself principally manifest in the opinion which he incidentally shows himself to entertain concerning his own rank and claims as an author. Herein, as in many other points, a contrast is noticeable between him and the great Italian masters, who were so sensitive as to the esteem in which they and their poetry were held. Who could fancy Chaucer crowned with laurel, like Petrarch, or even, like Dante, speaking with proud humility of "the beautiful style that has done honour to him," while acknowledging his obligation for it to a great predecessor? Chaucer again and again disclaims all boasts of perfection, or pretensions to pre-eminence, as a poet. His Canterbury Pilgrims have in his name to disavow, like Persius, having slept on Mount Parnassus, or possessing "rhetoric" enough to describe a heroine's beauty; and he openly allows that his spirit grows dull as he grows older, and that he finds a difficulty as a translator in matching his rhymes to his French original. He acknowledges as incontestable the superiority of the poets of classical antiquity:—

> Little book, no writing thou envý,
> But subject be to all true poësy,
> And kiss the steps, where'er thou seest space
> Of Virgil, Ovid, Homer, Lucan, Stace.

But more than this. In the *House of Fame* he expressly disclaims having in his light and imperfect verse sought to pretend to "mastery" in the art poetical; and in a charmingly expressed passage of the *Prologue* to the *Legend of Good Women* he describes himself as merely following in the wake of those who have already reaped the harvest of amorous song, and have carried away the corn:—

> And I come after, gleaning here and there,
> And am full glad if I can find an ear
> Of any goodly word that ye have left.

Modesty of this stamp is perfectly compatible with a certain self-consciousness which is hardly ever absent from greatness, and which at all events supplies a stimulus not easily dispensed with except by sustained effort on the part of a poet. The two qualities seem naturally to combine into that self-containedness (very different from self-contentedness) which distinguishes Chaucer, and which helps to give to his writings a manliness of tone, the direct opposite of the irretentive querulousness found in so great a number of poets in all times. He cannot, indeed, be said to maintain an absolute reserve concerning himself and his affairs in his writings; but as he grows older, he seems to become less and less inclined to take the public into his confidence, or to speak of himself except in a pleasantly light and incidental fashion. And in the same spirit he seems, without ever folding his hands in his lap, or ceasing to be a busy man and an assiduous author, to have grown indifferent to the lack of brilliant success in life, whether as a man of letters or otherwise. So at least one seems justified in interpreting a remarkable passage in the *House of Fame*, the poem in which, perhaps, Chaucer allows us to see more deeply into his mind than in any other. After surveying the various company of those who had come as suitors for the favours of Fame, he tells us how it seemed to him (in his long December dream) that some one spoke to him in a kindly way,

> And saidë: 'Friend, what is thy name?
> Art thou come hither to have fame?'
> 'Nay, forsoothë, friend!' quoth I;
> 'I came not hither (grand merci!)
> For no such causë, by my head!
> Sufficeth me, as I were dead,
> That no wight have my name in hand.
> I wot myself best how I stand;
> For what I suffer, or what I think,
> I will myselfë all it drink,
> Or at least the greater part
> As far forth as I know my art.'

With this modest but manly self-possession we shall not go far wrong in connecting what seems another very distinctly marked feature of Chaucer's inner nature. He seems to have arrived at a clear recognition of the truth with which Goethe humorously comforted Eckermann in the shape of the proverbial saying, "Care has been taken that the trees shall not grow into the sky." Chaucer's, there is every reason to believe, was a contented faith, as far removed from self-torturing unrest as from childish credulity. Hence his refusal to trouble himself, now that he has arrived at a good age, with original research as to the constellations. (The passage is all the more significant since Chaucer, as has been seen, actually possessed a very respectable knowledge of astronomy.) That winged encyclopaedia, the Eagle, has just been regretting the poet's unwillingness to learn the position of the Great and the Little Bear, Castor and Pollux, and the rest, concerning which at present he does not know where they stand. But he replies, "No matter!

> '... It is no need;
> I trust as well (so God me speed!)
> Them that write of this matter,
> As though I knew their places there.'

Moreover, as he says (probably without implying any special allegorical meaning), they seem so bright that it would destroy my eyes to look upon them. Personal inspection, in his opinion, was not necessary for a faith which at some times may, and at others must, take the place of knowledge; for we find him, at the opening of the *Prologue* to the *Legend of Good Women,* in a passage the tone of which should not be taken to imply less than its words express, writing as follows:—

> A thousand timës I have heard men tell,
> That there is joy in heaven, and pain in hell;
> And I accordë well that it is so.
> But nathëless, yet wot I well alsó,
> That there is none doth in this country dwell
> That either hath in heaven been or hell,
> Or any other way could of it know,
> But that he heard, or found it written so,
> For by assay may no man proof receive.
>   But God forbid that men should not believe
> More things than they have ever seen with eye!
> Men shall not fancy everything a lie
> Unless themselves it see, or else it do;
> For, God wot, not the less a thing is true,
> Though every wight may not it chance to see.

The central thought of these lines, though it afterwards receives a narrower and more commonplace application, is no other than that which has been so splendidly expressed by Spenser in the couplet:—

> Why then should witless man so much misween
> That nothing is but that which he hath seen?

The *negative* result produced in Chaucer's mind by this firm but placid way of regarding matters of faith was a distrust of astrology, alchemy, and all the superstitions which in the *Parson's Tale* are noticed as condemned by the Church. This distrust on Chaucer's part requires no further illustration after what has been said elsewhere; it would have been well for his age if all its children had been as clear-sighted in these matters as he, to whom the practices connected with these delusive sciences seemed, and justly so from his point of view, not less impious than futile. His *Canon Yeoman's Tale,* a story of imposture so vividly dramatic in its catastrophe as to have suggested to Ben Jonson one of the most effective passages in his comedy *The Alchemist,* concludes with a moral of unmistakeable solemnity against the sinfulness, as well as uselessness, of "multiplying" (making gold by the arts of alchemy):—

> Whoso maketh God his adversáry,
> As for to work anything in contràry
> Unto His will, certes ne'er shall he thrive,
> Though that he multiply through all his life.

But equally unmistakeable is the *positive* side of this frame of mind in such a passage as the following—which is one of those belonging to Chaucer himself, and not taken from his French original—in *The Man of Law's Tale*. The narrator is speaking of the voyage of Constance, after her escape from the massacre in which, at a feast, all her fellow-Christians had been killed, and of how she was borne by the "wild wave" from "Surrey" (Syria) to the Northumbrian shore:—

> Here men might askë, why she was not slain?
> Eke at the feast who might her body save?
> And I answérë that demand again:
> Who savèd Daniel in th' horríble cave,
> When every wight save him, master or knave,
> The lion ate—before he could depart?
> No wight but God, whom he bare in his heart.

"In her," he continues, "God desired to show His miraculous power, so that we should see His mighty works; for Christ, in whom we have a remedy for every ill, often by means of His own does things for ends of His own, which are obscure to the wit of man, incapable, by reason of our ignorance, of understanding His wise providence. But since Constance was not slain at the feast, it might be asked: Who kept her from drowning in the sea? Who, then, kept Jonas in the belly of the whale till he was spouted up at Ninive? Well do we know it was no one but He who kept the Hebrew people from drowning in the waters, and made them to pass through the sea with dry feet. Who bade the four spirits of the tempest, which have the power to trouble land and sea, north and south, and west and east, vex neither sea nor land nor the trees that grow on it? Truly these things were ordered by Him who kept this woman safe from the tempest, as well when she awoke as when she slept. But whence might this woman have meat and drink, and how could her sustenance last out to her for three years and more? Who, then, fed Saint Mary the Egyptian in the cavern or in the desert? Assuredly no one but Christ. It was a great miracle to feed five thousand folk with five loaves and two fishes; but God in their great need sent to them abundance."

As to the sentiments and opinions of Chaucer, then, on matters such as these, we can entertain no reasonable doubt. But we are altogether too ill acquainted with the details of his personal life, and with the motives which contributed to determine its course, to be able to arrive at any valid conclusions as to the way in which his principles affected his conduct. Enough has been already said concerning the attitude seemingly observed by him towards the great public questions, and the great historical events, of his day. If he had strong political opinions of his own, or strong personal views on questions either of ecclesiastical policy or of religious doctrine—in which assumptions there seems nothing probable—he, at all events, did not wear his heart on his sleeve, or use his poetry, allegorical or otherwise, as a vehicle of his wishes, hopes, or fears on these heads. The true breath of freedom could hardly be expected to blow through the precincts of a Plantagenet court. If Chaucer could write the pretty lines in the *Manciple's Tale* about the caged bird and its uncontrollable desire for liberty, his contemporary Barbour could apostrophise Freedom itself as a noble thing, in words the simple manliness of which stirs the blood after a very different fashion. Concerning his domestic relations, we may regard it as virtually certain that he was unhappy as a husband, though tender and affectionate as a father. Considering how vast a proportion of the satire of all times—but more especially that of the Middle Ages, and in these again pre-eminently of the period of European literature which took its tone from Jean de Meung—is directed against woman and against married life, it would be difficult to decide how much of the irony, sarcasm, and fun lavished by Chaucer on these themes is due to a fashion with which he readily fell in, and how much to the impulse of personal feeling. A perfect anthology, or perhaps one should rather say, a complete herbarium, might be collected from his works of samples of these attacks on women. He has manifestly made a careful study of their ways, with which he now and then betrays that curiously intimate acquaintance to which we are accustomed in a Richardson or a Balzac. How accurate are such incidental remarks as this, that women are "full measurable" in such matters as sleep—not caring for so much of it at a time as men do! How wonderfully natural is the description of Cressid's bevy of lady-visitors, attracted by the news that she is shortly to be surrendered to the Greeks, and of the "nice vanity"—i. e., foolish emptiness—of their consolatory gossip. "As men see in town, and all about, that women are accustomed to visit their friends," so a swarm of ladies came to Cressid, "and sat themselves down, and said as I shall tell. 'I am delighted,' says one, 'that you will so soon see your father.' 'Indeed I am not so delighted,' says another, 'for we have not seen half enough of her since she has been at Troy.' 'I do hope,' quoth the third, 'that she will bring us back peace with her; in which case may Almighty God guide her on her departure.' And Cressid heard these words and womanish things as if she were far away; for she was burning all the time with another passion than any of which they knew; so that she almost felt her heart die for woe, and for weariness of that company.'" But his satire against women is rarely so innocent as this; and though several ladies take part in the Canterbury Pilgrimage, yet pilgrim after pilgrim has his saw or jest against their sex. The courteous *Knight* cannot refrain from the generalisation that women all follow the favour of fortune. The *Summoner,* who is of a less scrupulous sort, introduces a diatribe against women's passionate love of vengeance; and the *Shipman* seasons a story which requires no such addition by an enumeration of their favourite foibles. But the climax is reached in the confessions of the *Wife of Bath,* who quite unhesitatingly says that women are best won by flattery and busy attentions; that when won they desire to have the sovereignty over their husbands, and that they tell untruths and swear to them with twice the boldness of men; while as to the power of their tongue, she quotes the secondhand authority of her fifth husband for the saying that it is better to dwell with a lion or a foul dragon than with a woman accustomed to chide. It is true that this same *Wife of Bath* also observes with an effective *tu quoque:*—

> By God, if women had but written stories,
> As clerkës have within their oratòries,
> They would have writ of men more wickednéss
> Than all the race of Adam may redress;

and the *Legend of Good Women* seems, in point of fact, to have been intended to offer some such kind of amends as is here declared to be called for. But the balance still remains heavy against the poet's sentiments of gallantry and respect for women. It should, at the same time, be remembered that among the *Canterbury Tales* the two which are of their kind the most effective constitute tributes to the most distinctively feminine and wifely virtue of fidelity. Moreover, when coming from such personages as the pilgrims who narrate the *Tales* in question, the praise of women has special significance and value. The *Merchant* and the *Shipman* may indulge in facetious or coarse jibes against wives and their behaviour; but the *Man of Law,* full of grave experience of the world, is a witness above suspicion to the womanly virtue of which his narrative celebrates so illustrious an example, while the *Clerk of Oxford* has in his cloistered solitude, where all womanly blandishments are unknown, come to the conclusion that

> Men speak of Job, most for his humbleness,
> As clerkës, when they list, can well indite,
> Of men in special; but, in truthfulness,
> Though praise by clerks of women be but slight,
> No man in humbleness can him acquit
> As women can, nor can be half so true
> As women are, unless all things be new.

As to marriage, Chaucer may be said generally to treat it in that style of laughing with a wry mouth, which has from time immemorial been affected both in comic writing and on the comic stage, but which in the end even the most determined old bachelor feels an occasional inclination to consider monotonous.

In all this, however, it is obvious that something at least must be set down to conventionality. Yet the best part of Chaucer's nature, it is hardly necessary to say, was neither conventional nor commonplace. He was not, we may rest assured, one of that numerous class which in his days, as it does in ours, composed the population of the land of Philistia—the persons so well defined by the Scottish poet, Sir David Lyndsay (himself a courtier of the noblest type):—

> Who fixèd have their hearts and whole intents
> On sensual lust, on dignity, and rents.

Doubtless Chaucer was a man of practical good sense, desirous of suitable employment and of a sufficient income; nor can we suppose him to have been one of those who look upon social life and its enjoyments with a jaundiced eye, or who, absorbed in things which are not of this world, avert their gaze from it altogether. But it is hardly possible that rank and position should have been valued on their own account by one who so repeatedly recurs to his ideal of the true gentleman, as to a conception dissociated from mere outward circumstances, and more particularly independent of birth or inherited wealth. At times, we know, men find what they seek; and so Chaucer found in Boethius and in Guillaume de Lorris that conception which he both translates and reproduces, besides repeating it in a little *Ballade*, probably written by him in the last *decennium* of his life. By far the best-known and the finest of these passages is that in the *Wife of Bath's Tale*, which follows the round assertion that the "arrogance" against which it protests is not worth a hen; and which is followed by an appeal to a parallel passage in Dante:—

> Look, who that is most virtuous alway
> Privy and open, and most intendeth aye
> To do the gentle deedes that he can,

Take him for the greatest gentleman.
Christ wills we claim of Him our gentleness,
Not of our elders for their old richés.
For though they give us all their heritáge
Through which we claim to be of high paráge,
Yet may they not bequeathë for no thing—
To none of us—their virtuous living,
That made them gentlemen y-callèd be,
And bade us follow them in such degree.
Well can the wisë poet of Florénce,
That Dante hightë, speak of this senténce;
Lo, in such manner of rhyme is Dante's tale:
'Seldom upriseth by its branches small
Prowess of man; for God of His prowéss
Wills that we claim of Him our gentleness;
For of our ancestors we no thing claim
But temporal thing, that men may hurt and maim.'[1]

By the still ignobler greed of money for its own sake, there is no reason whatever to suppose Chaucer to have been at any time actuated; although, under the pressure of immediate want, he devoted a *Complaint* to his empty purse, and made known, in the proper quarters, his desire to see it refilled. Finally, as to what is commonly called pleasure, he may have shared the fashions and even the vices of his age; but we know hardly anything on the subject, except that excess in wine, which is often held a pardonable peccadillo in a poet, receives his emphatic condemnation. It would be hazardous to assert of him, as Herrick asserted of himself, that though his "Muse was jocund, his life was chaste;" inasmuch as his name occurs in one unfortunate connexion full of suspiciousness. But we may at least believe him to have spoken his own sentiments in the Doctor of Physic's manly declaration that

Of all treason sovereign pestilence
Is when a man betrayeth innocence.

His true pleasures lay far away from those of vanity and dissipation. In the first place, he seems to have been a passionate reader. To his love of books he is constantly referring; indeed, this may be said to be the only kind of egotism which he seems to take a pleasure in indulging. At the opening of his earliest extant poem of consequence, the *Book of the Duchess,* he tells us how he preferred to drive away a night rendered sleepless through melancholy thoughts, by means of a book, which he thought better entertainment than a game either at chess or at "tables." This passion lasted longer with him than the other passion which it had helped to allay; for in the sequel to the well-known passage in the *House of Fame,* already cited, he gives us a glimpse of himself at home, absorbed in his favourite pursuit:—

> Thou go'st home to thy house anon,
> And there, as dumb as any stone,
> Thou sittest at another book,
> Till fully dazèd is thy look;
> And liv'st thus as a hermit quite,
> Although thy abstinence is slight.

And doubtless he counted the days lost in which he was prevented from following the rule of life which elsewhere he sets himself, "to study and to read alway, day by day," and pressed even the nights into his service when he was not making his head ache with writing. How eager and, considering the times in which he lived, how diverse a reader he was, has already been abundantly illustrated in the course of this volume. His knowledge of Holy Writ was considerable, though it probably, for the most part, came to him at second-hand. He seems to have had some acquaintance with patristic and homilectic literature; he produced a version of the homily on Mary Magdalene, improperly attributed to Origen; and, as we have seen, emulated King Alfred in translating Boethius's famous manual of moral philosophy. His Latin learning extended over a wide range of literature, from Virgil and Ovid down to some of the favourite Latin poets of the Middle Ages. It is to be feared that he occasionally read Latin authors with so eager a desire to arrive at the contents of their books that he at times mistook their meaning—not far otherwise, slightly to vary a happy comparison made by one of his most eminent commentators, than many people read Chaucer's own writings now-a-days. That he possessed any knowledge at all of Greek may be doubted, both on general grounds and on account of a little slip or two in quotation of a kind not unusual with those who quote what they have not previously read. His *Troilus and Cressid* has only a very distant connexion, indeed, with Homer, whose *Iliad,* before it furnished materials for the mediæval Troilus-legend, had been filtered through a brief Latin epitome, and diluted into a Latin novel, and a journal kept at the seat of war, of altogether apocryphal value. And, indeed, it must in general be conceded that, if Chaucer had read much, he lays claim to having read more; for he not only occasionally ascribes to known authors works which we can by no means feel certain as to their having written, but at times he even cites (or is made to cite, in all the editions of his works) authors who are altogether unknown to fame by the names which he gives to them. But then it must be remembered that other mediæval writers have rendered themselves liable to the same kind of charge. Quoting was one of the dominant literary fashions of the age; and just as a word without an oath went for but little in conversation, so a statement or sentiment in writing acquired a greatly enhanced value when suggested by authority, even after no more precise a fashion than the use of the phrase "as old books say." In Chaucer's days the equivalent of the modern "I have seen it said *somewhere*"—with, perhaps, the venturesome addition: "I *think*, in Horace"—had clearly not become an objectionable expletive.

Of modern literatures there can be no doubt that Chaucer had made substantially his own the two which could be of importance to him as a poet. His obligations to the French singers have probably been over-estimated—at all events, if the view adopted in this essay be the correct one, and if the charming poem of the *Flower and the Leaf,* together with the lively, but as to its meaning not very transparent, so-called *Chaucer's Dream,* be denied admission among his genuine works. At the same time, the influence of the *Roman de la Rose* and that of the courtly poets, of whom Machault was the chief in France and Froissart the representative in England, are perceptible in Chaucer almost to the last, nor is it likely that he should ever have ceased to study and assimilate them. On the other hand, the extent of his knowledge of Italian literature has probably till of late been underrated in an almost equal degree. This knowledge displays itself not only in the imitation or adaptation of particular poems, but more especially in the use made of incidental passages and details. In this way his debts to Dante were especially numerous; and it is curious to find proofs so abundant of Chaucer's relatively close study of a poet with whose genius his own had so few points in common. Notwithstanding first appearances, it is an open question whether Chaucer had ever read Boccaccio's *Decamerone,* with which he may merely have had in common the sources of several of his *Canterbury Tales.* But as he certainly took one of them from the *Teseide* (without improving it in the process), and not less certainly, and adapted the *Filostrato* in his *Troilus and Cressid,* it is strange that he should refrain from naming the author to whom he was more indebted than to any one other for poetic materials.

But wide and diverse as Chaucer's reading fairly deserves to be called, the love of nature was even stronger and more absorbing in him than the love of books. He has himself, in a very charming passage, compared the strength of the one and of the other of his predilections:—

And as for me, though I have knowledge slight
In bookës for to read I me delight,
And to them give I faith and full credénce,
And in my heart have them in reverence
So heartily, that there is gamë none
That from my bookës maketh me be gone,
But it be seldom on the holiday—
Save, certainly, when that the month of May
Is come, and that I hear the fowlës sing,
And see the flowers as they begin to spring,
Farewell my book, and my devotión.

Undoubtedly the literary fashion of Chaucer's times is responsible for part of this May-morning sentiment, with which he is fond of beginning his poems (the Canterbury pilgrimage is dated towards the end of April—but is not April "messenger to May?"). It had been decreed that flowers should be the badges of nations and dynasties, and the tokens of amorous sentiment; the rose had its votaries, and the lily, lauded by Chaucer's *Prioress* as the symbol of the Blessed Virgin; while the daisy, which first sprang from the tears of a forlorn damsel, in France gave its name *(marguerite)* to an entire species of courtly verse. The enthusiastic adoration professed by Chaucer, in the *Prologue* to the *Legend of Good Women,* for the daisy, which he afterwards identifies with the good Alceste, the type of faithful wifehood, is, of course, a mere poetical figure. But there is in his use of these favourite literary devices, so to speak, a variety in sameness significant of their accordance with his own taste, and of the frank and fresh love of nature which animated him, and which seems to us as much a part of him as his love of books. It is unlikely that his personality will ever become more fully known than it is at present; nor is there anything in respect of which we seem to see so clearly into his inner nature as with regard to these twin predilections, to which he remains true in all his works and in all his moods. While the study of books was his chief passion, nature was his chief joy and solace; while his genius enabled him to transfuse what he read in the former, what came home to him in the latter was akin to that genius itself; for he at times reminds us of his own fresh Canace, whom he describes as looking so full of happiness during her walk through the wood at sunrise:—

What for the season, what for the morning
And for the fowles that she hearde sing,
For right anon she wiste what they meant
Right by their song, and knew all their intent.

If the above view of Chaucer's character and intellectual tastes and tendencies be in the main correct, there will seem to be nothing paradoxical in describing his literary progress, so far as its *data* are ascertainable, as a most steady and regular one. Very few men awake to find themselves either famous or great of a sudden, and perhaps as few poets as other men, though it may be heresy against a venerable maxim to say so. Chaucer's works form a clearly recognisable series of steps towards the highest achievement of which, under the circumstances in which he lived and wrote, he can be held to have been capable; and his long and arduous self-training, whether consciously or not directed to a particular end, was of that sure kind from which genius itself derives strength. His beginnings as a writer were dictated, partly by the impulse of that imitative faculty which, in poetic natures, is the usual precursor of the creative, partly by the influence of prevailing tastes and the absence of native English literary predecessors whom, considering the circumstances of his life and the nature of his temperament, he could have found it a congenial task to follow. French poems were, accordingly, his earliest models; but fortunately (unlike Gower, whom it is so instructive to compare with Chaucer, precisely because the one lacked that gift of genius which the other possessed) he seems at once to have resolved to make use for his poetical writings of his native speech. In no way, therefore, could he have begun his career with so happy a promise of its future as in that which he actually chose. Nor could any course so naturally have led him to introduce into his poetic diction the French idioms and words already used in the spoken language of Englishmen, more especially in those classes for which he in the first instance wrote, and thus to confer upon our tongue the great benefit which it owes to him. Again, most fortunately, others had already pointed the way to the selection for literary use of that English dialect which was probably the most suitable for the purpose; and Chaucer, as a Southern man (like his *Parson of a Town),* belonged to a part of the country where the old alliterative verse had long since been discarded for classical and romance forms of versification. Thus the *Romaunt of the Rose* most suitably opens his literary life—a translation in which there is nothing original except an occasional turn of phrase, but in which the translator finds opportunity for exercising his powers of judgment by virtually re-editing the work before him. And already in the *Book of the Duchess,* though most unmistakeably a follower of Machault, he is also the rival of the great French *trouvere,* and has advanced in freedom of movement not less than in agreeableness of form. Then, as his travels extended his acquaintance with foreign literatures to that of Italy, he here found abundant fresh materials from which to feed his productive powers, and more elaborate forms in which to clothe their results;

while at the same time comparison, the kindly nurse of originality, more and more enabled him to recast instead of imitating, or encouraged him freely to invent. In *Troilus and Cressid* he produced something very different from a mere condensed translation, and achieved a work in which he showed himself a master of poetic expression and sustained narrative; in the *House of Fame* and the *Assembly of Fowls* he moved with freedom in happily contrived allegories of his own invention; and with the *Legend of Good Women* he had already arrived at a stage when he could undertake to review, under a pleasant pretext, but with evident consciousness of work done, the list of his previous works. "He hath," he said of himself, "made many a lay and many a thing." Meanwhile the labour incidentally devoted by him to translation from the Latin, or to the composition of prose treatises in the scholastic manner of academical exercises, could but little affect his general literary progress. The mere scholarship of youth, even if it be the reverse of close and profound, is wont to cling to a man through life, and to assert its modest claims at any season; and thus Chaucer's school-learning exercised little influence either of an advancing or of a retarding kind upon the full development of his genius. Nowhere is he so truly himself as in the masterpiece of his last years. For the *Canterbury Tales,* in which he is at once greatest, most original, and most catholic in the choice of materials as well as in moral sympathies, bears the unmistakeable stamp of having formed the crowning labour of his life—a work which death alone prevented him from completing.

It may be said, without presumption, that such a general view as this leaves ample room for all reasonable theories as to the chronology and sequence, where these remain more or less unsettled, of Chaucer's indisputably genuine works. In any case, there is no poet whom, if only as an exercise in critical analysis, it is more interesting to study and re-study in connexion with the circumstances of his literary progress. He still, as has been seen, belongs to the Middle Ages, but to a period in which the noblest ideals of these Middle Ages are already beginning to pale and their mightiest institutions to quake around him; in which learning continues to be in the main scholasticism, the linking of argument with argument, and the accumulation of authority upon authority, and poetry remains to a great extent the crabbedness of clerks or the formality of courts. Again, Chaucer is mediaeval in tricks of style and turns of phrase; he often contents himself with the tritest of figures and the most unrefreshing of ancient devices, and freely resorts to a mixture of names and associations belonging to his own times with others derived from other ages. This want of literary perspective is a sure sign of medievalism, and one which has amused the world, or has jarred upon it, since the Renascence taught men to study both classical and Biblical antiquity as realities, and not merely as a succession of pictures or of tapestries on a wall. Chaucer mingles things mediæval and things classical as freely as he brackets King David with the philosopher Seneca, or Judas Iscariot with the Greek "dissimulator" Sinon. His Dido, mounted on a stout palfrey paper-white of hue, with a red-and-gold saddle embroidered and embossed, resembles Alice Perrers in all her pomp rather than the Virgilian queen. Jupiter's eagle, the poet's guide and instructor in the allegory of the *House of Fame,* invokes "Saint Mary, Saint James," and "Saint Clare" all at once; and the pair of lovers at Troy sign their letters *"la vostre T."* and *"la vostre C."* Anachronisms of this kind (of the danger of which, by the way, to judge from a passage in the *Prologue* to the *Legend of Good Women,* Chaucer would not appear to have been wholly unconscious) are intrinsically of very slight importance. But the morality of Chaucer's narratives is at times the artificial and overstrained morality of the Middle Ages, which, as it were, clutches hold of a single idea to the exclusion of all others—a morality which, when carried to its extreme consequences, makes monomaniacs as well as martyrs, in both of which species, occasionally, perhaps, combined in the same persons, the Middle Ages abound. The fidelity of Griseldis under the trials imposed upon her by her, in point of fact, brutal husband is the fidelity of a martyr to unreason. The story was afterwards put on the stage in the Elizabethan age; and though even in the play of *Patient Grissil* (by Chettle and others) it is not easy to reconcile the husband's proceedings with the promptings of common sense, yet the playwrights, with the instinct of their craft, contrived to introduce some element of humanity into his character, and of probability into his conduct. Again, the supra-chivalrous respect paid by Arviragus, the Breton knight of the *Franklin's Tale,* to the sanctity of his wife's word, seriously to the peril of his own and his wife's honour, is an effort to which probably even the Knight of La Mancha himself would have proved unequal. It is not to be expected that Chaucer should have failed to share some of the prejudices of his times as well as to fall in with their ways of thought and sentiment; and though it is the *Prioress* who tells a story against the Jews which passes the legend of Hugh of Lincoln, yet it would be very hazardous to seek any irony in this legend of bigotry. In general, much of that *naivete* which to modern readers seems Chaucer's most obvious literary quality must be ascribed to the times in which he lived and wrote. This quality is, in truth, by no means that which most deeply impresses itself upon the observation of any one able to compare Chaucer's writings with those of his more immediate predecessors and successors. But the sense in which the term *naif* should be understood in literary criticism is so imperfectly agreed upon among us, that we have not yet even found an English equivalent for the word.

To Chaucer's times, then, belongs much of what may at first sight seem to include itself among the characteristics of his genius; while, on the other hand, there are to be distinguished from these the influences due to his training and studies in two literatures—the French and the Italian. In the former of these he must have felt at home, if not by birth and descent, at all events by social connexion, habits of life, and ways of thought; while in the latter he, whose own country's was still a half-fledged literary life, found ready to his hand masterpieces of artistic maturity lofty in conception, broad in bearing, finished in form. There still remain, for summary review, the elements proper to his own poetic individuality—those which mark him out not only as the first great poet of his own nation, but as a great poet for all times.

The poet must please; if he wishes to be successful and popular, he must suit himself to the tastes of his public; and even if he be indifferent to immediate fame, he must, as belonging to one of the most impressionable, the most receptive species of humankind, live, in a sense, *with* and *for* his generation. To meet this demand upon his genius, Chaucer was born with many gifts which he carefully and assiduously exercised in a long series of poetical experiments, and which he was able felicitously to combine for the achievement of results unprecedented in our literature. In readiness of descriptive power, in brightness and variety of imagery, and in flow of diction, Chaucer remained unequalled by any English poet, till he was surpassed—it seems not too much to say, in all three respects—by Spenser. His verse, where it suits his purpose, glitters, to use Dunbar's expression, as with fresh enamel, and its hues are variegated like those of a Flemish tapestry. Even where his descriptive enumerations seem at first sight monotonous or perfunctory, they are, in truth, graphic and true in their details, as in the list of birds in the *Assembly of Fowls,* quoted in part on an earlier page of this essay, and in the shorter list of trees in the same poem, which is, however, in its general features, imitated from Boccaccio. Neither King James I. of Scotland, nor Spenser, who after Chaucer essayed similar *tours de force,* were happier than he had been before them. Or we may refer to the description of the preparations for the tournament and of the tournament itself in the *Knight's Tale,* or to the thoroughly Dutch picture of a disturbance in a farm-yard in the Nun's *Priest's.* The vividness with which Chaucer describes scenes and events as if he had them before his own eyes, was no doubt, in the first instance, a result of his own imaginative temperament; but one would probably not go wrong in attributing the fulness of the use which he made of this gift to the influence of his Italian studies—more especially to those which led him to Dante, whose multitudinous characters and scenes impress themselves with so singular and immediate a definiteness upon the imagination. At the same time, Chaucer's resources seem inexhaustible for filling up or rounding off his narratives with the aid of chivalrous love or religious legend, by the introduction of samples of scholastic discourse or devices of personal or general allegory. He commands, where necessary, a rhetorician's readiness of illustration, and a masque-writer's inventiveness, as to machinery; he can even (in the *House of Fame*) conjure up an elaborate but self-consistent phantasmagory of his own, and continue it with a fulness proving that his fancy would not be at a loss for supplying even more materials than he cares to employ.

But Chaucer's poetry derived its power to please from yet another quality; and in this he was the first of our English poets to emulate the poets of the two literatures to which, in the matter of his productions and in the ornaments of his diction, he owed so much. There is in his verse a music which hardly ever wholly loses itself, and which at times is as sweet as that in any English poet after him.

This assertion is not one which is likely to be gainsaid at the present day, when there is not a single lover of Chaucer who would sit down contented with Dryden's condescending mixture of censure and praise. "The verse of Chaucer," he wrote, "I confess, is not harmonious to us. They who lived with him, and some time after him, thought it musical; and it continues so, even in our judgment, if compared with the numbers of Lydgate and Gower, his contemporaries: there is a rude sweetness of a Scotch tune in it, which is natural and pleasing, though not perfect." At the same time, it is no doubt necessary, in order to verify the correctness of a less balanced judgment, to take the trouble, which, if it could but be believed, is by no means great, to master the rules and usages of Chaucerian versification. These rules and usages the present is not a fit occasion for seeking to explain.[2]

With regard to the most important of them, is it not too much to say that instinct and experience will very speedily combine to indicate to an intelligent reader where the poet has resorted to it. *Without* intelligence on the part of the reader, the beautiful harmonies of Mr. Tennyson's later verse remain obscure; so that, taken in this way, the most musical of English verse may seem as difficult to read as the most rugged; but in the former case the lesson is learnt not to be lost again; in the latter, the tumbling is ever beginning anew, as with the rock of Sisyphus. There is nothing that can fairly be called rugged in the verse of Chaucer.

And, fortunately, there are not many pages in this poet's works devoid of lines or passages the music of which cannot escape any ear, however unaccustomed it may be to his diction and versification. What is the nature of the art at whose bidding ten monosyllables arrange themselves into a line of the exquisite cadence of the following:—

And she was fair, as is the rose in May?

Nor would it be easy to find lines surpassing in their melancholy charm Chaucer's version of the lament of Medea when deserted by Jason—a passage which makes the reader neglectful of the English poet's modest hint that the letter of the Colchian princess may be found at full length in Ovid. The lines shall be quoted *verbatim*, though not *literatim*; and perhaps no better example, and none more readily appreciable by a modern ear, could be given than the fourth of them of the harmonious effect of Chaucer's usage of *slurring*, referred to above:—

> Why liked thee my yellow hair to see
> More than the boundes of mine honesty?
> Why liked me thy youth and thy fairness
> And of thy tongue the infinite graciousness?
> O, had'st thou in thy conquest dead y-bee(n),
> Full myckle untruth had there died with thee.

Qualities and powers such as the above have belonged to poets of very various times and countries before and after Chaucer. But in addition to these he most assuredly possessed others, which are not usual among the poets of our nation, and which, whencesoever they had come to him personally, had not, before they made their appearance in him, seemed indigenous to the English soil. It would, indeed, be easy to misrepresent the history of English poetry, during the period which Chaucer's advent may be said to have closed, by ascribing to it a uniformly solemn and serious, or even dark and gloomy, character. Such a description would not apply to the poetry of the period before the Norman Conquest, though, in truth, little room could be left for the play of fancy or wit in the hammered-out war-song, or in the long-drawn Scriptural paraphrase. Nor was it likely that a contagious gaiety should find an opportunity of manifesting itself in the course of the versification of grave historical chronicles, or in the tranquil objective reproduction of the endless traditions of British legend. Of the popular songs belonging to the period after the Norman Conquest, the remains which furnish us with direct or indirect evidence concerning them hardly enable us to form an opinion. But we know that (the cavilling spirit of Chaucer's burlesque *Rhyme of Sir Thopas* notwithstanding) the efforts of English metrical romance in the thirteenth and fourteenth centuries were neither few nor feeble, although these romances were chiefly translations, sometimes abridgments to boot— even the Arthurian cycle having been only imported across the Channel, though it may have thus come back to its original home. There is some animation in at least one famous chronicle in verse, dating from about the close of the thirteenth century; there is real spirit in the war-songs of Minot in the middle of the fourteenth; and from about its beginnings dates a satire full of broad fun concerning the jolly life led by the monks. But none of these works or of those contemporary with them show that innate lightness and buoyancy of tone which seems to add wings to the art of poetry. Nowhere had the English mind found so real an opportunity of poetic utterance in the days of Chaucer's own youth as in Langland's unique work, national in its allegorical form and in its alliterative metre; and nowhere had this utterance been more stern and severe.

No sooner, however, has Chaucer made his appearance as a poet, than he seems to show what mistress's badge he wears, which party of the two that have at most times divided among them a national literature and its representatives he intends to follow. The burden of his song is "Si douce est la marguerite:" he has learnt the ways of French gallantry as if to the manner born, and thus becomes, as it were without hesitation or effort, the first English love-poet. Nor—though in the course of his career his range of themes, his command of materials, and his choice of forms are widely enlarged—is the gay banner under which he has ranged himself ever deserted by him. With the exception of the *House of Fame,* there is not one of his longer poems of which the passion of love, under one or another of its aspects, does not either constitute the main subject or (as in the *Canterbury Tales)* furnish the greater part of the contents. It is as a love-poet that Gower thinks of Chaucer when paying a tribute to him in his own verse; it is to the attacks made upon him in his character as a love-poet, and to his consciousness of what he has achieved as such, that he gives expression in the *Prologue* to the *Legend of Good Women,* where his fair advocate tells the God of Love:—

> The man hath servèd you of his cunníng,
> And furthered well your law in his writing,
> All be it that he cannot well indite,
> Yet hath he made unlearnèd folk delight
> To servë you in praising of your name.

And so he resumes his favourite theme once more, to tell, as the *Man of Law* says, "of lovers up and down, more than Ovid makes mention of in his old *Epistles."* This fact alone—that our first great English poet was also our first English love-poet, properly so called—would have sufficed to transform our poetic literature through his agency.

What, however, calls for special notice, in connexion with Chaucer's special poetic quality of gaiety and brightness, is the preference which he exhibits for treating the joyous aspects of this many-sided passion. Apart from the *Legend of Good Women,* which is specially designed to give brilliant examples of the faithfulness of women under circumstances of trial, pain, and grief, and from two or three of the *Canterbury Tales,* he dwells, with consistent preference, on the bright side of love, though remaining a stranger to its divine radiance, which shines forth so fully upon us out of the pages of Spenser. Thus, in the *Assembly of Fowls* all is gaiety and mirth, as indeed beseems the genial neighbourhood of Cupid's temple. Again, in *Troilus and Cressid,* the earlier and cheerful part of the love-story is that which he develops with unmistakeable sympathy and enjoyment; and in his hands this part of the poem becomes one of the most charming poetic narratives of the birth and growth of young love which our literature possesses—a soft and sweet counterpart to the consuming heat of Marlowe's unrivalled *Hero and Leander.* With Troilus it was love at first sight—with Cressid a passion of very gradual growth. But so full of nature is the narrative of this growth, that one is irresistibly reminded at more than one point of the inimitable creations of the great modern master in the description of women's love. Is there not a touch of Gretchen in Cressid, retiring into her chamber to ponder over the first revelation to her of the love of Troilus?—

> Cressid arose, no longer there she stayed,
> But straight into her closet went anon,
> And set her down, as still as any stone,
> And every word gan up and down to wind,
> That he had said, as it came to her mind.

And is there not a touch of Clärchen in her—though with a difference—when from her casement she blushingly beholds her lover riding past in triumph:

> So like a man of armës and a knight
> He was to see, filled full of high prowéss,
> For both he had a body, and a might
> To do that thing, as well as hardiness;
> And eke to see him in his gear him dress,
> So fresh, so young, so wieldly seemèd he,
> It truly was a heaven him for to see.
> His helm was hewn about in twenty places,
> That by a tissue hung his back behind;
> His shield was dashed with strokes of swords and
>   maces,
> In which men mightë many an arrow find

That piercèd had the horn and nerve and rind;
And aye the people cried: 'Here comes our joy,
And, next his brother, holder up of Troy'

Even in the very *Book of the Duchess,* the widowed lover describes the maiden charms of his lost wife with so lively a freshness as almost to make one forget that it is a *lost* wife whose praises are being recorded.

The vivacity and joyousness of Chaucer's poetic temperament, however, show themselves in various other ways besides his favourite manner of treating a favourite theme. They enhance the spirit of his passages of dialogue, and add force and freshness to his passages of description. They make him amusingly impatient of epical lengths, abrupt in his transitions, and anxious, with an anxiety usually manifested by readers rather than by writers, to come to the point, "to the great effect," as he is wont to call it. "Men," he says, "may overlade a ship or barge, and therefore I will skip at once to the effect, and let all the rest slip." And he unconsciously suggests a striking difference between himself and the great Elizabethan epic poet who owes so much to him, when he declines to make as long a tale of the chaff or of the straw as of the corn, and to describe all the details of a marriage-feast *seriatim:*

The fruit of every tale is for to say:
They eat and drink, and dance and sing and play.

This may be the fruit; but epic poets, from Homer downwards, have been generally in the habit of not neglecting the foliage. Spenser, in particular, has that impartial copiousness which we think it our duty to admire in the Ionic epos, but which, if the truth were told, has prevented generations of Englishmen from acquiring an intimate personal acquaintance with the *Fairy Queen.* With Chaucer the danger certainly rather lay in an opposite direction. Most assuredly he can tell a story with admirable point and precision, when he wishes to do so. Perhaps no better example of his skill in this respect could be cited than the *Manciple's Tale,* with its rapid narrative, its major and minor catastrophe, and its concise moral, ending thus:—

My son, beware, and be no author new
Of tidings, whether they be false or true;
Whereso thou comest, among high or low,
Keep well thy tongue, and think upon the crow.

At the same time, his frequently recurring announcements of his desire to be brief have the effect of making his narrative appear to halt, and thus, unfortunately, defeat their own purpose. An example of this may be found in the *Knight's Tale,* a narrative poem of which, in contrast with its beauties, a want of evenness is one of the chief defects. It is not that the desire to suppress redundancies is a tendency deserving anything but commendation in any writer, whether great or small; but rather, that the art of concealing art had not yet dawned upon Chaucer. And yet few writers of any time have taken a more evident pleasure in the process of literary production, and have more visibly overflowed with sympathy for, or antipathy against, the characters of their own creation. Great novelists of our own age have often told their readers, in prefaces to their fictions or in quasi-confidential comments upon them, of the intimacy in which they have lived with the offspring of their own brain, to them far from shadowy beings. But only the *naivete* of Chaucer's literary age, together with the vivacity of his manner of thought and writing, could place him in so close a personal relation towards the personages and the incidents of his poems. He is overcome by "pity and ruth" as he reads of suffering, and his eyes "wax foul and sore" as he prepares to tell of its infliction. He compassionates "love's servants" as if he were their own "brother dear;" and into his adaptation of the eventful story of Constance (the *Man of Law's Tale)* he introduces apostrophe upon apostrophe, to the defenceless condition of his heroine—to her relentless enemy the Sultana, and to Satan, who ever makes his instrument of women "when he will beguile"—to the drunken messenger who allowed the letter carried by him to be stolen from him—and to the treacherous Queen-mother who caused them to be stolen. Indeed, in addressing the last-named personage, the poet seems to lose all control over himself.

> O Domegild, I have no English digne
> Unto thy malice and thy tyranny:
> And therefore to the fiend I thee resign,
> Let him at length tell of thy treachery.
> Fye, mannish, fye!—Oh nay, by God, I lie;
> Fye fiendish spirit, for I dare well tell,
> Though thou here walk, thy spirit is in hell.

At the opening of the *Legend of Ariadne* he bids Minos redden with shame; and towards its close, when narrating how Theseus sailed away, leaving his true-love behind, he expresses a hope that the wind may drive the traitor "a twenty devil way." Nor does this vivacity find a less amusing expression in so trifling a touch as that in the *Clerk's Tale,* where the domestic sent to deprive Griseldis of her boy becomes, *eo ipso* as it were, "this ugly sergeant."

Closely allied to Chaucer's liveliness and gaiety of disposition, and in part springing from them, are his keen sense of the ridiculous and the power of satire which he has at his command. His humour has many varieties, ranging from the refined and half-melancholy irony of the *House of Fame* to the ready wit of the sagacious uncle of Cressid, the burlesque fun of the inimitable *Nun's Priest's Tale,* and the very gross salt of the *Reeve,* the *Miller,* and one or two others. The springs of humour often capriciously refuse to allow themselves to be discovered; nor is the satire of which the direct intention is transparent invariably the most effective species of satire. Concerning, however, Chaucer's use of the power which he in so large a measure possessed, viz., that of covering with ridicule the palpable vices or weaknesses of the classes or kinds of men represented by some of his character-types, one assertion may be made with tolerable safety. Whatever may have been the first stimulus and the ultimate scope of the wit and humour which he here expended, they are *not* to be explained as moral indignation in disguise. And in truth Chaucer's merriment flows spontaneously from a source very near the surface; he is so extremely diverting, because he is so extremely diverted himself.

Herein, too, lies the harmlessness of Chaucer's fun. Its harmlessness, to wit, for those who are able to read him in something like the spirit in which he wrote—never a very easy achievement with regard to any author, and one which the beginner and the young had better be advised to abstain from attempting with Chaucer in the overflow of his more or less unrestrained moods. At all events, the excuse of gaiety of heart—the plea of that *vieil esprit Gaulois* which is so often, and very rarely without need, invoked in an exculpatory capacity by modern French criticism—is the best defence ever made for Chaucer's laughable irregularities, either by his apologists or by himself. "Men should not," he says, and says very truly, "make earnest of game." But when he audaciously defends himself against the charge of impropriety by declaring that he must tell stories *in character,* and coolly requests any person who may find anything in one of his tales objectionable to turn to another:—

> For he shall find enough, both great and small,
> Of storial thing that toucheth gentleness,
> Likewise morality and holiness;
> Blame ye not me, if ye should choose amiss—

we are constrained to shake our heads at the transparent sophistry of the plea, which requires no exposure. For Chaucer knew very well how to give life and colour to his page without recklessly disregarding bounds the neglect of which was even in his day offensive to many besides the *"precious* folk" of whom he half derisively pretends to stand in awe. In one instance he defeated his own purpose; for the so-called *Cook's Tale of Gamelyn* was substituted by some earlier editor for the original *Cook's Tale,* which has thus in its completed form become a rarity removed beyond the reach of even the most ardent of curiosity hunters. Fortunately, however, Chaucer spoke the truth when he said that from this point of view he had written very differently at different times; no whiter pages remain than many of his.

But the realism of Chaucer is something more than exuberant love of fun and light-hearted gaiety. He is the first great painter of character, because he is the first great observer of it among modern European writers. His power of comic observation need not be dwelt upon again, after the illustrations of it which have been incidentally furnished in these pages. More especially with regard to the manners and ways of women, which often, while seeming so natural to women themselves, appear so odd to male observers, Chaucer's eye was ever on the alert. But his works likewise contain passages displaying a penetrating insight into the minds of men, as well as a keen eye for their manners, together with a power of generalising, which, when kept within due bounds, lies at the root of the wise knowledge of humankind so admirable to us in our great essayists, from Bacon to Addison and his modern successors. How truly, for instance, in *Troilus and Cressid,* Chaucer observes on the enthusiastic belief of converts, the "strongest-faithed" of men, as he understands! And how fine is the saying as to the suspiciousness characteristic of lewd (i. e., ignorant) people, that to things which are made more subtly

> Than they can in their lewdness comprehend,

they gladly give the worst interpretation which suggests itself! How appositely the *Canon's Yeoman* describes the arrogance of those who are too clever by half; "when a man has an over-great wit," he says, "it very often chances to him to misuse it!" And with how ripe a wisdom, combined with ethics of true gentleness, the honest *Franklin,* at the opening of his *Tale,* discourses on the uses and the beauty of long-suffering:—

> For one thing, sirës, safely dare I say,
> That friends the one the other must obey,
> If they will longë holdë company.
> Love will not be constrainèd by mastery.
> When mastery comes, the god of love anon
> Beateth his wings—and, farewell! he is gone.
> Love is a thing as any spirit free.
> Women desire, by nature, liberty,
> And not to be constrainèd as a thrall;

And so do men, if I the truth say shall.
Look, who that is most patiént in love,
He is at his advantage all above.
A virtue high is patiénce, certain,
Because it vanquisheth, as clerks explain,
Things to which rigour never could attain.
For every word men should not chide and plain;
Learn ye to suffer, or else, so may I go,
Ye shall it learn, whether ye will or no.
For in this world certain no wight there is
Who neither doth nor saith some time amiss.
Sickness or ire, or constellatión,
Wine, woe, or changing of complexión,
Causeth full oft to do amiss or speak.
For every wrong men may not vengeance wreak:
After a time there must be temperance
With every wight that knows self-governance.

It was by virtue of his power of observing and drawing character, above all, that Chaucer became the true predecessor of two several growths in our literature, in both of which characterisation forms a most important element—it might perhaps be truly said, the element which surpasses all others in importance. From this point of view the dramatic poets of the Elizabethan age remain unequalled by any other school or group of dramatists, and the English novelists of the eighteenth and nineteenth centuries by the representatives of any other development of prose-fiction. In the art of construction, in the invention and the arrangement of incident, these dramatists and novelists may have been left behind by others; in the creation of character they are, on the whole, without rivals in their respective branches of literature. To the earlier at least of these growths Chaucer may be said to have pointed the way. His personages—more especially, of course, as has been seen, those who are assembled together in the *Prologue* to the *Canterbury Tales*—are not mere phantasms of the brain, or even mere actual possibilities, but real human beings, and types true to the likeness of whole classes of men and women, or to the mould in which all human nature is cast. This is, upon the whole, the most wonderful, as it is perhaps the most generally recognised, of Chaucer's gifts. It would not of itself have sufficed to make him a great dramatist, had the drama stood ready for him as a literary form into which to pour the inspirations of his genius, as it afterwards stood ready for our great Elizabethans. But to it were added in him that perception of a strong dramatic situation, and that power of finding the right words for it, which have determined the success of many plays, and the absence of which materially detracts from the completeness of the effect of others, high as their merits may be in other respects. How thrilling, for instance, is that rapid passage across the stage, as one might almost call it, of the unhappy Dorigen in the *Franklin's Tale!* The antecedents of the situation, to be sure, are, as has been elsewhere suggested, absurd enough; but who can fail to feel that spasm of anxious sympathy with which a powerful dramatic situation in itself affects us, when the wife, whom for truth's sake her husband has bidden be untrue to him, goes forth on her unholy errand of duty? "Whither so fast?" asks the lover:

> And she made answer, half as she were mad:
> 'Unto the garden, as my husband bade,
> My promise for to keep, alas! alas!'

Nor, as the abbreviated prose version of the *Pardoner's Tale* given above will suffice to show, was Chaucer deficient in the art of dramatically arranging a story; while he is not excelled by any of our non-dramatic poets in the spirit and movement of his dialogue. The *Book of the Duchess* and the *House of Fame,* but more especially *Troilus and Cressid* and the connecting passages between some of the *Canterbury Tales,* may be referred to in various illustration of this.

The vividness of his imagination, which conjures up, so to speak, the very personality of his characters before him, and the contagious force of his pathos, which is as true and as spontaneous as his humour, complete in him the born dramatist. We can see Constance as with our own eyes, in the agony of her peril:—

> Have ye not seen some time a pallid face
> Among a press, of him that hath been led
> Towards his death, where him awaits no grace,
> And such a colour in his face hath had,
> Men mightë know his face was so bested
> 'Mong all the other faces in that rout?
> So stands Constánce, and looketh her about.

And perhaps there is no better way of studying the general character of Chaucer's pathos than a comparison of the *Monk's Tale* from which this passage is taken, and the *Clerk's Tale,* with their originals. In the former, for instance, the prayer of Constance, when condemned through Domegild's guilt to be cast adrift once more on the waters, her piteous words and tenderness to her little child as it lies weeping in her arm, and her touching leave-taking from the land of the husband who has condemned her—all these are Chaucer's own. So also are parts of one of the most affecting passages in the *Clerk's Tale*— Griseldis' farewell to her daughter. But it is as unnecessary to lay a finger upon lines and passages illustrating Chaucer's pathos as upon others illustrating his humour.

Thus, then, Chaucer was a born dramatist; but fate willed it, that the branch of our literature which might probably have of all been the best suited to his genius was not to spring into life till he and several generations after him had passed away. To be sure, during the fourteenth century the so-called miracle-plays flourished abundantly in England, and were, as there is every reason to believe, already largely performed by the trading-companies of London and the towns. The allusions in Chaucer to these beginnings of our English drama are, however, remarkably scanty. The *Wife of Bath* mentions plays of miracles among the other occasions of religious sensation haunted by her, clad in her gay scarlet gown—including vigils, processions, preachings, pilgrimages, and marriages. And the jolly parish-clerk of the *Millers Tale*, we are informed, at times, in order to show his lightness and his skill, played "Herod on a scaffold high"—thus, by-the-bye, emulating the parish clerks of London, who are known to have been among the performers of miracles in the Middle Ages. The allusion to Pilate's voice in the *Miller's Prologue*, and that in the *Tale* to

> The sorrow of Noah with his fellowship
> That he had ere he got his wife to ship,

seem likewise dramatic reminiscences; and the occurrence of these three allusions in a single *Tale* and its *Prologue* would incline one to think that Chaucer had recently amused himself at one of these performances. But plays are not mentioned among the entertainments enumerated at the opening of the *Pardoner's Tale;* and it would in any case have been unlikely that Chaucer should have paid much attention to diversions which were long chiefly "visited" by the classes with which he could have no personal connexion, and even at a much later date were dissociated in men's minds from poetry and literature. Had he ever written anything remotely partaking of the nature of a dramatic piece, it could at the most have been the words of the songs in some congratulatory royal pageant such as Lydgate probably wrote on the return of Henry V. after Agincourt; though there is not the least reason for supposing Chaucer to have taken so much interest in the "ridings" through the City which occupied many a morning of the idle apprentice of the *Cook's Tale,* Perkyn Revellour. It is, perhaps, more surprising to find Chaucer, who was a reader of several Latin poets, and who had heard of more, both Latin and Greek, show no knowledge whatever of the ancient classical drama, with which he may accordingly be fairly concluded to have been wholly unacquainted.

To one further aspect of Chaucer's realism as a poet reference has already been made; but a final mention of it may most appropriately conclude this sketch of his poetical characteristics. His descriptions of nature are as true as his sketches of human character; and incidental touches in him reveal his love of the one as unmistakeably as his unflagging interest in the study of the other. Even these May-morning *exordia*, in which he was but following a fashion—faithfully observed both by the French *trouveres* and by the English romances translated from their productions, and not forgotten by the author of the earlier part of the *Roman de la Rose*—always come from his hands with the freshness of natural truth. They cannot be called original in conception, and it would be difficult to point out in them anything strikingly original in execution; yet they cannot be included among those matter-of-course notices of morning and evening, sunrise and sunset, to which so many poets have accustomed us since (be it said with reverence) Homer himself. In Chaucer these passages make his page "as fresh as is the month of May." When he went forth on these April and May mornings, it was not solely with the intent of composing a roundelay or a *marguerite*; but we may be well assured he allowed the song of the little birds, the perfume of the flowers, and the fresh verdure of the English landscape, to sink into his very soul. For nowhere does he seem, and nowhere could he have been, more open to the influence which he received into himself, and which in his turn he exercised, and exercises upon others, than when he was in fresh contact with nature. In this influence lies the secret of his genius; in his poetry there is *life*.

Notes

1. The passage in Canto viii. of the Purgatorio is thus translated by Longfellow:

> Not oftentimes upriseth through the branches
> The probity of man; and this He wills
> Who gives it, so that we may ask of Him.

Its intention is only to show that the son is not necessarily what the father is before him; thus, Edward I. of England is a mightier man than was his father Henry III. Chaucer has ingeniously, though not altogether legitimately, pressed the passage into his service.

2. It may, however, be stated that they only partially connect them
   selves with Chaucer's use of forms which are now obsolete—more
   especially of inflexions of verbs and substantives (including several
   instances of the famous final *e)*, and contractions with the negative *ne*
   and other monosyllabic words ending in a vowel, of the initial syllables
   of words beginning with vowels or with the letter *h*. These and other
   variations from later usage in spelling and pronunciation—such as the
   occurrence of an *e* (sometimes sounded and sometimes not) at the end
   of words in which it is now no longer retained, and, again, the frequent
   accentuation of many words of French origin in their last syllable, as in
   French, and of certain words of English origin analogously—are to be
   looked for as a matter of course in a last writing in the period of our
   language in which Chaucer lived. He clearly foresaw the difficulties which
   would be caused to his readers by the variations of usage in spelling and
   pronunciation—variations to some extent rendered inevitable by the fact
   that he wrote in an English dialect which was only gradually coming to
   be accepted as the uniform language of English writers. Towards the close
   of his *Troilus and Cressid* he thus addresses his "little book," in fear of the
   mangling it might undergo from scriveners who might blunder in the
   copying of its words, or from reciters who might maltreat its verse in the
   distribution of the accents:—

> And, since there is so great diversity
> In English, and in writing of our tongue,
> I pray to God that none may miswrite thee
> Nor thee mismetre, for default of tongue,
> And wheresoe'er thou mayst be read or sung,
> That thou be understood, God I beseech.

But in his versification he likewise adopted certain other practices which
had no such origin or reason as those already referred to. Among them
were the addition, at the end of a line of five accents, of an unaccented
syllable; and the substitution, for the first foot of a line either of four or
of five accents, of a single syllable. These deviations from a stricter system
of versification he doubtless permitted to himself, partly for the sake of
variety, and partly for that of convenience; but neither of them is peculiar
to himself, or of supreme importance for the effect of his verse. In fact,
he seems to allow as much in a passage of his *House of Fame*—a poem
written, it should, however, be observed, in an easy-going form of verse
(the line of four accents) which in his later period Chaucer seems, with

this exception, to have invariably discarded. He here beseeches Apollo to make his rhyme

Somewhat agreéable,

Though some verse fail in a sylláble.

But another of his usages—the misunderstanding of which has more than anything else caused his art as a writer of verse to be misjudged—seems to have been due to a very different cause. To understand the real nature of the usage in question it is only necessary to seize the principle of Chaucer's rhythm. Of this principle it was well said many years ago by a most competent authority—Mr. R. Home—that it is "inseparable from a full or fair exercise of the genius of our language in versification." For though this usage in its full freedom was gradually again lost to our poetry for a time, yet it was in a large measure recovered by Shakespeare and the later dramatists of our great age, and has since been never altogether abandoned again—not even by the correct writers of the Augustan period—till by the favourites of our own times it is resorted to with a perhaps excessive liberality. It consists simply in *slurring* over certain final syllables—not eliding them or contracting them with the syllables following upon them, but passing over them lightly, so that, without being inaudible, they may at the same time not interfere with the rhythm or beat of the verse. This usage, by adding to the variety, incontestably adds to the flexibility and beauty of Chaucer's versification.

—Adolphus William Ward, "Characteristics of Chaucer
and His Poetry," Chaucer, 1879, pp. 146–88

Matthew Arnold (1880)

Matthew Arnold (1822–88) was an important Victorian author who is perhaps best known for his poem "Dover Beach." In his *Essays on Criticism*, Arnold writes of his admiration for Chaucer's stylistics and form, and students writing on those subjects would do well to cite this critic. Arnold begins by noting, as many other critics do, that Chaucer is the father of English poetry: "With him is born our real poetry." Arnold emphasizes both Chaucer's word choice and his fluid use of rhythm and meter: "[Chaucer] is our 'well of English undefiled,' because by the lovely charm of his diction, the lovely charm of his movement, he makes an epoch and founds a tradition." In particular, Arnold identifies among Chaucer's strengths his "liquid diction," the poet's ability to choose not only the precise word in a given line of poetry but also to ensure that the poetry flows with a natural fluid sense.

Despite this praise, Arnold concludes that Chaucer "is not one of the great classics." Arnold adds: "The substance of Chaucer's poetry, his view of things and his criticism of life, has largeness, freedom, shrewdness, benignity; but it has not . . . high seriousness." Citing Aristotle, Arnold defines "high seriousness" as the poet's ability to write of what he or she experiences with enough magnitude to ensure that the poem's readers will take the work as gravely as the poet does. Many students find Chaucer's sense of humor and playful satire his most endearing qualities; conversely, works such as *Troilus and Criseyde* or "The Parson's Tale" seem to imbibe the seriousness that Arnold suggests is lacking in Chaucer. Students may thus find it useful to debate Arnold on these issues and conclude for themselves whether Chaucer possesses a "high seriousness," or whether it is precisely this lack of "high seriousness" that makes Chaucer such an appealing poet.

The predominance of French poetry in Europe, during the twelfth and thirteenth centuries, is due to its poetry of the *langue d'oil*, the poetry of northern France and of the tongue which is now the French language. In the twelfth century the bloom of this romance-poetry was earlier and stronger in England, at the court of our Anglo-Norman kings, than in France itself. But it was a bloom of French poetry; and as our native poetry formed itself, it formed itself out of this. The romance-poems which took possession of the heart and imagination of Europe in the twelfth and thirteenth centuries are French; 'they are,' as Southey justly says, 'the pride of French literature, nor have we anything which can be placed in competition with them.' Themes were supplied from all quarters; but the romance-setting which was common to them all, and which gained the ear of Europe, was French. This constituted for the French poetry, literature, and language, at the height of the Middle Ages, an unchallenged predominance. The Italian Brunetto Latini, the master of Dante, wrote his *Treasure* in French because, he says, 'la parleure en est plus delitable et plus commune a toutes gens.' . . .

Yet it is now all gone, this French romance-poetry, of which the weight of substance and the power of style are not unfairly represented by this extract from Christian of Troyes. Only by means of the historic estimate can we persuade ourselves now to think that any of it is of poetical importance.

But in the fourteenth century there comes an Englishman nourished on this poetry, taught his trade by this poetry, getting words, rhyme, metre from this poetry; for even of that stanza which the Italians used, and which Chaucer derived immediately from the Italians, the basis and suggestion was probably given in France. Chaucer (I have already named him) fascinated his contemporaries, but so too did Christian of Troyes and Wolfram of Eschenbach. Chaucer's power of fascination, however, is enduring; his poetical importance does not need the assistance of the historic estimate; it is real. He is a genuine source of joy and strength, which is flowing still for us and will flow always. He will be read, as time goes on, far more generally than he is read now. His language is a cause of difficulty for us; but so also, and I think in quite as great a degree, is the language of Burns. In Chaucer's case, as in that of Burns, it is a difficulty to be unhesitatingly accepted and overcome.

If we ask ourselves wherein consists the immense superiority of Chaucer's poetry over the romance-poetry—why it is that in passing from this to Chaucer we suddenly feel ourselves to be in another world, we shall find that his superiority is both in the substance of his poetry and in the style of his poetry. His superiority in substance is given by his large, free, simple, clear yet kindly view of human life,—so unlike the total want, in the romance-poets, of all intelligent command of it. Chaucer has not their helplessness; he has gained the power to survey the world from a central, a truly human point of view: We have only to call to mind the Prologue to *The Canterbury Tales*. The right comment upon it is Dryden's: 'It is sufficient to say, according to the proverb, that *here is God's plenty*.' And again: 'He is a perpetual fountain of good sense.' It is by a large, free, sound representation of things, that poetry, this high criticism of life, has truth of substance; and Chaucer's poetry has truth of substance.

Of his style and manner, if we think first of the romance-poetry and then of Chaucer's divine liquidness of diction, his divine fluidity of movement, it is difficult to speak temperately. They are irresistible, and justify all the rapture with which his successors speak of his 'gold dew-drops of speech.' Johnson misses the point entirely when he finds fault with Dryden for ascribing to Chaucer the first refinement of our numbers, and says that Gower also can show smooth numbers and easy rhymes. The refinement of our numbers means something far more than this. A nation may have versifiers with smooth numbers and easy rhymes, and yet may have no real poetry at all. Chaucer is the father of our splendid English poetry; he is our 'well of English undefiled,' because by the lovely charm of his diction, the lovely charm of his movement, he makes an epoch and founds a tradition. In Spenser, Shakespeare, Milton, Keats, we can follow the tradition of the liquid diction, the fluid movement, of Chaucer; at one time it is his liquid diction of which in these poets we feel the virtue, and at another time it is his fluid movement. And the virtue is irresistible.

Bounded as is my space, I must yet find room for an example of Chaucer's virtue, as I have given examples to show the virtue of the great classics. I feel disposed to say that a single line is enough to show the charm of Chaucer's verse; that merely one line like this—

O martyr souded in virginitee!

has a virtue of manner and movement such as we shall not find in all the verse of romance-poetry;—but this is saying nothing. The virtue is such as we shall not find, perhaps, in all English poetry, outside the poets whom I have named as the special inheritors of Chaucer's tradition. A single line, however, is too little if we have not the strain of Chaucer's verse well in our memory; let us take a stanza. It is from 'The Prioress's Tale', the story of the Christian child murdered in a Jewry —

> My throte is cut unto my nekke-bone
> Saidè this child, and as by way of kinde
> I should have deyd, yea, longè time agone;
> But Jesu Christ, as yc in bookès finde,
> Will that his glory last and be in minde,
> And for the worship of his mother dere
> Yet may I sing O *Alma* loud and clere.

Wordsworth has modernised this Tale, and to feel how delicate and evanescent is the charm of verse, we have only to read Wordsworth's first three lines of this stanza after Chaucer's—

> My throat is cut unto the bone, I trow.
> Said this young child, and by the law of kind
> I should have died, yea, many hours ago.

The charm is departed. It is often said that the power of liquidness and fluidity in Chaucer's verse was dependent upon a free, a licentious dealing with language, such as is now impossible; upon a liberty, such as Burns too enjoyed, of making words like *neck, bird,* into a dissyllable by adding to them, and words like *cause, rhyme,* into a dissyllable by sounding the *e* mute. It is true that Chaucer's fluidity is conjoined with this liberty, and is admirably served by it; but we ought not to say that it was dependent upon it. It was dependent upon his talent. Other poets with a like liberty do not attain to the fluidity of Chaucer; Burns himself does not attain to it. Poets, again, who have a talent akin to Chaucer's, such as Shakespeare or Keats, have known how to attain to his fluidity without the like liberty.

And yet Chaucer is not one of the great classics. His poetry transcends and effaces, easily and without effort, all the romance-poetry of Catholic Christendom; it transcends and effaces all the English poetry contemporary with it, it transcends and effaces all the English poetry subsequent to it down to the age of Elizabeth. Of such avail is poetic truth of substance, in its natural and necessary union with poetic truth of style. And yet, I say, Chaucer is not one of the great classics. He has not their accent. What is wanting to him is suggested by the mere mention of the name of the first great classic of Christendom, the immortal poet who died eighty years before Chaucer,— Dante. The accent of such verse as

> In la sua volontade è nostra pace

is altogether beyond Chaucer's reach; we praise him, but we feel that this accent is out of the question for him. It may be said that it was necessarily out of the reach of any poet in the England of that stage of growth. Possibly; but we are to adopt a real, not a historic, estimate of poetry. However we may account for its absence, something is wanting, then, to the poetry of Chaucer, which poetry must have before it can be placed in the glorious class of the best. And there is no doubt what that something is. It is the *spoudaiotē,* the high and excellent seriousness, which Aristotle assigns as one of the grand virtues of poetry. The substance of Chaucer's poetry, his view of things and his criticism of life, has largeness, freedom, shrewdness, benignity; but it has not this high seriousness. Homer's criticism of life has it, Dante's has it, Shakespeare's has it. It is this chiefly which gives to our spirits what they can rest upon; and with the increasing demands of our modern ages upon poetry, this virtue of giving us what we can rest upon will be more and more highly esteemed. A voice from the slums of Paris, fifty or sixty years after Chaucer, the voice of poor Villon out of his life of riot and crime, has at its happy moments (as, for instance, in the last stanza of 'La Belle Heaulmiere') more of this important poetic virtue of seriousness than all the productions of Chaucer. But its apparition in Villon, and in men like Villon, is fitful; the greatness of the great poets, the power of their criticism of life, is that their virtue is sustained.

To our praise, therefore, of Chaucer as a poet there must be this limitation; he lacks the high seriousness of the great classics, and therewith an important part of their virtue. Still, the main fact for us to bear in mind about Chaucer is his sterling value according to that real estimate which we firmly adopt for all poets. He has poetic truth of substance, though he has not high poetic seriousness, and corresponding to his truth of substance he has an exquisite virtue of style and manner. With him is born our real poetry.

—Matthew Arnold, *Essays in Criticism,*
1880, Second Series, pp. xxx–xxxvi

GERARD MANLEY HOPKINS
"LETTER TO ROBERT BRIDGES" (1880)

I have not studied Wyatt, but Surrey I used to read: he, I think, is a greater man. He was an accomplished rhythmist, not that the experiments in couplets of long twelves and thirteens are pleasing, though this is better than couplets both twelves or both thirteens. He has a very fine style free from Euphuism. However, to speak of the sample you send, I must say that I think you have missed the clue. You take the rhythm for free triple time, iambs and anapaests say, and four feet to a line (except the refrain). But to get this you have to skip, in two lines out of these few, a whole foot as marked and stressy as any other foot. This is a licence unpardonable by the reader and incredible in the writer.

Before offering my own thoughts I must premise something. So far as I know triple time is in English verse a shy and late thing. I have not studied *Piers Ploughman* and so cannot pronounce how far triple time is boldly employed in it; at least it must have been suggested. But on the Romance side of our versification triple time appeared, I think, late. It may have been suggested by *Piers Ploughman's* rhythm, as I have said, but partly I conjecture it arose from a simple misunderstanding or misreading of Chaucer and the verse of that date and thereabouts. Chaucer and his contemporaries wrote for a pronunciation fast changing (everybody knows that final *e* for instance has often to be sounded in Chaucer, but everybody does not know that mostly it is *not* to be sounded and that the line which scans by its aid is really to be scanned another way). Their versification was popular and hit the mark in its time, but soon, as far as I can see, became obsolete, and they being much read and not rightly scanned thus came to suggest rhythms which they never thought of. The same sort of thing has, I think, happened often in the history of verse. And so far, Wyatt's piece might be scanned as you scan it—but for the two lines with a foot too much.

Now in particular I suppose that the verse called doggrel (in which the play of *Royster Doyster* is written and parts of *Love's Labour*, the *Shrew*, etc) arose in this way: I do not know how else such a shapeless thing can have arisen. If it were a spontaneous popular growth it wd. [be] simpler and stronger. It must be the corruption or degeneration of something literary misunderstood or disfigured. Its rule is: couplets, with a pause dividing each line and on either side of this either two or three (perhaps sometimes even more) stresses, so that the line may range from four to six feet, and the rhythm variable too, iambic or anapaestic.

This wretched doggrel I think Surrey was systematising and raising in that couplet of his of which I spoke above and, to come to the point, I conjecture that Wyatt is dealing with the same thing here. The main point is the pause or caesura; on that the line turns. The notion of pause or caesura had come to English versification from two different quarters; from *Piers Ploughman* and the older native poetry on the one hand, where it is marked by a sort of Greek colon or by a stroke, and from France on the other, where it is essential both to the Alexandrine and to the old ten-syllable or five-foot line of the Chansons and is marked after the fourth syllable, I find.

—Gerard Manley Hopkins, "Letter to Robert Bridges,"
1880, The Letters of Gerard Manley Hopkins
to Robert Bridges, 1935, ed. Abbott, pp. 106–07

ALGERNON CHARLES SWINBURNE
"SHORT NOTES ON ENGLISH POETS" (1880)

Algernon Charles Swinburne (1837–1909) was a noted Victorian poet and prose author. In this excerpt, Swinburne offers criticisms of Chaucer, suggesting that, ultimately, much of Chaucer's work is "borrowed" from the continental writers of the Middle Ages. The arguments Swinburne raises regarding poetic form and social class may be of particular interest to students.

Swinburne begins this piece by taking issue with the work of William Rossetti, who listed Chaucer with William Shakespeare, John Milton, and Percy Shelley as the originators and best practitioners of varying poetic forms in English. Swinburne acknowledges that Chaucer may have originated the narrative form Rossetti credits to him, but believes that form to be "avowedly inferior" to the other poetic forms listed, and thus suggests that Chaucer should not be included with such illustrious company.

Swinburne goes on to write that much of Chaucer's work originated in other writers. Swinburne is referring to the very common practice of medieval and Renaissance writers basing their own works on stories and legends that had been previously recorded; this was common for Shakespeare as well as for numerous other authors. Swinburne believes this to be a particular fault in Chaucer, that in "all his poems of serious or tragic narrative we hear a French or Italian tongue speaking with a Teutonic accent through English lips," and that "Chaucer was in the main a French or Italian poet." Perhaps most interestingly, Swinburne writes that Chaucer as a poet represented the middle class of the Middle Ages, and that "the English middle class, being incomparably the happiest and the wisest, is indisputably, considering the common circumstances of their successive times, the least likely [of any social class] to have left us the highest example of all poetry then possible to men." Students working with issues related to Chaucer and class may find Swinburne's observations on the subject of interest; they may also find it useful to compare Swinburne's words to those of William Morris (1888), who wrote that Chaucer's poetry reflected the life of the upper class court, and not the middle class.

Swinburne concedes that Chaucer was the greatest English poet of the Middle Ages, but he suggests that this is not enough to place him into the category of the greatest English poets of all time.

<hr />

Having before this had occasion to remark in terms of somewhat strong deprecation on the principle adopted by Mr. William Rossetti in his revision and rearrangement of the text of our greatest lyric poet, I am the more desirous to bear witness to the elevation and the excellence of his critical workmanship in his *Lives of Famous Poets*. On some points I differ gravely from his estimate; once or twice I differ from it on all points; but on the whole I find it not acceptable merely but admirable as the very best and most sufficient ever yet given of some at least among the leading names of our poets.

Four of these are by him selected as composing the supreme quadrilateral of English song. It is through no lack of love and reverence for the name of Chaucer that I must question his right, though the first narrative poet of England, to stand on that account beside her first dramatic, her first epic, or her first lyric poet. But, being certainly unprepared to admit his equality with Shakespeare, with Milton, and with Shelley, I would reduce Mr. Rossetti's mystic four to the old sacred number of three. Pure or mere narrative is a form essentially and avowedly inferior to the lyrical or the dramatic form of poetry; and the finer line of distinction which marks it off from the epic marks it also thereby as inferior.

Of all whose names may claim anything like equality of rank on the roll of national poets—not even excepting Virgil—we may say that Chaucer borrowed most from abroad, and did most to improve whatever he borrowed. I believe it would be but accurate to admit that in all his poems of serious or tragic narrative we hear a French or Italian tongue speaking with a Teutonic accent through English lips. It has utterly unlearnt the native tone and cadence of its natural inflections; it has perfectly put on the native tone and cadence of a stranger's; yet is it always what it was at first—*lingua romana in bocca tedesca*. It speaks not only with more vigour but actually with more sweetness than the tongues of its teachers; but it speaks after its own fashion no other than the lesson they have taught. Chaucer was in the main a French or Italian poet, lined thoroughly and warmly throughout with the substance of an English humorist. And with this great gift of specially English humour he combined, naturally as it were and inevitably, the inseparable twin-born gift of peculiarly English pathos. In the figures of Arcite and Grisilde, he has actually outdone Boccaccio's very self for pathos: as far almost as Keats was afterwards to fall short of the same great model in the same great quality. And but for the instinctive distaste and congenital repugnance of his composed and comfortable genius from its accompanying horror, he might haply have come nearer than he has cared or dared to come even to the unapproachable pathos of Dante. But it was only in the world of one who stands far higher above Dante than even Dante can on the whole be justly held to stand above Chaucer, that figures as heavenly as the figures of Beatrice and Matilda could move unspotted and undegraded among figures as earthly as those of the Reve, the Miller, and the Wife of Bath: that a wider if not keener pathos than Ugolino's or Francesca's could alternate with a deeper if not richer humour than that of Absolon and Nicholas.

It is a notable dispensation of chance—one which a writer who might happen to be almost a theist might designate in the deliriously comical phrase of certain ambiguous pietists as 'almost providential'—that the three great typical poets of the three great representative nations of Europe during the dark and lurid lapse of the Middle Ages should each afford as complete and profound a type of a different and alien class as of a different and alien people. Vast as are the diversities of their national and personal characters, these are yet less radical than the divergences between class and class which mark off each from either of his fellows in nothing but in fame. Dante represents, as its best and highest, the upper class of the dark ages not less than he represents their Italy; Chaucer represents their middle class at its best and wisest, not less than he represents their England; Villon represents their lower class at its worst and its best alike, even more than he represents their France. And of these three the English middle class, being incomparably the happiest and the wisest, is indisputably, considering the common circumstances of their successive times, the least likely to have left us the highest example of all poetry then possible to men. And of their three legacies, precious and wonderful as it is, the Englishman's is accordingly the least wonderful and the least precious. The poet of the sensible and prosperous middle class in England had less to suffer and to sing than the theosophic aristocrat of Italy, or the hunted and hungry vagabond who first found articulate voice for the dumb longing and the blind love as well as for the reckless appetites and riotous agonies of the miserable and terrible multitude in whose darkness lay dormant, as in a cerecloth which was also a chrysalid, the debased and disfigured god-head which was one day to exchange the degradation of the lowest populace for the revelation of the highest people—for the world-wide apocalypse of France. The golden-tongued gallows-bird of Paris is distinguished from his two more dignified compeers by a deeper difference yet—a difference, we might say, of office and of mission no less than of genius and of gift. Dante and Chaucer are wholly and solely poets of the past or present—singers indeed for all time, but only singers of their own: Villon, in an equivocal and unconscious fashion, was a singer also of the future; he was the first modern and the last mediaeval poet. He is of us, in a sense in which it cannot be said that either Chaucer or Dante is of us, or even could have been; a man of a changing and self-transforming time, not utterly held fast, though still sorely struggling, in the jaws of hell and the ages of faith.

But in happy perfection of manhood the great and fortunate Englishman almost more exceeds his great and unfortunate fellow-singers than he is exceeded by them in depth of passion and height of rapture, in ardour and intensity of vision or of sense. With the single and sublimer exception of Sophocles, he seems to me the happiest of all great poets on record; their standing type and sovereign example of noble and manly happiness. As prosperous indeed in their several ages and lines of life were Petrarca and Ariosto, Horace and Virgil; but one only of these impresses us in every lineament of his work with the same masculine power of enjoyment. And when Ariosto threw across the windy sea of glittering legend and fluctuant romance the broad summer lightnings of his large and jocund genius, the dark ages had already returned into the outer darkness where there is weeping and gnashing of teeth—the tears of Dante Alighieri and the laughter of François Villon. But the wide warm harvest-field of Chaucer's husbandry was all glorious with gold of ripening sunshine while all the world beside lay in blackness and in bonds, throughout all those ages of death called ages of faith by men who can believe in nothing beyond a building or a book, outside the codified creeds of a Bible or the œcumenical structures of a Church.

—Algernon Charles Swinburne, "Short Notes on
English Poets: Chaucer; Spenser; The Sonnets of
Shakespeare; Milton" (1880), *Complete Works*, 1926,
Volume 4, pp. 97–101

GERARD MANLEY HOPKINS (1881)

I have found that Chaucer's scanning, once understood, is extremely smooth and regular, much more so than is thought by Mr. Skeat and other modern Chaucerists, and they think it regularity itself compared to what Dryden and older critics thought of it.

—Gerard Manley Hopkins, Letter to R.W. Dixon, 1881,
*The Correspondence of Gerard Manley Hopkins and
R.W. Dixon,* 1935, ed. Abbott, pp. 66–67

ALGERNON CHARLES SWINBURNE
"CHAUCER LACKS SUBLIMITY" (1886)

In this excerpt, Swinburne compares Chaucer unfavorably to William Wordsworth, concluding that Wordsworth's work was more capable of emotional expression than Chaucer's. While Swinburne declares that "[o]n all other points Chaucer is of course almost immeasurably the superior of Wordsworth," whenever a subject calls for an expressive depth of feeling, Wordsworth is the better of the two. This distinction, in Swinburne's estimation, makes Wordsworth the superior poet. His observation is certainly useful for any students comparing these two great writers.

On all other points Chaucer is of course almost immeasurably the superior of Wordsworth; in breadth of human interest, in simplicity of varied sympathies, in straightforward and superb command of his materials as an artist, the inspired man of the world as much excels the slow-thoughted and self-studious recluse as in warmth and wealth of humour, in consummate power of narrative, and in childlike manfulness of compassionate or joyous emotion; but their usual relations are reversed when the subject treated by Wordsworth exacts a deeper and intenser expression of feeling, or when his thought takes wing for higher flights of keener speculation, than the strong, elastic, equable movement of Chaucer's thought and verse could be expected to achieve or to attain. In a word, the elder singer has a thousand advantages over the later, but the one point on which the later has the advantage is worth all the rest put together: he is the sublimer poet of the two.

—Algernon Charles Swinburne,
"Chaucer Lacks Sublimity," *Miscellanies,* 1886, p. 152

George Dawson "Chaucer" (1887)

George Dawson (1821–76) was a prominent, nonconformist English preacher and occasional lecturer on British literature at the Birmingham and Midland Institute. He was most known for his *Biographical Lectures*, two volumes of which were published after his death. In his lecture on Chaucer, Dawson calls the medieval author "the Adam of English poetry," and declares that Chaucer was one of the four greatest English poets of all time (along with Spenser, Shakespeare, and Milton). Dawson also praises Chaucer's ability to create stirring characters (like Ascham, Hughes, Ogle, and Blake before him, among others) and reflects on his "love of nature" (like Hunt).

If Chaucer had had the good fortune to write in Latin or Greek, the English nation would have given themselves great pains to interpret his meaning; but as he had the misfortune to write in English at an early period, there are few, even educated people, who put themselves to the trouble of comprehending his great and glorious poems.

As our time is limited, it will be very wise to confine our attention to two or three distinct points. I wish first to convince you that Chaucer was not only a great poet considering his age, but one of the five great poets the world ever produced. Then I shall have to show you that Chaucer may be read fluently in his own peculiar language, without the modernising aid of Dryden, who was unequal to the task, or of Pope, who could not do it though he tried. Afterwards I shall put before you certain passages to justify any eulogiums I may pass.

Of the man, very little is known; and though whole quartos have been written about him, like many other biographies there is very little in them. Honestly speaking, the life of Chaucer might be written in a very small compass; but it is so mixed up and involved with the political history of his noble friend and patron, John of Gaunt, that if one does not know much of the latter one cannot know much of the former; and if one does, then there is hardly any necessity to speak about Chaucer in this respect.

We will, therefore, dismiss very briefly what is acknowledged in the poet's career—his education at Cambridge and Oxford, his studies in the Temple, his admission to the splendid and brilliant court of Edward III. as a page, his there becoming a protege of the powerful Duke of Lancaster, his rapid rise and growth in favour with the chivalrous monarch under whom he served, his successful mission as ambassador to Genoa, his subsequent rewards and pensions, his acquisition of wealth, his reduction to poverty by the death of

John of Gaunt and the King, and, finally, his death in quietude and seclusion in the country. When dying, he wrote those beautiful and oft-quoted verses known as "The good counsel of Geoffrey Chaucer," which will show with what true piety and with what admirable knowledge of the world this good man went out of it.

> Fly from the press, and dwell with soothfastness;
> Suffice unto thy good, though it be small;
> For hoard hath hate, and climbing fickleness,
> Praise hath envy, and weal is blent owre all;
> Savour no more than thee behovë shall,
> Rede well thyself that other folk canst rede—
> And truth thee shall deliver, it is no drede.
> Painë thee not each crooked to redress,
> In trust of her that turneth as a ball:
> Great rest standeth in little business,
> Beware also to spurn against a nail,
> Strive not as doth a crockë with a wall.
> Doomë thyself that doomest others dede,
> And truth thee shall deliver, it is no drede.
> That thee is sent receive in buxomness;
> The wrestling of this world asketh a fall:
> Here is no home, here is but wilderness—
> Forth, pilgrim, forthë beast, out of thy stall.
> Look up on high, and thankë God for all,
> Weivë thy lusts, and let thy ghost thee lede,
> And truth thee shall deliver, it is no drede.

It is with Chaucer as a poet that we have most to do; and I do protest against an error which some people entertain relative to Chaucer. When speaking of him, they are apt to say that, "considering the circumstances of the age in which he lived, he was a great poet." Now, don't let us make any allowance or apology of this sort for Chaucer; don't say of him, as they did in the time of Pope, that considering he was "the morning star," he was a great poet. The fact is, Chaucer was absolutely one of the greatest poets the world ever brought forth; he was one of the four great English poets; and he was not merely one of the first of these, but of the universe, and one of the noblest.

Before proceeding next to notice some of the distinctive peculiarities of the ancient poet, I must pause to pay a tribute to the patriotic benefit he conferred upon the English language and the English people; and in doing so I must advert to the Norman Conquest, and the yoke put upon the bluff, hard-handed, simple Saxons by their cool, chivalrous, gentlemanly invaders. Whilst that yoke was new, and the hand of William was strong, there were two languages spoken in the country— the Saxon and the Norman French. Saxon book-making was interrupted; but the Saxon spirit remained uncontaminated and untouched: the two rivers ran side by side unmingled. The consequence was that by-and-bye the national life began to revive. Not many years after the Conquest, the Norman gentleman had to learn Saxon; and, with the resuscitation of the national spirit came the revival of the Saxon literature. Chaucer's lot was a peculiar one. He became a national poet. He was Norman by descent, a courtier by profession, a scholar by acquirement, a favourite with the learned, and the darling of the nobles; and yet he became the poet of the people. There is so much talk now-a-days about "poets of the people," that it is gratifying to find in what respect this great man was essentially worthy of that denomination. He combined the speech of the Norman gentleman with the Saxon poetry of the people; he turned himself to the people, and he did more than any other man in history in the admirable task of binding together the classes of the nation. That man does a more beautiful work who joins the hands of classes, than he who, by irate or harsh language, causes them to keep apart. Apart from being a poet, he laid his one white hand in the open, broad, brown palm of the Saxon, and the other in the fair hand of the Norman lady; he did wed together these people; and he did choose to write in the great old English tongue; he was not only England's great poet, but he was England's great patron.

Since his time the question has been settled that the man who writes a great book must write it in the popular speech, in the people's ways and manners. When Chaucer took up the people, he discovered his burgher and his miller, and so made the Canterbury Tales such a grand picture of national manners, as that Homer himself might almost "pale his ineffectual fire" before his genius. Homer lived early and sang about the early Greeks; Chaucer lived later, and he took some of the old stories of England for his themes. If we cannot give him the credit of being an inventor, yet he was the sweetest narrator of old popular legends that ever lived. But Chaucer wrote for the people in the language and spirit of a gentleman. In these days it is said you must put on fustian and go down to the people. Chaucer did not do that. His poems, to speak in a common phrase of the present day, had a "run," and he familiarised the Anglo-Norman in England. He himself said, "Let their clerks indite in Latin, for they have propriety of sense and knowledge, and let the French also in their French indite, for it is kindly in their mouths; but let us show our phantasies in such words as we have learned in our dame's tongue." To which I say a loud Amen.

Chaucer was the first author who discovered character, and drew it individually. We often hear it said of a person, "He is a character." This is no ill compliment; for it means that he is original, strong, individual, unmistakable; you cannot take him for anybody else. He is no mere John Jones, but one by himself. Look at Chaucer's works. How thoroughly individual, how truly flesh and blood his people are. There is as much difference between Chaucer and Boccaccio as there is between Homer and Virgil. Homer is grand, truthful, and life-like; Virgil is a delusion, full of magic-lantern slides and shadows. Chaucer is the Homer of England; his characters are so thoroughly real and life-like. He exercised a great influence on the drama, as he was the first of modern writers who thoroughly individualised.

As Shelley said of Shakespeare, it may well be said of Chaucer that he carries the palm over the Greek drama by the introduction of a large and genial humour into his poetry. Chaucer abounds in pathos, but it only serves to lead to his humour; and the flashes of his English humour only serve to show there are slumbrous depths of true feeling and true sympathy beneath. He was best humoured amongst men. Let him go to a dance, and all the girls wished he would dance with them first. In battle foremost, in retreat the last. In the house of God meek in his humility, great in his piety. Such was Chaucer. Shakespeare embodies the alternate play of passion, pathos, and humour; for in the case of all English humour its tears and laughter are happily intermingled: and all this is eminently displayed by Chaucer. Whilst capable of touching pathos, he had a downright hearty, genial love of fun in him.

Chaucer was the great national poet of olden time, and the best, the fairest, the truest painter of nature. He was the Adam of English poetry, and he walked in the early dew of the Paradise of poesy. He was the Homer of England. He saw things as they were, and wrote them down. He knew life well. If you wanted a courtly pageant, he could depict it; but if you wanted a portrait of a man, Montaigne could not come up to him, nor could Swift equal him. He was the type of all sorts of writers who came after him. As it is said that an overture foreshadows the best part of an opera, his was the solemn overture to English literature.

Chaucer was very unconventional; he was, moreover, frank, and if he told his hearers a dull story he gaped and told them so. It is perfect rest to get away from the laboured strains of Gray, Pope, and company, and lend oneself for a while to the freshness and sweetness of the verse of this early man. It may be said that you cannot read him; but I want to inspire you with faith enough to attempt to crack Chaucer's quaint English. There is not half the difficulty in reading Chaucer that there is in reading French; who then would

be unrational enough to waste time over French and whine that Chaucer
is difficult? In illustration of this, I will read you an exquisite passage from
Chaucer's "Death of Emily," in the original language:

> His beard was well begunnen for to spring;
> His voice was as a trumpë thundering.
> Contrast this with Dryden's reproduction of the same lines:
> Whose voice was heard around
> Loud as a trumpet with a silver sound.

. . . I place Chaucer amongst the four fine old fathers of English poesy, and
I class Chaucer and Spenser, Shakespeare and Milton, in one category. He
was, in fact, almost the best fruit the old English tree ever grew. Let us take
his works in proof of this. His merit is that he was the first poet that drew
character individually, well discriminated, and withal correct. In reading the
Canterbury Tales, the great charm is that one can recognise every one of its
people as every-day characters. One knows the features of every individual
even to the cut of his nose, and can perceive all that glorious reality of life in
them which only a true artist can impart. Chaucer showed Shakespeare how to
depict: Shakespeare, it is true, delineated character well, as he did everything
well; but Chaucer is the oldest, the truest-hearted, most deep, pathetic, and
unconventional poet England ever produced. He was a new man, a first man,
a fresh man, an unconventional man. He wrote down things exactly as he
saw them, and as they had effect upon him—not what correct people now-a-
days would say *ought* to have been the effect. Chaucer was the sincerest poet
that ever lived; and it is right pleasant to get away into his hearty, frank, jolly,
jovial verses, full as they are of fine old unconventional English words. The
man had a wonderful idea of satire; he was a dear lover of nature, and was,
moreover, an awful "quiz." He had all the merits of Montaigne, more than the
wit of Swift, and Wordsworth's love of nature as well. Whether we begin with
nature or go on to character, the hand of a master is perceptible.

But he had one great misfortune to contend with—he had the bad luck
to be an Englishman. If he had been a delicate Virgil, or a feeble Ennius,
people in the present day might have taken the trouble perhaps to read him.
But why should we not comprehend old English as well as Greek or French?
Chaucer wrote in a language that is fast becoming dead to us who live in these
modern times. It is true it is awkward and annoying to be obliged to turn to
a dictionary in the middle of a line; but have we not often to do that with
Homer? How, I will ask, do Englishmen read Burns? Many do, and do it by
study. Why not with a national poet like Chaucer? The excuse that you cannot
make out his language ought only to be made use of by lazy people. The

proper understanding of the value of words is essential to proper speaking and proper writing; and the best study of primitive English will be found in Chaucer. Why should we mouth over a Roman pot, or go "mooning" to Kenilworth, if we neglect to familiarise ourselves with a curious and beautiful antiquity like Chaucer's poems? In a word, we ought to be acquainted with the language in which our forefathers talked, with which they rallied in the battle-field, and in which they prayed and worshipped.

To justify the view I have expressed of Chaucer's character and writings, I will give to you a series of selected and various quotations from his pages. I give them to you as a few lessons in Chaucerian reading, in the hope of convincing you of its ease and simplicity. However, I will first of all lay down a few simple rules for reading Chaucer with fluency. You must pay particular attention to the plurals and genitives, and the variation of the final syllables. You must be Teutonic in your pronunciation, and if you will call "drops" "droppes," and "streams" "streames," &c, you will easily manage Chaucer. The language, partly Teutonic and partly Saxon as it is, may in some cases be considered vulgar; but it may be heard in use, by the country folk, in some counties, even in the present day; and it is so beautifully intermixed that each word has its full meaning, whilst the harmony of the lines,—though occasionally short of a foot, perhaps—is quite refreshing and thoroughly English.

In illustrating Chaucer's characteristics, we will commence with his love of nature, and for this we may take his exquisite lines on "The Daisy"; while quotations from the *Canterbury Tales* and *Troilus and Cresseide* will show his mastery in description of incidents in common life, and in delineating individual character. First then, about the daisy:

> And as for me, though that I can but lite,
> On bookës for to read I me delight,
> And to them give I faith and full credénce,
> And in mine heart have them in reverence
> So heartily, that there is gamë none
> That from my bookës maketh me to gone.
> But it be seldom, on the holy day,
> Save certainly when that the month of May
> Is comen, and I hear the fowlës sing
> And that the flow'rës 'ginnen for to spring,—
> Fare well my book and my devotiön.
>   Now have I then eke this condition
> That, above all the flow'rës in the mead,
> Then love I most those flow'rës white and red

Such that men callen daisies in our town.
To them have I so great affectiön,
As I said erst, when comen is the May,
That in my bed there daweth me no day
That I n'am up and walking in the mead,
To see this flow'r against the sunnë spread.
When it upriseth early by the morrow,
That blissful sight softeneth all my sorrow,
So glad am I when that I have présénce
Of it, to do it all reverence
As she that is of all flow'rës the flow'r,
Fulfillëd of all virtue and honóur,
And ever alikë fair and fresh of hue
As well in winter as in summer new,
This love I ever, and shall until I die
Al' swear I not of this, I will not lie.

These beautiful lines, from the prologue to the *Legend of Good Women,* may serve to illustrate Chaucer's love of nature.

[Prominent among the qualities of his poetry is the ruggedly picturesque. Short and rapid strokes of the brush are usually more powerful than they are polished: but in Chaucer the ruggedness is compensated by the concentration. He crams into a big bulging line the meaning which, in Spenser, would fill a stanza or a page. In the description of the Temple of Mars, in the *Knight's Tale,* every line is a picture, and resembles the boss upon a buckler, or the knob on a rough goblet of gold:—

There stood the temple of Mars Armipotent,
Wrought all of burnëd steel, of which th' entry
Was long and strait, and ghastly for to see;
The northern light in at the doorë shone,
For window on the wall ne was there none,
Through which men mighten any light-discern;
The door was all of adamant etern.
What figures are carved there! There is
The smiler with the knife under the cloak;

and—

The slayer of himself yet saw I there.
His hearte blood hath bathëd all his hair;

and—

> Woodness laughing in his rage:

and ghastlier still—

> The sow fretting the child right in the cradle;
> The cook yscalded, for all his long ladle.
> Nought was forgot by th' infortune of Martë,
> The carter overridden with his cartë,
> Under the wheel full low he lay adown.

When he follows the humourous style, Chaucer is equally sententious and striking. Thus he says of his Franklin:—

> Withouten bake-meat never was his house,
> Of fish and flesh, and that so plenteous,
> *It snowëd in his house of meat and drink.*

Of the Miller—

> His beard as any sow or fox was red,
> And thereto broad as though it were a spade,
> Upon the cop right of his nose he had
> A wart, and thereon stood a tuft of hairs,
> Red as the bristles of a sowës ears.
> His mouth widë was as a furnace.

And of the Friar—

> Somewhat he lispëd for his wantonness,
> To make his English sweet upon his tongue,
> And in his harping, when that he had sung,
> His eyen twinkled in his head aright
> As do the starrës in a frosty night.

In this broad yet condensed style of pictorial representation Chaucer resembles Bunyan, as well as in some other qualities of his brawny genius. Bunyan, too, writes like a man of business—deals in direct strokes—puts much into few, and these simple words—has an eye for sly humour as well as for bold allegory—and with comparatively little fancy, has an immense deal of essential imagination. How different at first view the Canterbury from the Christian Pilgrims—the Friar from Evangelist—the Franklin from Great-heart—the Miller from Christian—the Sompnour from Hopeful—the Manciple from Gaius mine host—the Nun from Mercy—and the Wife of

Bath from Christiana! And yet, in one very important point, they are alike; they are no cold abstractions—no stiff, formal, and half-animated figures— they are, both the pious and profane, intensely natural, and bursting at every pore with life.

Troilus and Cresseide is a lengthy poem in five books. It tells essentially the same story with the play of Shakespeare bearing the same name, but in a very different spirit. Shakespeare's great object in his drama is to laugh; and he seems for the nonce to exchange places with its real hero Thersites. Chaucer, on the other hand, extracts the pathos that is in the story, and uses it in his own fine way, "painting the afflicting circumstances slowly and assiduously, and descending exploringly into the caverns of tears." As a whole, however, the poem is tedious, although fine passages are frequent. One often quoted is that which describes Cresseide's yielding and acknowledging her love:—

> And as the now abashëd nightingale
> That stinteth first when she beginneth sing,
> When that she heareth any herdë's tale,
> Or in the hedges any wight stirring,
> And after sicker doth her voice outring:
> Right so Cresseide, when that her dreadë stent;
> Open'd her heart and told him her intent.

Let us quote, too, a passage in which we find the germ of his coming "comedy"—*The Canterbury Tales*:—

> Go, little book, go, little tragedy;
> There God my Maker yet ere that I die
> So send me might to make *some comedy;*
> But little book, make thou thee none envy,
> But subject ben unto all poesy,
> And kiss the steps where as thou seest pace
> Of Virgil, Ovid, Homer, Lucan, Stace.][1]

In conclusion, the object I have had in view has been to show the completeness and universality of the man, and also to induce you to read him for yourselves, in his own language— for no translation, however good, can do him justice. If you think well of this, you may, in the course of the ensuing winter, form a Chaucer club, and spend an evening now and then together, in reading his works, and not pass a line without thoroughly understanding every word in it.

Notes

1. The paragraphs in brackets are filled in conjecturally, from Rev. George Gillman's *Critical Dissertation,* but there can be little doubt about their identification.—GEORGE ST. CLAIR

—George Dawson, "Chaucer," *Biographical Lectures,*
ed. St. Clair, 1887, pp. 205–16

WILLIAM MORRIS "FEUDAL ENGLAND" (1888)

A prolific Victorian novelist, poet, short story writer, critic, and essayist, William Morris (1834–96) saw Chaucer as the epitome of the medieval courtly poet, the culmination of high or courtly medieval culture in one author. Nonetheless, Morris notes that Chaucer is very much a product of his class, and that the ballad poetry of the English fourteenth-century working class and "Lollard poetry," a type of work critical of the social and religious culture of the day typified by William Langland's *Piers Plowman,* make good "corrective[s]" to Chaucer's work. Morris's comments are particularly useful when compared to those of William Webbe (1586).

The successor of the deposed king, the third Edward, ushers in the complete and central period of the Middle Ages in England. The feudal system is complete: the life and spirit of the country has developed into a condition if not quite independent, yet quite forgetful, on the one hand of the ideas and customs of the Celtic and Teutonic tribes, and on the other of the authority of the Roman Empire. The Middle Ages have grown into manhood; that manhood has an art of its own, which, though developed step by step from that of Old Rome and New Rome, and embracing the strange mysticism and dreamy beauty of the East, has forgotten both its father and its mother, and stands alone triumphant, the loveliest, brightest, and gayest of all the creations of the human mind and hand.

It has a literature of its own too, somewhat akin to its art, yet inferior to it, and lacking its unity, since there is a double stream in it. On the one hand is the court poet, the gentleman, Chaucer, with his Italianizing metres, and his formal recognition of the classical stories; on which, indeed, he builds a superstructure of the quaintest and most unadulterated mediaevalism, as gay and bright as the architecture which his eyes beheld and his pen pictured for us, so clear, defined, and elegant it is; a sunny world even amidst its violence and passing troubles, like those of a happy child, the worst of them an amusement rather than a grief to the onlookers; a world that scarcely needed hope in its eager life of adventure and love, amidst the sunlit blossoming meadows, and green woods, and white begilded manor-houses. A kindly and human muse is Chaucer's, nevertheless, interested in and amused by all life, but of her very nature devoid of strong aspirations for the future; and that all the more, since, though the strong devotion and fierce piety of the ruder Middle Ages had by this time waned, and the Church was more often lightly mocked at than either feared or loved, still the *habit* of looking on this life as part of another yet remained: the world is fair and full of adventure; kind men and true and noble are in it to make one happy; fools also to laugh at, and rascals to be resisted, yet not wholly condemned; and when this world is over we shall still go on living in another which is a part of this. Look at all the picture, note all and live in all, and be as merry as you may, never forgetting that you are alive and that it is good to live.

That is the spirit of Chaucer's poetry; but alongside of it existed yet the ballad poetry of the people, wholly untouched by courtly elegance and classical pedantry; rude in art but never coarse, true to the backbone; instinct with indignation against wrong, and thereby expressing the hope that was in it; a protest of the poor against the rich, especially in those songs of the Foresters, which have been called the mediaeval epic of revolt; no more gloomy than the gentleman's poetry, yet cheerful from courage, and not content. Half a dozen stanzas of it are worth a cartload of the whining introspective lyrics of today; and he who, when he has mastered the slight differences of language from our own daily speech, is not moved by it, does not understand what true poetry means nor what its aim is.

There is a third element in the literature of this time which you may call Lollard poetry, the great example of which is William Langland's *Piers Plowman*. It is no bad corrective to Chaucer, and in *form* at least belongs wholly to the popular side; but it seems to me to show symptoms of the spirit of the rising middle class, and casts before it the shadow of the new master that was coming forward for the workman's oppression.

—William Morris, "Feudal England,"
Signs of Change, 1888, pp. 73–75

Henry Morley (1890)

A prominent scholar of English literature, Henry Morley (1822–94) was esteemed in his lifetime for his ten-volume *English Writers* (1864–94). In the following excerpt from that work, Morley examines Chaucer's place in the pantheon of English authors and provides commentary on two of Chaucer's primary texts, *Troilus and Criseyde* and *The Canterbury Tales*, which students today will find of particular use.

Morley begins his essay on Chaucer by noting that, "No English poet equal to him had preceded him, or lived in his own day. Only one writer since his time has risen to his level, and he rose yet higher" (Morley is here referring to Shakespeare). He praises Chaucer's wit, his depiction of character, and notes that, "Of Chaucer's there is not a thought coloured by prejudice or passion," declaring that Chaucer's strength as a writer came from his "genial spirit of companionship."

Still, students will likely find Morley's work on *Troilus and Criseyde* and *The Canterbury Tales* most helpful. Regarding *Troilus*, Morley notes that while the work was based on Boccaccio's *Il Filostrato*, "Chaucer Englished it" through several key alterations. These alterations include not only lengthening the piece, but also important modifications to the three principal characters of Troilus, his love Criseyde, and their go-between Pandarus (Morley is particularly impressed by how Chaucer altered this last character).

Morley then suggests that there are two obstacles to studying Chaucer's *The Canterbury Tales*. The first "is the essentially dramatic spirit in which he occupied himself with his design, giving to his pilgrims of either sex all the variety of rank and character that he could fairly group into a single company, in order that, through them and their stories, he might reach to a broad view of life in its most typical forms, fleshly and spiritual." Morley sees this aspect especially reflected in Chaucer's portrayal of women in the *Tales*. He writes: "It is a part of the same quality that makes noticeable in Chaucer . . . the variety and truth of his different creations of women. [T]he range of Chaucer is from the ideal patience of the wife Griselda, or the girlish innocence and grace of Emelie in "The Knight's Tale," to the Wife of Bath and lower; and in . . . [this] great poet the predominating sense is of the beauty and honour of true womanhood . . . the poet's sense of the worth and beauty of womanhood very greatly predominates over his satire of the weaknesses of women." Many critics have often commented on Chaucer's female characters, and many students often choose to write about Chaucer's depictions of women; Morley's views on the subject should provide useful fodder for writing on this topic.

Morley's second obstacle to studying *The Canterbury Tales* is that, even to this day, scholars are not quite sure of the correct order of the entire work. Morley rightly points out that Chaucer likely had a scheme of how the work should be presented in his mind, and this overall construction is vitally important to understanding the text. Morley concludes the section on *The Canterbury Tales* by again comparing Chaucer's work to one of its potential inspirations, Boccaccio's *Decameron*, and demonstrates why *The Canterbury Tales* exceeds the work it was based on.

The genius of Geoffrey Chaucer is not to be likened to a lone star glittering down on us through a rift in surrounding darkness, or to a spring-day in the midst of winter, that blossoms and fades, leaving us to wait long for its next fellow. He had in his own time for brother writers Wyclif, Langland, Gower, some of the worthiest men of our race, and the light of the English mind was not quenched when he died. Nor is it natural in any way whatever to think of Chaucer as an isolated man. No English poet equal to him had preceded him, or lived in his own day. Only one writer since his time has risen to his level, and he rose yet higher. But much of Chaucer's strength came of a genial spirit of companionship. It was his good-will to humanity, and his true sense of his own part in it, that gave him his clear insight into life. In him the simple sturdiness of the dutiful God-seeking Anglo-Saxon is blended intimately with the social joyousness of wit. Chaucer worked to the same end as Langland and Gower; not less religiously, though with much less despair over the evils that he saw. He does not see far who despairs of any part of God's creation. Having the sympathetic insight that is inseparable from genius at its best, and entering more deeply than his neighbour poets into characters of men, Chaucer could deal with them all good-humouredly; for he had the tolerance that must needs come of a large view of life, exact in its simplicity. Of Chaucer's there is not a thought coloured by prejudice or passion. He paints, in his chief work, character in all its variety, without once giving us, under some other name, a covert reproduction of himself. When he attacks hypocrisy that trades upon religion, and in so doing strips vice of its cloak, the sharpest note of his scorn has in it a rich quality of human kindliness. In perception of the ridiculous, he is beforehand with the most fastidious of his countrymen, and with his own native instinct he knows where an Englishman would turn with laughter or displeasure from words or thoughts that might seem good to any other people. Earnest as he was— disposed at times even to direct religious teaching—Chaucer was quick to see the brighter side of life, and ready to enjoy it in the flesh. When he was rich he seems to have delighted freely and naturally in whatever good things wealth would bring him; and when stripped of substance he set up no mean wailing of distress, but quietly consoling himself with a keener relish of the wealth that was within him, he dined worse and wrote his *Canterbury Tales*. . . .

His *Troylus and Criseyde* is an enlarged English version of the *Filostrato*, remarkable, as we shall find, for the illustration it affords of Chaucer's character in his treatment of the Italian original, and for its evidence of growth of the dramatic element in Chaucer's power as a writer. A tradition has come down to us on the authority of Lydgate, who was young when Chaucer died,[1] that

In youth he made a translacion
Of a boke whiche called is Trophe[2]
In Lumbarde tonge, as men may rede and se;
And in our vulgar, long er that he deyde,
Gave it the name of Troylus and Creseyde.

Gower, writing between 1393 and 1398, represents it as a common pastime of young ladies "to rede and here of Troylus,"[3] and it was natural to ascribe to the young days of its writer that which became the favourite love-poem of the cultivated English youth. But comparison with its original will show in Chaucer's *Troylus and Criseyde* a ripeness, both of purpose and invention, that connects it with the work of his maturer years. I cannot think that Chaucer was of unripe age when he produced this poem. . . .

(The) profoundly earnest close to the book is, with every touch of purity of thought contained in it, Chaucer's own, and is the final setting of the English seal to our own version of the Italian poem. Chaucer interpolates also, before the stanza tell- ing of the death of Troilus at the hand of Achilles, his "Go, little book," his reverence for the great poets of antiquity, and his own hope that he might live to write a comedy—that is, a poem ending cheerfully. Professor ten Brink sees here a reference to the *House of Fame* as a work modelled playfully upon the *Divine Comedy* of Dante; but Chaucer may have been looking forward to some such achievement as the framework of the *Canterbury Tales*. Also he prays, that through the diversity in English and in writing of our tongue—diversity conspicuous when we compare the English of these early poems of his with the contemporary Vision *of Piers Plowman*—he might not be miswritten or have his metre spoilt by bad pronunciation. Then he tells of the death of Troilus, which he has reserved for the purpose of attaching his own English moral to the tale of fleshly passion and the sand on which it builds. Boccaccio draws no moral from his story but that (also of one of our own modern Italian songs, "La donna e mobile") woman is changeable; and he adds a dedication of it to his Fiammetta, from whom he expects faith. Chaucer follows the soul of Troilus to heaven, and shows it looking down upon the transitory passions of the flesh; then, turning from the paynim Greeks and Trojans to the Christian creed, tells of the love unchangeable that is the Christian's stay, while dedicating his book to his two earnest friends and brother poets, John Gower and Ralph Strode. . . .

(T)he original of Chaucer's *Troilus and Cressida* was written by Boccaccio, a man of thirty-four or five, when the English poet was about sixteen years old. The original, written at the court of a lascivious and fascinating murderess, and produced to please the taste of a corrupt society, was but a livelier, and, in many passages, less modest form of the conventional court poetry that rang the changes upon love. Now let us see, through alterations that he made, in what spirit the right-hearted Chaucer Englished it.

In the first place, Chaucer's version is more than half as long again as its original. The varied invocations at the opening of Chaucer's first three books, and the invocation preceding the fourth book, which is common to the fourth and fifth, are not in Boccaccio's poem. Boccaccio invokes, at the outset of the poem, Fiammetta, who is his Jove and Apollo, and whose absence caused him to write of deserted Troilus. A few details will show Chaucer's manner of enlargement. Boccaccio begins the story in the seventh and eighth stanzas of the first part of the *Filostrato,* which are expanded into three stanzas of *Troylus and Criseyde.* Two stanzas are then translated closely; then a stanza is again expanded into two; five stanzas are then translated stanza for stanza, after which three stanzas are expanded into six. Then the translation is very direct, stanza for stanza, until Chaucer digresses to the comparison, which is his own, of the prince who disdains love, with proud Bayard, first in the trace, who skips on the way until the whip reminds him that he must pull with his fellows. This stanza is interpolated, and so are the following stanzas of reflection upon love. Presently there is another incidental interpolation of what Troilus had said to lovers. The next interpolation is the sonnet of Petrarch's, translated as "the Song of Troilus," in three stanzas. But we return to Boccaccio, at the stanza beginning, "And to the God of Love, thus sayed he." Eighteen stanzas are then closely translated, except that the Complaint of Troilus is in five stanzas instead of seven. Here ends the first part of *Il Filostrato;* the first stanza of the second part being that in which Pandarus first appears. From this stanza Chaucer has struck out the description of Pandarus as a brave young Trojan of high lineage. He brings him to Troilus as simply "a friend of his." His question, to which Boccaccio gives two lines, Chaucer expands into ten, with seven more of comments. He is to be Cressida's garrulous uncle, humorous, lachrymose, tricky, worldly wise according to the wisdom of the base; the sentimental comradeship with Troilus being an oddity which we may refer, if we please, to the fact that Troilus was a king's son, who might have any form of parasite. The next nine stanzas of dialogue are closely translated. Chaucer then interpolates the five stanzas beginning, "A whetstone is no carving instrument." The next two stanzas represent one stanza of Boccaccio's, then a stanza is translated pretty closely, and then five stanzas more are added by Chaucer to the argument of Pandarus. The next six stanzas of Boccaccio (xv.–xxii.) are expanded by Chaucer into the twenty-two beginning, "Yet Troilus, for all this, no word said," the narrative being overlaid by the garrulity of Pandarus. In Boccaccio, Griseida is represented as the cousin of Pandarus; Chaucer makes her his niece, and ascribes to him craft of age instead of the fresh valour of youth. Even when he translates closely, he gives to the dialogue a more colloquial character, although he burdens it with disquisitions, and impedes the progress of a narrative that in the verse of Boccaccio runs with a light, even, graceful step, from the first stanza to the last.

Outwardly graceful, inwardly graceless. In the next stanzas Boccaccio represents, what English Chaucer would not represent, Pandarus as a noble youth, offering help in winning his cousin's assent to dishonest love. Chaucer is not content with having taken the generosity of youth and manly dignity out of the character of Pandarus: he also modifies the character of his first offer to help Troilus. Three stanzas of Boccaccio (Bk. II. st. xxi.–xxiii.) are expanded into four, in order to secure a cleansing of the third of them. Chaucer interpolates the nine stanzas beginning, "But well is me," before he comes to the stanzas in which Pandarus proceeds with an argument concerning honour in women, better adapted to the court of Queen Giovanna of Naples than to the homes in which English-women had read to them Chaucer's *Troylus and Criseyde*. Five stanzas are here translated with omission, alteration, and interpolation. The rest of Chaucer's first book, "When Troilus heard," &c, expands and modifies five stanzas of Boccaccio (Bk. II. st. xxix.–xxxiii.), in which Pandarus laughs at modest professions made by Troilus, and Troilus embraces him as a wise friend who knows how to end his grief.

Chaucer closes his first book in the middle of the second book of *Filostrato*, and opening his own second book with an added invocation to Clio, comes altogether in his own way to the visit of Pandarus to Cressida. Boccaccio simply makes him go to her, look hard in her face, and begin offhand to call on her to forget the dead to whom her love was pledged, and think of the love torment of Troilus, to yield her love to him. Chaucer makes this part of the story, by a great deal, more dramatic as well as more honest and natural. The first thirty-two stanzas of the second book are Chaucer's own. The scene of the wily uncle's morning call upon his niece, where he

> found two other ladies set and shee
> Within a pavéd parlour, and they three
> Herden a maiden hem reden the geste
> Of the siége of Thebés, while hem leste,

the light familiar colloquy through which Pandarus makes subtle approach to his subject, the uncle's art of awakening curiosity, and the shrewd, half-comic suggestions of his worldly cunning, are all Chaucer's own, and there is nothing equal to them to be found in *Il Filostrato*. Chaucer's opening of the second book of *Troylus and Criseyde* is, indeed, evidence that—if he really wrote it in the earlier part of his life—at the time when he was bending to the fashion of the day, and writing or translating poems in the conventional way of the court, Chaucer was already a wise humourist, with a keen sense of character, and much of the original power that at last had full expression in the Prologue to the *Canterbury Tales*.

It is only in Chaucer's thirty-third stanza of the second book that Pandarus looks on Cressida "busie wise;" and we have translations again, though not close, from Boccaccio. The version is then very free till we come to the description of the grief of Troilus, "Tho (then) Pandarus a little gan to smile." Here there are several stanzas very closely followed, but there is change and amplification, and Chaucer does not represent Cressida as conquered by the description. After the departure of Pandarus, Boccaccio at once represents Cressida in love debate with herself. Chaucer prepares for this by bringing the martial figure of Troilus outside her window as he comes through the street, with broken helm and battered shield, from putting the Greeks to rout. He makes that picture of bright manliness suggestive, but even yet refuses to show Cressida as wholly won.

> For I say not that she so sodainly
> Yafe him her love, but that she gan encline
> To liken him tho, and I have told you why:
> And after that, his manhode and his pine
> Madé that love within her gan to mine.

Boccaccio made her yield at the mere hearing of "his pine." Chaucer adds the sight of him in his manhood "next his brother, holder up of Troy," before he tells somewhat of the thoughts of Cressida "'as mine auctour listeth to endite." He strikes out "mine auctour's" representation of her dwelling on the beauties of Troilus, her own beauty, the fleeting of youth, the honour of secrecy. He strikes out her licentious doctrine that it is no sin to do as others do; her objection to a husband; her sense of the wisdom of preserving liberty, and of the sweetness of stolen waters. What the English poet substitutes for all this is a sense of honour and a dread of the untruth of men. Cressida's going down into the garden and hearing from Antigone the Trojan song of love, with the song itself, the coming on of night, the singing of the nightingale upon the cedar-tree, and Cressida's dream, are all added by Chaucer to the poem. The letter of Troilus to Cressida, written at the suggestion of Pandarus, is condensed, after the previous counselling of Pandarus had been amplified, and touches of humour added to the dialogue—every change being on the side of wholesomeness.

Chaucer's dealing with the next incidents is equally remarkable. Boccaccio's Cressida receives the letter of Troilus as a gallant of the court of Joan of Naples would desire a lady of the same court to receive it; and her letter in reply broadly suggests that assurance of secrecy is all her honour needs. Chaucer invents a garden dialogue, in which he adds more touches to his character of Pandarus, sets Pandarus and his niece to dine together, and by suggestions of delicate humour gives an honest picture of the slow yielding of Cressida's mind to the suit pressed on her. Again also he supplements bare imagination with a picture of Troilus riding by; this time not as a battered hero, but as a knight in all his bravery. Instead of translating the long letter of lust disguised as half refusal, Chaucer describes it in five lines, thus:

> She thonkéd him, of all that he well ment
> Towardés her, but holden him in bond
> She nolde not, ne make her selven bond
> In love, but as his suster him to please
> She wold ay faine to don his herte on ease.

And it was with modest womanly reserves that Cressida gave the letter to the go-between. After its delivery, according to Boccaccio, Pandarus again talked to his cousin, obtaining an assignation with her for Troilus by simple assurance of his secrecy. And in the next book, the fourth of Boccaccio's ten, Cressida simply rises at night after all are gone to bed, to meet Troilus with open arms in a dark, solitary place, and be with him till cockrow. After this there is nothing in the Italian poem but a continued dwelling on illicit passion, till we come presently to the claim of Calchas for the delivery of Cressida, which incident occurs at the opening of Boccaccio's fifth book. What, then, is Chaucer's story of the wiles of Pandarus, with detail of the trick of the threatened lawsuit, of the dinner at the house of Deiphobus, the feigned sickness of Troilus, the interview with him in his chamber, and the final treachery of Pandarus on occasion of the supper at his own house, and the storm? These are dramatic incidents which the English poet has invented, to the end that he may substitute as long as he can, for the base Italian ideal, a picture, suited to his own and the best English mind, of woman's grace and innocence.

But that is not all, or nearly all. When at last animal passion has its triumph, Chaucer draws upon his author for a picture of such bliss as it can give; and, as he continues to translate, still modifying, humanising, and enriching with dramatic touches, blending suggestions of womanly delicacy that yet lingers about the fallen Cressida, he proceeds with that which is for him and for his readers part of the stern moral of the story, Cressida's loss of honesty towards her lover also. In so doing, he strengthens the grace of fidelity in Troilus, to whose character he had added many a touch of manliness. For these he had no warrant in his "author Lolius," who makes Troilus fall as struck by lightning when he hears that the demand for Cressida is granted by the Trojan Senate. And, after all, he sums up with a lesson on the perishableness of earthly passion, as he points heavenward to the love that is unchanging. Religious earnestness, honour to the pure beauty of womanhood, English humour and dramatic vigour, Chaucer adds to the *Filostrato;* but in so doing, it must be granted—as a set-off to the charm of his dramatic alteration and enrichment of the character of Pandarus, wherever it touches his remodelled Cressida—that by enlargement of the dialogues between Pandarus and Troilus, equally well meant, but less interesting to himself and us, he destroys the swiftness and grace with which the original poem, immoral though it be, runs in one strain of accordant music from the opening until the close.

Chaucer's additions to the story of Cressida in the Greek camp, and her dialogue with Diomede and with her father, indicate his reading in the first romance which contained the tale of *Troilus and Cressida*, the *Geste de Troie* of Benott de Sainte-Maure, or the Latin prose version of it by Guido Colonna. But throughout the poem the essential changes are of his own making, and directly illustrative of those qualities which we have found thus far, and shall find to the end, characteristic of the people whose best mind is expressed in the Literature whereof some part of the story is here being told.

In *The House of Fame* Chaucer sustains a lofty flight of original thought with playful homeliness of speech. Throughout his verse there is the true poet's disinclination to think upon stilts. Chaucer's English is that of the cultivated townsman. His mind had a wider range of perception and expression than that of any of his contemporaries and of the greater number of his after-corners, but in his grace and tenderness and in his strongest flights of fancy or feeling, as in broadest mirth, the natural man speaks with his own unforced humour. There is no muffling of power in thick wrappers of a far-fetched phraseology; strength that lies in the thought itself wears no misfitted clothing of an artificial eloquence. The beauty and dignity of human thought moves freely in all its native grace.

As far as regards the use of words, good writing excels good speaking, because it is compelled, by a more exact fitting of the words themselves to the thought spoken, and to the energy with which it is conceived, to atone for the absence of those personal aids of eye, voice, gesture, which enforce the word of mouth. But the strength comes of making written language more not less true to the natural mind of the writer. It does not come at all of keeping a closet in one's mind for best-company words and phrases, only to be set out in impressive array on state occasions. Good written English is the home language of Englishmen intensified by the care taken to make it perfectly expressive. It should be coloured more, not less, than spoken English with that which the hearer of the spoken language also sees in trick of eye and hears in tone of voice; temper, that is, and humour of the mind which seeks to utter itself truly. All that lives in the tones and modulations of the natural voice and brightens the aspect of the speaker who is interested in his subject, the writer also, be he poet, historian, philosopher, must endeavour not to keep out of his writing in the name of a dignity that is conventional and insincere, but to keep in it, in the name of truth, which is first of the dignities of God. The true writer's question to himself is never, "Am I like all other people who look fine?" But it is, "Am I like myself when truest to a duty?" "If I have matter to sing, or to record, or reason out, is it," he asks of himself when he desires to test his work, "my own whole and exact thought that I utter, with the variations in degree of force that belong really to my own perception of the parts of it, and with the simplicity essential to that plain and full expression which begets the readiest and truest sympathy of understanding in the minds of others?"

Such doctrine may now pass unquestioned, but it is in several respects the opposite of that preached by the critics fifty or a hundred years ago. The simple directness of speech that makes Chaucer himself seem always to be walking by his reader's side, we know now for a sign of power. His fancy travels a far road, for example, in his poem of *The House of Fame;* and, in the days when periwigs were worn, readers who went to a book with their heads preoccupied by critical rules of propriety, only half saw how true to English nature was the light strain veiling depth of thought, the homely saying or good-humoured air of jest nerving the strenuous labour of an upward climb, and making the appreciation of all great thoughts that proceed out of it only the more sure and true. I say this in apt connexion with one work of Chaucer's, but it was true of his work from the first, and now, as his independent strength asserts itself more and more clearly, becomes truer and truer. . . .

The *Canterbury Tales* express the whole power of Chaucer; yet it is only by such a study as we have now made of the sequence of his other works, that we can be fairly qualified to understand the poet while we are delighting in this chief group of his poems.

There are two obstacles to a study of Chaucer himself in the *Canterbury Tales.*

One is the essentially dramatic spirit in which he occupied himself with his design, giving to his pilgrims of either sex all the variety of rank and character that he could fairly group into a single company, in order that, through them and their stories, he might reach to a broad view of life in its most typical forms, fleshly and spiritual. Had the mind of Chaucer stirred among us in the days of Queen Elizabeth, his works would have been plays, and Shakespeare might have found his match. But, except in the miracle plays and mysteries, which seldom represented ordinary human life, there was in Chaucer's time no writing formally dramatic. Dramatic genius could only speak through such poems as were acceptable to the readers of that generation; and through such poems, therefore, Chaucer poured his images of life, bright with variety of incident, and subtle in perception of all forms of character. He had that highest form of genius which can touch every part of human life, and, at the contact, be stirred to a simple sympathetic utterance. Out of a sympathy so large, good humour flows unforced, and the pathos shines upon us with a rare tranquillity. The meanness or the grandeur, fleshly grossness or ideal beauty, of each form of life, is reflected back from the unrippled mirror of Chaucer's *Canterbury Tales,* as from no other work of man, except the Plays of Shakespeare. Chaucer alone comes near to Shakespeare in that supreme quality of the dramatist which enables him to show the characters of men as they are betrayed by men themselves, wholly developed as if from within, not as described from without by an imperfect and prejudiced observer. It is a part of the same quality that makes noticeable in Chaucer, as in Shakespeare, the variety and truth of his different creations of women. As the range of Shakespeare was from Imogen to Dame Quickly and lower, so the range of Chaucer is from the ideal patience of the wife Griselda, or the girlish innocence and grace of Emelie in the *Knight's Tale,* to the Wife of Bath and lower; and in each of these great poets the predominating sense is of the beauty and honour of true womanhood.

If there were many Englishmen who read what we have of the *Canterbury Tales* straight through, it would not be necessary to say that, even in the fragment as it stands, expression of the poet's sense of the worth and beauty of womanhood very greatly predominates over his satire of the weaknesses of women. His satire, too, is genial. For the lowest he has no scorn, as he has for the hypocrisies of men who wear religion as the cloak to their offences. We have seen something of this in his transformation of Boccaccio's impure Cressida into a woman whose true dignity and perfect delicacy is slowly undermined. So, too, the transformed Pandarus jests, gossips, proses, and plots through the poem, being shown dispassionately as a character that we might see in life, and of which we are to think as we think of our living neighbours. Yet he is so shown, that, as Sir Philip Sidney said, we have "the Terentian Gnatho and our Chaucer's Pandar so exprest, that we now use their names to signify their trades."[4] And let us not forget that Boccaccio described his Pandar, unconscious of infamy in his part, as a young and honourable knight. It was only when we compared the English poem with its Italian original, and saw thereby in what spirit Chaucer had worked, that we could distinguish the mind of the English poet while we read his *Troylus and Chseyde.* And thus it is that, to a considerable extent, although not altogether, in the *Canterbury Tales,* as in the plays of Shakespeare, the dramatic genius of Chaucer has obscured his personality.

The second obstacle to a study of Chaucer himself in the *Canterbury Tales* is the fact that we have but little indication of the order in which they were written, or of the relation of any one of them to a particular time of his life. The works of his which have been hitherto discussed were usually upon themes more or less personal, and we were seldom without some indication of the time when they were written. Therefore it was possible so far to connect them with his life, as slowly, point by point, to make them furnish cumulative evidence as to a few essential features in his character. We have seen, for example, that, in a sense of his own, he takes the Daisy for his flower; and rises high above all poets of his age in honour to marriage, and praise of the purity of the wife's white daisy crown. But stories written by Chaucer at wide intervals, and very various in merit, were, in the last years of his life, being transformed into *Canterbury Tales.* These express all his power, represent his whole mind, from the lightest jest to the profoundest earnest. They gather rays, as it were, out of all the quarters of his life; but its horizon is not to be measured in the little sun they form. . . .

Geoffrey Chaucer, who had taken delight from his youth up in the lively genius of Boccaccio, while repelled by the reflection of Italian morals in his images of life, had drawn from Boccaccio's *Decameron* the first hint of his crowning effort as a writer. He would form a collection of the stories he had rhymed or might yet rhyme, which he could leave behind him firmly bound together by a device like that which has, for all time, made one work of the hundred tales of the *Decameron.* But Chaucer's plan was better than that of the *Decameron,* and looked to a much greater result. "Forth, pilgrim, forth!" The English poet must have felt his mastery as he set his pilgrims on their way, and had every incitement to proceed with a work in which he was so perfectly achieving that which he had set himself to do. He could not have laid the *Canterbury Tales* aside for work of less account. And if he did, where is it? The last line that Chaucer wrote, when he sat for the last time at his desk as poet, pen in hand, must have been some one of the lines of the *Canterbury Tales.* Perhaps the sense of his approaching death caused him to end his labour among men with the discourse, or translation of a discourse, concerning sin, confession, and penance, which closes the work as we now have it, under the name of the "Parson's Tale." If so, the last words Chaucer wrote at his desk—certainly the last words of the *Canterbury Tales* as we now read them—look to the Heaven "ther as the body of man that whilom was seek and frel, feble and mortal, is immortal, and so strong, and so hool, that ther may no thing empeire it; ther nys neyther honger, ne thurst ne colde, but every soule replenisched with the sight of the parfyt knowyng of God. This blisful regne may men purchase by poverte espirituel, and the glorie by lowenes, the plente of joye by hunger and thurst, and reste by travaile, and the lif by deth and mortificacioun of synne. To thilke lyf he us brynge, that boughte us with his precious blode. Amen."

Boccaccio, who died twenty-five years before Chaucer, placed the scene of his *Decameron* in a garden to which seven fashionable ladies had retired with three fashionable gentlemen, during the plague that devastated Florence in 1348.[5] The persons were all of the same class, young and rich, with no concern in life beyond the bandying of compliments. They shut themselves up in a delicious garden of the sort common in courtly inventions of the middle ages, and were occupied in sitting about idly, telling stories to each other. The tales were not seldom dissolute, often witty, sometimes exquisitely poetical, and always told in simple charming prose. The purpose of the story-tellers was to help each other to forget the duties from which they had turned aside, and stifle any sympathies they might have had for the terrible griefs of their friends and neighbours, who were dying a few miles away.

Chaucer substituted for the courtly Italian ladies and gentlemen who withdrew from fellowship with the world, as large a group as he could form of English people, of ranks widely differing, in hearty human fellowship together. Instead of setting them down to lounge in a garden, he mounted them on horseback, set them on the high road, and gave them somewhere to go and something to do. The bond of fellowship was not fashionable acquaintance and a common selfishness. It was religion; not, indeed, in a form so solemn as to make laughter and jest unseemly, yet, according to the custom of his day, a popular form of religion—the pilgrimage to the shrine of Thomas à Becket—into which men entered with much heartiness. It happened to be a custom which had one of the best uses of religion, by serving as a bond of fellowship in which conventional divisions of rank were, for a time, disregarded; partly because of the sense, more or less joined to religious exercise of any sort, that men are equal before God, and also, in no slight degree, because men of all ranks trotting upon the high road with chance companions, whom they might never see again, have been in all generations disposed to put off restraint, and enjoy such intercourse as might relieve the tediousness of travel.

Boccaccio could produce nothing of mark in description of his ten fine ladies and gentlemen. Some of them are pleasantly discriminated: that is all. The procession of Chaucer's pilgrims is the very march of man on the high road of life. "Forth, pilgrim, forth!" There are knight and squire, sailor and merchant, parson and doctor, monk and nun, the ploughman who tills the earth, the bailiff who garners its corn and the miller who grinds it.

Finally, Chaucer's Tales, except a moral and a religious treatise each in prose, are poems, which, though they include such incidents as were thought most merry in his time, excel the tales of the *Decameron* in their prevailing tone.

Notes

1. Lydgate's Prologue to the *Fall of Princes*, st. 41.
2. Lydgate's use of "Trophe" as a name for the story of Troylus and Criseyde, points to Criseyde's perfidy, and is related to *trope*, a turning. In modern Italian the word is *truffa*, "slight, roguery, roguish trick;" its synonyms being, according to the Delia Cruscan Vocabulary, *inganno* and *furberia*.
3. Morley, *English Writers*, 1890, iv., 223.
4. Sidney's *Defence of Poesie*.
5. Morley, 1890, iv., 35, 36.

—Henry Morley, *English Writers*, 1890,
Volume 5, pp. 83–85, 186–282

BERNHARD TEN BRINK "PRELUDE TO REFORMATION AND RENAISSANCE" (1893)

Bernhard Egidius Konrad ten Brink (1841–92) was a Dutch-born German philologist and scholar whose critical work on Chaucer in the 1870s and 1880s and whose critical edition of the General Prologue to *The Canterbury Tales* sparked a revival of interest in Chaucer's work. Like the preceding excerpt by Henry Morley, Brink's discussion focuses on two key Chaucerian texts—in this case, "The Knight's Tale" from *The Canterbury Tales* and *Troilus and Criseyde*—and examines how in his versions of these tales, Chaucer altered the original sources as found in Boccaccio. Any student exploring either of these works would do well to cite Brink, who has long been noted as one of the nineteenth century's most astute and insightful writers on Chaucer.

In describing the subject matter of "The Knight's Tale," Brink writes of "the love which seizes Palamon and Arcite with such violence, which dominates their entire being, separates them from their own past and strangely decides their fates; this love is Chaucer's proper theme." When comparing "The Knight's Tale" to its main source, Boccaccio's *Teseide*, Brink notes especially Chaucer's alterations to the characters in the text, as well as to how certain events—such as the lead-up to the battle between Palamon and Arcite—are presented.

Brink also focuses on the changes Chaucer makes to character in *Troilus and Criseyde*, especially to the three main characters of Troilus, Criseyde, and Pandarus. Like Morley before him, Brink is especially struck by the differences in the portrayal and representation of Pandarus between Chaucer's work and Boccaccio's *Il Filostrato*, noting that, "In this character the creative power of the poet is most strongly expressed." Brink concludes that, "This developed art . . . enables us to appreciate how much Chaucer owes to the Italian Renaissance, of which he may be called the first English pupil—not, indeed, as scholar, but as poet."

Anyone turning from the *Teseide* to the *Knight's Tale* feels that he is turning from a world of impossibilities to a world, if not of realities, at least of inner truth. The discrepancy between form and contents, between modern sentiment and ancient costume, between antique and mediaeval manners, between the tone of the classical epics and the love romances, appears suppressed. Chaucer's whole story breathes the atmosphere of a romantic tale; the whole action of all the participating personages belongs to a world which is composed indeed of very different elements—antique, Byzantine, mediaeval—and which is in an educational and historical sense full of gross anachronisms, but which bears, nevertheless, a uniform poetic impress— viz., the impress of a fantastic period of the Renaissance. This uniformity lies in the soul of the poet, whose many-sided and somewhat checkered education is concentrated in a living interest for what is thoroughly human, and in an increasing perception of the beautiful. Unlike Boccaccio, Chaucer makes no pretensions whatever to the epic style; yet his narrative nevertheless breathes a potent epic charm, because he does no violence to his nature, but writes just as his interest is excited, and either tarries lovingly upon details or makes summary contractions, sometimes letting the story progress with energy, sometimes branching out loquaciously into reflections and amplifications.

The sentimental temperature of the internal action has been considerably lowered by Chaucer—his characters are more realistic, and in the way they express their feelings the poet's own sovereign humor is frequently revealed. In the conflict between friendship and love, he puts friendship entirely in the background; the love which seizes Palamon and Arcite with such violence, which dominates their entire being, separates them from their own past and strangely decides their fates; this love is Chaucer's proper theme; this he presents with keen participation, and at the same time with a roguish wink. His Palamon is much more passionate and jealous, much less magnanimous than the corresponding character in Boccaccio, and Arcite also becomes much more positive and violent in his hands. Chaucer even puts the following words in his mouth against Palamon (line 319 ff.):

> "We stryve, as dide the houndes for the boon,
> They foughte al day, and yet hir part was noon:
> There cam a kyte, whil that they were so wrothe,
> And bar away the boon betwixt hem bothe.
> And tharfore at the kynge's court, my brother,
> Eche man for himself, ther is noon other."

Chaucer succeeded, nevertheless, in bringing out with the utmost sharpness the contrast made by Boccaccio between the melancholy Arcite and the choleric Palamon; but while Boccaccio openly prefers the first, placing him always in the foreground and making him much more interesting than his rival, Chaucer strives to be equally just to both, and is able by well-timed, happy little touches to show off their characters by contrasts, and to warm the heart of the reader for each. Certain motives which are, indeed, contained in the Italian poem—as, for example, the difference in the prayers offered by the two heroes before the tournament—are first worked out with their full effect by Chaucer.

Compared with her two lovers, Emilia is kept more in the background by Chaucer than by Boccaccio. But we see enough of this lovely figure—whose heart is first inflamed by the fight of the rivals, and who nevertheless does not know her own mind, but hesitates in uncertainty between the two till the last—to appreciate the love of Palamon and Arcite.

As we have already said, Chaucer relieved his Theseus of one part of his heroic role. We do not see him fighting against the Amazons for power and glory for his own sake; the only fight in which we see him engaged is in the interests of humanity. He is thus so much the better suited for the impartial role assigned to him by Chaucer. This role is of a double nature— on the one side Theseus represents a sort of earthly Providence, on the other he is a sort of privileged exponent of Chaucer's humor and worldly wisdom. Nor does he stand on the conventional ideal dignity or in the narrow limits of his Italian prototype; like an English knight of the fourteenth century, he can fly into a passion with great violence. But under a somewhat rude exterior he conceals an excellent heart and sturdy manhood, sound common sense and noble

humanity. He shows exquisite humor in his reflections on the fierce duel of
Palamon and Arcite:

> Behold for Godde's sake that sitteth above,
> See how they bleed! be they not well arrayed?
> Thus hath their lord, the god of love, them paid
> Their wages, and their fees for their service.
> And yet they weenen for to be full wise,
> That serven love, for aught that may befall.
> And yet is this the beste game of all,
> That she for whom they have this jollity
> Can them therefore as muchel thank as me.
> She wot no more of all this hote fare,
> By God, than wot a cuckoo or an hare.
> But all must be assayed hot or cold;
> A man must be a fool either young or old.[1]

The creations of even the most objective poets do not belie their family
resemblance and parentage. Shakspere's characters, with the exception of the
typical clowns,—and these, also, in their way,—are all clever; and most of
Chaucer's personages are inclined to philosophical reflections, in which they
like to mix up scholastic arguments and learned quotations with popular
phrases and old proverbs. In the *Knight's Tale* not only do Theseus and his
father Ægeus philosophize in this way, but also the two lovers, and perhaps in
a way not always adapted to their situation and rank. But we must not fail to
mention here that, in this respect, the poet knows how to draw the light and
shade, and in such things his works show a decided progress toward a greater
truthfulness of characterization.

Chaucer has bestowed a great amount of care on certain descriptive
portions of his poem. This is specially true of the delineation of the
amphitheater built by Theseus for the tournament, with its three temples for
Mars, Venus, and Diana; on this occasion the English poet differs from his
predecessor in a remarkable way. The description of the three temples and
the pictures or statues therein contained shows us on the one hand excellent
models of characteristic amplification, and on the other hand passages which
betray the influence of the Renaissance in its growing taste for plastic beauty.

The description of the tournament is given in a more general—we might
almost say, in a sort of typical—style, but is nevertheless extremely vivid.

But most exquisite is the manner in which Chaucer compensates us
for what was missing in his poem, viz., the enumeration and description
of the heroes going to the tournament at Athens. Instead of the long and

unattractive catalogue which occupies nearly the whole of the sixth book of the *Teseide,* he gives us, as it were for a symbolical characterization of both parties, two carefully executed portraits ornamented with romantic and even fabulous magnificence. Attention has been often called to the beauty of these delineations. Yet the main point seems to have been overlooked, viz., the inner relation between the appearance of King Lycurgus of Thrace and the character of Palamon, and between the character of Emetreus of India and Arcite. The appearance of Lycurgus is manly, imposing, even terrible; Emetreus unites the charm of youthful beauty with a lion-like glance and a voice of thunder.

And so everywhere there is seen a great delicacy of meaning, a conscious art, which is only fully revealed by a continued study, for it delights to hide itself under a certain gayety of tone, and in a simple though always vivid and significant diction.

By supplying so much of his own, Chaucer unavoidably sacrificed many of the beauties of his original. Whoever wishes to study Boccaccio's amiable manner, even in his imperfect creations, must read the original. But whoever wishes above all things for aesthetic pleasure, and yet still prefers the *Teseide* to the *Knight's Tale* after one or even several readings, deserves greater praise for his patience than for his literary taste. . . .

Boccaccio has created a thoroughly original and highly significant work from an episode in the Troy legend. But Chaucer succeeded in the still more astonishing performance of recreating the Italian's epic, without in any way essentially altering the story or moving the centre of interest, into a new and equally significant, perhaps a little less harmonious, but yet a deeper and richer poem *(Troilus and Cryseyde).*

The tragic element in Boccaccio's presentation seems to have attracted Chaucer most. The inclination to bring this element into greater prominence mainly determines the changed conception of the characters of the two lovers. In Boccaccio, Troilus is a somewhat weakly disposed young worldling, who has passed through the ordinary school of Amor. In Chaucer, he is of an equally weak disposition. But as the conception of young heroes of this stamp is generally formed in the German mind, so here, too, he is a kind of Hippolytus before the decisive moment when he perceives Cryseyde in the splendor of her beauty. Believing himself invulnerable to the tenderer passions, he amuses himself by mocking with sovereign humor the poor wretches who bear Amor's yoke. Then he is overtaken by his nemesis—with sudden violence he is smitten by the arrow of the god, who now pays him back for all the scorn he had previously heaped upon his servants. His whole being now seems changed; his mental elasticity is broken. Hope first inspires him again with new life, and the delight of love restores the young knight to his former vigor. But the sudden change of his fortunes, the pain of separation, the gnawing desire, the anxious fear, are almost more than his nature can endure. And when at last he learns that his beloved has turned out unfaithful, his first impulse is not the wish for vengeance, but the desire for death; and he seeks in battle for this delivering friend with not less ardor than for his deadly foe Diomedes.

The character of Griseida has changed more under Chaucer's hands than Troilus. As in Boccaccio, she is a widow, but this trait is brought much less into prominence than in the *Filostrato*. The English Cryseyde is more innocent, less experienced, less sensual, more modest, than her Italian prototype. What a multitude of agencies were needed to inflame her love for Troilus; what a concatenation of circumstances, what a display of trickery and intrigue, to bring her at last to his arms! We see the threads of the web in which she is entangled drawing ever closer around her; her fall appears to us excusable, indeed unavoidable. And if afterwards, after the separation, she does not resist the temptation of Diomedes—how is she accountable, if her mind is less true and deep than that of Troilus? how is she accountable, when that first fall robbed her of her moral stay? Only unwillingly, and with hesitation, does Chaucer tell of her unfaithfulness, as if he himself were not convinced of it, and only admitted the testimony of his authorities with reluctance. And he eagerly picks up points from Benoit's story which may tend to the exculpation of his heroine. She only gives her heart to Diomedes when touched with sympathy for the wounds he had received from Troilus; and her infidelity is immediately followed by repentance. She thus appears as the victim of Destiny, she, not less than Troilus; and the finger of Destiny is perceived by the poet at all the turning-points of his story. He does not go so far as to wish to deny the freedom of the human will; and yet the question, how it can exist along with the fixed and firmly locked concatenation of events and the omniscience of Providence is for him an insoluble riddle. He therefore makes his hero enunciate thoughts—in that supreme moment, when he is under the weight of his sudden misfortune and forebodes still worse disasters in the future—which Boethius himself uses in his prison. The reply of "Philosophy," which should explain the riddle and dispel the doubt, has not been given us. It is his tragic intensiveness that leads the poet into such depths, and makes him express ideas in sonorous verses, which agitated deeply the most eminent minds of the age—ideas which touch strongly on the doctrine of predestination, such as Wyclif conceived it in following Augustine and Bradwardine. Not unworthy of notice is this coincidence between the great poet at the height of his artistic maturity and the great reformer who was then in Lutterworth closing the great life-account of his thoughts and actions.

Fortune, "who executes the ordinances of Fate, and is the shepherdess placed by God over men," finds in Chaucer's poem an appropriate instrument in Pandarus. In this character the creative power of the poet is most strongly expressed. It is a work of such intellectual boldness and assurance as can only be found equaled in the productions of the greatest masters. The more innocent Cryseyde is, the more inexperienced and helpless Troilus is, the greater grows the role of him who brings them together. Pandarus is here properly adapted for a pimp, and his name has remained in language as a synonym for this word. He is an elderly gentleman with great experience of life, uncle to Cryseyde, not—as in Boccaccio—her cousin. It is the poet's intention to excuse, or at least to explain, the part he plays, by the intimate friendship between him and Troilus. How far one can go out of friendship— especially to high personages—in the domain of moral concessions, how hard it is to make a halt at the right point, Chaucer himself had probably found out well enough in his relations with John of Gaunt. He presents the matter in the most objective form, but yet in such a way that the aesthetic charm given to the character of Pandarus helps us over the impression of the offense to morality in the same way as in Shakspere's Falstaff. To the insipid and somewhat cynical views of an old worldling, Pandarus unites a good dose of *naivete*. And Chaucer makes him push his trade of pimp as naively as possible. When he sees Troilus, formerly the chivalrous and lusty youth, physically and morally sinking under the weight of an unexplained disease, and going actually to ruin, he feels for him the sincerest sympathy. And when, by close interrogation, he finds at length the cause of his disease, when he knows that it is solely his hopeless love for Cryseyde which is killing him, then he feels comforted and his decision is immediately made. In his opinion the whole business is not worth so much bother; but a man's mind is his kingdom; this man can be helped, and Pandarus is firmly determined to help him. Then he commences his work, and carries it triumphantly through with the greatest mastery. He has the necessary talents and the necessary liking for the play of intrigue, and knows well how to hide his roguishness under the mask of a somewhat rough good nature and a paternal recklessness.

These qualities unite excellently with the other traits lent to him by the poet. A strange combination of Polonius, Mercutio, and Sancho Panza, he is garrulous, rather vain of his homespun wisdom, but at the same time gifted richly with sound common sense and wit—he is a thoroughly humorous figure. And thus he answers the arrangement of the poem from every point of view. He is the lever that keeps the action in movement up to the climax;

'tis he who ties the tragic knot, and also he who brings the comic element into the tragedy. His practical views of life are everywhere opposed to the enthusiasm of Troilus, just as Sancho Panza forms the contrast to Don Quijote, and Jean de Meung to Guillaume de Lords; they help us pleasantly over the onesidedness of an idealism which ignores the world, and free us from the oppressive feeling with which we are satiated by the spectacle of a self-consuming passion. It is, indeed, remarkable how this contrast is sometimes so formed that Pandarus represents the superior wisdom as opposed to the shortsightedness of Troilus when dominated by his passion. It is not difficult to prove that for some scenes between the two Chaucer had in his mind's eye the figures of "Philosophy" and the imprisoned Boethius; for besides containing innumerable popular sayings and many tit-bits from different classical writers, the speeches of Pandarus also contain not a little from the *Consolatio.* The clever head thus knows how to take advantage of everything.

Finally, Pandarus is the figure who helps most to develop the dramatic life of the action. Just as Chaucer recognized the tragic elements in the story, so also did he perceive the dramatic possibilities which lay hidden in Boccaccio's tale. His whole genius must have forced him on to bring them to light and to make them paramount. Almost all the changes, transpositions, interpolations that he made in his original tend, if not exclusively, at least concurrently, in this direction. For, with him, all the wheels catch on to each other; one stroke strikes a thousand springs. It is mostly in the dramatic scenes, which are sometimes of a monologue sort, but are more often acted out between two or more persons, that the characters are evolved and the situations developed. The narrative portions, which serve to bind those dramatic scenes together, are of a comparatively subordinate importance. These scenes are set off with the most realistic truthfulness, even to the smallest detail, and work with the most instantaneous power; they are full of fire and force, making us shake with laughter, and rousing our interest to the highest pitch. In the fifth or last book the description falls off considerably. The situations are too unrefreshing, and partly also too undramatic. The Cryseyde-Diomedes episode gave the poet little pleasure. Troilus is condemned to passivity, and Pandarus also is *au bout de son Latin.* To make the terror of a tragic pathos die powerfully away was not Chaucer's affair. And every tragic fate is not adapted to the tragic muse. This subject was deficient in grandeur, in all that exalts. It is sufficient, therefore, if the art of the poet was able to ennoble the ambiguous or even the offensive elements of the story by the charm of a realistic, and at the same time highly poetical presentation.

How well does the poet here show himself equal to his task! If we consider the truthfulness in conception and expression, the delicacy of the motives, the well planned arrangement of the whole, and then the abundance of diversified ideas and situations, the astonishing wealth and pliancy of the language, which, in seeming to go at random, does accurate justice to every thought and situation, the broad and smoothly flowing rush of the stanza, which is responsive to every shade of feeling—then we shall thoroughly understand the wish that Chaucer sends forth along with his poem and towards its end: "And since there is so great diversity in English, and in writing of our tongue, so pray I God that none may copy thee wrongly, nor spoil the metre by false reading. And wherever thou art read or sung, God grant that thou be understood."

Troilus and Cryseyde was a book for learned and unlearned, for the poet and the philosopher, the courtier and the man of action. The "moral" Gower and the "philosophical" Strode, to whom the author addressed the work in an envoy, must have been delighted with it—each from his own point of view. But John of Gaunt was, perhaps, better able than they to appreciate the whole; and it was only natural that his family should hold the work in honor. We regard with pleasure the ornamental characters and the rich arabesques of that *Troilus* manuscript which John's grandson, the later conqueror of Agincourt, had in his possession when Prince of Wales; and, moreover, we recall with pleasure how this same poem, which delighted the hero in the time of his extravagant youth, also exercised a mighty influence on Shakspere, the great singer of this hero. Nor is it astonishing that Sidney, who pointed out with high enthusiasm the noble mission of poesie at a time when the great era of English poetry was in its morning glow, should have looked with admiration on the poet of *Troilus,* who, in such a benighted century, had followed the correct road so surely.

This developed art—compared with which the doings of most of his contemporaries appear childlike, or, indeed, childish, and even a work like *Sir Gawayne and the Green Knight* seems as the effort of a novice—enables us to appreciate how much Chaucer owes to the Italian Renaissance, of which he may be called the first English pupil—not, indeed, as scholar, but as poet.

Note

1. Tyrwhitt, *Canterbury Tales,* 1802–14, *Knight's Tale,* 942 ff.

—Bernhard ten Brink, "Prelude to Reformation and
Renaissance," *History of English Literature,*
tr. William Clarke Robinson, 1893, pp. 68–96

H. Simon "Chaucer a Wicliffite" (1868–94)

H. (Hugo) Simon (1828–97) was a prominent German scholar and author of the influential essay "Chaucer a Wicliffite." Like the works by Maurice and Foxe, Simon's essay examines Chaucer's relationship with John Wycliffe (c. 1320–84), an English theologian and church reformer and direct contemporary of Chaucer's whose ideas eventually helped to spark the Protestant Reformation. Wycliffe's followers, known as Lollards, were incredibly controversial in Chaucer's day, and the idea that Chaucer may have been a Lollard or at least sympathetic to Wycliffe's ideals has long been a hotly debated scholarly issue. Simon argues that Chaucer was, in fact, a Lollard, and offers several proofs of this. Simon points out the "biting acid of [Chaucer's] satire" directed at many members of the ecclesiastic class who accompany the pilgrimage to Canterbury; likewise, he mentions Chaucer's associations with individuals such as John of Gaunt, one of his primary patrons, who was also an important friend of Wycliffe's. Much of Simon's evidence rests on the fact that he believes Chaucer's character of the Parson in *The Canterbury Tales* was a Lollard, which Simon declares is evidenced several times in the text. Simon's argument is certainly compelling, but students are well advised that this matter is still debated by scholars, and many contemporary scholars staunchly disagree with Simon's assessment. Thus while Simon's work may be helpful to students examining Chaucer's association with Wycliffe or the Church in general, it is prudent for them to examine the other works in this volume on the issue and other reliable sources as well.

———

Notwithstanding the immense amount of work done, from the days of Caxton down to our own time, for the study of the second greatest English poet, and in spite of the meritorious publications of *Tyrwhitt, Warton, Sir Harris Nicolas, Bradshaw, Furnivall, Ten-Brink,* and others, many a problem concerning him remains still unsolved, and—considering the want of sure information about his life, and the fragmentary state in which we possess his principal work—this is not to be wondered at.

One of the questions to which no satisfactory answer has yet been given is: *What was Chaucer's relation to the Church?*

In commenting on Speght's *Life of Chaucer* Tyrwhitt *(Introd. Disc.[1])* speaking of the preface to the *Plowman's Tale,* makes the following remark: "Though he (Chaucer) and Boccace have laughed at some of the abuses of religion and the disorders of Ecclesiastical persons, it is quite incredible that either of them, or even Wicliff himself, would have railed at the whole government of the Church, in the style of the *Plowman's Tale.* If they had been disposed to such an attempt, their times would not have borne it; but it is probable that Chaucer, though he has been pressed into the service of Protestantism by some zealous writers, was as good a Catholic as men of his understanding and rank in life have generally been. The necessity of auricular Confession, one of the great scandals of Popery, cannot be more strongly inculcated than it is in the following *Persones Tale*." Professor *Seeley*[2] believes that the Plowman of the *Prologue* is, or is founded on, the ideal Piers Plowman; but with regard to Chaucer's relation to the Church, all the principal English Chaucerians seem to share Tyrwhitt's opinion. Of course, nobody can help perceiving the strong contrast between the *Parson's Tale* and Chaucer's well-known enmity against the clergy, as shown in many parts of the *Canterbury Tales,* but it has not, as yet, given rise to any suspicion, the generally accepted opinion being that Chaucer, bowed down by poverty, age, and infirmity, made his peace with the Church; and Mr Furnivall suggests that he got the lease of the little house in the garden of St Mary's chapel, Westminster, as a reward for his penitence and the *Parson's Tale*. I cannot help doubting this. An engraving of the lease has been published by the Society of Antiquaries. The monk Robert Hermodesworth, who was keeper of St Mary's, and made the contract with the consent of the abbot and convent, reserved a rent of £2 13s. *Ad.,*—but this was, I imagine, a high rent for a little house, at that time, when money had ten times more value than now[3],—and he expressly reserved for himself, or the monastery, the ordinary power in leases, to distrain, if Chaucer should be in arrear with any part of the payment of rent for the space of 15 days[4] Does that look like a reward?

A prominent German scholar, Professor *Pauli,* seems to hold an opinion opposed to that stated above. In his *Bilder aus Altenland* (VII. 209) he says that the great political and religious questions of his time didn't puzzle Chaucer like his friend Gower, or drive him to the opposite extreme; that, on the contrary, he saw perfectly clearly, and endeavoured to treat these questions objectively, according to his nature. The American Reed[5] says that Chaucer greeted Wicliffe's work of reform with joy; Gatschenberger[6] unconditionally calls him Wicliffe's intimate friend;—I don't know his reasons; to my direct inquiry I received no answer. Ebert, Kissner, and Hertzberg have, to my knowledge, not examined this point; Ten-Brink has not yet given his opinion; of his excellent *Chaucerstudien* only one volume is out.

To get at the truth, we must first recollect what was the public opinion in England, in the second half of the 14th century, with regard to the Pope and the Church. The reign of Edward III., in which Chaucer's youth and early manhood fell, is one of the grandest and most glorious periods in English history. During the preceding 300 years the gifted Normans had been completely amalgamated with the morally noble and bodily powerful Anglo-Saxons, and the nation thus grown into existence offered a rare image of health and strength[7]. A lively consciousness of their belonging to one another—which expressed itself in the common use of a rich and powerful, though still somewhat unwieldy, language,—had taken the place of the former hatred between the conqueror and the conquered, and, in consequence of the exercise of constitutional rights for above a hundred years, the brilliant victories in France, Spain, and Italy, the fast growing culture, the development of arts, and the increase of wealth produced by commerce, had intensified itself into a strong national feeling, into a high, but justified, self-esteem. In such times of spiritual and material progress, new ideas irresistibly make their way, overthrowing everything opposed to the general tendency—however venerable may be the traditions upon which it is founded. It was a time like that we have now in Germany; and even as the conflict with Popery has now broken out with us, so did it then rage in England; only much more furiously, because the bull *Unam sanctam* had soon been followed by the "Babylonian Exile"; the immoderate pretension of the popes, depending, as they did, on England's deadly foe, could not but be doubly felt, and the awful moral depravity of all the clergy, as well as the great Schism, must at last have filled the whole nation with contempt.

The general abhorrence vented itself in poems like the *Vision of Piers Plowman,* in the writings of Wicliffe, in Chaucer's *Canterbury Tales.* When, in this immortal work, we see Chaucer pour the biting acid of his satire on the representatives of Rome, and especially the friars, he most decidedly appears as the second and avenger of him who in his pamphlet *De otio et mendacitate*[8] had mercilessly exposed the foulest sore of the Roman Church. All the clerical and semi-clerical pilgrims are made to feel his weighty scourge; the only[9] exception—a brilliant one—is

The Parson

By the side of the repulsive characters of the friars and clergy and their officials, the Parson of the *Prologue* appears like a bright figure of sublime beauty. Nobody, perhaps, has read this delicate yet pithy picture without emotion; hundreds of times the Parson has been quoted as the ideal of Christian charity and humility, evangelical piety, unselfish resignation to the high calling of a pastor.

It cannot be that Chaucer unintentionally produced this bright image with so dark a background. Involuntarily it occurs to us, as to former critics, that a Wicliffite, perhaps the great reformer himself, sat for the picture; and the more we look at it, the more striking becomes the likeness. This observation

is not new; to say nothing of English critics, *Pauli* (Bilder, VII. 202) says
that the likeness of the Parson has decidedly Lollardish traces, and *Lechler*
(Iohann von Wiclif, I. 408 ff.) expressly declares it to be Wicliffe's portrait,
though he says, at the same time, that it is not only doubtful, but improbable,
that Chaucer should have sympathized with, or really appreciated, Wicliffe's
great ideas of and efforts for reform. Both scholars, however, principally refer
to the description in the *General Prologue;* but the Parson is mentioned also
in the *Shipman's* prologue and in that to the *Parson's Tale;* and it is exactly
in the latter two that we find the most striking proofs of his unquestionably
Wicliffite character.

The General Prologue

as a whole, and its description of the Parson, are the best-known parts of the
Canterbury Tales. I can, therefore, be brief about it.

In three passages it is stated with great emphasis that the Parson took his
doctrine from the gospel:

> v. 481. That Cristes gospel gladly[10] wolde preche.
> v. 498. Out of the gospel he tho wordes caughte.
> v. 527. But Cristes lore, and his apostles twelve
>   He taught, and ferst he folwed it himselve.

This was a pointedly distinguishing characteristic of a Wicliffite; for the
gospel was the foundation-stone of their doctrine and sermons. Wicliffe
himself was indefatigable in drawing general attention to it[11]; he and his
associates translated the Bible; with this sword and shield the great "Dr
Evangelicus" attacked the Roman dogmas and statutes, and refuted the
accusation of heresy; while the orthodox Catholic clergy never allowed
the Scripture to be looked upon as the only source of Christian truth, and,
especially in Chaucer's time, mostly moved on the barren sands of subtle
scholastic theology. In their sermons, instead of preaching the gospel, they
frequently amused their hearers by telling fables, romances, and jests.

Moreover, the Parson was a holy man; he made the gospel, as we know
from v. 528, his rule of thought and life. The whole prologue proves it; I only
quote two more passages:

> v. 479. But riche he was of holy thought and werk.
> v. 505. And though he holy were, and vertuous,

Wicliffe and his disciples distinguished themselves by an irreproachable
life; even their worst enemies were obliged to acknowledge that. How very
different were the orthodox clergy in this point! The secular clergy, indeed,

were better than the monks, but it was exactly among them that Wicliffe found many most zealous followers, and out of their number he recruited his itinerant preachers[12]

> v. 480   brings a new characteristic:
> He was also a lerned man, a clerk.

Wicliffe and his school did not indulge in the illusion that learning was unnecessary for holy purposes; they loved and cherished it; in the ranks of their antagonists reigned incapacity and ignorance.
Finally we have a peculiar outward mark:

> v. 495. Upon his feet, and in his hond a staf.

A chronicler of those times, Knighton, a prebendary of Leicester, says that the Wicliffite Aston "vehiculum equorum non requisivit, sed *pedestris effectus cum baculo incedens* ubique ecclesias regni—indefesse cursitando visitavit, ubique in ecclesiis regni praedicans."—*Hist. angl. Scriptores,* X. London, 1652, vol. III. col. 2658 f. (in Lechler, I. 421, Note). Th. Walsingham describes the associates of Wicliffe, "talaribus indutos vestibus de ruseto, insignum perfectionis amplioris, *incedens nudis pedibus,* qui suos errores iji populo ventilarent et palam ac publice in suis sermonibus praedicarent."—*Hist, angl,* ed. Riley, 1863, I. 324 (ibid.). And Pauli says (Bilder, VII. 243) that Archbishop *Courtenay* in 1382, after Wat Tyler's insurrection, when trying to pass the bill against heretics, expressly stated in his speech in parliament, that the Wicliffite itinerant clergy walked about in plain apparel of coarse reddish cloth, *barefoot* and *staff in hand.*

This contradicts at the same time the assumption that Wicliffe himself had been the Parson's prototype; for it was no peculiarity of his to walk about on foot and with a staff; in fact, he never was "a pore Persoun" (v. 478), for the King's favour amply provided for his wants.

The Shipmans Prologue
proves plainly that the Parson was a Wicliffite. When he earnestly, and yet mildly, rebukes the host for taking the Lord's name in vain, Henry Bailey exclaims derisively,

> v. 10. . . . . O Iankyn be ye there?
> Now, goode men, . . . herkneth me;
> I smel a *loller* in the wind,

and as the Parson makes no reply, he repeats the invective with a new oath, as if to try if he would put up with it:

> v. 13. Abideth for Goddes digne passion,
>   For we schul have a predicacion;
>   *This loller* heer wol[de] prechen us somwhat.

He does not "smell a loller" only, he sees him now, points him out! Even now
the Parson remains silent. This silence speaks very plainly. For the nickname
applied to him was in those times as generally used for "Wicliffite," as now,
for instance, "quaker" is for a member of the Society of Friends[13] The heaviest
charge imaginable that could be brought against any priest had been thrown
in the Parson's face: He was branded as a heretic!

For an orthodox clergyman it would have been impossible to put up with
this epithet; even the most peaceful and long-suffering must have resented it,
if only for the sake of the laymen who witnessed the scene, and who would,
in consequence of it, and if need were, have been able to cite the example of
an heretical priest as an excuse for their own heresy. But the Parson remained
silent. Here we may alter the proverb: *Qui tacet consentire videtur,* and say:
Qui tacet consentit, or in ordinary English phrase, "Silence gives consent."

There can be no doubt, I think, that the Shipman was of the same opinion,
as we may see by

> v. 16. 'Nay by my father soule! that schal he nat,'
>   Sayde the Schipman[14]; 'heer schal he naught
>   preche,
>   He schal no gospel glosen heer ne teche.
>   We levyn al in the gret God,' quod he.
>   'He wolde sowen som difficulte,
>   Or springen cokkil[15] in our clene corn.'

Three times he protests energetically against the Lollard's expected sermon[16],
against his 'gospel glosing,' that would only disturb the peaceful harmony of
the pilgrims (or the conformity of their faith). With the skilful remark "We
levyn al in the gret God," and the decided declaration that he himself is going
to tell a tale now, he prevents the pending quarrel.

Who used to 'glose' on the gospel in those times? Who grounded on it a
doctrine differing from that of the Church, and which was sure to produce
the most violent disputes, as soon as it was pronounced before orthodox ears?
Who else but the Wicliffites?

The Parson's Prologue

at last removes all doubt. The host, who only a short time before used very
passionate language against the Monk, and spoke "with rude speech and
bold" to the Nonne-priest, behaves very respectfully to the Parson. Not till

all the other pilgrims have told their tales, and then in a conciliatory manner, does he ask him:

> v. 20.   I pray to God to yeve him right good chaunce,
> That tellith us his tale lustily.

Had the quiet dignity of the Lollard made an impression upon him, or had he been struck by the idea that a religious persuasion enabling to suffer insults so quietly, could not be quite objectionable? 'Sir prest,' he says, perhaps still somewhat in doubt, owing to the Parson's peculiar dress,

> v. 22. . . . . artow a vicory?
> Or artow a persoun[17]? say soth, by thy fay.

Perhaps he thought he might yet have done the Parson wrong, and was anxious to give him an opportunity to clear himself of the suspicion of heresy by explaining his real station. But the Parson did not avail himself of the opportunity. What could he have said? Tell an untruth he would not; and to declare himself a Wicliffite in this society would have been neither safe nor advisable. The host, however, instead of growing impatient, as was his wont, passes over this painful silence, saying: "Be what thou be, ne breke thou nought oure play" (v. 24); he even flatters him:

> v. 27.   For trewely me thinketh by thy chier,
> Thou scholdist wel knyt up a gret matier.

Chaucer couldn't have paid more delicate homage to the Lollard, nor shown more forcibly the powerful influence of the Wicliffite preachers over the minds of others, than by the effect which the dignified bearing of the Parson had upon this unlicked cub of an innkeeper who had clumsily trodden on the corns of all the other tale-tellers, and even now could not quite renounce his innate coarseness. The Host asks for a fable. Now, at last, the Parson bursts out:

> v. 31.   Thou getist fable noon i-told for me,
> For Poul, that writeth unto Timothé,
> Repreveth hem that weyveth sothfastnesse,
> And tellen fables, and such wrecchednesse.
> 35.   Why schuld I sowen draf out of my fest,
> Whan I may sowe whete, if that me lest?
> For which I say, if that yow lust to hiere
> Morality and vertuous matiere,
> And thanne that ye will yeve me audience,
> 40.   I wot ful fayn at Cristis reverence

> Do yow plesaunce leful, as I can.
> But trusteth wel, I am a suthern man,
> I can not geste, rum, ram, ruf, by letter,
> Ne, God wot, rym hold I but litel better.
> 45.   And therfor, if yow lust, I wol not glose,
> I wol yow telle a mery tale in prose,
> To knyt up al this fest, and make an ende;
> And Ihesu, for his grace, wit me sende
> To schewe yow the way, in this viage,
> 50.   Of thilke parfyt glorious pilgrimage
> That hatte Ierusalem celestial.

To understand the whole weight of these words, we must read what Lechler (I. von W., I. 395 ff.) says about the Wicliffites' manner of preaching, as opposed to that of the Romish priests. Instead of preaching the word of God, the latter used to tell episodes from universal, or pieces of natural, history, the *Gesta Romanorum,* all sorts of legends, romances, and fables, from profane sources, as Ovid's *Metamorphoses,* sometimes even jokes, for the amusement, if not for the edification, of their hearers. The form of these sermons was as worldly as their contents, verses in alliteration and in rhyme alternating with each other. This sort of preaching Wicliffe denounced with all the fervour of his pious, evangelical heart, with all the power of his mighty word. . . .

Condemning . . . strictly the "fables and such wrecchednesse" told by the clerical pilgrims; choosing for his "meditacioun" the same subject that Wicliffe treated in his "Wicket"; following, as to form and contents, the rules given by Wicliffe in a hundred passages of his works; and doing all this not only in the spirit and manner, but partly with the very words, of the great reformer[18], the Parson, in my opinion, *declares himself as unequivocally to be a Wicliffitte, as it was possible to do without using the name.*

One essential point, however, is still to be mentioned: the Parson's citing the epistles of St Paul to Timothy in vindication of his refusal to tell a fable. In this condemnation, seemingly directed only against the tales of the clerical pilgrims, he, by this allusion, strikes the whole Roman Church a blow as with a club. For in no other part of the Bible do we find such emphatic, nay, imploring exhortations to cling to the gospel; nowhere is the necessity of the clergy's leading a holy life so forcibly urged; nowhere are the false doctrines and ecclesiastical statutes, as they were afterwards smuggled into Christianity from Rome, more decidedly condemned! What could be the use of all this, if he intended to follow the beaten paths of church-doctrine? There is no sense in it, except it be said to introduce some new doctrine; and it is perfectly in character with a Wicliffite whose master also, at the beginning of 1378, before the inquisition in Lambeth Hall, declared his readiness to retract as soon as they should convince him of the fallacy of his religious belief[19].

Not till the pilgrims consent to hear his meditacioun does the host invite him to begin, but to be brief[20].

I have now to discuss the seeming inconsistency in the Parson's taking part in the pilgrimage.

Canterbury had, besides the tomb of the "martyr," many attractions, even for a Wicliffite. Beda tells us that at the time of the Romans, one of the first, if not the first, Christian church in Britain had been erected in Canterbury and dedicated to St Martin; there Augustin with his 40 monks had first preached the gospel, and the first Christian King of England had there received holy baptism; there lay, besides Becket's, the remains of Augustin, Æthelbert, Stephen Langton (to whom England chiefly owes her Magna Charta), and the Black Prince, the idol of the nation, which only a short time before had been plunged in the deepest grief by his untimely death[21]. And must not Canterbury, as a far-famed place of pilgrimage, powerfully attract a Wicliffite preacher, whether he wished to see with his own eyes how the "miracles" were wrought, or hoped to find a particularly rich field of labour in a city so much frequented from religious reasons?

One thing more. All the historians of English literature agree in maintaining that the *Canterbury Tales* were intended to be a great picture of the morals and customs of those times, and by this they excuse many things that would otherwise throw a bad light on our poet. But what should we think of this picture, if, by the side of so many persons from all classes of society, and of such different intellectual standing, it wanted a representative of that prodigious world-known movement, which the great Wicliffe, according to directions from the King and parliament, first raised on a question of politics, but which, with internal necessity, soon reached the department of religion, and almost overthrew the government and doctrine of the Established Church? Even if Chaucer himself was no Wicliffite, such a character would have been indispensable in his immortal picture of his times.

But we can scarcely suppose that our poet was not heartily attached to Wicliffe's tenets. If such were the case, how could he depict the "Lollard"[22] so ideally, and, at the same time, display, as we have seen, such knowledge of the reformer's writings and way of thinking? His near connection with Wicliffe's protector, John of Gaunt, who took the learned professor as his assistant with him to Bruges, and, in 1377, delivered him, with peril to himself, from the hands of the court of inquisition at St Paul's; the interest he took in the political struggles of his nation; his journeys to Italy, in which he, perhaps, passed Avignon and closely saw the hierarchical Babel, but which, at any rate, made him acquainted with the more enlightened religious views of prominent Italians[23]; his high sense of right and truth; lastly, the beginning of the great Schism which deprived Popery of the last remnant of esteem;—all these tended to alienate him from the Pope and the Church, and make him join the great reformer with whom he was very probably personally acquainted[24].

All that his works seem to contain to the contrary, vanishes upon closer examination. Thus his A B C and the *Legende of Seint Cecile* are earlier productions[25]; his *Mother of God* and the *Story of Custance* are most likely so too; and it is doubtful whether the latter was meant to form part of the *Canterbury Tales*[26] After the pathetic, though 'bait-the-Jews,' legend of the Prioress, Chaucer lets fly his fantastic Sir *Topas,* as if to show that it deserves to be thrown into the same pot with the Fabliaux; he has not a single word of praise for this nor for the rest of the "fables and such wrecchednesse" told by the other Romists, and the Monk's water-fall of tragedies is roughly interrupted, while even the *Miller's* and *Reve's* tales are applauded. But the *friars are* treated more despicably than all the others. We have only to remember the place of abode assigned to them in hell, and the punishment they incur by their greediness (Sompnour's Prol. and Tale). A hatred so furious, a contempt passing so far beyond all bounds, are not to be explained by the Sompnour's irritation, nor by Chaucer's dislike of the clergy in general. They must have their peculiar cause. We need not look long for it: the synod held at Blackfriars, which, in May 1382, condemned Wicliffe's doctrines, consisted for the greatest part of friars; they preached against heresy, after the Whitsuntide procession; they published the resolutions of that synod at Oxford; they were the beadles who executed them; they helped to obtain Wicliffe's excommunication, and to condemn him to lose his place as professor[27].

That Chaucer himself takes part in the pilgrimage may be accounted for by what was said about Canterbury.

The words in the General Prologue:

> v. 17.   The holy blisful martir for to seeke;
>   That hem hath holpen whan that they were seeke;

are certainly the repetition of a current phrase rather than his own sincere opinion. He knew better what to think of a pilgrimage: he makes the Parson simply call it a 'viage' (v. 49, P. Prol.), and in the Wife's Prologue he has preserved for us a proverb still applicable in our own time:

v. 655. Who that buyldith his hous al of salwes,
       And pricketh his blynde hors over the falwes,
       And suffrith his wyf go seken halwes,
       Is worthy to ben honged on the galwes.

Nay, it is not impossible that the *Canterbury Tales* were intended to hold pilgrimage up to ridicule and contempt, by showing what loose and sinful people took part in it, and what unholy conversation used to shorten the way.

The Parson's Tale

The strictly orthodox contents of the Parson's Tale are consequently the only remaining proof that Chaucer either remained always true to the Roman creed, or at least died an orthodox Catholic. A man who could write a sermon on Penitence in which the necessity of auricular confession is so emphatically enjoined, cannot have been of Wicliffe's persuasion. True. But is it so sure that Chaucer did write it? That he wrote it as it now lies before us[28]? If it can be shown that there is a great dissimilarity between the parts, that some of them are dry, poor of thought, clumsy, yet full of paltry subtlety and hairsplitting, full of inconsistencies with the Parson's way of thinking, the Bible, common sense, and the scheme of the treatise, full of grammatical and stylistic mistakes; if the remainder can be shown to form a genuine, evangelical *De Poenitentia*—short, powerful, coming from, and going to, the heart, with a completely exhaustive and well worked-out scheme, containing nothing of auricular confession; if the probability of a falsification, and the fact that it was easy to perpetrate it, can alike be proved—will it then still be possible to adduce the Parson's Tale as a proof of Chaucer's orthodox catholicism? . . .

Conclusion

With the orthodox *Parson's Tale* falls the last and principal argument that can be adduced in favour of Chaucer's orthodoxy at his death. For the probability of his having been a Wicliffite I have given many reasons, but not all. I have yet to mention the great number and influence of the Wicliffites, according to the certainly unexceptionable testimony of *Walsingham* and *Knighton*[29]; further, the estrangement between Chaucer and his once intimate friend Gower, which has not as yet been sufficiently accounted for, but appears very natural, if we suppose Chaucer to have adopted Wicliffe's doctrines. For Gower, though a zealous advocate for the reformation of the clergy, was no friend to Wicliffe's tenets; we may see this in the second book of his Vox *Clamantis,* and in the Prologue to his *Confessio Amantis,* where he speaks contemptuously of "this new secte of Lollardie[30]." Finally, there is the beautiful poem "Fie fro the pres, and duelle with sothfastnesse," with the burden "And trouthe the schal delyver, hit ys no drede." This poem, apparently containing the gist of Chaucer's philosophy, agrees perfectly with Wicliffe's way of thinking, and does not show a trace of orthodox Catholicism. That Henry IV, the persecutor of the Lollards, let fall a ray of his favour on the poet who was then on the brink of the grave, does not contradict my assumption; for Henry was the son of the Duchess Blanche, whose death-song Chaucer sang; he was, too, the son of Chaucer's protector, John of Gaunt; and, besides, it is not necessary to suppose that the poet openly displayed his religious persuasion.

I'm perfectly aware that my solution of the problem: *What was Chaucer's relation to the Church?* is neither exhaustive nor undoubtedly correct. I did not intend it to be so; for in the present state of our knowledge of Chaucer, a thorough investigation of the question is not yet possible, since a great many other questions must first be answered, before we can be positively sure on this point. But so long as they are not answered in a sense contrary to my expectation, I think I may, without presumption, maintain, that in his heart at least

Chaucer was a Wicliffite.

Notes

1. Morris's edition, I. 249, Note 42.
2. Chaucer Soc. Rep. 1873.
3. "In 1350 the average price of a horse was 18s. 4c/.; of an ox, 1/. 4s. 6c/.; of a cow, 17s. *Id.;* of a sheep, 2s. 6c/.; of a goose, 9c/.; of a hen, 2c/.; of a day's labour in husbandry, 3d."—(Morris, *Introd. to Ch.*, Clar. Press Series ed., p. vii.)
4. Sir H. Nicolas, *Life of Ch.*, in Morris, I. 41.
5. *Engl. Lit., p.* 69.
6. *History of Engl. Lit.*, I. 157.
7. See Macaulay's brilliant paragraphs on this subject in his Introduction to his *Hist. of England*, i. 16–20, ed. 1849.
8. Wycliffe.
9. The companions of the Prioress seem to make an exception also; this semblance is, however, completely destroyed by what Tyrwhitt says in his *Introd. Disc.* (Morris, I. 209 ff., with the notes).
10. Tyrwhitt and the Six-Text edition have "trewely," which is, perhaps, still more convenient for a Wicliffite.
11. *Wicliffe's Festpredigten*, No. 22, fol. 42: Idem est spiritualiter pascere auditorium *sine sententia evangelica*, ac si quis faceret *convivium sine pane* . . . and: Quando praedicatum est ab apostolis *evangelium*, crevit ecclesia in virtute; sed modo ex defectu spirituals seminis, continue

decrescit.—*Vermischte Predigten,* No. 9, fol. 207: sacerdos Domini missus ad gignendum et nutriendum populum *verbo vitae.*—(In *Lechler,* I. v. Wiclif, I. 401.) See also p. 422.

12. *Pauli,* Bilder, VII. 202. *Lechler,* I. 417 f. and 421.

13. From Harl. Cat. 1666: "And to absteyne fro othes nedeles and unleful and repreve sinne by way of charite, is cause now why Prelates and sum Lordes sclaunderen men, and clepen hem *Lollardes,* Eretikes, etc." Tyrwhitt concludes (p. 349, note 1) that *'Lollard'* was a common invective. Common enough it was, no doubt; but to denote *a Wicliffite!* All the historical works on that time prove it. Thus Knighton says: "sicque a vulgo Wyclyf discipuli et Wicliviani sive *Lollardi* vocati sunt." (Lechler, II. 5, where some more passages to this effect are to be found, among which is one from an official document. See also p. 55!)

14. Only Arch. Seld. B. 14 has "Schipman"; 18 of the 22 MSS. of the Six-Text print have Squire, 3 Sompnour, 2 of them in opposition to the headings. It is, however, not material who spoke.

15. Lollium, in allusion to the then general derivation of "Lollard."

16. Some Protestants hate evangelical sermons as much as Papists do.

17. The Vicar took only the small tithes of his parish, while the great ones went to a Monastery or Cathedral, &c. The Parson or Rector took both the great and small tithes.

18. Concerning the expression "leful" (v. 41) see *Lechler,* II. 17 f., and especially *Knighton,* col. 2664.

19. *Pauli,* Bilder, VII. 227 ff.

20. The variations in the Six-Text print of the *Parson's Prologue* (Blank-Parson Link) are immaterial as to the sense; they all spring from mistakes of the copyists or their different orthography.

21. *Pauli,* Bilder, VII. "Canterbury."

22. I assume that the reader admits the validity of my evidence and argument.

23. *Kissner,* Ch. in seinen Beziehungen zur italienischen Literatur, p. 78.

24. What Wicliffe thought of the Schism we see in his work *De quatuor sectis novellis,* MS. 3929, fol. 225, col. 3: "Benedictus Deus, qui—divisit *caput serpentis,* movens unam partem ad aliam conterendam. . . . Consilium ergo sanum videtur permittere *has duaspartes Antichristi* semet ipsas destruere."—(In Lechler, I. 650.) That he dared to write thus, shows plainly what was the public opinion about Popery in England.

25. *Furnivall,* Recent Work at Chaucer (in *Mac Millan's Magazine,* 1873), p. 6: B. *ten-Brink,* Chaucerstudien, p. 130, and Tyrwhitt (Morris, I. 240).

26. I only mention one reason: *Man of Law's Prol.*, v. 90, "I speke in *prose* and let him rymes make;" the Story of Custance being *in rhyme.* To solve the difficulty by supposing v. 90 to mean "I make no rhymes myself, but I will tell you a rhymed story of his," is impossible, for he *does* make rhymes in his *Prologue;* and, besides, if he was going to tell one of Chaucer's rhymed stories, he could not have said: "Though I come after him *with hawebake*" (v. 95).

27. *Pauli,* Bilder, VII. 242 ff.

28. The title it bears according to Tyrwhitt (Morris's ed., I. 251) in some MSS.: "Tractatus de Poenitentia pro fabula, ut dicitur, Rectoris," may possibly be meant to convey a doubt.

29. *Walsingham,* Hist, angl., II. 188 (ed. Riley), "1389: . . . Lollardi—in errorem suum plurimos seduxerunt." *Knighton,* V. col. 2644: "Mediam partem populi, aut majorem partem, sectae suae adquisiverunt." Ibid., col. 2666: "Secta ilia in maximo honore illis diebus habebatur, et in tantum multi-plicata fuit, quod vix duos videres in via, quin alter eorum discipulus Wicliffe fuerit."

30. Pauli's Introd. Essay to his edition of Gower's works. He also touches the altered relation between the two poets, but says that it was the consequence of political differences.

—H. Simon, "Chaucer a Wicliffite," *Essays on Chaucer,*
1868–94, pp. 229–46

JOHN CHURTON COLLINS (1895)

John Churton Collins (1848–1908) was a prominent English literary critic. In the following excerpt, students will find a useful discussion of Chaucer's waxing and waning fame. Collins examines Chaucer's popularity from the end of the Middle Ages through the Victorian period, noting his surprise that while Chaucer was not particularly admired in the eighteenth century, only fifty years later he is considered, along with Shakespeare and Milton, one of the three greatest English authors of all time. Students may find it interesting to place the other excerpts in this volume into Collins's timeline and see if what he notes holds true.

We have often thought that a curiously interesting book might be written on the posthumous fortune of poets. In the case of prose writers, the verdict of the age which immediately succeeds them is, as a rule, final. Their reputation is subject to few fluctuations. Once crowned, they are seldom deposed;

once deposed, they are never reinstated. Time and accident may affect their popularity, but the estimate which has been formed by competent critics of their intrinsic worth remains unmodified. How different has been the fate of poets! Take Chaucer. In 1500 his popularity was at its height. During the latter part of the sixteenth century it began to decline. From that date till the end of William III. 's reign—in spite of the influence which he undoubtedly exercised over Spenser, and in spite of the respectful allusions to him in Sidney, Puttenham, Drayton, and Milton—his fame had become rather a tradition than a reality. In the following age the good-natured tolerance of Dryden was succeeded by the contempt of Addison and the supercilious patronage of Pope. Between 1700 and 1782 nothing seemed more probable than that the writings of the first of England's narrative poets would live chiefly in the memory of antiquarians. In little more than half a century afterwards we find him placed, with Shakspeare and Milton, on the highest pinnacle of poetic renown.

—John Churton Collins, *Essays and Studies*, 1895, pp. 106–07

W.P. Ker "The Poetry of Chaucer" (1895)

A prominent Scottish literary scholar and essayist, W.P. (William Paton) Ker (1855–1923) adds his voice to the common Victorian discussion regarding Chaucer and his sources, a topic discussed by Morley and Brink in previous extracts and in the Peter Borghesi excerpt from 1903. In an article from *The Quarterly Review* about Skeats's edition of Chaucer's work, Ker alters the tone of this discussion, noting that such research into source origins is only fruitful when speaking of an author like Chaucer "[i]f the result . . . is to bring out Chaucer's independence more in relief by the subtraction of his loans, and to prove the limitations of this historical method when it is made to confront the problems of original and underived imagination."

Ker reinforces this point by discussing several of Chaucer's works and the relationship these works have to their sources. Ker acknowledges the debt that Chaucer's *House of Fame* owes to Dante's *Divine Comedy*, but hastens to add that the *House of Fame* is "a poem inexplicable by any references to the poem from which it was borrowed, a poem as different from the *Divine Comedy* as it is possible to find in any Christian tongue." Ker's point, which students working on this particular topic should find helpful, is that Chaucer may have been inspired by other works, but that his poems, far from being translations or rehashings of earlier works, are significant poetic achievements in their own right.

After *House of Fame*, Ker turns his attention to *Troilus and Criseyde* and "The Knight's Tale." Ker writes, "Chaucer is always at his best when he is put on his mettle by Boccaccio." The sections comparing these two works to Boccaccio's originals are best read along with the excerpts by Morley, Brink, and Borghesi.

Ker concludes his discussion on Chaucer's poetry by addressing *The Canterbury Tales* in general and several entries in particular, including "The Man of Law's Tale" and "The Tale of Melibee (Melibeus)". These discussions may prove especially useful to students, as neither work has been discussed in other entries in this volume.

It is easily possible to be tired of the historical criticism that plies its formulas over the sources and origins of poetry, and attempts to work out the spiritual pedigree of a genius. It cannot, however, be seriously argued that enquiries of this sort are inept in the case of Chaucer, whose obligations to his ancestors are manifest in every page, not to speak of those debts that are less obvious. If the result, in most instances, is to bring out Chaucer's independence more in relief by the subtraction of his loans, and to prove the limitations of this historical method when it is made to confront the problems of original and underived imagination, there is no great harm done, but the contrary. It is the result to be looked for.

These volumes of Chaucer (Skeat's edition) present one interesting case where the enquiry into origins has scored one conspicuous success, and in an equal degree has found its limits and proved its inability, after all, to analyse the inexplicable. The *House of Fame* has been subjected to laborious study, and one important set of facts has been brought to evidence about it. The relation of the poem to the *Divine Comedy* has been considered and discussed by Sandras, Ten Brink, and other scholars, and is here explained by Mr. Skeat. The proof is decisive. There is no remnant of doubt that Chaucer had been reading Dante when he wrote the *House of Fame;* that he derived from the suggestions of Dante the images and the pageants of his dream, and many of the phrases in which it is narrated. Here, however, the proof comes to an end. The historical enquiry can do no more. And when all is said and done, the *House of Fame* still stands where it stood—a poem inexplicable by any references to the poem from which it was borrowed, a poem as different from the *Divine Comedy* as it is possible to find in any Christian tongue. The true criticism of the poem has to begin where the historical apparatus leaves off. If its quiddity is to be extracted, the *House of Fame* must be taken, first of all, as the poem it is, not as the poem from which it is derived.

It is in this way that the works of Chaucer afford the most delightful tests of ingenuity and of the validity and right use of the methods of criticism. No task is more dangerous for a critic who has his own private device for the solution of all problems. The problems in Chaucer are continually altering, and the ground is one that calls for all varieties of skill if it is to be tracked out and surveyed in all its changes of level.

The appearance of Chaucer's works at last in this satisfactory and convenient form, with the blemishes of the vulgate texts removed, and everything made easy for every one who is not too anxious about his ease, can hardly fail to call out some new devotion to the great master of stories. Chaucer is always being discovered, like Homer, Shakespeare, and the book of Baruch; and his discoverers are not to be pitied, though one may be inclined to ask them to deal gently with their ignorant friends, and not to be vexed because of the obdurate who say that Chaucer was a hack and a translator.

After the first discovery of all, there is none more pleasant than the discovery how little Chaucer's genius is exhausted in the *Canterbury Tales,* and how far his great book is from being his greatest poem, or from representing his genius to the full. It is only by looking at the *Canterbury Tales* from the vantage-ground of the other works that the magnitude of Chaucer can be in any way estimated aright.

The *Canterbury Tales,* which include so much, do not include the whole of Chaucer. Some of his masterpieces are there, and there is nothing like the Prologue anywhere else; but outside of the group of the Tales is to be found the finest work of Chaucer in the more abstract and delicate kind of poetry Anelida'; the most massive and the richest of his compositions, which is *Troilus;* and the most enthralling and most musical of all his idylls, in the Prologue to the *Legend of Good Women,* with the balade of Alcestis, 'sung in carolwise':

Hyd, Absolon, thy gilte tresses clere.

The poem of 'Anelida and the false Arcite,' it may be suspected, is too often and too rashly passed over. It has a good deal of the artificial and exquisite qualities of the court poetry; it appears to be wanting in substance. Yet for that very reason the fineness of the style in this unfinished poetical essay gives it rank among the greater poems, to prove what elegance might be attained by the strong hand of the artist, when he chose to work in a small scale. Further, and apart from the elaboration of the style, the poem is Chaucer's example of the abstract way of story telling. It is the light ghost of a story, the antenatal soul of a substantial poem. The characters are merely types, the situation is a mathematical theorem; yet this abstract drama, of the faithless knight who leaves his true love for the sake of a wanton shrew, is played as admirably, in its own way, as the history of the two Noble Kinsmen, or the still nobler Troilus.

It is difficult to speak moderately of Chaucer's *Troilus*. It is the first great modern book in that kind where the most characteristic modern triumphs of the literary art have been won; in the kind to which belong the great books of Cervantes, of Fielding, and of their later pupils,—that form of story which is not restricted in its matter in any way, but is capable of taking in comprehensively all or any part of the aspects and humours of life. No other mediaeval poem is rich and full in the same way as *Troilus* is full of varieties of character and mood. It is a tragic novel, and it is also strong enough to pass the scrutiny of that Comic Muse who detects the impostures of inflated heroic and romantic poetry. More than this, it has the effective aid of the Comic Muse in that alliance of tragedy and comedy which makes an end of all the old distinctions and limitations of narrative and drama.

The original of *Troilus,* the *Filostrato* of Boccaccio, is scarcely more substantial in its dramatic part, though it is longer and has a more elaborate plot, than Chaucer's 'Anelida.' The three personages of the one poem are not more definite than the three of the other. The *Filostrato* is not merely 'done into English' in Chaucer's *Troilus and Criseyde.* Chaucer has done much more than that for the original poem; he has translated it from one form of art into another,—from the form of a light romantic melody, vague and graceful, into the form of a story of human characters, and of characters strongly contrasted and subtly understood by the author. The difference is hardly less than that between the Italian novels and the English tragedies of *Romeo* or *Othello,* as far at least as the representation of character is concerned. Chaucer learned from Boccaccio the art of construction: the design of the *Filostrato* is, in the main outline, the design of Chaucer's *Troilus and Criseyde;* but in working out his story of these 'tragic comedians,' the English poet has taken his own way, a way in which he had no forerunners that he knew of, and for successors all the dramatists and novelists of all the modern tongues.

No other work of Chaucer's has the same dignity or the same commanding beauty. It would be difficult to find in any language, in any of the thousand experiments of the modern schools of novelists, a story so perfectly proportioned and composed, a method of narrative so completely adequate. Of the dramatic capacities of the original plot, considering the use made of it in Shakespeare's *Troilus and Cressida,* there is little need to say anything. Boccaccio chose and shaped the plot of his story with absolute confidence and success; there is nothing to break the outline. The general outline is kept by Chaucer, who thus obtains for his story a plan compared with which the plan of Fielding's greatest novel is ill-devised, awkward, and irregular; while the symmetry and unity of Chaucer's story is compatible with a leisure and a profusion in the details not less than Shakespeare's, and in this case more suitably bestowed than in Shakespeare's *Troilus*. There is nothing in the art of any narrative more beautiful than Chaucer's rendering of the uncertain faltering and transient moods that go to make the graceful and mutable soul of Cressida; nothing more perfect in its conception and its style than his way of rendering the suspense of Troilus; the slowly-rising doubt and despair keeping pace in the mind of Troilus with the equally gradual and inevitable withdrawal and alteration of love in the mind of his lady, till he comes to the end of his love-story in Cressida's weak and helpless letter of defence and deprecation.

Besides the triumph of art in the representation of the characters, there are more subsidiary beauties in *Troilus* than anywhere else in Chaucer; as in the effective details of the less important scenes, the ladies reading the romance of Thebes together, the amateur medical advice for the fever of Troilus, the visit of Helen the queen, the very Helen of the *Odyssey*, to show kindness to Troilus in his sickness. There are other poems of Chaucer, the *Knight's Tale* for instance, in which Chaucer relies more consistently throughout on the spell of pure romance, without much effort at strong dramatic composition. But it is in *Troilus*, where the art of Chaucer was set to do all its utmost in the fuller dramatic form of story, that the finest passages of pure romance are also to be found; in *Troilus*, and not in the story of Palamon and Arcite, or of Constance, or of Cambuscan, or any other. At least it may be imagined that few readers who remember the most memorable passage of pure narrative in *Troilus*, his entrance into Troy from the battle without, will be inclined to dispute the place of honour given to it by Chaucer's last disciple, in his profession of allegiance in the *Life and Death of Jason*. The 'tragedie' of the lovers is embellished with single jewels more than can be easily reckoned; with scenes and pictures of pure romance; with the humours and the 'ensamples' and opinions of Pandarus; with verses of pure melody, that seem to have caught beforehand all the music of Spenser:

> And as the newe abaysshed nightingale
> That stinteth first when she biginnith singe;

with many other passages from which the reader receives the indefinable surprise that is never exhausted by long acquaintance, and that makes the reader know he is in the presence of one of the adepts. But all these single and separable beauties are nothing in comparison with the organic and structural beauty of the poem, in the order of its story, and in the life of its personages.

Chaucer is always at his best when he is put on his mettle by Boccaccio. He is well enough content in other instances to borrow a story ready made. In his appropriation of Boccaccio he is compelled by his sense of honour to make something as good if he can, in a way of his own. He learns from the Italian the lesson of sure and definite exposition; he does not copy the Italian details or the special rhetorical prescriptions. The story of *Palamon and Arcite*, on which Chaucer appears to have spent so much of his time, is a different sort of thing from *Troilus*; the problems are different; the result is no less fortunate in its own way. The *Teseide*, the original of the *Knight's Tale*, is reduced in compass under Chaucer's treatment, as much as the *Filostrato* is strengthened and enlarged. The *Teseide*, unlike the *Filostrato*, is an ambitious experiment, no less than the first poem in the solemn procession of modern epics according to the rules of the ancients; an epic poem written correctly, in twelve books, with epic similes. Olympian machinery, funeral games, and a catalogue of the forces sent into the field, all according to the best examples. Chaucer brings it down to the form of a romance, restoring it, no doubt, to the form of Boccaccio's lost original, whatever that may have been; at any rate to the common scale of the less involved and less extravagant among the French romances of the twelfth or thirteenth century. For Boccaccio's *Theseid*, with all its brilliance, is somewhat tedious, as an epic poem may be; it is obviously out of condition, and overburdened in its heroic accoutrements. The *Knight's Tale* is well designed, and nothing in it is superfluous. There are some well-known instances in it of the success with which Chaucer has changed the original design: reducing the pompous and unwieldy epic catalogue of heroes to the two famous contrasted pictures 'in the Gothic manner', the descriptions of Lycurgus and Emetreus, and rejecting Boccaccio's awkward fiction in the account of the prayers of Palamon, Arcita, and Emilia. But the most significant part of Chaucer's work in this story is the deliberate evasion of anything like the drama of *Troilus and Cressida*.

The *Knight's Tale* is a romance and nothing more; a poem, a story, in which the story and the melody of the poem are more than the personages. Chaucer saw that the story would not bear a strong dramatic treatment. The Comic Muse was not to be bribed: neither then, nor later, when the rash experiment of Fletcher in the *Two Noble Kinsmen* proved how well the elder poet was justified in refusing to give this story anything like the burden of *Troilus*. The Lady Emilia, most worshipful and most shadowy lady in the romance, is too cruelly put to the ordeal of tragedy: the story is refuted as soon as it is made to bear the weight of tragic passion or thought. Chaucer, who found the story of *Troilus* capable of bearing the whole strength of his genius, deals gently with the fable of the *Theseid*; the characters are not brought forward;

instead of the drama of *Troilus,* there is a sequence of pictures; the landscapes of romance, the castles and the gardens, are more than the figures that seem to move about among them. There is pathos in the *Knight's Tale,* but there is no true tragedy. How admirably Chaucer tells the pathetic story may be seen at once by comparing the meeting of Palamon and Arcita in the wood with the corresponding scene in Fletcher's play:—

> Ther nas no good day, ne no saluing;
> But streight, withouten word or rehersing,
> Everich of hem halp for to armen other,
> As freendly as he were his owne brother.

This simplicity of style is the perfection of mere narrative, as distinguished from the higher and more elaborate forms of epic poetry or prose. The situation here rendered is one that does not call for any dramatic fullness or particularity: the characters of Palamon and Arcita in any case are little qualified for impressive drama. But the pathos of the meeting, and of the courtesy rendered to one another by the two friends in their estrangement, is a pathos almost wholly independent of any delineation of their characters. The characters are nothing: it is 'any friend to any friend,' an abstract formula, used by Chaucer in this place with an art for which he found no suggestion in Boccaccio, nor obtained any recognition from Fletcher. In the *Teseide* the rivals meet and argue with one another before the duel in which they are interrupted by Theseus; in the play of the *Two Noble Kinsmen* they converse without any apparent strain. In Chaucer's poem the division between them is made deeper, and indicated with greater effect in four lines, than in the eloquence of his Italian master or his English pupil.

Such is the art of Chaucer in the *Knight's Tale:* perfect in its own kind, but that kind not the greatest. It needs the infinitely stronger fable of his *Troilus and Criseyde* to bring out the strength of his imagination. *Troilus,* to use a familiar term of Chaucer's own, cannot but 'distain' by comparison the best of the *Canterbury Tales. Troilus* is not a romance, but a dramatic story, in which the characters speak for themselves, in which the elements that in the *Canterbury Tales* are dissipated or distributed among a number of tales and interludes are all brought together and made to contribute in due proportion to the total effect of the poem. In the *Canterbury Tales* the comic drama is to be found at its best outside of the stories, best of all in the dramatic monologues of the 'Wife of Bath' and the 'Pardoner.' It takes nothing away from the glory of those dramatic idylls to maintain that Chaucer's Pandarus belongs to a higher and more difficult form of comic imagination. The 'Wife of Bath' and the 'Pardoner' are left to themselves as much, or very nearly as much, as the 'Northern Farmer' or 'Mr. Sludge the Medium.' Pandarus has to acquit himself as well as he may on the same stage as other and more tragic personages, in a story where there are other interests besides that of his humour and his proverbial philosophy. This is not a question of tastes and preferences; but a question of the distinction between different kinds and varieties of narrative poetry. It is open to any one to have any opinion he pleases about the value of Chaucer's poetry. But the question of value is one thing; the question of kinds is another. The value may be disputed indefinitely; the kind may be ascertained and proved. The kind of poetry to which *Troilus* belongs is manifestly different from that of each and all of the *Canterbury Tales*, and manifestly a richer and more fruitful kind; and for this reason alone the poem of *Troilus* would stand out from among all the other poems of its author.

The problems regarding Chaucer's methods of composition are inexhaustible. They are forced on the attention, naturally, by this collected edition of his writings, which makes the contradictions and paradoxes of Chaucer's life more obvious and striking than they ever were before. *Boece* and *Troilus*, which are mentioned together by Chaucer himself, are here associated in the same volume: the *Treatise on the Astrolabe* goes along with the *Legend of Good Women*. Of all the critical problems offered by this great collection of the works of a great master there is none more fascinating and none more hopeless than the task of following his changes of mood and his changes of handling. *Troilus* is followed by the *House of Fame*, a caprice, a fantasy, the poet's compensation to himself for the restraint and the application bestowed on his greater poem. 'Ne jompre eek no discordant thing yfere,' is the advice of a literary critic in the book of *Troilus* itself: the critic knew the mediaeval temptation to drag in 'termes of physik' and other natural sciences, whether they were required or not. The *House of Fame* is an indulgence, after *Troilus*, in all the mediaeval vanities that had been discouraged by the ambitious and lordly design of that poem. Allegory, description, painted walls, irrelevant science, pageants and processions of different kinds, everything that the average mediaeval book makes play with,—these are the furniture of the *House of Fame*; and, in addition to these and through all these, there is the irony of the dream, and the humorous self-depreciation which gives to the *House of Fame* the character of a personal confession. It is one of the most intimate as well as one of the most casual of all his works; a rambling essay in which all the author's weaknesses of taste are revealed, all his fondness for conformity with his age and its manners, while at the same time there is no other poem of Chaucer's so clear and so ironical in its expression of his own view of himself. On the one hand, it is related to all the dreariest and stalest mediaeval fashions; on the other, to the liveliest moods of humorous literature. The temper of Chaucer in his tedious description of the pictures from the *Aeneid*, in the first book, is in concord with all the most monotonous and drawling poets of the mediaeval schools; his wit in the colloquy with the eagle in the second book is something hardly to be matched except in literature outside the mediaeval conventions altogether. The disillusion of the poet, when he imagines that he is going to heaven to be 'stellified,' and is undeceived by his guide, is like nothing in the world so much as the conversation with Poseidon in Heine's *Nordsee*, where the voyager has his fears removed in a manner equally patronising and uncomplimentary.

The contradictions and the problems of the *House of Fame*, in respect of its composition and its poetical elements, are merely those that are found still more profusely and more obviously in the *Canterbury Tales*. There is little need for any one to say more than Dryden has said, or to repeat what every reader can find out for himself, about the liveliness of the livelier parts of the collection. The Prologue, the Interludes of conversation and debate, the Host's too masterful good humour, the considerate and gentle demeanour of the Monk, the Shipman's defence of true religion, the confessions of the Wife of Bath and the Pardoner, the opinions of the Canon's Yeoman,—of all this, and of everything of this sort in the book, it is hopeless to look for any terms of praise that will not sound superfluous to people with eyes and wits of their own. It is not quite so irrelevant to enquire into the nature of the separate tales, and to ask how it is that so many of them have so little of the character of Chaucer, if Chaucer is to be judged by the Prologue and the Interludes.

Some of the Tales are early works, and that explains something of the mystery. Still the fact remains that those early works were adopted and ratified by Chaucer in the composition of his great work, when he made room for the Life of St. Cecilia, and expressly set himself to bespeak an audience for the gravity of *Melibeus*. Here again, though on a still larger scale, is the contradiction of the elements of the *House of Fame*, the discord between the outworn garment of the Middle Ages and the new web from which it is patched.

There is nothing in all the *Canterbury Tales* to set against the richly varied story of *Troilus and Cressida*. There are, however, certain of the *Canterbury Tales* which are not less admirable in respect of mere technical beauty of construction, though the artistic skill is not shown in the same material as in *Troilus*. The *Knight's Tale* preserves the epic, or rather the romantic unities of narrative, as admirably as the greater poem. The *Nun's Priest's Tale* is equally perfect in its own way, and that way is one in which Chaucer has no rival. The story of Virginia, the story of the fairy bride, the story of the revellers who went to look for Death, and many others, are planned without weakness or faltering in the design. There are others which have an incurable fault in the construction, a congenital weakness, utterly at variance from the habit of Chaucer as shown elsewhere, and from the critical principles which he had clearly mastered for his own guidance in his study of Boccaccio.

The *Man of Law's Tale,* the story of Constance, is a comparatively early work, which Chaucer apparently did not choose to alter as he altered his first version of *Palamon and Arcite.* At any rate, the story declares itself as part of a different literary tradition from those in which Chaucer has taken his own way with the proportions of the narrative. The story of Constance has hardly its equal anywhere for nobility of temper; but in respect of unity and harmony of design it is as weak and uncertain as the *Knight's Tale* is complete, continuous, and strong. Chaucer, whose modifications of Boccaccio are proof of intense critical study and calculation of the dimensions of his stories, here admits, to rank with his finished work, a poem beautiful for everything except those constructive excellences on which he had come to set so much account in other cases. The story of Constance follows the lines of a dull original. It has the defects, or rather the excesses, of most popular traditional fairy-tales. Chaucer, who afterwards refused to translate Boccaccio literally, here follows closely the ill-designed plot of a writer who was not in the least like Boccaccio. The story repeats twice over, with variations in detail, the adventure of the princess suffering from the treacherous malice of a wicked mother-in-law; and, also twice over, her voyage in a rudderless boat; the incident of her deliverance from a villain, the Northumbrian caitiff in the first instance, the heathen lord's steward in the second, is also repeated; while the machinery of the first false charge made against Constance by the Northumbrian adversary goes some way to spoil the effect of the subsequent false charge made by the queen-mother, Donegild. The poem has beauties enough to make any one ashamed of criticism; yet it cannot be denied that its beauties are often the exact opposite of the virtues of Chaucer's finished work, being beauties of detail and not beauties of principle and design. The *Man of Law's Tale* with all the grace of Chaucer's style has also the characteristic unwieldiness of the common mediaeval romance; while the *Knight's Tale,* which is no finer in details, is as a composition finished and coherent, with no unnecessary or irrelevant passages.

Besides the anomalies of construction in the *Canterbury Tales,* and not less remarkable than the difference between the neatness and symmetry of the *Knight's Tale* and the flaccidity of the *Man of Law's,* there is an anomaly of sentiment and of mood. *Melibeus* may be left out of account, as a portent too wonderful for mortal commentary: there are other problems and distresses in the *Canterbury Tales,* and they are singular enough, though not altogether inexplicable or 'out of all whooping,' like that insinuating 'little thing in prose' by which Sir Thopas was avenged on his detractors.

The *Knight's Tale* is an artifice, wholly successful, but not to be tampered with in any way, and above all things not to be made into a drama, except for the theatre of the mind. Chaucer refused to give to Emilie and her rival lovers one single spark of that imaginative life which makes his story of *Troilus* one of the great narrative poems of the world, without fear of comparison with the greatest stories in verse or prose. By the original conception of the *Knight's Tale,* the Lady Emilie is forbidden to take any principal part in the story. This is an initial fallacy, a want of dramatic proportion, which renders the plot impossible for the strongest forms of novel or of tragedy. But Chaucer saw that the fable, too weak, too false for the stronger kind, was exactly right when treated in the fainter kind of narrative which may be called romance, or by any other name that will distinguish it from the order of *Troilus,* from the stronger kind of story in which the characters are true.

In some of the other Tales the experiment is more hazardous, the success not quite so admirable. What is to be said of the *Clerk's Tale?* what of the *Franklin's?* That the story of Griselda should have been chosen by the author of *Troilus* for an honourable place in his *Canterbury Tales* is almost as pleasant as the publication of *Persiles and Sigismunda* by the author of *Don Quixote.* Chaucer had good authority for the patience of Griselda; by no author has the old story been more beautifully and pathetically rendered, and his 'Envoy' saves him from the suspicion of too great solemnity: but no consideration will ever make up for the disparity between the monotonous theme and the variety of Chaucer's greater work, between this formal virtue of the pulpit and the humanities outside. In the *Franklin's Tale* again, in a different way, Chaucer has committed himself to superstitions of which there is no vestige in the more complex parts of his poetry. As Griselda represents the abstract and rectilinear virtue of mediaeval homilists, the *Franklin's Tale* revolves about the point of honour, no less gallantly than Prince Prettyman in the *Rehearsal.* The virtue of patience, the virtue of truth, are there impaled, crying out for some gentle casuist to come and put them out of their torment. Many are the similar victims, from Sir Amadace to Hernani: 'the horn of the old Gentleman' has compelled innumerable romantic heroes to take unpleasant resolutions for the sake of a theatrical effect. That the point of honour, the romantic tension between two abstract opposites, should appear in Chaucer, the first of modern poets to give a large, complete, and humorous representation of human action, is merely one of the many surprises which his readers have to accept as best they may. It is only one of his thousand

and one caprices: the only dangerous mistake to which it could possibly lead, would be an assumption that the *Franklin's Tale* can stand as a sample of Chaucer's art in its fullest expression; and the danger of such an error is small. The beginning of right acquaintance with Chaucer is the conviction that nothing represents him except the whole body of his writings. So one is brought round to Dryden's comfortable and sufficient formula: 'Here is God's plenty.' From the energy and the volume of his Trojan story, as glorious as his Trojan river:

> And thou, Simoys, that as an arwe clere
> Through Troie rennest ay downward to the se;

from the passion and the music of that 'tragedie' to the doleful voices of *Melibeus,* there is no form or mood, no fashion of all the vanities, that is not in some way or other represented there. The variety of the matter of Chaucer may possibly to some extent have hindered a full and general recognition of the extraordinary variety in his poetical and imaginative art. It may be doubted whether there is any general appreciation of the height attained by Chaucer in the graver tragic form of story, or of the perfection of his style in all the manifold forms in which he made experiments. If there be any such established injustice in the common estimate of Chaucer as makes it possible for reasonable but misguided people to think of him as merely a 'great translator,' then the refutation will come best of all, without clamour or heat, from the book in which Chaucer's work is presented in the most adequate way. Mr. Skeat in his edition has excluded a number of critical questions which might be maintained to be as capable of argument as the subject of Chaucer's dialect and his practice in the composition of English verse. But although the problems of Chaucer's poetry are not exhausted, and many of them untouched, in this edition, it is still to this edition that appeal will be made for many a year to come. Its value as the first critical text of the whole of Chaucer will scarcely be much impaired by the future edition of a hundred years hence, which shall stand in the same relation to this edition as this to Tyrwhitt's, not to disparage its work, but to complement it. The spirit of the editor is fortunately such as to make him disinclined to rest on his accomplishments. It is evident from many signs that these six volumes are not yet the end of his studies, and that it will probably be something even more strongly equipped than these six volumes which will be left by him to the next age as the final version of his work.

—W.P. Ker, "The Poetry of Chaucer,"
The Quarterly Review, April 1895, pp. 521–48

Frank Jewett Mather "Introduction" (1899)

Frank Jewett Mather (1868–1953) was an American scholar and art critic. His discussion of Chaucer's poetic style is helpful to students who are writing about the ways in which Chaucer uses words and constructs images and characters.

At the beginning of the excerpt, Mather declares that considerations of style are what separate genius poets from others and adds that, "The analysis of a few passages will only confirm the feeling that Chaucer has that beauty and appropriateness of phrase which is proper to the great poets." Mather then examines Chaucer's use of word and sound and the manner in which he fashions characters, with a particular emphasis on the General Prologue to *The Canterbury Tales*. Mather then briefly interjects his thoughts on the "borrowing" issue that had become such a hotly debated topic in late Victorian scholarly circles, believing, like Ker, that "everything [Chaucer] borrowed speedily became his own."

Mather concludes that it is "the supreme ease of his poetry that gives him his unique position among English poets. Certain it is that no other poet of the first rank gives so much, requiring of the reader so little effort in return." This is all a result, Mather suggests, of Chaucer's unique and effortless style.

The test of style is ultimate in the determination of genius. By this we mean that there must be perfect accord between the thought in the writer's mind and the words that express that thought to the reader. Mere originality, nobility even of thought, hardly lie to their creator's credit, unless he has for them words equally novel and lofty. It is chiefly this command of style in the larger sense that gives the poet his advantage over the average fine-souled man—that makes a Burke greater than a Pitt. The first question that we ask ourselves, then, after the immediate relish of curiosity is passed, is, "Has this new writer the supreme gift of style that separates him from the writers of the day?" And this is the question we must sooner or later raise concerning Chaucer. Is his immediate and lasting charm the result of the finest genius, or, as it appears, wayward and almost accidental?

The analysis of a few passages will only confirm the feeling that Chaucer has that beauty and appropriateness of phrase which is proper to the great poets. His style bears all the traces of conscious art. Take this description of a bristling forest,—

> First on the wal was peynted a forest,
> In which ther dwelleth neither man nor best,

> With knotty, knarry, bareyn treës olde
> Of stubbes sharpe and hidous to biholde;
> In which ther ran a rumbel in a swough,
> As though a storm sholde bresten every bough.[1]

How well the harsh and angular adjectives express the gnarled trees; when Chaucer will describe the continuous roaring of the wind in the branches, how he fills the line with resonant and prolonged consonants, "m's," "n's," and "r's," and finally the crash of the "st's" in "storm," "bresten," which renders the crack of great branches torn from the parent stem! Here are the exact words to express what the eye and the ear gather from the wild scene.

I would willingly quote entire the scene of Arcite's death, the perfect sincerity and simplicity of which has touched generations of readers.[2] Note only the force of the redundant "Al-lone, withouten any compaignye" when put in the mouth of one upon whom had just smiled the prospect of a life in Emily's company:—

> What asketh man to have,
> Now with his love now in his colde grave
> Allone withouten any compaignye?[3]

In the following lines the very structure of the verse, the balanced participles, "giggynge," "lacynge," etc., the clause that overruns its line to end abruptly and strangely with "gnawynge," all heightens the effect of bustle and breathless preparation for the tournament:—

> Ther maystow seen . . .
> Knyghtes, of retenue, and eek squyeres
> Nailynge the speres, and helmes bokelynge,
> Giggynge of sheeldes, with layneres lacynge;
> Ther as need is, they weren nothyng ydel;
> The fomy steedes on the golden brydel
> Gnawynge, and fast the armurers also
> With fyle and hamer prikyng to and fro, *etc.*[4]

Let these few examples suffice for many.

> Single lines show the same felicity. We are told of the Monk that—
>   whan he rood men myghte his brydel here
> Gynglen in a whistlynge wynd as clere,
> And eek as loude as dooth the chapel belle,
> Ther as this lord was kepere of the celle;[5]

and the very whistling of the wind is in the second line with its thin "i" and "e" sounds and its resonant "n's." Or in the description of the Miller—

> He was short-sholdered, brood, a thicke knarre[6]—

the verse with its weighty compound word and its halting rhythm moves with the hulking carriage of the Miller's powerful frame.

In these instances we are dealing with no narrowly rhetorical matters; it is this mastery of his instrument that marks the great artist.

From a very early time men have noted and admired the realism of Chaucer, and probably the time will never come when lovers fail to recognize something of themselves in Troilus, and men cease to find their neighbors among the Canterbury pilgrims. Perhaps the handsomest tribute ever paid to this quality of Chaucer's is that of a very poor poet of the succeeding century, the anonymous writer of *The Book of Curtesye* (E. E. T. S., Ext. Ser. No. iii. ll. 337–343), . . .

> Our arsenal would have sounded and resounded
> With bangs and thwacks of driving bolts and nails,
> Of shaping oars and holes to put the oars in;
> With hacking, hammering, clattering, and boring;
> Words of command, whistles, and pipes and fifes.
> (Frere's Translation.)

> Redith his bokes fulle of all pleasaunce,
>   Clere in sentence, in longage excellent,
> Brefly to write suche was his suffesaunce,
>   What-ever to sey he toke in his entent,
>   His longage was so feyre and pertinent,
> That semed unto mennys heryng
> Not only the worde, but verrely the thing.

It would be hard to better the last line. It is the complete fusion of the word in the thing that makes Chaucer not only one of the great artists, but one of the great realists.

We may well carry our analysis of this recognized quality a point further and ask, What are the methods of observation and setting-forth that make the *Prologue* and the best of the *Canterbury Tales* unique for vividness and reality? We may say at the outset that Chaucer never sought the cheaper and more obvious methods of modern realism. We never find anything like an inventory of the moral qualities of the Canterbury pilgrims; we seldom have a complete account even of their dress and physical characteristics. Of

the Shipman we are told only that he rode badly, was dressed in a long coat
of rough cloth, with a dagger by his side, that he was tanned and weather-
beaten. The rest is description of his "easy" handling of a wine cargo, of his
piratical traits, and of his seamanship, except for the single line,—

> With many a tempest hadde his berd been shake.[7]

Yet what a sea-picture there is in this simple statement. I need no more than
this to see the Shipman, legs wide-braced on a heaving deck, eyes, under
beaten brows, strained out into the storm, while the gale sweeps a great beard
back over his shoulders.

After we have learned how the Friar lived by his wits and pleased his very
dupes, we part from him with the lines,—

> And in his harpyng, whan that he hadde songe,
> His eyen twynkled in his heed aryght
> As doon the sterres in the frosty nyght.[8]

We have seen the snap of his eye and know why everybody liked him, and a
poor widow would give the fellow her last farthing.

Arcite has been cruelly crushed under his horse. Chaucer says simply,—

> Tho was he corven out of his harneys,[9]—

and we shudder. No surgeon's exact description of the hurt could so move us.

Two lines express the whole restless character of the Man of Law,—

> Nowher so busy a man as he ther n' as,
> And yet he semed bisier than he was.[10]

You cannot forget that the Reeve is "sclendre" when you have seen his legs
through Chaucer's homely simile,—

> Ful longe were his legges and ful lene,
> Y-lyk a staf, ther was no calf y-sene.[11]

Nor will you doubt that the Prioress is sentimental and tenderhearted when
you learn that a trapped mouse claimed her tears, that the death or even the
chastisement of one of her lapdogs caused bitter weeping, finally that the
same "smale houndes," on a diet of "rosted flessh, or milk, and wastel bred,"
fared better than a mistress who kept ascetic rules for herself,—not for her
pets. Can you finally imagine a better simile for Chaucer's lover and soldier-
squire than the almost commonplace,—

He was as fresh as is the monthe of May?[12]

It is this faculty of seizing upon the characteristic attitude or action that makes Chaucer's descriptions so vivid. He wastes no time upon the things that might be said of any lawyer or any miller, but goes straight to the traits that mark his particular lawyer and miller. We all have some way of looking or acting that reveals us; often the idiosyncrasy is so slight as to escape even our closest friends until a skilful mimic shows that this mere trick of expression marks us as our very selves. Chaucer's power lay in the unerring observation of such peculiarities. It is a method closely allied to that of caricature, and as such, much abused even by the better students of human eccentricity,—witness Dickens and Balzac. This pitfall Chaucer measurably escapes. Of course we know that the Miller's mouth was not literally "wyde . . . as a greet forneys;" the comparison none the less renders unforgettable its bigness and redness.

At the risk of repetition we must insist that Chaucer seldom tries gradually to build up a character; that he could have done so Chriseyde is abundant proof. His method then differs essentially from that of the modern novelist. His presentation of character, on the contrary, comes instantaneously through illuminating flashes, and the great masters of the short story, such as Maupassant, are in technique his true successors. It is this power of flashing truth into a description that our poet of the *Book of Curtesye* had in mind when he spoke of Chaucer's "longage" as being so "pertinent" that it conveyed

Not only the word but verrely the thing.

The most serious passages of his poetry are seldom without a sub-quality of humor, while usually this quality is unrestrained. But Chaucer's humor rarely passes over into satire. At most he is finely ironical toward the offender against the congruous, sincerely loving and even respecting him against whom he has turned the laugh. It is this unshaken good-humor and friendliness which is most characteristic of the poet's attitude toward men. He loves to laugh at them, but he loves them too. And his humor is so fine and pervasive that it claims oftener a smile than a laugh.

Alert as this humor is, its touch is kindly. The Prioress escapes with only a fling at her airs and graces; the Monk provokes only an ironical approval of his hunting; so the Friar is commended for loving a barmaid better than a leper: the Doctor loves gold because it has medicinal value:—

For gold in physik is a cordial,
Therfore he loved gold in speciall.[13]

Sometimes this humor takes the form of burlesque. What more delicious and yet what more realistic than the description of Chaunticleer?—

> His comb was redder than the fyn coral,
> And batailled as it were a castel wal;
> His byle was blak, and as the jeet it shoon;
> Lyk asure were his legges and his toon;
> His nayles whiter than the lylye flour.
> And lyk the burned gold was his colour.[14]

So the old romancers loved to describe a Sir Lybeau or a Lancelot; and Chaucer must have observed the cock with a real admiration for his splendor, though seeing too the fun of cock character. Vain pedant that he is, the cock deigns to rally anxious Dame Pertelote in Latin, and to add the interpretation:—

> *Mulier est hominis confusio:*
> Madame, the sentence of this Latin is,
> Woman is mannes joye, and al his blis.[15]

We can see what Mr. Robert Grant has aptly named "the furtive conjugal smile."

Few characters fail to challenge Chaucer's genial irony; and yet there are those, such as the Knight, the Parson, and the Plowman, that are treated with perfect seriousness. Souls so finely simple and genuine are impregnable even to the kindest ridicule. They disarm the humorist. "Sitting beside them the Comic Muse is grave and sisterly," is Mr. Meredith's fine word.

The frank realism of Chaucer's humor brings him at times into conflict with modern standards of the fitting, and even of the permissible. In the *Prologue* (1.731), he has already warned us that—

> Whoso shal telle a tale after a man,
> He moot reherce as ny as ever he can,
> Everich a word, if it be in his charge,
> Al speke he never so rudeliche and large.

Consequently he lets the Miller tell on freely his "cherles tale;" nor does he hold the rein on the Miller's coarser fellows. Many of these stories, that "sownen unto" a now decorously covered sin, are quite redeemed by the brilliancy and humor of the telling. Chaucer is too much the artist to be coarse for coarseness' sake, and often lends a special refinement of manner to matter sufficiently dubious. Yet the reader of no too squeamish taste will find certain parts of these tales obtrusively nasty. Nor can he wholly excuse the poet on the ground of old-time freedom of expression; for Chaucer knew perfectly well what he was about in treating the Somnour as realistically as he did the Prioress: the choice and the responsibility were his alone. It is, however, fair to say that such work is small in amount, and to the average reader a negligible quantity. The closer student will condemn this portion of his work, or hold it justified, according to his opinion of the realistic doctrine; while those who have experienced some of life's compromises will be rather tolerant toward one whose "gipoun," unlike that of the Knight, bears stains other than those of the crusader's "habergeoun."

Supremely inventive Chaucer proved himself just once—in the *Prologue* and the plan of the *Canterbury Tales*. Elsewhere he prefers to rest upon the authority of other men, and to use his great literary powers in the re-shaping and bringing to perfection of well-known stories. He possibly never invented a plot, and when, as in the *House of Fame*, he lacked a direct model, the story quite ran away with him. Pillaging literature with a freedom that reminds us of Shakespeare digging *Macbeth* out of a chronicle, or transforming a popular novel into As You *Like It*, Chaucer now borrowed the plot of an Italian epic, now used a Latin tale of Petrarch's, now re-wrote a French *fableau*; or again a legend of Ovid, or an "example" from a monkish compilation was his theme.

But everything he borrowed became speedily his own. The *Knight's Tale* emerged a very different thing from the *Teseide*; Boccaccio would have recognized only with difficulty in *Troilus* his *Filostrato*. Even in those cases where he follows an original closely, the grace of the telling, the picturesqueness and genial humor which permeate the old material transmute it into another and far finer substance. Every one knows that inventiveness is the smallest part of the story-teller's gift. The most indifferent tale may be redeemed by the resources of the narrator's art; the most ingenious spoiled through inadequate telling. So the story-teller's business lies chiefly in presentation, very little in absolute invention. *Or dient et content et fabloient,* "Now they say and relate and tell the tale," stands at the chapter-heads of that blithest of early stories, *Aucassin and Nicolette.* Let this artless redundancy of words for telling indicate that therein lies the whole opus and labor of a difficult art. So a man tell his story supremely well, be he a Chaucer, an Ariosto, a La Fontaine, the question "Where did he get it?" troubles little the reader. He is foolish who seeks too narrowly the antecedents of bookish treasure-trove. 'T is the bookworm's, not the gentle reader's part. And be it said that such rummaging among Chaucer's "olde bokes" only illustrates his genius. Many-sided as is his genius, he must be judged, or better, enjoyed primarily, as the master of those who tell. In olden times the French trouvere of recognized preeminence received the title of king. So Adenes proudly signs himself *li rois.* Chaucer had no need to claim a title that posterity has never refused him.

We have found in Chaucer an unusual power of style, the *eloquentia* of the humanist whom Chaucer in temperament often foreshadows. And here be it said that when Matthew Arnold denied to him the possession of the "grand style," he spoke from imperfect knowledge or appreciation. As well deny this gift to Horace because he prefers the note of comedy. To style in the narrower sense Chaucer adds extraordinary descriptive power, dealing however rather in the significant line than in the elaborated study. Finally, the texture of his invention is undershot with a humor peculiarly genial and humane. The result is a style unequalled for ease and charm. This naturalness has frequently passed for *naivete*. There could be no greater mistake. The great poets have no "wood-notes wild," and Chaucer is of their company, *della loro schiera*.

It is, I believe, the supreme ease of his poetry that gives him his unique position among English poets. Certain it is that no other poet of the first rank gives so much, requiring of the reader so little effort in return. And this ease lies deeper than facts of style and methods of composition; it comes from a nature finely adjusted to the world in which it finds itself. When we think of the man Chaucer we are inevitably reminded of the Horace of the *Satires* and *Epistles*. We divine a man who has loved the world much, not wholly trusting it, who knows tears but prefers smiles. We recognize an experience, mellowing where embitterment were possible, which has yielded worldly wisdom of the most amiable sort. It is these qualities that make Chaucer of all our poets the friendliest.

Notes
1. *Knight's Tale*, 11. 1117ff.
2. *Knight's Tale*, 11. 1907ff.
3. "How does the repetition and amplification give force and bitterness to the thought, as if Arcite must need dwell on his expected loneliness in order to feel it fully!"—Lowell, *Conversations*, p. 17.
4. *Knights Tale*, 11. 1644ff. My friend, Dr. M.C. Satphen, kindly supplies a parallel from Aristophanes,—the description of a busy arsenal,—which presents similar stylistic features.
5. *Prologue*, 11. 174ff.
6. *Prologue*, 1. 549.
7. *Prologue*, 1. 406.
8. *Prologue*, 11. 266ff.
9. *Knights Tale*, 1. 1858.
10. *Prologue*, 11. 321f.
11. *Prologue*, 11. 592ff.

12. *Prologue,* 1. 92.
13. *Prologue,* 11. 43f.
14. *Nun's Priest's Tale,* 11. 39ff.
15. *Nun's Priest's Tale,* 11. 343ff.

—Frank Jewett Mather, "Introduction,"
*The Prologue, The Knight's Tale and
the Nun's Priest's Tale,* 1899, pp. ix–xlvii

THE TWENTIETH CENTURY

George Saintsbury (1901)

An important literary critic of the late nineteenth and early twentieth centuries, George Saintsbury (1845–1933) writes in *The Earlier Renaissance* that
"Chaucer came too early." Saintsbury believed that the Middle English language of Chaucer's day had not yet developed into a tongue fully capable
of supporting the height of English poetry, and that only Chaucer, through
his sheer genius, rose above the inherent difficulties that were to be found
within the language itself.

It is by no means out of accordance with the rule of things in literature and
life that the English Renaissance, which was to produce by far the greatest
literary results of the whole movement, had an overture, and even something
much more than an overture, of portentous and almost unexampled length
and dulness. . . .

The first, the most obvious, the most important, of these reasons, but
perhaps still one not quite completely recognised, is the peculiar character of
the English language—a character on which mere philology throws very little
light, if, indeed, it does not distinctly obscure the field and distort the vision.
Modern English is, of all great literary languages, the least of a natural growth
or even a chemical compound, the most of a mechanical blend or adjustment.
The purely English or Anglo-Saxon, the French, and the Latin elements in
it, not to mention the smaller constituents, have simply taken their shapes
by a secular process of rolling and jumbling together, like the pebbles on
the sea-shore or the sweetmeats in a confectioner's copper basin. From this
mere attrition, this mere shaking together, English grammar, English prose
style, and English prosody have resulted. And this process took—could not
but take—centuries before it could turn out results suitable for a Spenser
or a Shakespeare, a Hooker or a Bacon. The real reason why the results of a
method so apparently accomplished as Chaucer's were mere botch-work in
the hands of his purely native followers, was that Chaucer came too early, and
when this process of attrition had not gone on long enough. Dante, dealing
with a language like Italian, homogeneous in itself, however various in
dialect, was able to do his work once for all—not that Dante gives us complete
modern Italian, either in grammar or even in prosody, but that there are no
fundamental differences. Chaucer could do nothing of the kind. The phi-
lologers who ask "Whether Chaucer did not know his own language?" and so
force on him chimerical uniformities of rhyme and syntax, may be asked in
turn, "How, then, do you account for what followed?" They cannot account
for it. The literary historian can.

In other words, Chaucer, by main force and gigantic dead-lift of individual genius, had got the still imperfectly adjusted materials of English into a shape sufficient for architecture of permanent and beautiful design. But when this force and this skill were taken away, the rough-edged or crumbling materials of language, the not fully organised devices of grammar and metre, were insufficient to make anything but more or less shapeless heaps. Skelton may have evaded the difficulty by adopting rococo forms; Surrey and, earlier still, Wyatt, by taking liberties with accent or quantity on the one hand, improving grammar on the other, and borrowing the constraining stay of the sonnet or the liberty of blank verse from more accomplished languages like Italian, may have made actual progress towards the true English style. But all this demanded time, experiment, unsuccessful as well as successful, and an amount of individual genius which simply did not happen to be available for the moment, or for many moments.

The prose-writers had an apparently more difficult but really easier task. They were not misled, in the very act of being assisted, by intrinsically consummate, but relatively premature and exceptional, work like Chaucer's. Chaucer's own prose, interesting and important as it is, has nothing of the exceptional and almost portentous character of his verse. It fits (with due allowance for the exceptional talent of its author) easily and naturally into the succession of its kind, from the *Ancren Riwle* and the various theological exercises of the thirteenth and early fourteenth centuries. It is itself succeeded as naturally by fresh applications and developments. The prose-writers of the fifteenth century are not, like the verse-writers of it, endeavouring to draw a bow which is not only too strong for them, but of which the yew is dry-rotted and the string frayed by time and weather. They have a great deal to do; they have not done very much as yet. But they are putting prose more and more to its naturally multifarious or rather infinite uses; they are accumulating the vocabulary; they are discovering, either by mere practice, or by borrowing, sensibly or insensibly, from the French and Latin originals, whom they almost inevitably follow, the varieties of style; they are shaping grammar by using it. In one great instance—that of Malory—they have already done a great deal more than this: they have actually made, once for all, a style that cannot be surpassed for its particular purpose. And now, in our own period, in Fisher and in Berners, we find them achieving something only less great. Berners, indeed, like Malory, "comes to the end": of the myriad purposes of prose he has found one which he can discharge excellently, but which will not need, in that particular way and style, to be discharged again. Fisher is much less positively satisfactory and interesting to us; but he is even more important to history, because he is trying the rhetorical devices, forming the tools of style, for purposes other than his own, as well as for his own itself.

—George Saintsbury, *The Earlier Renaissance,* 1901, pp. 231–36

PETER BORGHESI (1903)

Peter (Pietro) Borghesi was an esteemed Italian scholar of English medieval and Italian Renaissance literature. His most significant work, *Boccaccio and Chaucer,* is excerpted here. Like the entries by Henry Morley and Bernhard ten Brink, Borghesi wrote about the relationship between several of Chaucer's texts and their sources, both proven and supposed, from Boccaccio's works. Any student writing about these two poets or about "The Knight's Tale" and *Troilus and Criseyde* in general would do well to carefully examine what these three scholars all say on the subject. Borghesi writes, "We do not know of any two other writers more similar, or more equal in their general characteristics than Boccaccio and Chaucer." Borghesi sees the two writers as twin poetic souls, "closer than friends, than master and disciple, than father and son, than two brothers." Borghesi's excerpt begins by examining the then-ongoing discussion regarding Chaucer's knowledge of the Italian language itself. While Chaucer clearly knew French and Latin, his knowledge of Italian is a matter for debate. Borghesi declares that Chaucer knew Italian, and that his use of Boccaccio as a source for several of his most important texts only serves to ratify this point.

Like Morley and Brink, Borghesi focuses primarily on "The Knight's Tale" and *Troilus and Criseyde* and their respective forerunners in Boccaccio: *Teseide* and *Il Filostrato.* As with his predecessors, Borghesi compares the two works, especially the alterations in form and character; ultimately, Borghesi seems to conclude that "The Knight's Tale," though the alterations Chaucer introduced were necessary, is a lesser text than its source, while *Troilus and Criseyde,* which Borghesi calls a "recasting" of *Il Filostrato,* is a superior work. When Borghesi begins to discuss the possible influences that Boccaccio's *Decameron* had on *The Canterbury Tales,* he strays into an area that requires more supposition than his previous discussion. Borghesi is an ardent admirer of *The Canterbury Tales:* "Chaucer's *Canterbury Tales* is his master-piece, because when he wrote it he had then become possessed of more knowledge of life, his style had improved and become firmer, clearer, more flexible, more expressive and was above all things most popular. He is subtle, various, sprightly; he gives gorgeous descriptions and passages with a profound and exquisite delicacy and pathos." Borghesi also notes Chaucer's penchant for writing about women: "If in many instances Chaucer has exposed women to derision, perhaps to correct their ridiculous habits, in this book he gives a solid proof of knowing how much a virtuous woman is deserving of praise and how superior she is to every eulogy." Certainly many modern students of Chaucer might have a different perspective than Borghesi on the women in *The Canterbury Tales*.

Borghesi's excerpt is also of use to students because of his frequent mentions of numerous other Chaucerian scholars featured in this volume, including Morley, Speght, Warton, and Dryden. Students may find it valuable to compare what Borghesi claims these men say about Chaucer and what they actually state in their own words.

It has been recorded by several critics and Nicolas Harris is one of these, that Chaucer did not know Italian. We think that nothing can be more absurd. The only reason they give worth considering is that he never intermingled a single Italian word in his works, whilst he used so many French and Latin words.

Not only was Chaucer able to distinguish the superiority of the Italian literature over the French, but he could also choose the very best Italian books. As regards style the *Teseide* is one of Boccaccio's best works[1] In spite of its classical imitations, the narrative is always simple and bright, the verse and the octave rhyme are generally good and this work was the forerunner of Ariosto and Tasso.

Chaucer knew at once that it was a masterpiece, although the plot in itself is not very interesting; he saw that the characters were not cold, as some are inclined to think, but passionate and full of life; he knew that it was "the first long narrative heroic poem written by a man of genius[2]". What a difference between the allegory of the *Roman de la Rose* and the human characters of the *Teseidel* It was a great step towards a better form of literature. Chaucer read this poem, he understood all its superiority, and he began to translate it. But it is most probable that he did not translate it in the form which we now possess in the *Canterbury Tales* under the title of the *Knight's Tale*. This tale is most probably a recasting of an earlier translation, now lost, which he made before and which he mentions in his *Legend of Good Women*.

Here the usual great question arises, the question of source, as Chaucer only says that he took his work from "old stories" and from "old books", which would not be true, if, as we believe, Boccaccio's *Teseide* was his original. But was it really so?

Many eminent critics answer that it was, but a few are not of this opinion. The latter say that Boccaccio's *Teseide* and Chaucer's *Knight's Tale* have a common source. Craik is one of these and he claims to prove his assertion by saying that the *Teseide* "extends to about 12,000 octosyllabic verses" whilst Chaucer's poem extends "to not many more than 2,000 decasyllabic ones" He adds that the English work is much less detailed than the Italian and that "the two versions differ in some of the main circumstances" In another passage he says that what is thought to be translated or imitated from Boccaccio is very little and insignificant and only leads one to suppose that they were drawn from a common source. All this is absolutely denied by Furnivall, who says that the original of the *Knight's Tale* is only the Italian *Teseide,* and he adds that it is impossible to think of a French origin of the fable of the *Teseide* and therefore of the *Knight's Tale.*

Happily we are not obliged to give much weight to Craik's remarks. In the first phase we must say that he had but very little acquaintance with the Italian language. Everybody knows that Boccaccio's *Teseide* is not written in octosyllabic verses, and that it has not 12,000 verses, but only 9,896, to which we must add fifteen sonnets, and we must also add that there are 2,350 in the *Knight's Tale.*

It is also necessary to state here, that we do not say that Chaucer translated Boccaccio's *Teseide* for his *Knight's Tale,* we say that Boccaccio's *Teseide* is Chaucer's original, that therefore he knew this poem: we say that much is translated and imitated from it, and we add also that Chaucer follows the Italian poem in its general features in such a way as to show his original very clearly.

In the second place, as to the shortness of the English poem as compared with the Italian one it is necessary to know that the *Knight's Tale* is at the beginning of Chaucer's *Canterbury Tales,* which is a collection of tales told, in order to pass the time cheerfully, by at least 29 persons travelling from London to Canterbury. Now Chaucer's *Knight's Tale* is shorter than Boccaccio's *Teseide* for two reasons: first because a long tale would not amuse, secondly because the time was very limited and it was polite and necessary to leave to every member of the company sufficient time to tell two tales in going and two in returning as had been agreed upon. Therefore many secondary and even main circumstances must differ in the two versions, but it is beyond all doubt that Chaucer knew Italian, and his *Knight's Tale* has its source in the *Teseide,* as he literally translated from it about 270 verses, and either imitated or paraphrased about 500[3].

To prove this assertion we could give here a long list of many, or all the passages in the *Teseide* with Chaucer's English translations or paraphrases, but this work has already been done by Tyrwhitt, Rossetti, Skeat and others, and therefore it is unnecessary for us to do so.

After the proofs that the most learned students of Chaucer have given us, after the comparisons which have been made between the Italian

and the English poems, it is impossible not to admit that Chaucer knew
Italian and that the *Teseide* is the true source of the *Knight's Tale*. If many
beautiful passages in the *Teseide* are not to be found in the *Knight's Tale*,
it is, as we have already pointed out, because he wanted to shorten it very
much, as he often says at the beginning of his tale, and also because many
passages had already been inserted in other works of his. For example,
from the description of the temple of Venus Chaucer took very little for
his *Knight's Tale*, as he had already inserted a very close imitation of it in
his *Assembly of Fowls*[4], namely from verse 183 to verse 287, and these lines
"are translated in a way that places beyond question Chaucer's knowledge
of Italian. The turn of the phrase makes it quite evident that Chaucer wrote
with the Italian original before him[5]". So in the same poem a list of birds
and a shorter list of trees are taken or closely imitated from the *Teseide*, and
many passages from this poem are to be found here and there in Chaucer's
works. In the same way some of the reminiscences of the *Teseide* are also
to be found in Chaucer's *Troylus and Cryseide*. The 260.th, 261.st and 262.nd
stanzas of this poem are taken from the first three stanzas of the eleventh
canto of the *Teseide*.

The poem of *Queen Anelida and False Arcite* bears a striking resemblance
to the *Knight's Tale* and therefore to the *Teseide* "chiefly in the opening lines[6]"
so that the 1.st, 2.nd and 3.rd stanzas of *Queen Anelida* correspond to the 3.rd,
2.nd and 1.st of the *Teseide*.

All this explains the gaps that are found here and there in the *Knight's
Tale* and it explains also that even if Chaucer had had a mind to translate the
Teseide literally for his *Canterbury Tales*, he could not have done so.

From all this we may infer also that Boccaccio's *Teseide* is the poem which
most pleased Chaucer and from which he borrowed as much as he could.

Here another question arises: when Chaucer altered, did he alter for the
worse or for the better? The answer is a very difficult one, but something
also may be said on this point. There is no doubt that Boccaccio's *Teseide*
has one great defect; this defect lies in the effort to remove, to keep at a
distance the conclusion of the action, which is already foreseen from the
middle of the poem[7]. Generally speaking, to curtail the story was to improve
it, therefore many critics have praised him inasmuch as he avoided many
tiresome descriptions, which, if useful or tolerable in a long poem, are not
so in a short one. But in several cases, in his curtailing and in his alterations
he was not guided by very good taste, as he does not avoid several of the
above mentioned descriptions, he seems to delight in rhetorical tirades full
of mythology and biblical quotations and expressions[8], defects which were
however very common during the Middle-ages. Perhaps it was in considering

these defects that Sandras was induced to say that Chaucer did not improve the *Teseide*, in fact he says that the English poet diminished its poetic merit, omitted the finest features of the fable and spoiled the truth of the story.

But, in spite of its defects, the *Knight's Tale,* which leads the series of the *Canterbury Tales,* and which in spirit as well as in language is the translation of Boccaccio's *Teseide,* had a great success in England and a great influence on English literature, as it was the basis of Fletcher's drama, of Dryden's poem, and of many other compositions.

If Chaucer took very much from the *Teseide* for his *Knight's Tale,* he certainly did not take less from the *Filostrato* for his *Troylus and Cryseide.* He did not literally translate it as he was an inventor though a disciple, an original writer though a translator[9].

Chaucer's work could not be called a translation, but it is rather a recasting of Boccaccio's *Filostrato.* . . .

Boccaccio's *Filostrato* contains 5,704 lines and Chaucer's *Troylus and Cryseide* 8,246. Chaucer adapted from the *Filostrato* 2,730 lines which he condensed into 2,583 so that only 5,663 lines belong almost exclusively to Chaucer. Therefore one third of *Troylus and Cryseide* is taken from Boccaccio and two thirds are either Chaucer's own, or taken from Boethius, Dante and Petrarch, besides many imitations from Ovid.

It is true that many passages and episodes of Boccaccio's *Filostrato* are not to be found in the English poem, but we must always bear in mind that Chaucer was not a mere translator, and it will be easy for us to understand all the difference which exists between the two poems. We must consider that if between the two poems there are differences there are also many resemblances: so the leading incidents are the same, there are minute coincidences of expression which could not exist if Chaucer had not translated from Boccaccio, and we must not forget that Chaucer could not translate literally as he wrote poetry.

In many instances Chaucer has helped scholars to find out the sources of his works, but in the case of *Troylus and Cryseide* he rather puts them at a loss. He does not claim any merit of invention in this poem as in one passage he says that he translated it "out of Latin", but by the word Latin he might also have meant the *Latino volgare* or Italian. In other passages he incidentally refers to Homer, Dares Phrygius, Dictus Cretensis, but he certainly did not take anything from them. He states also that the author of his original was Lollius, but no one appears to recognize this as the name of a writer from whom Chaucer may have taken anything, and no one can presume to say, as Tyrwhitt does, that Lollius may be another name for Boccaccio as our great prose-writer was never so called.

Now, why does not Chaucer mention Boccaccio in any place though he owes so much to him?

It was not only Chaucer's wish to be a Court poet, but he also looked to this for his means of livelihood: he was not a man of action, not a man of great courage: he was not inclined to write anything that might displease the Court. We see this in the translation of the *Roman de la Rose*, if the translation now extant is his, where he omits all passages casting reflections on Kings or other authorities. For a certain time Boccaccio was not in favour with those in authority, with the clergy and religious men in general, and this was chiefly before he expressed regret at having written the *Decameron*. Although in 1373, either just before or soon after the departure of Chaucer from Florence, Boccaccio was appointed to explain Dante to the public and his renown was reestablished, yet some rumours of his being a man of corrupt and loose habits must have reached Chaucer, who thought that these reports might get to England: he feared the King's reproaches had he mentioned that man as his master, therefore he never mentioned Boccaccio, and perhaps translated from him less than he would otherwise have done. Besides this, although it is quite certain that Chaucer knew Boccaccio's works, yet it cannot be actually proved that he knew his name, or that he knew him personally, or indeed that he ever knew he was the author of his works, as many of the manuscripts of the Middle-ages were published anonymously.

The supposition that Chaucer purposely avoided mentioning the name of Boccaccio gains strength when we remember that Chaucer's idea of decorum was superior to Boccaccio's. In Boccaccio's *Filostrato* Cryseide is a comparatively commonplace person. This rich, young, beautiful and gay widow did not wish to reject the advances of a young man of distinction: she could not live the life of a nun, and if other women amused themselves with intrigue, why should she not do the same? On being assured that her reputation would not suffer, she yields at once, and makes excuses for her reluctance. In Boccaccio's work Cryseide is bad, faithless, vicious and lustful: in Chaucer's she is not "a nun to whom earthly love is a sin", but she is rather a "victim of fate". After having read Boccaccio we despise or hate such wanton women, but Chaucer's Cryseide possesses every quality which entitles a woman to love and respect: she is won with difficulty and overcome only by surprise. The English poet rather teaches us to pity her and he endears her to his readers.

Boccaccio's Pandarus is the most despicable of men; Chaucer's is a good natured, loquacious, rather unscrupulous man, a man who knows the world and who means to enjoy life; he is quite a new creation, a good character for a good comedy, the right man in the right place.

Boccaccio's Troylus is an ordinary man, rather destitute of refined feeling, self-indulgent and practised in the art of intrigue: Chaucer's on the contrary loves with all the ardour and freshness of youth, he is the personification of what a lover ought to be.

Boccaccio does not waste words in the first part of his poem, but he loiters in the second, chiefly after the catastrophe, when all the interest of the poem has passed away. On the contrary Chaucer dwells at length on the most moral and charming part of the poem, where Cryseide is falling in love, but he so curtails the sorrowful conclusion that the fifth or last book of his poem corresponds to four of Boccaccio's cantos.

So, in justice to Chaucer, although a translation, we look upon his *Troylus and Cryseide* as a new creation, and, although Scott thought it a rather tedious work, we think it is a very good one, and we think that Rossetti is right to judge it the finest of ancient English love poems. Certainly in this work there springs up a new life, and we should say a life more moral and purer than in the Italian poem. It could not be otherwise, as Chaucer dedicates it to "the moral Gower and the philosophical Strode", and it shows also, to Chaucer's honour, that he did not require the aid of vulgarity or triviality to give expression to that vivacity and humour which are his chief characteristics.

We have pointed out that Chaucer's *Troylus and Cryseide* is more moral than Boccaccio's *Filostrato,* but it was not moral enough for the English of that time, and especially for many of the ladies of the Court. This justifies us in our supposition that Chaucer neither dared mention Boccaccio, nor admit that he was his principal master. Indeed, he knew that his poem was not well received at Court, and he wrote *The Legend of Good Women,* by the Queen's order, it is said, to remove the odium which *Troylus and Cryseide* had brought on him.

And here another question arises: is Chaucer's *Troylus and Cryseide* superior to Boccaccio's *Filostrato?*

If we consider separately the several points of Chaucer's work, perhaps, as we have already pointed out, in many passages in this poem Chaucer is superior to Boccaccio, and also, perhaps, if we consider the poem taken as a whole. In many instances Chaucer "has eminently shown his good sense and judgment in rejecting the superfluities and improving the general arrangement of the story. He frequently corrects and softens Boccaccio's manners and it is with singular address he has often abridged the Italian poet's ostentatious and pedantic parade of ancient history and mythology[10]". Perhaps this is saying too much; but at least it is partly true. On the other hand Chaucer is wanting in every respect in unity; unity of composition, unity of delineation, unity of character, unity of style;

whereas unity constitutes the peculiar attraction of Boccaccio. Chaucer is more monotonous, more diffuse, but he is "superior in depth of feeling and delineation of the passions[11]" and shows everywhere a closer knowledge of life. Boccaccio displays more "elegance of diction and ornament", and his work is and always will remain, an unrivalled master-piece.

Before speaking of the *Decameron* we think it necessary to say something about Chaucer's *Canterbury Tales,* to which we have already referred.

In Chaucer's time many persons, from all parts of England, went to Canterbury to visit the tomb of Thomas a Becket. On the sixth of May of a certain year Chaucer finds we do not know whether 29 or 30 of these pilgrims at the *Tabard,* an inn that was near London Bridge, in the South East of London, on the right bank of the Thames where in the same place, in High Street, Borough, at present stands the *Old Tabard,* a public house, but this building is very modern and there are no remains of the old one. Chaucer and the host joined the pilgrims, so that they then became either thirty-one or thirty-two and they agreed that every member of the company should tell two tales in going and two in returning from the pilgrimage. On the bright and green morning of the seventh day both journey and tales commenced.

Who does not see at once how grand is the idea, and one such as only a genius can conceive? It is not an easy task to write about 128 tales of licentious, and puts before us scenes which many would not care to see. Shall we find fault only with him, if at that time the Italian sense of delicacy was rather blunted? Shall we condemn Boccaccio if he represented society to us under the conditions that then existed and if he spoke the truth? And if we do not condemn Boccaccio, so much the less shall we rank among those who condemn Chaucer, because if the two authors wrote much which very old men might regret to have written, certainly Boccaccio had much more to regret than Chaucer. But who has not read the history of many a great man who muses sorrowfully on his best works? Chaucer's *Canterbury Tales* is his master-piece, because when he wrote it he had then become possessed of more knowledge of life, his style had improved and become firmer, clearer, more flexible, more expressive and was above all things most popular. He so excels in humour and imagination that only Shakespeare can be compared with him, only Shakespeare can pretend to rival him. He is subtle, various, sprightly; he gives gorgeous descriptions and passages with a profound and exquisite delicacy and pathos. He paints what he sees, and he knows so well how to mingle wisdom with humour that he amuses his readers, he endears them to him, and everyone feels sorry that he was able to write only so few of such tales. But, though unfinished, the work "contains about 17,000 verses, besides more than a fourth of that quantity in prose[12]". His verses are either decasyllabic or hendecasyllabic, and they are arranged either in couplets or in stanzas. Though unfinished it is the greatest of all his works and the most original, the one on which his fame stands as a rock against the ravages of time.

It can be proved, as we have seen, that Chaucer knew the *Teseide* and the *Filostrato,* but it has not yet been ascertained that he knew the *Decameron.* In all probability he did, and this is also the general opinion, but till now we have not found any material proof of it. What is certain, however, is that he did not translate from the *Decameron* as he did from the *Teseide* and the *Filostrato,* but this is no surprise to us: as Chaucer was a genius, he could not remain a translator all his life, and also because the conception of translating prose into poetry seems rather strange or awkward. What we say, what we believe, what we should like to demonstrate clearly and beyond doubt is, that Chaucer knew the *Decameron* and that from this work he took at least the idea of his *Canterbury Tales.*

Certainly the task is not an easy one, chiefly because Chaucer disowns his obligations to Boccaccio, for not only never does he mention his name, but he often seems, in this particular, to try to lead his students and critics astray. And in this he succeeds, because as both the English and the Italian poetry of that time was, generally speaking, either a translation or an imitation of that of France, so many critics were led to believe that Boccaccio and Chaucer were not much connected with each other.

It is certain that not a single one of the *Canterbury Tales* can be ascribed to Chaucer's own imagination, and although Craik says, that the fame of Italian song could hardly have reached Chaucer's ears and although Sir Harris Nicolas is almost of the same opinion, yet Ward, who is one of the best authorities on Chaucer, admits that Chaucer's indebtedness towards Italian literature and "Boccaccio in particular is considerable" and that it seems "hardly to admit of denial" Even Craik in a passage of his history of English literature says that "it must be considered very doubtful" if any one of Chaucer's tales was really derived from Italian, and in another place he says that "this may have been the case" Therefore we see that even those who do not admit of an Italian influence on Chaucer are nevertheless in considerable doubt in making such an assertion.

Let us look a little closer into the two works, and we shall find that the *Canterbury Tales* is a work of much the same kind as the *Decameron.* The *Decameron* is a species of comedy not intended for the stage and so is the *Canterbury Tales.* The subjects of the *Decameron* are of about the same kind as those of the *Canterbury Tales,* and although the framework is somewhat different, yet it has many striking resemblances.

And this resemblance in not only in the general idea, but moreover several of Chaucer's tales have some resemblance to those in the *Decameron*. In fact, the pardoner in the *Canterbury Tales* is an itinerant ecclesiastic of much the same stamp as Frate Cipolla in the *Decameron*, although Chaucer may have taken the outline of the very beautiful *Pardoners Tale* from the *Cento novelle antiche*.

The *Reeve's Tale* forms the basis of the sixth novel of the ninth day in Boccaccio's *Decameron*. The only difference is that Boccaccio's story is much more licentious than Chaucer's.

As to the *Shipman's Tale* Speght supposes that its original is the first novel of the eighth day of the *Decameron*. Although Morley frankly avows that it was taken from the *Decameron*, yet at the same time we must also record the fact that Tyrwhitt and Warton think it more probable that both Chaucer and Boccaccio derived the outline from a French *fabliau*. But, as we have said, if we believe that Chaucer had abandoned the idea of taking anything from France, it will not be difficult for us to take the side of Morley.

Chaucer asserts that he derived the *Franklin's Tale* from a Breton lay, but this lay is not known. Skeat says that "the subject seems to have survived in a popular *fabliau*, which Boccaccio has drawn upon in the *Decameron* and also introduced into the *Philocopo*", therefore also in this tale, if Chaucer did not take it from the *Decameron*, there is at least some connection with this work, namely with the fifth novel of the tenth day.

Several resemblances are also found between the *Merchant's Tale* and that of *Lidia and Nicostrato*, the seventh novel of the ninth day, and between the *Miller's Tale* and that of *Frate Puccio*, the third novel of the fourth day.

Although these resemblances are very striking, yet nothing definite can be proved, and if, for example, both Boccaccio and Chaucer find fault with the monks in similar matters, it does not of necessity follow that Chaucer borrowed from Boccaccio, but it may rather tend to show that the defects of the monks were as notorious in Italy as in England, as may be inferred from a letter written by Boniface IX in 1390, and it may be that both Boccaccio and Chaucer felt it was necessary to satirise and condemn these defects in order to put an end to them.

Furnivall says that, if Chaucer had known the *Decameron*, he would have translated and inserted some or at least one of its "racy *novelle*" in his *Canterbury Tales*. It seems to us that Furnivall and several others are inclined to wish Chaucer had translated more than he did. To some extent we have already answered this assumption when we spoke of the evolution of every author, namely when we said that almost every genius begins as a translator or as an imitator, and that it is only little by little that his own personality springs forth, but we have now another observation to make on this point. The *Canterbury Tales* is an unfinished work: there ought to be at least 120 tales, and we have only 24. Can we not suggest what Chaucer would have done if he had been allowed to finish his work? Could he not have thought of introducing some of the "racy *novelle*" into that portion of his book which he was not able to give us?

In conclusion if we look for material proofs that Chaucer knew the *Decameron,* we fail to find any as in all Chaucer's works there is no allusion to this book or to its author; neither a phrase nor a single word can be proved to have been taken from it, and the coincidences which the *Canterbury Tales* has with it are common to other books which were previously published and which Chaucer may have known. But when we consider the above coincidences, when we take into consideration Chaucer's love and enthusiasm for the Italian literature, and when we remember, as we have already pointed out, that he knew the *Teseide,* the *Filostrato* and Boccaccio's Latin works from which he took so much, we may conclude with some certainty that he knew also the *Decameron* or at least some of its tales. We can only conjecture this, but we feel that there is some ground for supposing that Morley, Mamroth and many others are right when they conclude that Chaucer owes to Boccaccio the framework of his *Canterbury Tales.*

The question has also arisen as to whether Chaucer's work is superior to Boccaccio's, and several English men of Letters have given judgment in favour of their own poet. We should like to say the contrary, but we cannot pass judgment on a question like this, because we do not feel called upon to pronounce too closely between the merits of these two geniuses, and also because it seems to us that it is very difficult to compare an unfinished work with a complete one. It has been said that in the *Canterbury Tales* there is more unity of idea, more unity of composition than in Boccaccio's *Decameron,* that the prologue is in strict accord with the following tales which are closely connected to one another. We certainly accept the suggestion that the prologue in the *Canterbury Tales* is in strict accord with the subsequent tales, and that the preface in the *Decameron* is not; but we do not see in the other portion of Chaucer's work more unity of composition than in Boccaccio's. It is so true, that Chaucer's tales are not much connected to one another that their order even is not the same in several old manuscripts. Notwithstanding this, let us grant that Chaucer's tales are a little more connected to one another than those in the *Decameron,* let us grant that Boccaccio's work is much less moral than Chaucer's, yet we do not think that this is enough to determine Chaucer's superiority.

The *Clerk's Tale*, which is one of the best in the *Canterbury Tales*, deserves special mention. It is the matchless story of patient *Griselda and Dioneo*, the last tale in the *Decameron*, about which Petrarch said that no one could read it without shedding tears. It pleased him so much that he translated it into Latin and it is from Petrarch's Latin prose that Chaucer took it. But how did Chaucer obtain this translation? He himself says that he went to Padua to see Petrarch, whom he calls his master, and he makes his Clerk say:

> I woll you tell a tale which that I
> Learned at Padowe of a worthy clerk,
> As preved by his wordes and his werk:
> He is now dead and nailed in his chest;
> I pray to God so yeve his soule rest.
> Francis Petrarch, the laureat poet
> Highte this clerk, whose rhethoricke sweet
> Enlumined all Itaille of poetrie.

Perhaps this time Chaucer, whose statements are often doubtful or unauthorized, has spoken the truth, because if it is true that Petrarch latinised this tale in 1373, it is rather difficult for Chaucer to have got hold of the translation in Florence before his departure from the town. Perhaps he really got it in Padua from Petrarch himself.

We have said that Chaucer's statement this time is true, but still it is not quite true, as his *Clerk's Tale* cannot be a version of only what he heard from Petrarch: he follows so closely Petrarch's Latin translation that he must have had it before him when he wrote.

The fact of not having taken it from Boccaccio is considered a great argument in favour of those who affirm that Chaucer knew neither the *Decameron* nor Italian. Indeed there is not in it a single phrase which leads us to suppose that Chaucer had already read it in the *Decameron*[13]; but, if it is true that Chaucer heard this tale from Petrarch himself, can it be that Petrarch did not speak to Chaucer of the original in the *Decameron*? It may be so, but we do not believe it.

As we have already pointed out, it may be possible that although Chaucer knew several of Boccaccio's tales he may not have known this particular one. It may be that when he wrote his *Clerk's Tale,* he had not yet finished reading the *Decameron*, but it is most likely that Chaucer was more familiar with Latin than with Italian, and that therefore he preferred to take this tale from Petrarch. To this add that at that time the *Decameron* was not very much esteemed by many people, that Boccaccio had already repented of having written it, and it will not be difficult to understand why he chose Petrarch's translation, and also why he never mentioned Boccaccio in his works.

It does not matter to us whether Boccaccio was the true originator of the story, or whether the story is very old, as Petrarch himself states, or whether it was taken from life and that Griselda really existed. For us it is enough to state with certainty, that Boccaccio originated this masterpiece which gave birth to many imitations and different compositions throughout Europe, chiefly in Italy, France, Germany and England, and that, after all, Chaucer's *Clerk's Tale,* in spite of being a translation from Petrarch, is nothing else than Boccaccio's *Decameron,* which he translated. It is therefore the art of Boccaccio that he brought to England, and besides the fact of having certainly heard the *Decameron* and its author spoken about is another argument in our favour to prove that Chaucer knew this work.

Yet Chaucer did not translate this splendid tale without curtailing much of what was of no use for his purpose and without adding something of his own. This was usual in Chaucer, who never was a "mere slavish translator[14]" Sometimes he altered for the worse and sometimes for the better. In this tale the changes he introduces really improve it: he omits a proem in which are many valuable, but, in this case, useless geographical notions, and he adds a passage on the fidelity of women, which gives so much pathos to the tale that many a critic has very much praised the English poet, and judged that the English version is perhaps superior to the Italian original. . . .

However that may be, the fact remains that he wrote this book, which does him credit, because, after Dante, Petrarch and Boccaccio, he was the first, and in England the very first, to appreciate the many good qualities of woman, and to raise her from the state of servitude and servility in which she was kept during the old and middle ages. According to him woman is a daisy in her modesty and has in her beautiful candour and sincerity the magic power of curing the wounds of the heart. If in many instances Chaucer has exposed women to derision, perhaps to correct their ridiculous habits, in this book he gives a solid proof of knowing how much a virtuous woman is deserving of praise and how superior she is to every eulogy. . . .

Our Carducci has stated that the *Decameron* is the human comedy just as Dante's work is the *Divine Comedy.* Even in this Chaucer resembles Boccaccio: if Chaucer had been born three centuries later, he would have been the English Moliere just as Boccaccio would have been another Goldoni if he had lived in the XVI or XVII century.

Unhappily for us, and for the English, at that time the modern drama was not yet born, and the miracle-plays of the XIV century could not be attractive either to Boccaccio or to Chaucer. Nay, there was not yet even the embryo of the modern drama, but the vividness of the imagination of these two writers, their humour, their scorn of hypocrisy, their cleverness in seeing deeply into the heart of man, caused them to be considered as true dramatists before drama existed.

It is so true that there is dramatic power in their compositions that afterwards some subjects which are common to both Boccaccio and Chaucer were successfully brought on the stage. . . .

He died, but his works did not. Not only is it not the place here, but it is also beyond our purpose to describe the influence which they had and are still having on English literature. Up to the beginning of the Elizabethan era nothing could compare with the *Canterbury Tales,* which has till now borne fruit in a long succession of prose writers, and poets and painters. In this respect we may say that Chaucer's influence in England was superior to Boccaccio's in Italy: Chaucer had no rival in his country, whilst in Italy Dante and Petrarch were at least as famous as Boccaccio.

We do not know of any two other writers more similar, or more equal in their general characteristics than Boccaccio and Chaucer: they approach to one another closer than friends, than master and disciple, than father and son, than two brothers. Nature had given them both qualities which no one can acquire by one's self: healthy, gay, sincere and high-minded, they seem to belong to a time in which mankind had fewer cares than at present. What can we say of Boccaccio that we cannot say also of Chaucer? Either little or nothing. They are two of the most learned men of their time. As to Boccaccio, his commentary on the first sixteen cantos of the *Divine Comedy* would suffice to prove this assertion. As to Chaucer his *Astrolabe* shows that he was something of an astronomer, his *Tale of the Chanon's Yeoman* shows that he was a philosopher, his *Parson's Tale* shows his knowledge of Divinity. There was no gloom in them, therefore they could easily penetrate to the heart of every man, and judge with certainty, and, as we have already pointed out, they are the true historians of their time. In their works there are pictures of public and domestic life: the clergyman is there represented in his good and his bad qualities, and so is the landlord and the poor workman, the great lady, the poor servant maid and the country-woman. On the scene of the world painted by these two authors we see in turn men and women of every social rank; now shameless vice and now modest virtue, now wickedness and deceit, now goodness, truthfulness, sincerity: all the different characters of mankind pass before our eyes as in life. And all this is brightly narrated with a freedom and vividness of imagination which our present novelists would be very proud to possess.

They were religious, but their religion, except perhaps in their later years, never approached bigotry or superstition. In any case they were always more moral than many other famous writers: indeed the only reproach which has been made to them is that in their youth they were rather unscrupulous in their love affairs. Severe critics and fearless accusers of the vices of the clergy, they were in their turn accused of having brought religion into contempt. It was not so: they reproached the vicious clergyman, but never religion itself, and if Chaucer ever espoused the cause of Wickliffe, it was certainly not for want of religion.

They both loved learning and books, but their love of nature was stronger and more absorbing, so that their works remain fresh and green, and can still be not only read, but studied with enthusiasm.

They are both the pioneers of a new language, of a new literature, we could say also of a new civilisation, and therefore they are full of natural inspirations. They copied directly from nature and put themselves between nature and the literary geniuses following them.

They were both good writers in prose and poetry, but Boccaccio wrote better prose and Chaucer better poetry. They both had great power of satire and great influence not only on literature, but also on morality and they deserve fully the monument of immortality erected to them by the generations that followed them.

Notes
1. Casini.
2. Morley.
3. Chiarini.
4. Tyrwhitt.
5. Morley.
6. Koch.
7. Casini.
8. Chiarini.
9. Taine.
10. Warton.
11. Skeat.
12. Craik.
13. Chiarini.
14. Ward.

—Peter Borghesi, *Boccaccio and Chaucer*, 1903, pp. 29–69

Sir Walter Raleigh
"Lecture on Chaucer" (1926)

Sir Walter Raleigh (1861–1922) was a prominent scholar of English poetry and a past president of Magdalen College of Oxford University. In his "Lecture on Chaucer," published posthumously, Raleigh makes the case for Chaucer as a humorist, a person who uses wit and comedy to comment on the happenings of his day.

In describing Chaucer's sense of humor, Raleigh notes, "he is not a railing wit, or a bitter satirist. His broad and calm philosophy of life, his delight in diversities of character, his sympathy with all kinds of people, and his zest in all varieties of experience—these are the qualities of a humorist." Though Raleigh decries that Chaucer's humor is "everywhere, even in places where it has no right to be," Raleigh delights in Chaucer's use of comedy in his texts: "Chaucer has the true humorist's gift—the gift of the wooden face. He utters a truism ('Honesty is the best policy') with a solemn air; and only the faintest twinkle in the eye makes one hesitate in believing him serious." Any student writing about Chaucer's use of humor will find much of use in Raleigh's discussion here.

Raleigh also enters into the ongoing debate about Chaucer's relationship to the English language. While many critics contend that Chaucer was a great innovator of English, Raleigh disagrees. He suggests that Chaucer's "English is plain, terse, homely, colloquial English, taken alive out of daily speech." Like Lindner, Raleigh believes that Chaucer's English represents the spoken language of his day, especially that of the middle and lower class people, and notes that, "The conclusion is that Chaucer's language is the language of his own day, like Gower's, but used by a quicker intelligence, and freer from repetition, artificial tags, flatnesses, etc."

—⁓— —⁓— —⁓—

Chaucer's strong sanity and critical commonsense, his quick power of observation, and his distaste for all extravagances and follies helped to make him a great comic poet. But he is not a railing wit, or a bitter satirist. His broad and calm philosophy of life, his delight in diversities of character, his sympathy with all kinds of people, and his zest in all varieties of experience— these are the qualities of a humorist.

Charles Lamb thought with misgiving of a heaven in which all irony and ironical modes of expression should be lacking. Certainly it would be no heaven for Chaucer. The all-pervading essence of his work is humour. Sometimes it breaks out in boisterous and rollicking laughter at the drunken and unseemly exploits of churls; sometimes it is so delicate and evanescent that you can hardly detect its existence. But it is everywhere, even in places where it has no right to be. The intellectual pleasure of standing aside and seeing things against an incongruous background was a pleasure he could not long forgo.

In this matter, and in this alone, Chaucer is sometimes guilty of what I shall call 'literary bad manners.' It is like the fault of distracted attention. Even at a funeral he must insinuate his jest. Now, it is quite excusable to jest at a funeral so long as it is regarded as a formal, official function; or if it is merely matter for thought. The suit of clay as the dwelling-house made for this creature a little lower than the angels is a jest of the Gods. But Chaucer will arouse deep feelings of pathos and sympathy, and in the atmosphere thus created, he will let off a little crackling penny jest, from pure love of mischief. This spirit of witty mischief is always breaking out.

Chaucer has the true humorist's gift—the gift of the wooden face. He utters a truism ('Honesty is the best policy') with a solemn air; and only the faintest twinkle in the eye makes one hesitate in believing him serious.

Chaucer's self-consciousness is of a piece with his critical art. Sometimes (as in *Troilus* and the *Knight's Tale*) he is fairly caught in the web of his own imagination, and forgets himself. Far more frequently he reminds you of his presence by some sly allusion to himself, or some ironical piece of self-depreciation. Then the tale becomes a mere tale again, and we come back into the company of the teller.

This is a common trait of the humorist. He sees much that is ridiculous in human life; what if he himself is ridiculous? So he anticipates criticism, and discounts the retort, by laughing at himself.

You will find this in Falstaff ('I do here walk before thee like a sow that hath overwhelmed all her litter but one.') You may find it in all the jackanapes tricks of Sterne, his posturings and grimaces. You will find it in Mr. Bernard Shaw, who cannot forget that laughter is generally a hostile weapon, and is unwilling to stand the push of it in championing his ideas. Being skilled with it, he over-values it and over-fears it. So, like Bob Acres, he stands edgeways, or turns his weapon against himself, that he may still be on the side of the laughers.

This furnishes excellent wit and comedy, but is not consistent with good epical work. The man who is afraid of being caught in a serious sentiment lest others should find it ridiculous, cannot tell a moving tale in a forthright, wholehearted way. His mind is a kingdom divided against itself,—under two kings, a warrior and a clown. A cavalry charge cannot be led by one who is thinking of the figure he cuts in the eyes of a bystander. The professions of reformer and humorist have never been successfully combined. A reformer does not care who laughs.

The escape from this sort of self-consciousness—the besetting sin of the professed humorist—is in the drama; and all Chaucer's best and deepest humour occurs in parts of his work that are dramatic in everything but form. The dramatist stands aside and has not to defend himself. He speaks through many voices, and is himself unseen. He looks at human life and portrays it, and smiles.

All profound dramatic humour depends on sympathy and breadth of view, that keeps sight of the whole even while it spends delighted attention on a part. A wit or a satirist can be angry and laugh; he can laugh at what he misunderstands and misrepresents. The dramatic humorist laughs because he understands and enjoys. Now there never was a poet whose zest and delight in life was fuller and broader than Chaucer's. He hates nothing that he has made; in the realms of his creation the sun shines upon the evil and the good. His characters, as they come alive, almost always find in him an admirer and abetter. Pandarus, it is to be supposed, was originally designed to be a base, broken lackey, just as Falstaff may have been designed for a shallow, vainglorious, lying heartless rascal. But Pandarus, like Falstaff, comes alive, and we end by almost loving him. He has the worldly wisdom, the shrewd humour, the tender affections, and the philosophic outlook of his creator. He is a good friend, and, like Falstaff, he too is a poet.

Anything fair to see or hear awakes Chaucer's enthusiasm. Of Troilus riding into Troy he says:—

> It was an hevene upon him for to see!

When the people applaud, Troilus blushes:—

> That to biholde it was a noble game.

When Antigone sings in the garden:—

> It an heven was hir voys to here.

Anything on a large and generous scale, such as the housekeeping of the Franklin ('It snewed in his hous of mete and drinke'), or the marriages of the Wife of Bath, arouses Chaucer's sympathy. He loves a rogue, so that the rogue be high-spirited and clever at his trade, and not a whey-faced, bloodless rascal. The Pardoner, in describing his own preaching, says:—

> Myn hondes and my tonge goon so yerne,
> That it is joye to see my bisiness,

and so Chaucer felt it. His joy is chronic and irrepressible.

Chaucer makes the most enormous claim on the sound sense and quick intelligence of his readers. He assumes that they are at one with him, and that it is unnecessary for him to expound his point of view. The natural form for the dramatic sense of humour is irony. Often enough Chaucer's 'irony is dramatic, as when the Carpenter, in the very act of being befooled by Nicholas the clerk, congratulates himself that he is a plain, unlearned man. But the best of Chaucer's irony is found in his own interpolated utterances. He seems to be telling the story simply and directly. Suspect him! He is conveying his own criticisms, expressing his own amusement, in touches—a word here and a word there—so subtle and delicate that eleven out of twelve men in any jury would acquit him of any comic intent. These quiet smiles that flicker over his face are so characteristic that I have ventured to call the passages where we can detect them *Chaucerisms*. Take the 'Shipman's Tale':—

> A Marchant whylom dwelled at Seint Denys,
> That riche was, for which men helde him wys,

Chaucer is at his work already.

> When the merchant returns from abroad,
> His wyf ful redy mette him atte gate
> As she was wont of olde usage algate.

How quietly, almost inaudibly, Chaucer indicates that she had no very lively affection for her husband!

It is impossible to overpraise Chaucer's mastery of language. Here at the beginning, as it is commonly reckoned, of Modern English literature, is a treasury of perfect speech. We can trace his themes, and tell something of the events of his life. But where did he get his style—from which it may be said that English literature has been (in some respects) a long falling away?

What is the ordinary account? I do not wish to cite individual scholars, and there is no need. Take what can be gathered from the ordinary text-books—what are the current ideas? Is not this a fair statement of them?

> English was a despised language little used by the upper classes.
> A certain number of dreary works written chiefly for homiletic
> purposes, or in order to appeal to the humble people, are to be found
> in the half century before Chaucer. They are poor and flat and feeble,
> giving no promise of the new dawn. Then arose the morning star!
> Chaucer adopted the despised English tongue and set himself to
> modify it, to shape it, to polish it, to render it fit for his purpose. He

imported words from the French; he purified the English of his time from its dross; he shaped it into a fit instrument for his use.

Now I have no doubt that a competent philologist examining the facts could easily show that this account *must be* nonsense, from beginning to end. But even a literary critic can say something certain on the point—perhaps can even give aid by divination to the philologists, and tell them where it will best repay them to ply their pickaxes and spades.

No poet makes his own language. No poet introduces serious or numerous modifications into the language that he uses. Some, no doubt, coin words and revive them, like Spenser or Keats in verse, Carlyle or Sir Thomas Browne in prose. But least of all great English poets did Chaucer mould and modify the speech he found. The poets who take liberties with speech are either prophets or eccentrics. From either of these characters Chaucer was far removed. He held fast by communal and social standards for literary speech. He desired to be understood of the people. His English is plain, terse, homely, colloquial English, taken alive out of daily speech. He expresses his ideal again and again, as when the Host asks what is the use of telling a tale that sends the hearers to sleep:—

> For certeinly, as that thise clerkes seyn,
> Where-as a man may have noon audience,
> Noght helpeth it to tellen his sentence.

The same admirable literary critic repeats Chaucer's creed when he instructs the Clerk:—

> Your termes, your colours, and your figures,
> Kepe hem in stoor till so be ye endite
> Heigh style, as whan that men to kinges write,
> Speketh so pleyn at this tyme, I yow preye,
> That we may understonde what ye seye.

Chaucer has expressed his views on the model literary style so clearly and so often, and has illustrated them so well in his practice, that no mistake is possible. His style is the perfect courtly style: it has all the qualities of ease, directness, simplicity, of the best colloquial English, in short, which Chaucer recognised, three centuries before the French Academy, as the English spoken by cultivated women in society. His 'facound,' like Virginia's, 'is ful womanly and pleyn.' He avoids all 'counterfeted terms,' all subtleties of rhetoric, and addresses himself to the 'commune intente.'

Examples of his plain, terse brevity are easy to find. Take one, from the *Monk's Tale*—of Hugelin of Pisa. (The imprisoned father bites his hands for grief; his young sons think it is for hunger):

> His children wende that it for hunger was
> That he his armes gnew, and not for wo,
> And seyde, 'Fader, do not so, alias!
> But rather ete the flessh upon us two;
> Our flesh thou yaf us, take our flesh us fro,
> And ete y-nough': right thus they to him seyde,
> And after that, with-in a day or two,
> They leyde hem in his lappe adoun, and deyde.

Now a style like this, and in this perfection, implies a society at the back of it. If we are told that educated people at the Court of Edward III spoke French and that English was a despised tongue, we could deny it on the evidence of Chaucer alone. His language was shaped for him, and it cannot have been shaped by rustics. No English style draws so much as Chaucer's from the communal and colloquial elements of the language. And his poems make it certain that from his youth up he had heard much admirable, witty talk in the English tongue.

The conclusion is that Chaucer's language is the language of his own day, like Gower's, but used by a quicker intelligence, and freer from repetition, artificial tags, flatnesses, etc. It was his good fortune to live at a time when bookish learning had not yet severed classes. He broke loose from the literary fashions which at all time affect the 'educated classes', and wrote the good English of peers and peasants. In this respect he comes near to the poets of Dryden's age.

This language was his own, not painfully acquired. Ease and skill of this kind is not attainable save in the birth tongue. Too much has been made of French; and of the dates of the 'adoption' of English for public documents, law courts, schools. The English language had throughout a healthy, full-blooded existence. Chaucer had no adequate *literary* predecessors in English. But how partial and poor a thing the manuscript literature of the time compared with the riches of spoken lore, proverb, tale and romance! As Chaucer helps us, by his portrait of the age, to correct the formal annalists, so he helps us, by his writing, to a truer appreciation of literary history.

If there is to be any profitable investigation of Chaucer's language it must be remembered that he is at the *end* of an age, not at the beginning. His pupils could make nothing of him, and the Renaissance brought in ideals which made him unintelligible. Like Burns, Chaucer is a culmination and a close. We can understand Burns only by remembering his debts to Fergusson, Ramsay, and scores of nameless poets. If we are to understand Chaucer, it must be by reference to a tribe of storytellers, songsters, traffickers in popular lore and moral maxims who, because they did not relate themselves to paper, have almost passed, except by inference, from our ken.

—Sir Walter Raleigh, "Lecture on Chaucer,"
On Writers and Writing 1926, ed. Gordon, pp. 108–19

Chronology

c. 1340	Born to John Chaucer, a prosperous London wine merchant.
1357	Page in the service of Elizabeth, countess of Ulster.
1359–60	Military service in France. Captured by the French, then ransomed by Edward III; enters the service of Edward's son Lionel, earl of Ulster.
1366	Marriage to Philippa.
1367–73	Esquire in King Edward III's household; granted an annuity.
1369–70	Writes *The Book of the Duchess*.
1372–73	Journey to Genoa and Florence.
1374–80	*House of Fame.*
1374–86	Pension from John of Gaunt. Daily pitcher of wine from Edward III. Residence over the gate of Aldgate. Appointed controller of wool custom and subsidy.
1375	Appointed guardian of Edmund Staplegate and of the heir of John Solys.
1377	Diplomatic service in France. Annuities and appointments confirmed by Richard II.
1378	In France; second journey to Italy.
1382	*Parliament of Fowls.*
1385–89	Justice of the peace for Kent.
1382–85	*Troilus and Criseyde.*
1385–86	*Legend of Good Women.*
1386	Gives up Aldgate and customs posts.
1387	Philippa Chaucer dies.
	Begins *The Canterbury Tales,* working on and off until 1400.
1389–91	Appointed clerk of the King's Works.

1390	Serves on commission surveying the banks of the Thames. Directed to repair St. George's Chapel, Windsor. Robbed by highwaymen.
1390–91	Substitute forester of the royal forest at North Petherton Park, Somerset.
1391	Surrenders clerkship of the Works.
1394	Awarded a new annuity by Richard II.
1398	Action of debt against Chaucer. Granted a butt of wine yearly by Richard II.
1399	Annuity and gift of wine confirmed by Henry IV and a further annuity granted him. Leases dwelling at Westminster.
1400	Dies. Burial at Westminster Abbey.

Index